◎Harden's

UK Restaurant
Guide 2011

"The UK's most helpful
and informative guide"
The Sunday Times

In association with **RÉMY MARTIN**
FINE CHAMPAGNE COGNAC

Survey-driven reviews of over 1,750 restaurants

RÉMY MARTIN
FINE CHAMPAGNE COGNAC

The Heart of Cognac

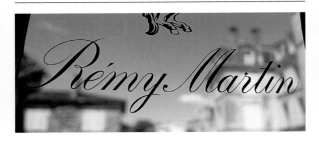

The appreciation of excellence

F ew business partnerships last as long as the co-operation between
Rémy Martin and Harden's. This is based on many things, but
particularly on authenticity, integrity and reliability, which are important
to both of us.

Harden's derives its authenticity from its annual nationwide survey of
restaurant-goers, leading to the creation of the UK's definitive democratic
restaurant guides and now, in association with The Sunday Times, the
UK's definitive Top 100 list. For Rémy Martin, it comes from three
centuries of tradition, its origins in the heart of Cognac and the unique
know-how of the cellar-master.

The Heart of Cognac

Since 1724, Rémy Martin – the only large cognac house still in family
ownership – has produced cognacs of exceptional quality and taste.
Alone, it sources 100% of its grapes from the very 'heart of Cognac'.
The 'heart' has its own official designation: 'Appellation Fine Champagne
Contrôllée'. 'Fine Champagne' indicates a blend of cognac from the two
best areas in the centre of the Cognac region, Grande Champagne (at
least half the blend) and Petite Champagne.

Champagne lends its name to these two Cognac areas because, like the
famous sparkling wine region, the soil is chalky. Over 80% of all the Fine
Champagne cognac produced in this designated area is used in Rémy
Martin Fine Champagne cognacs.

The result is three main characteristics which distinguish Rémy Martin:
the harmony between the complex aromas and the sweetness of the
flavours; the elegant richness of the aromas and palate; and the supreme
length of the finish.

Please enjoy Rémy Martin responsibly

This is why we believe that Rémy Martin captures the very heart of Cognac and it is this unswerving dedication to quality over nearly three centuries that has led Rémy Martin to become the worldwide leader in the most premium of cognacs.

The Centaur

The Sagittarius Centaur – a symbol of the alliance of man and nature – was adopted by the Rémy Martin family in 1870. Not only is Sagittarius the star sign of Rémy Martin's founding father, Paul-Émile Rémy Martin, but it is also representative of many of the values that the family upholds – courage, energy, audacity and generosity.

Artist and Artisan

The role of the cellar master commands huge respect. It demands a special combination of skills: knowledgeable viticultualist, skilled wine maker, master blender, and expert taster, all whilst never losing sight of the house style. Thanks to the skilled craftsmanship of generations of cellar masters, Rémy Martin has been able to anticipate the evolution of consumer tastes and adapt and innovate accordingly.

Spirit for Life

Much more than a digestif, Rémy Martin has a cognac to suit every mood and occasion from celebrations to moments of solace. Throw out the rule book: aperitif, digestif, cocktail or frozen, Rémy Martin captures the spirit for living.

RÉMY MARTIN
FINE CHAMPAGNE COGNAC

The Heart of Cognac

Rémy Martin V.S.O.P

This is the world's favourite V.S.O.P (Very Superior Old Pale) cognac and the benchmark by which all other V.S.O.P's are measured. Rémy Martin V.S.O.P shows near perfect balance of the three cornerstones of great cognac: floral, fruity and spice. Blended from over 240 eaux-de-vie, the result is a wonderfully balanced and smooth V.S.O.P.

Much more than simply a traditional digestif, the versatility of Rémy Martin V.S.O.P means it is perfect for many occasions. Why not try the recent trend from the US and impress friends by pulling a bottle out of the freezer and serving it chilled?

Enjoying Rémy Martin

Not only are Rémy Martin Fine Champagne cognacs the ideal choice to round off a wonderful meal, but Rémy Martin can also be enjoyed as a long drink before dinner or as the perfect accompaniment to fine food.

French Mojito

50 ml of Rémy Martin VSOP
Half a lime
4 small cane sugar cubes
(white or brown)
10 mint leaves
Crushed ice
Soda water

Method: build in a highball glass
Muddle (mash) the mint, lime and sugar together
Fill your glass with crushed ice
Pour the cognac and stir gently
Top up with a splash of soda water
Garnish with a mint sprig

RÉMY MAR

FINE CHAMPAGNE

V·S·O·

Fondée en 1724

PRODUCT OF FR

CHAMPAGNE

RÉMY MARTIN
FINE CHAMPAGNE COGNAC

The Heart of Cognac

The Rémy Martin V.S.O.P Award for the Best-Rated Newcomer remains the industry's most coveted recognition of up-and-coming restaurants. Rémy Martin is once again proud to be associated with the development of such a dynamic category.

Rémy Martin VSOP Award for Best Rated Newcomer – London

Winner

Viajante

There has been some very good cooking in London in recent years, but the cuisine of the capital's chefs has rarely been of note for its innovation. Not so with Nuno Mendes, a Portuguese chef who worked for a number of years with one of New York's most celebrated (and innovative) chefs, Jean-Georges Vongerichten. The name of Mendes's new restaurant means 'traveller', and the cuisine at his new East End dining room richly reflects his own peregrinations, and a special magic all of his own too.

Runners Up
Mooli's
Manson
Kitchen W8
Bistrot Bruno Loubet

Rémy Martin VSOP Award for Best Rated Newcomer – Rest of UK

Winner

Pea Porridge, Bury St Edmunds

This small restaurant in a modest-size market town is already making waves with the sheer consistency and quality of its 'offer'. It's a family production, with Justin Sharp – a Scot whose cv includes a stint at the famously crowd-pleasing Chez Bruce, in Wandsworth – at the stove, and his Lithuanian wife Jurga front-of-house. No set menu here. This is one of those restaurants which really has taken to heart the mantra of buying the finest produce of the moment, and turning it into the finest dishes possible.

Runner Up
Tuscan Kitchen, Rye

RÉMY MARTIN
FINE CHAMPAGNE COGNAC

Cœur de Cognac
THE HEART OF COGNAC

*Enticing notes of ripe summer fruits
with the promise of incredibly
smooth sensations*

A.O.C FINE CHAMPAGNE COGNAC

700 ml   40 % alc./vol.

Coeur de Cognac

Through expert blending, Rémy Martin has created a fruit-driven and succulent spirit – Coeur de Cognac. Fresher and lighter than traditional cognacs, the predominant flavours are of apricot, honey and vanilla. The first taste is like biting into a succulent, juicy apricot whilst the nose bursts with ripe summer fruits and the palate is rich and soft – without the fiery finish usually associated with spirits.

Coeur de Cognac is intended for sheer drinking pleasure to be enjoyed anytime, anywhere. Try it with an ice cube or two which will help to reveal all its complex flavours and make an ideal aperitif.

Developed with people who appreciate fine food and dining in mind, it is a natural accompaniment to fruity deserts like apricot tart or petits fours such as macaroons or fruit jellies.

RÉMY MARTIN
FINE CHAMPAGNE COGNAC

The Heart of Cognac

Now it its second year, the Rémy Martin Coeur de Cognac Award for the Best Dessert rewards a much overlooked, yet sublime, aspect of a complete dining experience.

Coeur de Cognac Award for Best Dessert – London

Winner

Marcus Wareing at the Berkeley
Warm chocolate moelleux, salted caramel

As a native Lancastrian – and having won recognition as London's top chef – it's particularly appropriate that Marcus Wareing should once again also carry off the prize for that most essential course in British cuisine: pudding. Marcus's skill for creating food that's both flawlessly presented and big on taste is showcased perfectly in his desserts. Indeed, with his fabled custard tart, he won the Award last year too.

Runners Up
The Ivy *(Baked Alaska with griotte cherries)*
Chez Bruce *(Cheeseboard)*
Murano *(Pistachio souffle with warm chocolate sauce)*
Le Caprice *(Iced berries with hot white chocolate sauce)*
Maze *(Peanut butter and cherry jam sandwich)*

Coeur de Cognac Award for Best Dessert – Rest of UK

Winner

Le Manoir aux Quat' Saisons, Great Milton
Raviole de fruits exotiques

Raymond Blanc is one of the great established names of British gastronomy, and his Oxfordshire restaurant-with-rooms is knows to his admirers everywhere simply as 'Le Manoir'. It's the establishment's all-round appeal which has made it such a big name, and this year it was his puddings which particularly fired the reporters' imagination. But then, after 15 years at Le Manoir, it's perhaps no great surprise that Executive Pastry Chef Benoit Blin is at the top of his game.

Runner Up
Fat Duck *(Taffety tart)*

RÉMY MARTIN
FINE CHAMPAGNE COGNAC

The Heart of Cognac

Rémy Martin XO

Sophisticated and beautifully balanced, Rémy Martin XO
Excellence (Extra Old) combines aromatic richness and
complexity with a wonderful velvety texture. The nose yields
hints of jasmine, ripe fig and candied orange and the palate
shows notes of cinnamon and freshly baked brioche.

Rémy Martin XO is aged for up to 37 years in Limousin oak cask
to achieve its maturity and balance.

XO is a wonderful digestif and the perfect partner to rich
hazelnut and cinnamon desserts. Rémy Martin XO truly is the
taste of extravagance.

FINE
CHAMPAGNE
COGNAC

RÉMY MARTIN

FINE CHAMPAGNE COGNAC

XO
EXCELLENCE

A.O.C. FINE CHAMPAGNE COGNAC.

RÉMY MARTIN
FINE CHAMPAGNE COGNAC

The Heart of Cognac

Now it its second year, the Rémy Martin XO Excellence Award is for the Best All Round Restaurant. This award is the result of painstaking analysis of the survey results, to identify the true crème de la crème – having regard to food, service and ambience – of the UK's dining scene.

Rémy Martin XO Excellence Award for Best All-Round Restaurant – London

Winner

Marcus Wareing at The Berkeley

Does anyone now recall that Marcus Wareing used to be mainly celebrated at number two to another famous chef? Well, those days are now all behind him, and Marcus Wareing, winner of the Rémy Martin XO Award for the second consecutive year, is now very definitely his own man, and his grand Knightsbridge dining room is now unassailably the capital's top all-round dining destination.

Runners Up
Le Gavroche
La Trompette
The Ledbury
Chez Bruce

Rémy Martin XO Excellence Award for Best All-Round Restaurant – Rest of UK

Winner

Gidleigh Park, Chagford

Runner-up last year, this grand country house may have an idyllic location on the fringe of Dartmoor, but it's Michael Caines's cooking that has really put it on the map. Michael is a 'local boy', trained in Exeter, and subsequently worked with some of the greats – including Raymond Blanc at Great Milton, and the late Bernard Loiseau in Saulieu – before become head chef at Gidleigh in 1994. He has subsequently gone into partnership with Andrew Brownsord (originally of greeting card fame) to establish the ABode hotel chain, each of whose outposts has a Michael Caines restaurant.

Runners Up

Le Manoir aux Quat' Saisons, Great Milton
Mr Underhill's, Ludlow
Waterside Inn, Bray
Hambleton Hall, Hambleton

RÉMY MARTIN
FINE CHAMPAGNE COGNAC
The Heart of Cognac

THE SUNDAY TIMES

The UK's 100 Best Restaurants

1 Gidleigh Park, Chagford
Winner Rémy Martin XO Award (Rest of UK)

2 Fat Duck, Bray
Winner Rémy Martin Coeur de Cognac Award (Rest of UK)

3 Marcus Wareing (The Berkeley), London SW1
Winner Rémy Martin XO Award (London)
and Rémy Martin Coeur de Cognac Award (London)

4 The Ledbury, London W11

5 Waterside Inn, Bray

6 Le Manoir aux Quat' Saisons, Great Milton
Winner Rémy Martin XO Award (Rest of UK)

7 Le Gavroche, London W1

8 L'Enclume, Cartmel

9 One-O-One (Sheraton Park Tower), London SW1

10 Kitchin, Edinburgh

11 Hambleton Hall, Hambleton

12 The Square, London W1

13 Restaurant Sat Bains, Nottingham

14 The Yorke Arms, Ramsgill-in-Nidderdale

15 Restaurant Martin Wishart, Edinburgh

16 Viajante, London/E2
Winner Rémy Martin VSOP Award (London)

17 Pied à Terre, London W1

18 Andrew Fairlie (Gleneagles Hotel), Auchterarder

19 Le Bécasse, Ludlow

20 Northcote, Langho

21 Sharrow Bay, Ullswater

22 Number One, Edinburgh

23 Murano, London W1

24 Mr Underhill's, Ludlow

25 Nobu (Metropolitan Hotel), London W1

26 L'Atelier de Joel Robuchon, London W1

27 Summer Lodge, Evershot

28 Midsummer House, Cambridge

29 Rasoi, London SW3

30 Three Chimneys, Dunvegan

RÉMY MARTIN

FINE CHAMPAGNE COGNAC

The Heart of Cognac

THE SUNDAY TIMES

The UK's 100 Best Restaurants

31 Hakkasan, London W1
32 Capital Restaurant (Capital Hotel), London SW3
33 Landau (The Langham), London W1
34 Roussillon, London SW1
35 Greenhouse, London W1
36 Simpsons, Birmingham
37 Zuma, London SW3
38 21212, Edinburgh
39 Bath Priory Hotel, Bath
40 Nobu Berkeley, London W1
41 Nahm (Halkin Hotel), London SW1
42 La Trompette, London W4
43 Le Champignon Sauvage, Cheltenham
44 The Ritz Restaurant (The Ritz), London W1
45 Hibiscus, London W1
46 Wiltons, London SW1
47 Chez Bruce, London SW17
48 Roka, London W1
49 L'Ortolan, Shinfield
50 The Seafood Restaurant, Padstow
51 Pearl, London WC1
52 Gordon Ramsay, London SW3
53 Morgan M, London N7
54 La Petite Maison, London W1
55 Texture, London W1
56 The Vineyard at Stockcross, Stockcross
57 Umu, London W1
58 Tom Aikens, London SW3
59 Anthony's, Leeds
60 The River Café, London W6
61 Kai Mayfair, London W1
62 Benares, London W1
63 Club Gascon, London EC1
64 Amaya, London SW1
65 Sheekey, London WC2
66 Petersham Nurseries, London

RÉMY MARTIN
FINE CHAMPAGNE COGNAC

The Heart of Cognac

THE SUNDAY TIMES

The UK's 100 Best Restaurants

As prepared by Harden's for The Food List. The UK's 100 Best Restaurants. In association with Rémy Martin and The Sunday Times.

Put us in your pocket!

Try our iPhone & BlackBerry editions

visit Blackberry app world or the iStore for more details

© **Harden's Limited 2010**

ISBN 978-1-873721-91-9

British Library Cataloguing-in-Publication data: a catalogue record for this book is available from the British Library.

Underlying UK map images ©MAPS IN MINUTES™/Collins Bartholomew (2008).

Printed in Spain by Graphy Cems

Design: Margaret Vanschaemelhout

Content Manager & Layout: Julie Pallot

Research assistants: Gaz Kllokoqi, Sarah Ashpole

Harden's Limited
14 Buckingham Street
London WC2N 6DF

The views expressed in the editorial section of this guide are exclusively those of Harden's Limited

Would restaurateurs (and PRs) please address communications to 'Editorial' at the above address, or ideally by email to: editorial@hardens.com

CONTENTS

Le Manoir aux Quat' Saisons

Viajante E2

RATINGS & PRICES

We see little point in traditional rating systems, which generally tell you nothing more than that expensive restaurants are 'better' than cheap ones, as they use costlier ingredients and attempt more ambitious dishes. You probably knew that already. Our system assumes that, as prices rise, so do diners' expectations.

£ Price
The cost of a three-course dinner for one person. We include half a bottle of house wine, coffee and service (or a 10% tip if there is no service charge).

Food
The following symbols indicate that, *in comparison with other restaurants in the same price-bracket*, the cooking at the establishment is:

 **Exceptional**

Very good

Some restaurants are worth a mention but, for some reason (typically low feedback) we do not think a rating is appropriate. These are indicated as follows:

 Tip

We also have a category for places which attract a notably high proportion of adverse comment:

Disappointing

Ambience
Restaurants which provide a setting which is very charming, stylish or 'buzzy' are indicated as follows:

Particularly atmospheric

Restaurant Rémy awards

 A Restaurant Rémy symbol signifies this year's winners – see front colour section

Small print

Telephone number – All numbers in the London section are (020) numbers.
Details – the following information is given where relevant:
Directions – to help you find the establishment.
Website – if applicable.
Last orders time – at dinner (Sun may be up to 90 mins earlier).
Opening hours – unless otherwise stated, restaurants are open for lunch and dinner seven days a week.
Credit and debit cards – unless otherwise stated, Mastercard, Visa, Amex and Maestro are accepted.
Dress – where appropriate, the management's preferences concerning patrons' dress are given.
Children – if we know of a specified minimum age for children, we note this.
Accommodation – if an establishment has rooms, we list how many and the minimum price for a double.

FROM THE EDITORS

To an extent we believe to be unique, this guide is written 'from the bottom up'. That is to say, its composition reflects the restaurants, pubs and cafés which people across the country – as represented by our diverse reporter base – talk about. It does not, therefore, concentrate on hotel restaurants (as does one of the major 'independent' guides whose publisher also does big business in paid-for hotel inspections). Nor does it 'overweight' European cuisines. Most restaurants in this country fall in the category usually called 'ethnic', but most guidebooks would lead you to think that such places are generally unworthy of serious commentary. It seems to us that this approach is positively wrong-headed in a country where the diversity of restaurant types is one of the most notable (and positive) features.

The restaurant revolution which began in London in the '90s has now had repurcussions right across the UK. Most major conurbations, for example, now have several ambitious restaurants good enough to be of note to visitors. The areas that are still truly 'culinary deserts' are becoming both smaller and more dispersed. Much as this is to be applauded, it does not make our task any easier, and we are keenly aware – as any honest publisher must acknowledge – that all guide books are imperfect. There will be deserving places missing, and opinions will be repeated that the passing of time has rendered redundant. However, we believe that our system – involving the careful processing of tens of thousands of reports – is the best available.

We are very grateful to each of our thousands of reporters, without whose input this guide could simply not have been written. Many of our reporters express views about a number of restaurants at some length, knowing full well that – given the concise format of the guide – we can seemingly never 'do justice' to their observations. We must assume that they do so in the confidence that the short – and we hope snappy – summaries we produce are as fair and as well-informed as possible. You, the reader, must judge – restaurant guides are not works of literature, and should be assessed on the basis of utility. This is a case where the proof of the pudding really is in the eating.

Given the growing scale of our task, we are particularly grateful for the continuing support we have received from Rémy Martin Fine Champagne Cognac in the publication of this guide. With their help, this is now well on the way to becoming the most comprehensive – as well as the most democratic and diverse – guide available to the restaurants of the UK.

All restaurant guides are the subject of continual revision. This is especially true when the restaurant scene is undergoing a period of rapid change, as at present. **Please help us to make the next edition even more comprehensive and accurate: sign up to join the survey by following the instructions overleaf.**

Richard Harden   Peter Harden

How This Book Is Organised

This guide begins in London, which, in recognition of the scale and diversity of its restaurant scene, has an extensive introduction and indexes, as well as its own maps. Thereafter, the guide is organised strictly alphabetically, without regard to national divisions – Ballater, Beaumaris, Belfast and Birmingham appear together under 'B'.

For cities and larger towns, you should therefore be able to turn straight to the relevant section. Cities which have significant numbers of restaurants also have a brief introductory overview, as well as entries for the restaurants themselves.

In less densely populated areas, you will generally find it easiest to start with the map of the relevant area at the back of the book, which will guide you to the appropriate place names.

How This Book Is Researched

This book is the result of a research effort involving thousands of 'reporters'. These are 'ordinary' members of the public who share with us summary reviews of the best and the worst of their annual dining experiences. This year, more than 8,000 people gave us some 87,000 reviews in total.

The density of the feedback on London (where many of the top places attract several hundred reviews each) is such that the ratings for the restaurants in the capital included in this edition are almost exclusively statistical in derivation. We have, as it happens, visited almost all the restaurants in the London section, anonymously, and at our own expense, but we use our personal experiences only to inform the standpoint from which to interpret the consensus opinion.

In the case of the more commented-upon restaurants away from the capital, we have adopted an approach very similar to London. In the case of less-visited provincial establishments, however, the interpretation of survey results owes as much to art as it does to science.

In our experience, smaller establishments are – for better or worse – generally quite consistent, and we have therefore felt able to place a relatively high level of confidence in a lower level of commentary. Conservatism on our part, however, may have led to some smaller places being underrated compared to their more visited peers.

How You Can Join The Survey

Register on our mailing list at www.hardens.com and you will be invited, in the spring of 2011, to participate in our next survey. **If you take part you will, on publication, receive a complimentary copy of Harden's Restaurant Guide 2012.**

London Introduction
& Survey Results

LONDON INTRODUCTION

How should I use this guide?

This guide can be used in many ways. You will often wish to use it to answer practical queries. These tend to be geographical – where can we eat near…? To answer such questions, the Maps (from page 153) and Area Overviews (from page 123) are the place to start. The latter tell you all the key facts about the restaurants – perhaps dozens – in a particular area in the space of a couple of pages.

But what if you'd like to be more adventurous and seek out new places purely for interest's sake or for a truly special occasion? That's the main point of this brief section – to give you a handy overview of London's dining scene, and also some thoughts as to how you can use the guide to lead you to eating experiences you might not otherwise have found (or perhaps even contemplated).

What makes London special?

This question would once have been easy to answer: London was the opposite of Paris. There you could eat one cuisine only – albeit in all its various regional glories – supremely well. London, like New York, was a city where nothing was done especially well, but at least the scene was cosmopolitan.

Well, London's cosmopolitanism has not gone away, and standards continue to improve across the board, but there are now at least two specialities of particular note. The first, chronologically speaking, was the cuisine of the Indian subcontinent, which is offered in London in greater variety, within a small geographical area, than anywhere else in the world. And the more recent speciality is…British cuisine! London is now the only city where you can consistently eat well in a varied idiom which is clearly British!

Which is London's best restaurant?

It's getting more and more difficult to say, because the old rules – which boiled down to French is Best – seem ever more inappropriate today. But let's stick with the traditional 'haute cuisine' definition. If you want the whole high-falutin' Gallic dining experience, the top all-rounder – no question – is *Marcus Wareing at the Berkeley*. In a rather more traditional style, London's original post-war grand restaurant, *Le Gavroche*, still has a lot going for it.

Following hard on their heels are a duo of restaurants from the same stable which have maintained very high quality for a good number of years and are still improving: *The Square* and *The Ledbury*. For something more adventurous, plan a trip to the East End, to the newly opened *Viajante*.

Other staples of quality dining include *Pied à Terre*, *Atelier de Robuchon*, *Launceston Place* and *The River Café*.

What about something a little more reasonably priced?

You can still have meals of exceptional quality – often memorable ones – a lot cheaper than at the establishments mentioned above.

As well as the aforementioned Square and Ledbury, Nigel Platts-Martin's empire includes not just 'Londoners' Favourite Restaurant', *Chez Bruce* (Wandsworth), but also the amazingly consistent *La Trompette* (Chiswick) and the similarly excellent *Glasshouse* (Kew).

For all of these establishments, you need to head out from the centre of town. Other hidden jewels out in Zones 2 and 3 include *Morgan M* (Islington), *Trinity* (Clapham), *Lambert's* (Balham), *Riva* (Barnes), the newly opened *Manson* (Fulham) or – if you really fancy a trip – *Petersham Nurseries* out just beyond Richmond. For somewhere still within the Circle Line, then consider *Clarke's*, *Moro*, *Angelus* or *Bistrot Bruno Loubet*.

What about some really good suggestions in the heart of the West End?

It used to be difficult to recommend places to dine well in the West End at reasonable cost, but the position has improved hugely in recent years. Names particularly to consider include *Arbutus*, *Giaconda Dining Room*, *Galvin Bistro de Luxe* and *Wild Honey*. If you're happy to eat in tapas style, add to this list such relatively recent arrivals as *Barrafina*, *Bocca di Lupo*, *Dehesa*, *Polpo*, *Sheekey's Oyster Bar* and *Terroirs*.

If you want a little more comfort and style, as well as pretty good food you're unlikely to go far wrong at the discreet *Caprice* (just behind the Ritz), or its siblings *J Sheekey* (hidden-away in Theatreland) and *Scott's* (a celebrity magnet on one of the grandest streets in Mayfair). These last are hardly bargain suggestions, but they do offer all-round value. For pure theatre, a visitor looking for that sort of style should probably try to eat at the *Wolseley* – the nation's 'grand café', by the Ritz – at some point.

Covent Garden is a tricky area, rich in tourist traps, but is now the unlikely home of a restaurant that's beginning to approach 'destination' status – *Clos Maggiore*.

And don't forget to lunch!

Particularly if you want to eat in the West End, it is very well worth considering whether you can do so at lunchtime, when there are some unlikely bargains available. Restaurants don't come much grander than *Le Gavroch*e, for example, and it famously offers a superb-value all-in lunch (even including some very decent wine), for less than many relatively run-of-the-mill establishments end up charging for a basic dinner.

And for the best of British?

As we hinted above, British food has only very recently emerged from a sort of tourist ghetto. If it's the grand end of that market you're looking for, seek out the Roast Beef of Olde England at *Simpson's-on-the-Strand*. Less impressive in scale, but much better, is nearby *Rules* – a beautiful old-timer, where game is the culinary speciality.

That, though, is not the sort of cooking, – often offal-rich and rediscovering historical dishes – that's making British one of the most fashionable cuisines in town. The pioneer establishment of the new-wave Brits – which for so long seemed to be crying in the wilderness – was *St John*. Over the last few years, however, the trend – often mixed in with 'gastropub' cooking in many people's minds – has become mainstream. Restaurants proper which may be said to be strongly influenced by the style include *Magdalen*, *Great Queen Street*, *Hereford Road* and *St John Bread & Wine*. It will probably also feature at the new, soon-to-open Heston Blumenthal restaurant, *Dinner*, at the swanky Mandarin Oriental Hotel. But a lot of this sort of cooking is taking place in gastropubs...

What are gastropubs?

These are essentially bistros in the premises of former pubs. They come in a variety of styles. What many people think of as the original gastropub (*The Eagle*, 1991) still looks very much like a pub with a food counter. At the other end of the scale, however, the 'pub' element is almost redundant, and the business is really just a restaurant housed in premises that happen once to have been a pub.

Few of the best gastropubs are particularly central. The reasonably handy location of the *Anchor & Hope*, on the South Bank, is no doubt part of the reason for its crazy popularity. Hammersmith and its environs, for some reason, have a particular concentration, with the *Anglesea Arms* the stand-out performer there. Two new stars are the *Bull & Last* (Kentish Town) and the *Harwood Arms* (Fulham).

Isn't London supposed to be a top place for curry?

London, as noted above, has a reasonable claim to being the world's top Indian restaurant city. Leading lights such as *Amaya*, *The Painted Heron*, *The Cinnamon Kitchen*, *Benares*, *Rasoi*, *Trishna* and *Zaika* are pushing back the frontiers, but – perfectly reasonably – charge the same as their European equivalents.

What's more exciting in terms of value are the many Indian restaurants where you can eat much more cheaply than you could eat European. Two top names in the East End are, however, almost legendary 'value' experiences – the *Lahore Kebab House* and *New Tayyabs*.

Any tips to beat the crunch?

● The top tip, already noted, is to lunch not dine. If you're a visitor, you'll find that it's better for your wallet, as well as your digestion, to have your main meal in the middle of the day. In the centre of town, it's one of the best ways you can be sure of eating 'properly' at reasonable cost.

● Think ethnic – for a food 'experience' at modest cost, you'll still generally be better off going Indian, Thai, Chinese or Vietnamese (to choose four of the most obvious cuisines) than French, English or Italian. The days when there was any sort of assumption that ethnic restaurants were – in terms of comfort, service and décor – in any way inferior to European ones is long gone.

● Try to avoid the West End. That's not to say that, armed with this book, you shouldn't be able to eat well in the heart of things, but you'll almost certainly do better in value terms outside the Circle line. Many of the best and cheapest restaurants in this guide are easily accessible by tube. Use the maps at the back of this book to identify restaurants near tube stations on a line that's handy for you.

● If you must dine in the West End, try to find either pre-theatre (generally before 7.30 pm) or post-theatre (generally after 10 pm) menus. You will generally save at least the cost of a cinema ticket, compared to dining à la carte. Many of the more upmarket restaurants in Theatreland do such deals.

● Use this book! Don't take pot luck, when you can benefit from the pre-digested views of thousands of other diners-out. Choose a place with a 'star' – or stars! – for food, and you're very likely to eat much better than if you walk in somewhere on spec' – this is good advice anywhere, but is most particularly so in the West End. Once you have decided that you want to eat within a particular area, use the Area Overviews (starting on p123) to identify the restaurants that are offering top value.

● Visit our website, www.hardens.com, for the latest reviews, and restaurant news.

SURVEY MOST MENTIONED

These are the restaurants which were most frequently mentioned by reporters. (Last year's position is given in brackets.) An asterisk* indicates the first appearance in the list of a recently-opened restaurant.

1   J Sheekey (1)
2   Scott's (3)
3   Chez Bruce (2)
4   Marcus Wareing (5)
5   Le Gavroche (8)
6   The Wolseley (4)
7   Hakkasan (6)
8= Galvin Bistrot de Luxe (9=)
8= Bleeding Heart (7)
10 The Ledbury (31)

J Sheeky

11 Terroirs (-)
12 La Trompette (15)
13 Clos Maggiore (24)
14 The Ivy (12=)
15 The Cinnamon Club (16)
16 Le Caprice (11)
17 Gordon Ramsay (9=)
18 La Poule au Pot (12=)
19 Oxo Tower (Rest') (20)
20 The Square (25)

Clos Maggiore

21 Bocca Di Lupo (36=)
22 The River Café (30)
23 Arbutus (17)
24 Andrew Edmunds (14)
25 Gordon Ramsay at Claridge's (20)
26 Zuma (18=)
27 The Anchor & Hope (27)
28 maze (18=)
29 Benares (26)
30 Moro (39)

The Anchor & Hope

31 Galvin at Windows (-)
32 L'Atelier de Joel Robuchon (22)
33 Murano (40)
34 Roussillon (-)
35 Amaya (34)
36= Yauatcha (23)
36= Galvin La Chapelle*
38 Polpo*
39 L'Anima (-)
40 Corrigan's Mayfair (35)

L'Atelier de Joel Robuchon

LONDON - HIGHEST RATINGS

FOOD	SERVICE

£80+

	FOOD			SERVICE
1	Marcus Wareing		1	Marcus Wareing
2	The Ledbury		2	Le Gavroche
3	Le Gavroche		3	The Ledbury
4	One-O-One		4	The Square
5	The Square		5	Pied à Terre

£60-£79

	FOOD			SERVICE
1	Chez Bruce		1	Chez Bruce
2	Morgan M		2	The Goring Hotel
3	Zuma		3	Assaggi
4	Amaya		4	Morgan M
5	Petersham Nurseries		5	J Sheekey

£45-£59

	FOOD			SERVICE
1	La Trompette		1	Oslo Court
2	Hunan		2	La Trompette
3	Lamberts		3	Sale e Pepe
4	Trinity		4	Tentazioni
5	Ken Lo's Memories		5	Trinity

£35-£44

	FOOD			SERVICE
1	Jin Kichi		1	Upstairs Bar
2	Dinings		2	Uli
3	Sushi-Say		3	Fabrizio
4	Barrafina		4	Yming
5	St John Bread & Wine		5	Bombay Palace

£34 or less

	FOOD			SERVICE
1	Asakusa		1	Mooli's
2	Pham Sushi		2	El Parador
3	Ragam		3	Golden Hind
4	Lahore Kebab House		4	Gung-Ho
5	Kastoori		5	Kastoori

AMBIENCE

1. The Ritz Restaurant
2. Galvin at Windows
3. Marcus Wareing
4. Le Gavroche
5. Hakkasan

1. Les Trois Garçons
2. Petersham Nurseries
3. Min Jiang
4. Galvin La Chapelle
5. Rules

1. Ffiona's
2. La Poule au Pot
3. Clos Maggiore
4. Blue Elephant
5. The Wallace

1. Andrew Edmunds
2. Upstairs Bar
3. The Oak
4. Randall & Aubin
5. Tate Modern, Level 7

1. Gordon's Wine Bar
2. Bar Italia
3. Polpo
4. Cork & Bottle
5. The Wine Library

OVERALL

1. Marcus Wareing
2. Le Gavroche
3. The Ledbury
4. The Square
5. The Ritz Restaurant

1. Chez Bruce
2. J Sheekey
3. Scott's
4. Min Jiang
5. Petersham Nurseries

1. La Trompette
2. Oslo Court
3. Clos Maggiore
4. Trinity
5. A Cena

1. Upstairs Bar
2. Barrafina
3. Babur
4. Caravan
5. Sushi Say

1. Mooli's
2. El Parador
3. Flat White
4. Taiwan Village
5. Polpo

SURVEY - NOMINATIONS

Top gastronomic experience

1. Marcus Wareing (1)
2. Le Gavroche (3)
3= Chez Bruce (2)
3= The Ledbury (8)
5= La Trompette (5)
5= Gordon Ramsay (4)
7. The Square (9)
8. L'Atelier de Joel Robuchon (7)
9. Roussillon (-)
10. Murano (10)

Le Gavroche

Favourite

1. Chez Bruce (1)
2. Galvin Bistrot de Luxe (7)
3= La Trompette (6)
3= Le Caprice (2)
5. The Wolseley (4=)
6. J Sheekey (3)
7. The Ivy (4=)
8. Moro (9)
9. The Ledbury (-)
10. The River Café (-)

Chez Bruce

Best for business

1. The Wolseley (1)
2. Coq d'Argent (4)
3. The Square (5)
4. Bleeding Heart (2)
5. The Don (3)
6. L'Anima (6)
7. Galvin Bistrot de Luxe (9)
8. Scott's (8)
9. Galvin La Chapelle*
10. The Ivy (-)

Bleeding Heart

Best for romance

1. La Poule au Pot (1)
2. Clos Maggiore (3)
3. Andrew Edmunds (2)
4. Bleeding Heart (4)
5. Galvin at Windows (9)
6. Chez Bruce (5)
7= Café du Marché (-)
7= Marcus Wareing (8)
9. Le Caprice (6)
10. Le Gavroche (10)

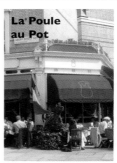

La Poule au Pot

OPENINGS AND CLOSURES

Restaurants in bold are included in the London section of this guide – for the full selection, see Harden's London Restaurants 2010 (£11.99), available in all good bookshops.

Openings (140)

A La Cruz
Abokado *W1, EC1, EC4*
Amico Bio
Angels & Gypsies
Antelope
L'Art du Fromage
Babbo
Bangalore Express *EC3*
Bar Boulud
Barbecoa
Barrica
The Battery
Benito's Hat *WC2*
Best Mangal *SW6*
Bistro K
Bistrot Bruno Loubet
Blues Kitchen
Boyd's Brasserie
Brasserie Battu
Brasserie Blanc
Brasserie De Ville
Brasserie Joël
Brasserie Toulouse-Lautrec
Byron *W1, WC2, SW3, SW7, N1, E14*
Café Luc
Cantina Laredo
Canton Arms
Caravan
Cassis
Cattle Grid *SW11, SW12*
Charlotte's Bistro
Chella
Chinese Cricket Club
Chipotle
Chiswick House Café
Circus
Cocorino
Colony
The Compass
Constancia
The Courtauld Gallery Café
Les Deux Salons
Dinner
Dishoom
The Dock Kitchen
Dose

Empress of Sichuan
Faanoos *W4*
Fire & Stone *E1*
Franco Manca *W4*
Gauthier Soho
Gelupo
Gessler at Daquise
Giant Robot
Ginger & White
Goldfish City *EC2*
Goodman *EC2*
Guerilla Burgers
Hakkasan *W1*
Hawksmoor *WC2*
Hazev
Hix
Hummus Bros *EC2*
HUNter 486
Jamie's Italian *WC2, W12*
Juniper Dining
JW Steakhouse
Kaffeine
Kiraku
Kitchen W8
Koffmann's
Koya
Kyashii
Lahore Karahi
Leong's Legends *W2*
Il Locale
London Wall Bar & Kitchen
Made in China
Manson
Mennula
Michael Nadra
Mien Tay *E2*
Monsieur M.
Mooli's
Mount Street Deli
My Dining Room
Needoo
North Road
The Northgate
Nottingdale
The Old Brewery
101 Pimlico Road
Otarian *W1, WC2*
Paramount

Openings (cont'd)

The Phene
Pinchito *WC1*
Pizza East
Pod *WC1, EC2, EC3*
Pollen Street
Polpetto
Polpo
Prince Albert
Princess of Shoreditch
Red Monkey
Red Pepper *SW1*
Redhook
Rocket *E14*
Rosa's Soho *E1*
Roux at Parliament Square
Saf *W8*
Santa Maria
Seven Park Place
Seventeen
Shaka Zulu
The Summerhouse

supperclub
Tatra
Tinello
Tom's Terrace
The Tommyfield
Tompkins
Trullo
Tsuru *EC2*
28-50
Valentina
Villandry Kitchen *W4*
W55
Wahaca *W1*
Wheeler's
William Curley Dessert Bar
Wright Brothers *W1*
Zilli Green
Zucca

Closures (72)

Admiralty
Alastair Little
Ambassade de L'Ile
Atrium
Bel Canto
Benihana *NW3*
Beotys
Boiled Egg & Soldiers
Bord'Eaux
Bowler Bar & Grill
Boxwood Café
Buchan's
Buddha Bar
Café du Jardin
Cha Cha Moon *W2*
Chinese Experience
Clerkenwell Dining Room
Comptoir Libanais *W2*
D Sum 2
Daquise
Daylesford Organic Café
Sloane Sq, SW1
Devonshire House
Dexter's Grill *SW4, SW17*
East Room
Eat & Two Veg
Establishment *SW6, SW11*
Farm
Fish Hook

Flâneur
Foliage
Frankie's Italian *SW15*
French House
Green Olive
Ground
L'Incontro
Lower East
Matsuri *WC1*
Noto Kikuya
Okawari *WC2*
1 Blossom Street
Ooze *W1*
Oriel
Papillon
Pappa Ciccia *SW15*
The Park
Pizza on the Park
Potemkin
Princess
Priory House
Provence
Quality Chop House
Salisbury
Shish *NW2, EC1*
Snazz Sichuan
Spacca Napoli
St Alban
St Germain

Salisbury
Shish *NW2, EC1*
Snazz Sichuan
Spacca Napoli
St Alban
St Germain
Sugar Reef
Swag & Tails

tamesa@oxo
Taro *SW3*
Tokyo City
Tootsies *all branches*
Vaporetto
Vivezza
Yi-Ban
Zetter

London Directory

A Cena TW1 £44
418 Richmond Rd 8288 0108
"Probably the best restaurant in Richmond" (if in fact over the bridge, in St Margaret's) — this *"comfortable modern Italian"* offers *"consistent"* cooking, and *"very warm"* service too.
/ **Details:** www.acena.co.uk; 10 pm; closed Mon L & Sun D; booking: max 6, Fri & Sat.

Abeno £37
47 Museum St, WC1 7405 3211 1–1C
17-18 Great Newport St, WC2 7379 1160 3–3B
66 Heath St, NW3 awaiting tel
"For a quick and unusual bite", try these *"courteous"* Japanese okonomiyaki (fancy omelette) diners — a *"sociable"* experience in which the *"novelty"* of having the dish cooked before your very eyes plays no small part. / **Details:** www.abeno.co.uk; 10 pm - 11 pm; WC2 no booking.

The Abingdon W8 £52
54 Abingdon Rd 7937 3339 4–2A
"Tucked-away off Kensington High Street", this *"lovely"* pub-conversion in a leafy backstreet is *"always a local favourite"*, thanks to its *"buzzy"* style and *"very competent"* food; try to book a booth at the back. / **Details:** www.theabingdonrestaurant.com; 11 pm, Mon 10.30 pm, Sun 10 pm.

About Thyme SW1 £45
82 Wilton Rd 7821 7504 1–4B
A Pimlico *"haunt"* that's *"going from strength to strength"*, thanks to its *"laid-back"* style, its *"smiley"* staff, and its *"wholesome and enjoyable"* Franco-Spanish fare.
/ **Details:** www.aboutthyme.co.uk; 11 pm; closed Sun.

Abu Zaad W12 £21
29 Uxbridge Rd 8749 5107 6–1C
An *"excellent bet for a cheap bite"*, this *"obliging"* café, near Shepherd's Bush Market, is of particular note for its *"wonderful, freshly-squeezed juices"* and its *"hearty"* Syrian fare.
/ **Details:** www.abuzaad.co.uk; 11 pm; no Amex.

Adams Café W12 £28
77 Askew Rd 8743 0572 6–1B

With its *"fry-ups by day, Tunisian/Moroccan fare by night"*, this *"little gem"* in Shepherd's Bush is *"a pleasure year after year"*; its all-round charms include some *"very drinkable"* wines, or you can BYO for small corkage. / **Details:** www.adamscafe.co.uk; 11 pm; closed Sun.

Addie's Thai Café SW5 £27 Ⓐ ⭐

121 Earl's Court Rd   7259 2620   4–2A

"What a bargain!" – this "buzzing" Thai café makes quite a discovery in the culinary desert around Earl's Court tube, thanks not least to its "cheap" but "incredibly flavourful" chow. / **Details:** *www.addiesthai.co.uk; 11 pm; closed Sat L & Sun L; no Amex.*

Aglio e Olio SW10 £37 ⭐

194 Fulham Rd   7351 0070   4–3B

"Hungry, or a homesick Italian?" – try this "always-crowded" and "ear-splittingly noisy" café, near the Chelsea & Westminster Hospital, which serves up "huge plates" of "very fresh-tasting" pasta, and at "low" prices too. / **Details:** *11.30 pm.*

Al-Waha W2 £34 ⭐

75 Westbourne Grove   7229 0806   5–1B

"Zingingly fresh mezze" and other "flavoursome" dishes have carved out quite a reputation for this low-key Bayswater Lebanese; it's sometimes hailed as "London's best" – doubters, though, feel it's a bit "hyped". / **Details:** *www.alwaharestaurant.com; 11 pm; no Amex.*

Alain Ducasse Dorchester W1 £108

53 Park Ln   7629 8866   2–3A

"How it gets three stars is a mystery!" – this "pretentious" Mayfair outpost of the Gallic über-chef's global empire is the epitome of an "over-rated Michelin destination", charging "comical" prices for an experience that's absolutely "nothing special" in any way. / **Details:** *www.alainducasse-dorchester.com; 10 pm; closed Mon, Sat L & Sun; jacket.*

Albertine W12 £27 Ⓐ

1 Wood Ln   8743 9593   6–1C

Long pre-dating neighbouring Westfield, this "very sweet and romantic wine bar" serves food that is only "passable", but its wine list offers some "reasonably-priced treasures". / **Details:** *10.30 pm; no Amex.*

Alisan HA9 £35 ⭐

The Junction, Engineers Way, Wembley   8903 3888

"Amazingly good" and "creative" dim sum dishes make a surprise find at this somewhat soulless contemporary oriental, by Wembley Stadium. / **Details:** *www.alisan.co.uk; 11 pm, Sat 11.30 pm, Sun 10.30 pm; closed Tue.*

Amaranth SW18 £27 ⭐

346 Garratt Ln   8874 9036

"One of the best Thais in SW London" – a "bustling" Earlsfield café where "willing" staff dole out "fresh" and "tasty" fare in double-quick time; "BYO too, so it can be a cheap night out". / **Details:** *11.30 pm; D only, closed Sun.*

Amaya SW1 £63 Ⓐ ⭐ ⭐

Halkin Arc, 19 Motcomb St   7823 1166   4–1D

"Exquisite", "tapas-style" dishes and a chic and "low-lit" setting make this "innovative" Belgravian the highest-rated Indian destination in town. / **Details:** *www.realindianfood.com; 11.30 pm, Sun 10.30 pm.*

43

The Anchor & Hope SE1   £38   ⭐⭐
36 The Cut   7928 9898
Thanks to its "inspired" and "gutsy" British cooking, London's No. 1 gastroboozer, near the Old Vic, is always "insanely busy"; basically "it's a scrum" – "get in early, and pounce when someone leaves!" / **Details:** *10.30 pm; closed Mon L & Sun D; no Amex; no booking.*

Andrew Edmunds W1   £39   Ⓐ
46 Lexington St   7437 5708   2–2D
"Where you go for a second date!" – this "very special" and "Bohemian" (and "squashed") Soho townhouse "remains the most romantic place in central London"; the "simple" food is "satisfactory", but is upstaged by the "surprisingly good" wine at "bargain" prices. / **Details:** *10.30 pm; no Amex; booking: max 6.*

Angels & Gypsies
Church Street Hotel SE5   £28   Ⓐ⭐
29-33 Camberwell Church St   7703 5984
"Getting a table is already a challenge", at this "star" newcomer, which forms part of a funky boutique hotel in "the middle of nowhere" (or Camberwell, as the locals call it); the "interesting" tapas are of "very good quality" and the tiled interior evokes "sunny Spanish climes".
/ **Details:** *www.churchstreethotel.com; 10.30 pm; closed Mon L; no Amex.*

Angelus W2   £67   Ⓐ⭐
4 Bathurst St   7402 0083   5–2D
"Punching well above expectations", ex-Gavroche sommelier Thierry Thomasin's "romantic" pub-conversion, tucked-away in a cul-de-sac near Lancaster Gate, rarely disappoints – he's a "most gracious host" and his "unusual" and "really lovely" wine collection accompanies "excellent" Gallic cuisine.
/ **Details:** *www.angelusrestaurant.co.uk; 11 pm, Sun 10 pm.*

The Anglesea Arms W6   £42   Ⓐ⭐⭐
35 Wingate Rd   8749 1291   6–1B
This "astonishingly good pub" in "the villagey part of Hammersmith" has long won acclaim with its "outstanding" cooking ("how do they do it from that minute kitchen?"), and its "charming", if always crowded, interior; "...and now you can even book!" / **Details:** *Tue-Sat 10.30 pm, Sat 10pm, Sun 9pm; no Amex; no booking.*

Anglo Asian Tandoori N16   £29   Ⓐ
60-62 Stoke Newington Church St   7254 3633
A stalwart Stoke Newington subcontinental, whose "lovely" food and "unfalteringly excellent" service inspire a devoted local following. / **Details:** *11.45 pm.*

L'Anima EC2   £67   ⭐
1 Snowden St   7422 7000   1–2B
"Perfect for a business lunch or dinner", Francesco Mazzei's "cool" and "creative" (and rather Manhattanite) City-fringe two-year-old is "one of the best new-wave Italians to open for quite a while"; its ratings drifted fractionally this year, though – let's hope its major mid-2010 expansion puts it back on track!
/ **Details:** *www.lanima.co.uk; 10.30 pm; closed Sat L & Sun.*

44

Annie's £45 Ⓐ
162 Thames Rd, W4   8994 9080
36-38 White Hart Ln, SW13   8878 2020
*Brace yourself for "death by Boden", but this "boho-chic" duo
have a big following among west London families, tempted
by "gorgeous" decor, and – rather incidentally – "decent
brasserie fare"; by night, they can make a "quirky" romantic
option too.* / **Details:** *www.anniesrestaurant.co.uk; 10 pm, Sat 10.30 pm.*

Apsleys
Lanesborough Hotel SW1 £88
1 Lanesborough Pl   7333 7254   4–1D
*This "opulent" Belgravia outpost of a big-name Roman chef has
been "much hyped", not least by Michelin's immediate credulous
award of a star – the reality, however, is "very average across
the board", and notably "overpriced" too.* / **Value tip:** *set brunch £59*
(FP). **Details:** *www.apsleys.co.uk; 10.30 pm; booking: max 12.*

aqua kyoto W1 £70
240 Regent St (entrance 30 Argyll St)   7478 0540   2–2C
*"Glamorous", "night-clubby" decor – and large terraces looking
down on Regent Street – give this "flash" yearling great
"occasion" appeal; the scene is too "trashy" for some tastes,
though, not helped by "average" oriental food being served
at "sky-high" prices.* / **Details:** *www.aqua-london.com; Mon-Wed 10.45 pm,
Thu-Sat 11.15 pm.*

Arbutus W1 £52 ★
63-64 Frith St   7734 4545   3–2A
*A "sensational" Soho bistro that's become a byword for value,
thanks to its consistently "creative" cooking (largely from offal
and cheaper cuts) and reasonable prices, plus "superb" wines
by the glass or carafe; the interior is "not the most dynamic",
but it does have "a nice buzz".* / **Value tip:** *set dinner £30*
(FP). **Details:** *www.arbutusrestaurant.co.uk; Mon-Sat 11pm, Sun 10.30 pm.*

Archipelago W1 £53 Ⓐ★
110 Whitfield St   7383 3346   1–1B

*"Exotic" decor and "crazy" dishes – zebra, ostrich, scorpion
or crocodile anyone? – make "ideal talking points for a date"
at this "eclectic" mini-gem, near the Telecom Tower; despite its
"outlandish" nature, though, the food is "surprisingly good".*
/ **Details:** *www.archipelago-restaurant.co.uk; 10.30 pm; closed Sat L & Sun.*

45

Ark Fish E18 £40 ★
142 Hermon Hill   8989 5345
"A massive selection of fish and seafood dishes cooked to the highest standard" have won a major following for this former pub in South Woodford; some find it "overlit" and "noisy", but the regular "queues" confirm they're doing something right. / **Details:** www.arkfishrestaurant.co.uk; Tue-Thu 9.45 pm, Fri & Sat 10.15 pm, Sun 8.45 pm; closed Mon; no Amex.

Asakusa NW1 £28 ★★
265 Eversholt St   7388 8533
"Getting a table is hard", and then "they cram you in", at this "slightly grim" establishment, near Euston; curiously, though, a visit to this family-run Japanese is usually "a real treat", thanks to "delicious, fresh" sushi, and so on, at "total-bargain" prices. / **Details:** 11.30 pm, Sat 11 pm; D only, closed Sun; no Amex.

Asia de Cuba
St Martin's Lane Hotel WC2 £86
45 St Martin's Ln   7300 5588   3–4C
Fans say it's "brilliant and wacky", but this Covent Garden fusion-scene can also seem "tired" nowadays, and those who say it's "an unsuccessful Nobu wannabe" complain of "insultingly overpriced" food and "non-existent" service. / **Details:** www.stmartinslane.com; midnight, Sun 11 pm.

Assaggi W2 £65 ★
39 Chepstow Pl   7792 5501   5–1B
"You'll struggle to find better, even in Italy!", say fans of this "quirky", hard-to-book room above a Bayswater pub, where "idiosyncratic" service adds brio to an "understated" setting; it lost its spot as London's No. 1 Italian this year, though, due to a few reports of "huge" bills for "lame" meals. / **Details:** 11 pm; closed Sun; no Amex.

Atari-Ya £18 ★★
20 James St, W1   7491 1178   2–1A
31 Vivian Ave, NW4   8202 2789
You get "the best cheap sushi in London", at these no-frills bars and take-aways, which are run by a leading firm of Japanese food importers; but "don't tell anyone!" – "tables are limited", and the Marylebone premises, in particular, are "already too crowded". / **Details:** www.atariya.co.uk; W1 8.30 pm, NW4 10 pm; NW4 closed Mon.

L'Atelier de Joel Robuchon WC2 £90 A★
13-15 West St   7010 8600   3–2B

"It's all WOW!" (including the bill, sadly), at this Covent Garden outpost of one of the world's greatest chefs, known for its "insanely good" Gallic tapas; the "very sexy" ground floor is probably the preferred destination – upstairs is a touch "subdued". / **Value tip:** set weekday L £48 (FP). **Details:** www.joelrobuchon.co.uk; midnight, Sun 10.30 pm; no trainers.

Athenaeum
Athenaeum Hotel W1　　　　£68　　　🅐⭐
116 Piccadilly　7499 3464　2–4B
It may be little known, but this "cosy, Art Deco-like" chamber is, say fans, "one of the best hotel dining rooms in town", thanks to its "refined" and "beautifully presented" cuisine and "exemplary" service; lunch and pre-theatre menus are "particularly good value". / **Details:** *www.athenaeumhotel.com; 10.30 pm.*

The Atlas SW6　　　　£37　　　🅐⭐
16 Seagrave Rd　7385 9129　4–3A
"A real pub", near Earl's Court 2, that still manages to be a really impressive all-rounder – it offers "excellent" Mediterranean fare, "interesting" wines and "real ales galore", and even has a "nice walled garden". / **Details:** *www.theatlaspub.co.uk; 10 pm; closed Sat D.*

Atma NW3　　　　£40　　　⭐
106c Finchley Rd　7431 9487
"A great 'posh' local curry house", in Belsize Park, with "high-quality" food and "friendly" service; "shame about the busy road-side location, but it's still very much worth a visit". / **Details:** *www.atmarestaurants.com; 11 pm; closed Mon.*

Aubergine SW10　　　　£92
11 Park Wk　7352 3449　4–3B
As our survey year coincided with the period during which new chef Christophe Remou was establishing himself at this once-celebrated Chelsea restaurant, we've left it un-rated; let's hope those who've reported the food to be "truly exceptional" are on to something! / **Value tip:** *set weekday L £38 (FP).* **Details:** *www.auberginerestaurant.co.uk; 10.30 pm; closed Mon & Sun; no trainers.*

Automat W1　　　　£53
33 Dover St　7499 3033　2–3C
"A real local staple for unfussy American food" – this "always buzzy" Mayfair diner does "lovely breakfasts" (one hour limit!) and "perfect burgers"; it can seem "pricey" for what it is, though, and service is sometimes "off-hand". / **Details:** *www.automat-london.com; midnight; closed Sat D & Sun D.*

L'Autre Pied W1　　　　£62　　　⭐
5-7 Blandford St　7486 9696　1–1A
"Dazzling dishes, full of flavour" make this "cheaper alternative to Pied à Terre" very popular; it's "less formal" than its parent, but its Marylebone premises can still seem "stilted". / **Value tip:** *set always available £39 (FP).* **Details:** *www.lautrepied.co.uk; 10.45 pm, Sun 9.30 pm.*

L'Aventure NW8　　　　£56　　　🅐⭐
3 Blenheim Ter　7624 6232
Catherine Parisot's "small", "sweet" and "classy" St John's Wood fixture is, for its many fans, "the zenith of romantic dining" (especially on the "magical" terrace); staff are "charming" too, and the Gallic fare they dish up "very reliable". / **Value tip:** *set weekday L £36 (FP).* **Details:** *11 pm; closed Sat L & Sun.*

Babbo W1 £70

39 Albermarle St 3205 1099 2–3C

Even some fans of the "comfort food" at this new, "more-Manhattan-than-Mayfair" Italian say it's overpriced; for critics, though, it's just a "rip-off", and with "arrogant service to boot".
/ **Details:** www.babborestaurant.co.uk; 11 pm; closed Sun.

Babur SE23 £39 Ⓐ ✪ ✪

119 Brockley Rise 8291 2400

"The best dining in south east London", say fans, is to be found "in the unsung suburb of Honor Oak Park" at this "deservedly popular Indian", which offers notably "refined" cuisine, and has staff who "couldn't be more accommodating".
/ **Details:** www.babur.info; 11.30 pm.

Babylon
Kensington Roof Gardens W8 £69 Ⓐ

99 Kensington High St 7368 3993 4–1A

"Wow, what a setting!" – "a stroll around gardens eight floors up" adds a "truly special" aura to a visit to this Kensington restaurant (which also has great views); obviously, you're "paying for the scenery", but the overall experience generally satisfies.
/ **Details:** www.virgin.com/roofgardens; 10.30 pm; closed Sun D.

Back to Basics W1 £48 ✪ ✪

21a Foley St 7436 2181 1–1B

"Like a seaside Cornish village restaurant transplanted into the middle of London!" (well, nearly) – this "very simple" and "cramped", but "relaxed", Marylebone corner spot serves up some "delicious fresh fish and seafood"; get there early!
/ **Value tip:** set always available £29 (FP). **Details:** www.backtobasics.uk.com; 10.30 pm; closed Sun.

Bam-Bou W1 £44 Ⓐ ✪

1 Percy St 7323 9130 1–1C

"Enter another world of French-Vietnamese colonialism"; this "dimly-lit" and seductive Fitzrovia townhouse – part of Richard Caring's empire – dishes up some "delicious" Asian/fusion cuisine, and there's a "fabulous" bar too.
/ **Details:** www.bam-bou.co.uk; midnight; closed Sat L & Sun; booking: max 6.

Banners N8 £39 Ⓐ

21 Park Rd 8348 2930

"Insanely large" breakfasts and "a lovely family-friendly environment", help win a devoted following for this "fun" diner in "trendy Crouch End"; its all-day World Food menu is "a bit like Giraffe on steroids". / **Details:** 11.30 pm, Fri & Sat midnight, Sun 11; no Amex.

Baozi Inn WC2 £18 ✪

25 Newport Ct 7287 6877 3–3B

"Heavenly pork buns" are the highlight of the "inexpensive and authentic" Sichuan street food on offer at this "miniscule" but characterful Chinatown two-year-old – you may find a queue, but "it's worth the wait". / **Details:** 10 pm, Fri-Sat 10.30; no credit cards; no booking.

Bar Boulud
Oriental Hyde Park SW1   **£50**
66 Knightsbridge   7201 3899   4–1D
NYC star-chef, Daniel Boulud's Manhattan/Paris-style brasserie concept has dazzled the critics (and impressed us too), not least with its "fantastic" charcuterie, and "smooth" service; Adam Tihany's design, however, does nothing to shake off the inevitable "basement" feel of its Knightsbridge setting. / **Details:** www.barboulud.com; 11 pm.

Bar Italia W1   **£20**   Ⓐ
22 Frith St   7437 4520   3–2A
"Still the coolest café in London" – this "lively" 24/7 Soho institution may do "the best coffee" and some "decent" bites, but it's the people-watching that makes it special (particularly in the wee hours). / **Details:** www.baritaliasoho.com; open 24 hours, Sun 4 am; no Amex; no booking.

Barrafina W1   **£43**   Ⓐ✪✪
54 Frith St   7813 8016   3–2A
The tapas are "so bloody good" – the seafood's "so fresh, you wonder if it's actually dead" – at the Hart brothers' "stunning" carbon copy of Barcelona's famous 'Cal Pep'; "go early!" – there's no booking… and only 23 seats. / **Details:** www.barrafina.co.uk; 11 pm, Sun 10.30 pm; no booking.

The Battery E14   **£70**
34 Westferry Circus   8305 3089
"Sublime river views" are the highlight of this pricey new Inc. Group outlet on the former Canary Wharf site of Ubon (RIP); even so, there's "not much atmosphere" but, for a business encounter, the food is "tasty enough". / **Details:** www.battery.uk.com; 10.30 pm; closed Sat & Sun.

Bellamy's W1   **£70**   Ⓐ
18-18a Bruton Pl   7491 2727   2–2B
Hidden-away in a mews, a posh Mayfair brasserie that achieves "formality without undue grandeur", and where the fare is pricey but quite "reliable"; "nicely spaced" tables make it a natural for business too. / **Details:** www.bellamysrestaurant.co.uk; 10.15 pm; closed Sat L & Sun.

Bellevue Rendez-Vous SW17   **£37**   Ⓐ✪
218 Trinity Rd   8767 5810
"Thriving after rebranding" – this "lovely" bistro near Wandsworth Common (previously called Mini Mundus) wins all-round praise for its "charming" service (from the French couple who own it), and its "simple" dishes at "good-value" prices. / **Details:** www.bellevuerendezvous.com; 10.30 pm; closed Mon L; no Amex.

Belvedere W8 £57

Holland Pk, off Abbotsbury Rd   7602 1238   6–1D

*For "old-world charm" ("I thought I might meet Poirot"),
this "lovely" Art Deco spot – a "wonderfully romantic oasis"
in leafy Holland Park – is "hard to beat"; the food does nothing
to detract from an "efficient and high-class" experience.*
/ **Details:** www.belvedererestaurant.co.uk; 10.30 pm; closed Sun D.

Benares W1 £75

12a Berkeley Square Hs, Berkeley Sq   7629 8886   2–3B

*"The post-fire refit has only added to the ambience" of Atul
Kochar's "slick" Mayfair dining room; that's not all that's
currently on a high, though – service is very "crisp" and his
"sophisticated" Indian cuisine "truly memorable".* / **Value tip:** set
weekday L £48 (FP). **Details:** www.benaresrestaurant.co.uk; 10.45 pm,
Sun 10.30 pm; no trainers.

Bentley's W1 £67

11-15 Swallow St   7734 4756   2–3D

*Relaunched by Richard Corrigan in recent years, this old veteran,
near Piccadilly Circus, is home, say fans, to "the best seafood
in the capital"; the "informal" ground-floor oyster bar, however,
is to be preferred to the "staid" dining room above.*
/ **Details:** www.bentleys.org; 10.30 pm; no jeans; booking: max 8.

Bevis Marks EC3 £61

Bevis Marks   7283 2220

*"An atmospheric location at the side of London's
oldest synagogue" helps make this modern kosher venture
a "useful" City rendezvous; this year's reports on the cuisine,
however, were rather up-and-down.*
/ **Details:** www.bevismarkstherestaurant.com; 8.30 pm; closed Fri D, Sat & Sun.

Bibendum SW3 £71

81 Fulham Rd   7581 5817   4–2C

*The "airy" and "well-spaced" first-floor dining room of this
Brompton Cross "landmark" is a "beautiful" space, and its
"talented" waiting staff, and "brilliant" wine list do nothing to let
it down; the food is "refined" too, and, if you visit for lunch,
can even be "good value".* / **Details:** www.bibendum.co.uk; 11 pm,
Sun 10.30 pm; booking: max 12 at L, 10 at D.

Bibendum Oyster Bar SW3 £56
81 Fulham Rd 7589 1480 4–2C
"Beautiful, super-fresh seafood" comes *"at a price, but one that's worth paying"*, at this elegant parlour, on the way in to the Brompton Cross Conran Shop – *"for best atmosphere, sit in the original space, not the entrance hall"*. / **Details:** www.bibendum.co.uk; 10.30 pm, Sun 10 pm; no booking.

The Bingham TW10 £70 Ⓐ
61-63 Petersham Rd 8940 0902
With its "bucolic" riverside location, this "lovely, bright and stylish" dining room makes a "beautiful setting for a special occasion" (particularly a "reasonably-priced" lunch); "oh, and the food's great too". / **Value tip:** set weekday L £41 (FP). **Details:** www.thebingham.co.uk; 10 pm; closed Sun D; no trainers.

Bistrot Bruno Loubet
The Zetter EC1 £42 Ⓐ ★ ★
St John's Square 86-88 Clerkenwell Rd 7324 4455
"Welcome back Bruno!"; this new Farringdon venture – from a chef who was big news in '90s London – is a *"bright and airy"* sort of place that's *"one of the rarities that gets everything right"*; his *"revved-up, classic French cuisine"* pleases almost all reporters, and the service is *"charming"* too.
/ **Details:** www.thezetter.com; 10.30 pm, Sun 10 pm.

Bistrotheque E2 £46 Ⓐ
23-27 Wadeson St 8983 7900
"Fun, fun, fun, and make sure you catch the cabaret at weekends" – this *"quirky"* bar/restaurant occupies a trendy, warehouse-style space and is *"first point of call"* for many East End hipsters, especially for brunch. / **Value tip:** set pre-theatre £31 (FP). **Details:** www.bistrotheque.com; 10.30 pm, Fri 11 pm; closed weekday L.

Blakes
Blakes Hotel SW7 £100 Ⓐ
33 Roland Gdns 7370 6701 4–2B
With its "dark and exotic" looks, this datedly glamorous (and nowadays rather forgotten) South Kensington dining room retains some allure as a romantic venue, despite the perennial risk of "ordinary" food; brace yourself, though, for some "open-wallet surgery". / **Details:** www.blakeshotels.com; 11.30 pm.

Bleeding Heart EC1 £51 Ⓐ ★
Bleeding Heart Yd, Greville St 7242 8238
"Oozing history", this hidden-away den, north of Holborn – a rambling warren of tavern, bistro and restaurant – is a venue *"with few equals"* for sheer consistency; with its *"classy"* Gallic fare and a *"serious"* wine list, it's *"great for business by day"* (and even better for *"an illicit date"* by night).
/ **Details:** www.bleedingheart.co.uk; 10.30 pm; closed Sun.

Blue Elephant SW6   £56

4-6 Fulham Broadway   7385 6595   4–4A

The "exotic tropical setting" – "almost a theme park" – provides a "stunning" and "romantic" backdrop to a meal at this "fun" Fulham veteran; its "well-prepared" food is back on better form of late too – "expensive, but worth it".
/ **Details:** www.blueelephant.com; 11.30 pm, Sun 10.30 pm.

Blue Jade SW1   £31

44 Hugh St   7828 0321   1–4B

"Bravo!" – this Pimlico backwoods Thai impresses all reporters with its "charm" and "reliability", not least of its "simple but tasty" fare. / **Details:** 11 pm; closed Sat L & Sun.

Bocca Di Lupo W1   £46

12 Archer St   7734 2223   2–2D

"Incredible", "earthy" Italian 'tapas' – "even my friends from Milan were surprised!" – have won a vast fan club for this "stellar" yearling, "hidden in a dingy street" in Soho; "consistency has slipped" since the early days, though, and conditions can seem "too squashed".
/ **Details:** www.boccadilupo.com; 11 pm; closed Sun D; booking: max 10.

Bombay Palace W2   £44

50 Connaught St   7723 8855   5-1D

"This is the real deal: just look at all the rich Indians around you!" – this "traditional" Bayswater veteran offers "fantastic" cooking, and service that's "prompt, discreet and friendly", albeit in a setting that's (authentically) "hotel-like".
/ **Details:** www.bombay-palace.co.uk; 11.30 pm.

Il Bordello E1   £38

81 Wapping High St   7481 9950

A "most busy and bustling" old-school Italian, in Wapping, which thrives on its "excellent, personal service", "inviting" atmosphere, and its "generous" and "affordable" dishes; "top-flight" pizzas a speciality. / **Details:** 11 pm, Sun 10.30 pm; closed Sat L.

La Bota N8   £24

31 Broadway Pde   8340 3082

A "genuine Spanish tapas place", in Hornsey, offering "excellent food" at "amazing prices"; no wonder it's "always packed".
/ **Details:** www.labota.co.uk; 11 pm, Fri-Sun 11.30 pm; no Amex.

Brady's SW18   £26 ⭐
513 Old York Rd   8877 9599
"First-rate fish" (battered or grilled), chips, mushy peas and puds, plus "welcoming" staff – no wonder this "happy" family-run chippy/fish bistro in Wandsworth retains a devoted local following. / **Details:** www.bradysfish.co.uk; 10.30 pm; closed Mon L & Sun; no Amex; no booking.

Brasserie Joël
Park Plaza Westminster Bridge SE1   £53
Westminster Bridge Rd   7620 7272   1–3D
A star London chef of the '90s, Joël Antunes, is now back in town after stints in Atlanta and New York; we didn't have a chance to sample his new dining room – part of a 1000+ bedroom hotel – before this guide went to press, but reactions in the newspapers have been mixed. / **Details:** www.brasseriejoel.co.uk; 10.30 pm, 11 pm Fri & Sat; D only.

Brasserie Toulouse-Lautrec SE11 £34 Ⓐ⭐
140 Newington Butts   7582 6800
"One of the few viable places to eat near Elephant & Castle"; this "fun" newcomer (from the same family as local legend the Lobster Pot) gets a big thumbs-up for its "surprisingly good" food, and "attentive" service; regular live music in the bar. / **Details:** www.lobsterpotrestaurant.co.uk; 10.30 pm.

Brick Lane Beigel Bake E1   £ 6   ⭐⭐
159 Brick Ln   7729 0616   1–1C
"Never-ending queues" are a hazard 24/7 at this famous slice of "the real East End"; star menu item – "the best salt beef beigels in town", at a price that's an "absolute steal". / **Details:** open 24 hours; no credit cards; no booking.

Brilliant UB2   £35   Ⓐ⭐⭐
72-76 Western Rd   8574 1928
Lost deep in suburban Southall, this large and "busy" Indian veteran justifies the schlep with its "superb" and "really authentic" dishes (plus healthy low-salt/fat/sugar alternatives); expect "Bollywood films on the plasmas" while you eat. / **Details:** www.brilliantrestaurant.com; 11.30 pm, Fri & Sat midnight; closed Mon, Sat L & Sun L; booking: weekends only.

(The Albemarle)
Brown's Hotel W1   £75
Albemarle St   7493 6020   2–3C
For a "clubby" meal, this "spacious" and "muted" Mayfair dining room – with its "rather splendid British dishes", and its "discreet" and "caring" service – is currently one of the best choices in town. / **Value tip:** set always available £45 (FP). **Details:** www.roccofortecollection.com; 11 pm, 10.30 pm.

Brula TW1   £43   Ⓐ⭐
43 Crown Rd   8892 0602
This "cosy" St Margaret's bistro remains a "favourite local haunt", thanks to its "delicious" Gallic cooking and "very friendly" service; "the set lunch is a steal". / **Value tip:** set weekday L £24 (FP). **Details:** www.brula.co.uk; 10.30 pm; closed Sun D.

Brunello
Baglioni Hotel SW7 £75
60 Hyde Park Gate   7368 5900   4–1B

Food that's sometimes "very good" is matched up with
an "extensive" (and "incredibly expensive") wine list, at this
Italian-owned boutique-hotel, near Kensington Gardens; doubters
find the approach a touch "arrogant", though, and reports are
few. / *Details: www.baglionihotellondon.com; 11 pm.*

Buen Ayre E8 £44 ⭐
50 Broadway Mkt   7275 9900
It's "not so cool now it's been discovered", but this Hackney
'parilla' is still a "hidden gem" – "amazing aromas" prepare you
for "the best steaks". / *Details: www.buenayre.co.uk; midnight.*

Bull & Last NW5 £43 Ⓐ⭐⭐
168 Highgate Rd   7267 3641
"Redefining the gastropub!", this Kentish Town phenomenon
dishes up "excellent, robust, modern-seasonal British cooking
with style and flair"; nowhere's quite perfect, though –
it's "far too noisy". / *Details: www.thebullandlast.co.uk; 10 pm; no Amex.*

Byron £31
97-99 Wardour St, W1   7297 9390   2–2D
33-35 Wellington St, WC2   7420 9850   3–3D
300 King's Rd, SW3   7352 6040   4–3C
75 Gloucester Rd, SW7   7244 0700   4–2B
93-95 Old Brompton Rd, SW7   7590 9040   4–2B
Westfield, Ariel Way, W12   8743 7755   6–1C
222 Kensington High St, W8   7361 1717   4–1A
341 Upper St, N1   7704 7620
Cabot Place East, E14   7715 9360
"There's a new best-burger in town" – and it's to be found
at this family-friendly, fast-growing chain of "weirdly chic diners";
trouble in the family, though – its ratings are even better than its
'gold standard' elder sibling, PizzaExpress.
/ *Details: www.byronhamburgers.com; 11 pm, Fri & Sat 11.30 pm,
Sun 10.30 pm; W12 8 pm, Thu & Fri 9 pm, Sun 5 pm; W12 closed Sun D;
no booking Sat & Sun L, W12 no booking.*

Café 209 SW6 £23 Ⓐ
209 Munster Rd   7385 3625
This "so cheap" Fulham Thai is always "really buzzing", thanks
not least to the feisty style of riotous owner Joy; "it's BYO too,
which is a big plus". / *Details: 10.30 pm; D only, closed Sun, closed Dec;
no Amex.*

Le Café Anglais
Whiteley's W2   £55   Ⓐ
8 Porchester Gdns   7221 1415   5–1C
*This "calm" Art Deco-style chamber – perched above the
hubbub of Whiteley's in Bayswater – appears to best advantage
by day; Rowley Leigh's "something-for-everyone" brasserie menu
(with "especially good" small plates) offers "affordable luxury"
for most reporters, but a minority remain deeply unconvinced;
new 50-seat oyster bar coming soon.*
/ **Details:** www.lecafeanglais.co.uk; 11 pm, Sun 10 pm.

Café del Parc N19   £16   Ⓐ⭐
167 Junction Road   7281 5684
*"Freshly-cooked" and "delicious" tapas win nothing but raves for
this Tufnell Park café (and the wine list is "particularly good"
too) – it's "quite astounding what they manage to achieve
in such a small space".* / **Details:** www.delparc.co.uk; 10.30 pm; no Amex.

Café du Marché EC1   £51   Ⓐ⭐
22 Charterhouse Sq   7608 1609
*With its "old-fashioned, bare brick walls" (and, at night,
"cool jazz"), this well-known "little-bit-of-France" in Smithfield
provides a "very convivial" and "romantic" destination;
its "rustic" Gallic fare has been "remarkably consistent for
decades".* / **Details:** www.cafedumarche.co.uk; 10 pm; closed Sat L & Sun;
no Amex.

Café Japan NW11   £30   ⭐⭐
626 Finchley Rd   8455 6854
*"My Japanese wife is willing to cross London for this!" –
a "basic" café, opposite Golder's Green tube, rightly acclaimed
for its "consistently exceptional" sushi at "great-value" prices.*
/ **Value tip:** set dinner £20 (FP). **Details:** 10 pm; closed Mon & Tue; no Amex.

Café Luc W1   £48   ⭐
50 Marylebone High St   7258 9878   1–1A
*This new Belgian-backed venture on the former Marylebone site
of Eat & Two Veg (RIP) is an upmarket (but tightly-packed)
brasserie of a type still rare in London; the menu looks
uninspired, but was realised – on our early-days visit – to the
high standard the prices demand.* / **Details:** www.cafeluc.com; 11 pm.

Café Spice Namaste E1   £44   ⭐
16 Prescot St   7488 9242
*"Forget the hawkers of Brick Lane" – if you're looking for
"sophisticated" and "imaginative" Indian cuisine, seek out Cyrus
Todiwala's "cheerful" and "colourful" veteran; with its
"beautifully-spiced" food, it's still "a winner after all these years".*
/ **Details:** www.cafespice.co.uk; 10.30 pm; closed Sat L & Sun.

Caffè Vergnano   £12   Ⓐ⭐
62 Charing Cross Rd, WC2   7240 8587   3–3B
Royal Festival Hall, SE1   7921 9339   1–3D
*"Must-have coffee and decadent hot choc", with "attractive"
snacks, win praise for these "upmarket coffee houses"; WC2 is
"small and crowded" – in SE1 there's also a restaurant with
more substantial fare (which is less of an attraction).*
/ **Details:** www.caffevergnano.com; SE1 midnight; WC2 8 pm, Fri & Sat midnight,
EC4 11 pm; EC4 Sat & Sun; no Amex.

Caleya Ibérica
Ibérica W1 £57 ★
195 Great Portland St   7636 8650   1–1B
"Quieter than the ground-floor tapas bar" — to the extent it has "no buzz" — this quality Spanish dining room wins praise for its "exemplary" service, and surprisingly "imaginative" and "well-executed" Spanish dishes. / Details: www.ibericalondon.co.uk; 11 pm.

Cambio de Tercio SW5 £52 Ⓐ★
163 Old Brompton Rd   7244 8970   4–2B
Everything is done "with gusto and élan" at this "excellent all-rounder" in South Kensington, not least the "enthusiastic" service, and "imaginative" Spanish cooking; "superb wine" too. / Details: www.cambiodetercio.co.uk; 11.30 pm.

Canton Arms SW8 £32 Ⓐ★
177 South Lambeth Rd   7582 8710
The arrival of this "little sister to the Anchor & Hope" (London's top gastropub) has been a boon to "poorly-served" Stockwell; it was instantly "super-busy", with most reporters acclaiming the "sheer inventiveness" of its "robust" fare. / Details: www.cantonarms.com; 10 pm; closed Mon L; no booking.

The Capital Restaurant
Capital Hotel SW3 £85
22-24 Basil St   7589 5171   4–1D
The jury's still out on the new culinary régime at this luxurious (but some feel "charmless") Knightsbridge dining room; fans say the place "retains its halo" under Jerome Ponchelle (once of the Connaught), but critics — citing "reduced portions" and "no inter-course freebies" — aren't so sure. / Details: www.capitalhotel.co.uk; 10 pm; no jeans or trainers.

Le Caprice SW1 £58 Ⓐ★
Arlington Hs, Arlington St   7629 2239   2–4C
With its "'80s-chic" brasserie styling, this famous "class act", near the Ritz, is still, by and large, the definition of "utter reliability"; of late, however, it has very occasionally seemed a tad "dull", "pretentious" or "passé" — perhaps the strain of nursing its new NYC sibling? / Details: www.caprice-holdings.co.uk; midnight, Sun 11 pm.

Caraffini SW1 £45 Ⓐ
61-63 Lower Sloane St   7259 0235   4–2D
"So welcoming and hospitable", this "crowded" trattoria, near Sloane Square, has staff who "make you feel like a VIP even on your first visit"; the "old-fashioned" Italian cooking is "reassuring" and "very tasty" too. / Details: www.caraffini.co.uk; 11.30 pm; closed Sun.

The Caramel Room
Berkeley Hotel SW1 £69
Wilton Pl   7235 6000   4–1D
The informal all-day eatery of London's foodiest hotel has achieved PR-prominence with its 'prêt-à-portea' afternoon tea ("cakes like mini-handbags, bikinis", …); it also does a "great Full English". / Details: www.the-berkeley.co.uk; 11 pm.

Caravan EC1   £35
11-13 Exmouth Mkt   7833 8115
"Unconventional", "fusion-esque" combos of "top-notch" ingredients – plus the "friendliest" service – help whip up a "great buzz" at this "casual" new Farringdon hang-out; like its predecessor Al's (RIP), it's an ace spot "for brunch and lazy weekend meals". / **Details:** www.caravanonexmouth.co.uk; 10.30 pm; closed Sun.

Le Cassoulet CR2   £46
18 Selsdon Rd   8633 1818
Malcolm John's "typical French bistro" is "a real find in a surprising location", say many South Croydon locals; not everyone is quite convinced, but even cynics generally concede the place offers "reasonable value for money". / **Value tip:** set Sun L £31 (FP). **Details:** www.lecassoulet.co.uk; 10.30 pm, Sat 11 pm, Sun 10 pm.

Catch
Andaz Hotel EC2   £70
40 Liverpool St   7618 7200   1–2B
"For conducting business", some reporters tip this "smart" venue, deep inside a hotel by Liverpool Street; "there's not enough separation" from the "noisy" bar, though, and the fish and seafood dishes can seem "bland" and "overpriced".
/ **Details:** www.andazdining.com; 10.15 pm; closed Sat & Sun.

Cecconi's W1   £55
5a Burlington Gdns   7434 1500   2–3C
"A magnet for Bond girls!" – this "slick" and "genial" Italian brasserie in Mayfair has an "all-day buzz" about it, starting at breakfast (which fans say is "better than at the Wolseley"); the rest of the day's "luxe" light menu is "competent", though, "rather than exciting". / **Value tip:** set brunch £37 (FP). **Details:** www.cecconis.co.uk; 1am, Sun midnight.

Cellar Gascon EC1   £35
59 West Smithfield Rd   7600 7561
"For a glass of vino plus nibbles", this Smithfield budget spin-off from nearby Club Gascon fits the bill perfectly, with its "heavenly", regional wine list at "good-value" prices, and "tasty tapas". / **Value tip:** set weekday L £18 (FP). **Details:** www.cellargascon.com; midnight; closed Sat & Sun.

Le Cercle SW1   £48
1 Wilbraham Pl   7901 9999   4–2D
"Brilliant Gascon tapas" and "cool" styling create a "sexy" all-round experience at this "sophisticated" basement, near Sloane Square; for romance, try to nab one of the curtained booths.
/ **Value tip:** set pre-theatre £30 (FP). **Details:** www.lecercle.co.uk; 11 pm; closed Mon & Sun.

Chamberlain's EC3   £55 ⭐

23-25 Leadenhall Mkt   7648 8690
*From the al fresco tables you can watch the world go by, at this
Leadenhall Market fish and seafood parlour; it seems
"more reasonably priced these days", winning higher ratings for
its "well-cooked, varied and original" cuisine.*
/ Details: www.chamberlains.org; 9.30 pm; closed Sat & Sun.

Champor-Champor SE1   £48 🅐⭐

62 Weston St   7403 4600
*A "sensational" take on Malaysian cuisine again inspires rave
reviews for this "small" and "hard-to-find" spot, "tucked away
near London Bridge"; with its "exotic" and "cluttered" interior,
it's "great for a special dîner-à-deux" too.*
/ Details: www.champor-champor.com; midnight; D only, closed Sun.

Chella W4   £39 ⭐

142 Chiswick High Rd   8994 6816   6–2A
*"Unusually modern decor for an eatery of this genre" helps
differentiate this new Chiswick Iranian – an "approachable"
operation, with "really tasty, high-quality food at reasonable
prices". / Details: www.chella-restaurant.co.uk; midnight; no Amex.*

Cheyne Walk Brasserie SW3   £63

50 Cheyne Walk   7376 8787   4–3C
*"Beautiful" decor lends a "sophisticated yet casual" air to this
glamorous Chelsea venture, and the "simple" Gallic fare –
largely from an open grill – is "extremely tasty"; sceptics,
though, find it "so very overpriced", and service is surprisingly
"variable". / Details: www.cheynewalkbrasserie.com; 10.30 pm; closed
Mon L & Sun D.*

Chez Bruce SW17   £62 🅐⭐⭐

2 Bellevue Rd   8672 0114
*Yet again voted Londoners' favourite destination, Bruce Poole's
admirably "unpretentious" star, by Wandsworth Common,
stands out for its "spot-on" seasonal food (plus "exceptional"
wines and "legendary" cheese) and its "considerate" service,
all at "reasonable prices"; let's hope the summer-2010
expansion only improves it! / Value tip: set weekday L £38
(FP). Details: www.chezbruce.co.uk; 10.30 pm, Sun 9.30 pm.*

Chez Liline N4   £38 ⭐⭐

101 Stroud Green Rd   7263 6550
*Ignore the decidedly "non-scenic" location – "every mouthful is a
taste sensation", at this "superb" Finsbury Park gem, where
chef/patron Sylvain Hong puts a super-spicy "Mauritian twist"
on some of the best fish dishes in town. / Value tip: set weekday L
£20 (FP). Details: ww.chezliline.co.uk; 11 pm; closed Mon.*

Chez Marcelle W14   £27 ⭐⭐

34 Blythe Rd   7603 3241   6–1D
*"The indomitable Marcelle" presides over this "one-woman
show" in an "IKEA-esque" room, behind Olympia, and her
"colossal" Lebanese dishes are "truly excellent"; "atrocious"
waits, however, may make take-away "the better option".
/ Details: 10 pm; closed Mon, Tue-Thu D only, Fri-Sun open L & D; no credit
cards.*

China Tang
Dorchester Hotel W1 **£75**
53 Park Ln 7629 9988 2–3A
"Like my neighbourhood Chinese, just 5x the price!" – it's very
hard to warm to Sir David Tang's *"grand"* and potentially
"glamorous" Mayfair basement, which sometimes seems merely
a *"pretentious, money-making machine"*. / **Value tip:** *set weekday L
£34 (FP).* **Details:** *www.thedorchesterhotel.com; 11.30 pm.*

Chisou W1 **£38** ✪
4 Princes St 7629 3931 2–1C
*It certainly looks "unassuming", but this "friendly" Japanese
café, near Oxford Circus, is "excellent" – the food (not just the
sushi and sashimi) is "wonderful", and there's a "great sake list"
too.* / **Details:** *www.chisou.co.uk; 10.30 pm; closed Sun.*

Cho-San SW15 **£39** ✪
292 Upper Richmond Rd 8788 9626
"A little piece of Japan in Putney!" – this *"shabby"* but
"welcoming" veteran has a *"very authentic feel"*, and its
"excellent, reasonably-priced" fare is *"the real thing"* too.
/ **Details:** *10.30 pm; closed Mon; no Amex.*

Chor Bizarre W1 **£43** 🅐✪
16 Albemarle St 7629 9802 2–3C
*A "bizarre" collection of "great furniture and fittings" –
the name means 'thieves' bazaar' – sets the "eccentric" tone for
this Mayfair Indian, where the food is generally "a cut above".*
/ **Details:** *www.chorbizarre.com; 11.30 pm; closed Sun L.*

Chutney SW18 **£28** ✪
11 Alma Rd 8870 4588
"An excellent local for Wandsworth" – a cosy Indian offering
"quality curry" that's quite a *"bargain"*.
/ **Details:** *www.chutneyrestaurant.co.uk; 11.30 pm; D only.*

Chutney Mary SW10 **£55** 🅐✪
535 King's Rd 7351 3113 4–4B
*Celebrating 20 years in business, World's End's "great all-
rounder" still offers "interesting and different" Indian food and
"attentive" service in a "serene" and "romantic" environment –
"get a conservatory table if you can".*
/ **Details:** *www.realindianfood.com; 11.30 pm, Sun 10.30 pm; closed weekday
L; booking: max 10.*

The Cinnamon Club SW1 **£67** 🅐✪
Old Westminster Library, Great Smith St 7222 2555 1–4C
*Thanks not least to its "adventurous" cuisine, this "chic" and
"clubby" outfit – in a former library near Westminster Abbey –
retains its status as London's top "posh Indian"; it's particularly
popular for business.* / **Value tip:** *set always available £42
(FP).* **Details:** *www.cinnamonclub.com; 10.45 pm; closed Sun; no trainers.*

Cinnamon Kitchen EC2 £55 Ⓐ⭐⭐
9 Devonshire Sq   7626 5000
The "vivid" Indian cuisine at this "slick" City yearling is actually "better than at the original Cinnamon Club" (itself no slouch); all this, plus a "hip and happening bar" and "great deck area for warm weather". / Details: www.cinnamon-kitchen.com; 11.30 pm; closed Sat L & Sun.

Cipriani W1 £78 ⓧ
25 Davies St   7399 0500   2–2B

*A "hilarious" Mayfair Eurotrash "zoo", where the prices are "a joke", but the people-watching is "fun" – "if you're not on the A-list, though, expect to be ignored, and charged for the privilege"; NB following legal action by the eponymous Venetian hotel, a name change is expected some time soon.
/ Details: www.cipriani.com; 11.45 pm.*

Clarke's W8 £57 Ⓐ⭐⭐
124 Kensington Church St   7221 9225   5–2B
"Back on form", Sally Clarke's "understated" veteran achieved dazzling ratings this year for its "caring" service – often from la patronne herself – and "terrific" Californian-inspired cuisine showcasing "top ingredients"; NB the basement is rather "dreary" compared to the ground floor. / Details: www.sallyclarke.com; 10 pm; closed Sun D; booking: max 14.

Clos Maggiore WC2 £52 Ⓐ⭐
33 King St   7379 9696   3–3C
*"If you don't feel romantic here, order some Viagra asap!"; the "stunning" conservatory is a high point of this "magical" and increasingly discovered "oasis", among the tourist traps of Covent Garden, where the whole experience is "first-rate"; brace yourself for a wine list which is "absurdly large". / **Value tip**: set weekday L £32 (FP). Details: www.closmaggiore.com; Mon-Sat 11.15 pm, Sun 10 pm.*

Club Gascon EC1 £71 Ⓐ⭐
57 West Smithfield   7796 0600
A "lovely" Smithfield fixture that matches up some "superb" and "complex" (and foie-gras heavy) Gascon tapas with "first-class" (and "unusual") Gallic wines; "between all the bankers, a romantic meal can be had…" / Details: www.clubgascon.com; 10 pm, Fri-Sat 10.30 pm; closed Sat L & Sun.

Coach & Horses EC1 £38 ⭐

26-28 Ray St   7278 8990

"Mouth-watering Scotch eggs" are a highlight of the *"earthy"* dishes on offer at this *"traditional"* and *"friendly"* Clerkenwell pub. / **Details:** www.thecoachandhorses.com; 10 pm; closed Sat L & Sun D.

Cocorino W1 £14 ⭐

18 Thayer St   7935 0810   2–1A

A new Fitzrovia gelateria/focacceria serving *"tempting"* treats at *"bargain"* prices; the only drawback? – it's *"a teeny, tiny space"*. / **Details:** www.cocorino.co.uk; 6 pm; no Mastercard.

Cocum SW20 £30 ⭐

9 Approach Rd   8540 3250

With its *"beautiful south Indian food"*, this Raynes Park spot is *"no run-of-the-mill curry house"*; it's a *"small place, and it can get crowded"*. / **Details:** www.cocumrestaurant.co.uk; no Amex.

Comptoir Gascon EC1 £43 Ⓐ⭐

63 Charterhouse St   7608 0851

"Cramped but cosy, and with an authentic bistro feel", Club Gascon's *"refined but fun"* Smithfield spin-off is much admired for its *"delightful"* service, and its *"robust"* portions of *"real French food"*. / **Details:** www.comptoirgascon.com; 10 pm, Thu & Fri 11 pm; closed Mon & Sun.

Coq d'Argent EC2 £62

1 Poultry   7395 5000

"To impress a client", many City-slickers tip this *"amazing"* 6th-floor D&D-group venue, with its extensive gardens and its *"stunning"* views; you pay *"a high premium"*, though, for *"safe"* food and *"efficient but charm-free"* service, in a dining room that manages – given the location – to feel remarkably *"sterile"*. / **Details:** www.coqdargent.co.uk; 9.45 pm; closed Sat L & Sun D.

Cork & Bottle WC2 £34 Ⓐ❌

44-46 Cranbourn St   7734 7807   3–3B

This *"quirky"* and *"buzzing"* old basement wine bar is something of a *"secret treasure"*, hidden away by a Leicester Square sex shop; the food is *"entirely beside the point"* – *"you're here for owner Don's impeccable wine list"*. / **Details:** www.corkandbottle.net; 11.30 pm; no booking after 6.30 pm.

Corrigan's Mayfair W1 £68

28 Upper Grosvenor St   7499 9943   2–3A

Richard Corrigan's Mayfair yearling provides a *"classy"* all-round experience; compared to the best of his 'Lindsay House' days, though, fans can find the *"gutsy"* cuisine *"a little underwhelming"*, and the overall style too obviously aimed at *"expense accounts"*. / **Details:** www.corrigansmayfair.com; 11 pm, Sun 9 pm; closed Sat L; booking: max 8.

Crazy Bear W1   £50   

26-28 Whitfield St   7631 0088   1–1C

"Exaggeratedly cool" decor (including "fantastic, if confusing, loos!") lends a "stylish" and "romantic" air to this Fitzrovia venture; the Thai/Chinese food is "lovely", too – if maybe "a tad overpriced" – and there's an "excellent cocktail bar".
/ **Details:** *www.crazybeargroup.co.uk; 10.30 pm; no shorts.*

Cyprus Mangal SW1   £26

45 Warwick Way   7828 5940   1–4B

"200 cab drivers can't be wrong!"; this Pimlico grill is hailed by the cognoscenti as offering "the best shish kebab in town" – "truly authentic" "scrumptious", and "cheap"! / **Details:** *Sun-Thu midnight, Fri & Sat 1 am; no Amex.*

Dans le Noir EC1   £69

29 Clerkenwell Grn   7253 1100

"Overall, eating in the dark is a phenomenal 'once-in-a-lifetime' experience", says one survivor of this "weird" Farringdon theme restaurant; once is enough, though – "the food couldn't be much worse!" / **Details:** *www.danslenoir.com; 9.30 pm; D only.*

Daphne NW1   £31

83 Bayham St   7267 7322

"On a summer evening on the terrace, you could believe yourself in Greece", at this "super-homely" Camden Town veteran – a "trustworthy" taverna, where the cooking is "a bit different from the run-of-the-mill". / **Value tip:** *set weekday L £18 (FP).* **Details:** *11.30 pm; closed Sun; no Amex.*

Daphne's SW3   £51

112 Draycott Ave   7589 4257   4–2C

"You just feel so relaxed", at this "perfect upmarket Italian" near Brompton Cross (which "has improved greatly" since the Caprice group took it over a few years ago) – service is "extremely courteous" and "there's nothing to fault" in the "reliable" cooking. / **Details:** *www.daphnes-restaurant.co.uk; 11.30 pm.*

Dean Street Townhouse W1   £45

69-72 Dean St   7434 1775   3–2A

An "unbelievably noisy bar" adds to the "cool" media vibe at this clubby Soho newcomer – instantly a key hang-out for those "who won't pay to join the parent Soho House club or the Graucho"; the menu is "upmarket school dinners" – "passable", but "not what the place is about".
/ **Details:** *www.deanstreettownhouse.com; Mon-Sat 11.30 pm, Sun 11 pm.*

Defune W1 **£41** ⭐⭐
34 George St   7935 8311   2–1A
You get some of "the best sushi in town", at this "slightly sterile" Marylebone Japanese, but "lordy you pay for it" – prices are "absurd". / *Details:* 10.30 pm.

Dehesa W1 **£40** Ⓐ⭐
25 Ganton St   7494 4170   2–2C
"A very slick and inspiring operation" – the Salt Yard's Soho sibling may be "squashed" and "always packed", but it has a "wonderful buzz", and offers "fabulous" Italian/Spanish tapas, plus "interesting" wines; should they turn the music down, though? / *Details:* www.dehesa.co.uk; 11 pm; closed Sun D.

Le Deuxième WC2 **£48**
65a Long Acre   7379 0033   3–2D
Near the Royal Opera House, this somewhat "austere" contemporary spot is ultra-"convenient" for a pre/post show bite, and quite well positioned for a "smart business lunch" too; the food, though is "not thrilling". / *Value tip:* set pre-theatre £29 (FP). *Details:* www.ledeuxieme.com; midnight, Sun 11 pm.

Dinings W1 **£37** ⭐⭐
22 Harcourt St   7723 0666
"Awesome!"; this tiny "concrete bunker", "hidden-away" in Marylebone, may not look much, but it is quite possibly "the best Japanese in town" – "fabulous" sushi is the highlight of its "really exciting" menu. / *Details:* www.dinings.co.uk; 10.30 pm; closed Sat L & Sun.

The Dock Kitchen
Portobello Dock W10 **£43** Ⓐ⭐
342 Ladbroke Grove   8962 1610
Steve Parle's "underground" café is tucked away in canal-side North Kensington studios (where the terrace is "delightful on a sunny day"); its "seasonal and eclectic" dishes are often "gorgeous". / *Details:* www.dockkitchen.co.uk; 11.30 pm; closed Sun.

$ EC1 **£42** Ⓐ
2 Exmouth Mkt   7278 0077
"Very good burgers" are the culinary highlight at this attractive Farringdon diner, which has a notably cosy cocktail bar, tucked-away in the basement. / *Details:* www.dollargrills.com; 11.30 pm, Tue & Wed 11 pm, Sun & Mon 10 pm.

The Don EC4 **£47** ⭐
20 St Swithin's Ln   7626 2606
"Tucked-away down an alley", near Bank, this "slick" operation – with its "solid" cooking and "extensive" and "interesting" wine list – is one of the City's top options for entertaining; there's a "smart" restaurant or a more informal bistro in the "atmospheric" cellar. / *Details:* www.thedonrestaurant.com; 10 pm; closed Sat & Sun; no trainers.

Donna Margherita SW11   £37   A ★ ★

183 Lavender Hill   7228 2660

Perhaps "the most authentic Neapolitan restaurant in London"; the pizza at this Battersea favourite is the real deal — "fresh and zingy toppings on wonderfully soft, springy and even crusts". / **Details:** www.donna-margherita.com; 10.30 pm, Fri-Sat 11 pm; closed weekday L.

Dorchester Grill
Dorchester Hotel W1   £85

53 Park Ln   7629 8888   2–3A

Reports from this "weirdly Scottish-themed" Mayfair dining room are surprisingly few and irreconcilably mixed — fans say it's "without doubt one of the best places in London", but sceptics put it more bluntly: "avoid!" / **Value tip:** set dinner £55 (FP). **Details:** www.thedorchester.com; 11 pm, Sun 10.30 pm; no trainers.

Dose EC1   £ 8   ★

69 Long Lane   7600 0382

"Best flat white in town", "best espresso on the planet"... — reporters positively rave over the caffeine highs at this "perfectionist" but "friendly" Farringdon "hole in the wall"; "excellent" light bites too. / **Details:** www.dose-espresso.com; L only; no credit cards.

Dotori N4   £28   ★

3 Stroud Green Rd   7263 3562

"Brilliant" Japanese/Korean dishes offer compensation for the "cramped" conditions at this "very busy" and "friendly" Finsbury Park spot. / **Details:** 11 pm; closed Mon; no booking.

Doukan SW18   £22   A ★

350 Old York Rd   8870 8280

It may have been a bit over-hyped by the Ramsay TV programme, but this inexpensive and "ultra-friendly" Moroccan is nevertheless hailed as a "real treat" — an "exotic" sort of place (by Wandsworth standards), where the food can be "great". / **Details:** www.doukan.co.uk; midnight, Mon & Sun 5 pm; no Amex.

Dragon Castle SE17   £35   ★ ★

114 Walworth Rd   7277 3388

"A welcoming and cheerful oasis of good-quality Chinese food", all the more worth remembering in the Elephant & Castle "desert"; a "hangar"-like "emporium", it is of most renown for "the best dim sum south of the river". / **Details:** www.dragoncastle.eu; 11 pm, Fri 11.30 pm, Sun 10.30 pm.

E&O W11   £46   A ★ ★

14 Blenheim Cr   7229 5454   5–1A

With its "exceptional" Asian-fusion dishes, gluggable cocktails, and "sophisticated" atmosphere, Will Ricker's "always-exciting" Notting Hill hang-out is one of those rare places that "never lets you down". / **Value tip:** set weekday L £24 (FP). **Details:** www.rickerrestaurants.com; 11 pm, Sun 10.30 pm; booking: max 6.

The Eagle EC1   **£25**   A

159 Farringdon Rd   7837 1353
"The original London gastropub" (1992), and "still one of the best" – this "chaotic" (and "more shabby than chic") Farringdon "haunt" has stood the test of time, thanks not least to its "extra-tasty" Mediterranean food. / **Details:** *10.30 pm; closed Sun D; no Amex; no booking.*

The Easton WC1   **£35**   A ⭐

22 Easton St   7278 7608
A "laid-back" gastropub in Farringdon, where "they really care", and the food is "very enjoyable" and "great value"; it can, however, get "very noisy". / **Details:** *10 pm, Sun 9.30 pm.*

Eastside Inn EC1   **£45**   ⭐

40 St John St   7490 9230
Chef/patron Bjorn van der Horst is successfully winning reporters over to his brave Smithfield yearling; he's re-formatted the original fine dining room as a bar, and the bistro is applauded for its "attentive" service and its "ambitious" and "vibrant" cuisine. / **Details:** *www.esilondon.com; 11 pm; closed Sun; no trainers.*

Edokko WC1   **£44**   ⭐

50 Red Lion St   7242 3490   1–1D
A "very Japanese" stalwart, "tucked-away" in Holborn, which retains a dedicated fan club for its "excellent" sushi and other fare; lunch deals are "really good value" too.
/ **Details:** *10 pm, Sat 9.30 pm; closed Sat L & Sun.*

Emile's SW15   **£38**   ⭐

96-98 Felsham Rd   8789 3323
Emile Fahy's "personal touch" is much in evidence at this "friendly", if perhaps "dated", prix-fixe restaurant, "hidden-away in deepest Putney" – stick to the "first-class signature dishes" (Beef Wellington, for instance), and you'll almost certainly have an "enjoyable" visit. / **Details:** *www.emilesrestaurant.co.uk; 11 pm; D only, closed Sun; no Amex.*

Enoteca Turi SW15   **£50**   ⭐

28 Putney High St   8785 4449
"One of the best all-Italian wine lists in the world" is the stand-out attraction of the Turi family's stalwart Italian, near Putney Bridge; actually, though, it "does everything right" – the food is "delicious", and service is notably "welcoming" too. / **Details:** *www.enotecaturi.com; 10.30 pm, Fri-Sat 11 pm; closed Sun.*

Eriki NW3   **£38**   ⭐

4-6 Northways Pde, Finchley Rd   7722 0606
A Swiss Cottage Indian with an unlovely location, but where the service is "attentive", and the "non-standard" cooking is "a definite notch above your typical curry house". / **Details:** *www.eriki.co.uk; 10.30 pm; closed Sat L; no Amex.*

L'Etranger SW7 £57 ✪

36 Gloucester Rd   7584 1118   4–1B

Prices may be "fancy", but the fusion fare is likewise, at this "slightly off-beat" but "consummately professional" Japanese/French venture, in South Kensington; what really wows reporters, though, is a wine list such as to "put any buff into seventh heaven". / **Value tip:** *set weekday L £36 (FP).* **Details:** *www.etranger.co.uk; 11 pm, Sun 10 pm.*

Fabrizio EC1 £38 ✪✪

30 Saint Cross St   7430 1503

Fabrizio Zafarana is an "incredibly welcoming" host, and his "well-prepared and generous comfort food" inspires the most positive reports on this "super-value", but still little-known, Sicilian, hidden-away north of Holborn. / **Details:** *www.fabriziorestaurant.co.uk; 10 pm; closed Sat L & Sun.*

The Farm Collective EC1 £ 7 ✪

91 Cowcross St   7253 2142

"Tired of Pret and Eat?" – this "bustling" Farringdon café offers "fantastic", "flavour-filled" bites ("sarnies, salads, hot food") from "a small, seasonal menu" that's "almost entirely sourced from the UK", and "excellent" coffee too; "pity about the lack of seats". / **Details:** *www.farmcollective.com; L only, closed Sat & Sun.*

El Faro E14 £44 ✪

3 Turnberry Quay   7987 5511

"Sumptuous" Spanish dishes (not just "fantastic" tapas), and a "lovely dockside setting" too, make it "worth the trip" to the Isle of Dogs to seek out this extremely "welcoming" outfit, near Crossharbour DLR; it took some flak this year, though, for "rising prices". / **Details:** *www.el-faro.co.uk; 11 pm; closed Sun D.*

Faulkner's E8 £27 ✪

424-426 Kingsland Rd   7254 6152

"Cracking fish 'n' chips" justify the reputation of this renowned and quite comfortable Dalston chippy. / **Details:** *10 pm; no Amex; need 8+ to book.*

Fernandez & Wells £25 Ⓐ✪✪

43 Lexington St, W1   7734 1546   2–2D

73 Beak St, W1   7287 8124   2–2D

This "tip-top" duo of "laid-back", "media-crowd" cafés in Soho offer a "refreshing take on sandwiches and coffee" (plus great cakes, wine, hams…) – "everything they do is excellent"; (there's also an espresso bar in nearby St Anne's Ct). / **Details:** *www.fernandezandwells.com; Lexington St 10 pm; Beak St 6 pm.*

Ffiona's W8 £45 Ⓐ

51 Kensington Church St   7937 4152   4–1A

"Larger-than-life" owner Ffiona creates a "uniquely charming" ambience at her candlelit Kensington bistro; in keeping with best dinner party manners, feedback rarely mentions the food, but it seems to go down pretty well. / **Details:** *www.ffionas.com; 11 pm, Sun 10 pm; D only, closed Mon; no Amex.*

Fifteen Dining Room N1 £85 ✖
15 Westland Pl 3375 1515 1–1A
Jamie Oliver's Hoxton training project is "so expensive"…
especially when you bear in mind the "indifferent" service,
the "disappointing" basement location, and the monumentally
"average" Italian cooking. / *Value tip:* set weekday L £37
(FP). **Details:** www.fifteen.net; 9.30 pm; booking: max 6.

La Figa E14 £37 ★
45 Narrow St 7790 0077
A "perennial favourite" pizza-and-pasta joint, in Wapping;
"portions are large, so you may want to share". / **Details:** 11 pm,
Sun 10.30 pm.

Fino W1 £52 🅐★
33 Charlotte St 7813 8010 1–1C

"Completely authentic" tapas
and a "huge range of marvellous
Iberian wines" again win rave
reviews for the Hart brothers'
"excellent" Fitzrovia basement
– a "low-lit" and "buzzy"
(if slightly "cavernous") space.
/ **Details:** www.finorestaurant.com;
10.30 pm; closed Sat L & Sun;
booking: max 12.

First Floor W11 £42 🅐
186 Portobello Rd 7243 0072 5–1A
"No date could fail to be charmed by the chandeliers,
high ceilings and groovy clientele" of this "boho-chic" old-timer,
overlooking Portobello Market; its "lovely" service,
and increasingly "assured" cooking play honourable supporting
roles. / **Details:** www.firstfloorportobello.co.uk; 11 pm.

Fish Club £33 ★
189 St John's Hill, SW11 7978 7115
57 Clapham High St, SW4 7720 5853
"Be it for traditional options, or something more modern and
tricksy", these south London refectories win bouquets for their
"brilliant-value" fish 'n' chips; they're pretty basic, though –
arguably "take-away is best". / **Details:** www.thefishclub.com; 10 pm,
Sun 9 pm; SW4 closed Mon L, SW11 closed Mon.

500 N19 £33 ★
782 Holloway Rd 7272 3406
"What a strange location for such a good restaurant!" –
a "wonderfully unpretentious" Sicilian trattoria in the
"gastronomic void" of Archway; its "cheerful and informative"
staff dish up "honest" and "clean-tasting" dishes, and at prices
which are "easy on the wallet" too. / **Details:** www.500restaurant.co.uk;
10 pm; closed Mon & Sun L.

Flat White W1 £9 🅐★
17 Berwick St 7734 0370 2–2D
"The best coffee on this or any nearby planet" draws addicts
to this "enthusiastic" Kiwi-run Soho coffee shop; "the cakes are
good too". / **Details:** www.flat-white.co.uk; L only; no credit cards.

Food for Thought WC2 £17 ⭐

31 Neal St 7836 0239 3–2C

"Still great vegetarian food", "still cramped", "still good value" –
thankfully this "wonderful" (if "claustrophobic") Covent Garden
basement is "still going strong"; BYO.
/ **Details:** www.foodforthought-london.co.uk; 8 pm, Sun 5 pm; no credit cards;
no booking.

The Forge WC2 £48

14 Garrick St 7379 1531 3–3C

This "attractive" Gallic dining room, in a "lovely old building"
in Covent Garden, wins a lot of praise as a "reliable pre- or post-
theatre destination"; à la carte, though, the fare may seem
no more than "adequate". / **Value tip:** set weekday L £24
(FP). **Details:** www.theforgerestaurant.co.uk; midnight.

The Fox and Anchor EC1 £37 Ⓐ

115 Charterhouse St 7250 1300

This "brilliant" old pub near Smithfield Market has been
"fabulously restored" of late; it may be famed for its
monumental breakfasts (washed down with a pint), but it's
most tipped nowadays for its daytime menu – "traditional",
"quite basic" dishes, often with "an amusing twist".
/ **Details:** www.foxandanchor.co.uk; 9.30 pm.

Franco Manca £17 ⭐⭐

144 Chiswick High Rd, W4 8747 4822 6–2A

Unit 4 Market Row, SW9 7738 3021

"The best pizza in the UK, hands
down!" – this tiny Brixton
phenomenon serves "fabulous,
fresh sourdough pizza" with
a "definitive" crust and
"stunning" toppings, all at "rock-
bottom" prices; its instantly
popular new W4 offshoot
– only a tad less highly rated –
is also "stonking value".
/ **Details:** www.francomanca.com;
SW9 5 pm; W4 11 pm; no Amex.

La Fromagerie Café W1 £39 Ⓐ

2-6 Moxon St 7935 0341 2–1A

"Amazing cheese" aside, the "lovely" café of this famous
Marylebone store offers a variety of dishes using "delicious fresh
produce", and makes a "fun" destination "for an out-of-the-
ordinary lunch" (or "delicious breakfast"); since expansion
last year, though, service has had its ups and downs.
/ **Details:** www.lafromagerie.co.uk; 7.30 pm, Sat 7 pm, Sun 6 pm; L only;
no booking.

Galvin at Windows
Park Lane London Hilton Hotel W1 £88 Ⓐ
22 Park Ln   7208 4021   2–4A
*With its "breathtaking panoramas", this 28th-floor Mayfair eyrie certainly has an "incomparable" setting; most reporters feel the cuisine "matches the view", but it's naturally "seriously pricey", and – for a few critics – "not quite what you'd expect from the Galvins". / **Value tip:** set always available £49*
(FP). **Details:** *www.galvinatwindows.com; 10.30 pm; closed Sat L & Sun D; no trainers.*

Galvin Bistrot de Luxe W1   £45   Ⓐ⭐⭐
66 Baker St   7935 4007   1–1A
*"Better than its Paris role-models!" – the Galvin brothers' "utterly professional" Marylebone "super-bistro" remains one of London's foremost all-rounders (and especially popular as a business destination). / **Value tip:** set pre-theatre £30*
(FP). **Details:** *www.galvinrestaurants.com; Mon-Wed 10.30 pm, Thu-Sat 10.45 pm, Sun 9.30 pm.*

Galvin La Chapelle E1   £62   Ⓐ⭐
35 Spital Sq   7299 0400   1–2B
*"A breathtakingly beautiful interior" – a chapel-like former school hall, in Spitalfields – helps make the Galvin brothers' acclaimed newcomer "a superb addition" to the City; the "poshed-up bistro food" rather plays second fiddle, but it is still very "competent"; (the "casual" Café à Vin next door is cheaper – formula price £47 – but "crowded" and "less pretty"). / **Details:** www.galvinrestaurants.com; Mon-Fri 10 pm, Sat & Sun 10.30 pm.*

Ganapati SE15   £31   Ⓐ⭐⭐
38 Holly Grove   7277 2928
Some of "the best south Indian food outside of south India!"; "people, rightly, cross town" to "squeeze into one of the shared tables" at this communal Peckham diner, to enjoy its "sumptuous" and "tangy" dishes.
*/ **Details:** www.ganapatirestaurant.com; 10.30 pm, Sun 10 pm; closed Mon; no Amex.*

Garrison SE1   £40   Ⓐ
99-101 Bermondsey St   7089 9355
*In an "über-trendy" corner of Bermondsey (near the Antiques Market), this "un-self-conscious", and "very friendly" gastropub is "always buzzing"; the food is "interesting", and the setting – though "cramped and very noisy" – "perfect for cosy get-togethers". / **Details:** www.thegarrison.co.uk; 10 pm, Sun 9.30 pm.*

The Gate W6   £40   ⭐
51 Queen Caroline St   8748 6932   6–2C
*So good you "never miss the meat", this Hammersmith veggie "gem" has many supporters; the "church hall"-style interior is quite "attractive" too, and in summer you can eat on a "delightful" terrace. / **Details:** www.thegate.tv; 10.30 pm, Sat 11 pm; closed Sat L & Sun.*

69

Le Gavroche W1 £112 Ⓐ⭐⭐

43 Upper Brook St   7408 0881   2–2A

The prices may be "staggering", but Michel Roux Jr's "reassuringly old-fashioned" Mayfair "institution" is "worth it" – with its "unashamedly classical" cuisine, its "biblical" wine list and its "dazzlingly pleasant" staff, it really is "the epitome of fine dining"; NB the set lunch is "the bargain of the century" too. / **Value tip:** set weekday L £69 (FP). **Details:** www.le-gavroche.co.uk; 11 pm; closed Sat L & Sun; jacket required.

Geeta NW6 £18

57-59 Willesden Ln   7624 1713

This threadbare South Indian café, in Kilburn, is "a lovely family-run business", say fans, with "authentic home-made dishes", impeccably "helpful" service, and "extraordinarily low" prices; some meals, however, have seemed uncharacteristically "ordinary" of late; BYO. / **Details:** 10.30 pm, Fri-Sat 11 pm; no Amex.

The Giaconda Dining Room WC2 £39 ⭐

9 Denmark St   7240 3334   3–1A

"A little place that packs a big punch"; this "unconventional" café/bistro – a "snug" spot in the "ghastly" environs of Centre Point – serves "seriously good food" at "great-value" prices. / **Details:** www.giacondadining.com; 9.15 pm; closed Sat & Sun.

Giant Robot EC1 £37 ⭐

45 Clerkenwell Rd   7065 6810

A Clerkenwell newcomer on the site of the once legendary cocktail bar Match, re-launched with a swish new interior, and a warm and funky vibe; on our early-days visit, culinary standards were much higher than the pick 'n' mix menu led us to expect; offshoots are already planned. / **Details:** www.gntrbt.com; midnight.

Gifto's Lahore Karahi UB1 £22 ⭐

162-164 The Broadway   8813 8669

With its "plain, Formica-topped" interior, this big, "buzzy" Indian diner is a Southall landmark, serving a wide-ranging menu of "superb" curries at "very reasonable" prices. / **Details:** www.gifto.com; 11.30 pm, Sat & Sun midnight.

Ginger & White NW3 £ 8 ⭐

4a-5a, Perrins Ct   7431 9098

"You wouldn't think Hampstead needs another coffee bar, but it does" – this prettily-sited new operation is hailed for its "fantastic" coffee, "great" cakes, and "boho-chic" atmosphere. / **Details:** www.gingerandwhite.com; L only; no Mastercard.

The Glasshouse TW9　　　£57　　⭐⭐
14 Station Pde　8940 6777
*"A splendid sibling of Chez Bruce"; this "tranquil" spot, by Kew Gardens tube, is "nothing too flashy, just a lovely place for a meal", with "cracking" food and "immaculate" standards generally; the "airy and relaxing" setting, however, can seem a teeny bit "boring". / **Value tip:** set weekday L £37 (FP). **Details:** www.glasshouserestaurant.co.uk; 10.30 pm, Sun 10 pm.*

Golden Hind W1　　　£22　　⭐⭐
73 Marylebone Ln　7486 3644　1–1A
*With its "unbeatable fish 'n' chips" and supremely "jolly" service, this "simple", "Formica-tabled" Marylebone chippy takes some beating for "a good cheap 'n' cheerful meal" near the West End (and it's BYO too!); it's obviously doing something right, as it's expanding into the next door premises. / **Details:** 10 pm; closed Sat L & Sun.*

Good Earth　　　£52　　⭐
233 Brompton Rd, SW3　7584 3658　4–2C
143-145 The Broadway, NW7　8959 7011
*In business since time immemorial, an "upmarket" mini-chain – in Knightsbridge and Mill Hill – that's still churning out very "competent", if "pricey", Chinese cuisine. / **Details:** www.goodearthgroup.co.uk; 11 pm, Sun 10.45 pm.*

Goodman　　　£67　　⭐
26 Maddox St, W1　7499 3776　2–2C
11 Old Jewry, EC2　7600 8220
*For "a US steakhouse-style" operation, it's hard to beat this Mayfair yearling (which, bizarrely, is Russian-owned), which offers "perfectly-cooked" meat (albeit "at a price"); its success has been such that a City branch is scheduled to open in late-2010. / **Value tip:** set weekday L £36 (FP). **Details:** 11 pm.*

Gordon Ramsay SW3　　　£123
68-69 Royal Hospital Rd　7352 4441　4–3D
*"All the whingers have got it wrong… this is still the best place in town!" – so say fans of the TV-chef's Chelsea HQ; there's a roughly equal and opposite camp, however, for whom it is just "an expensive yawn" nowadays – "not a disaster", but displaying "no flair", and offering "no excitement". / **Value tip:** set weekday L £72 (FP). **Details:** www.gordonramsay.com; 11 pm; closed Sat & Sun; no jeans or trainers; booking: max 8.*

Gordon Ramsay at Claridge's
Claridge's Hotel W1　　　£100
55 Brook St　7499 0099　2–2B
*Even fans who insist the food at this grand Mayfair dining room is "lovely" often feel it comes at "unjustified" prices; harsher critics are simply "amazed" that Ramsay puts his name to such a "clapped-out" venture – "please Claridge's, find another partner!". / **Value tip:** set weekday L £58 (FP). **Details:** www.gordonramsay.com; 11 pm, Sun 10 pm; no jeans or trainers; booking: max 8.*

Gordon's Wine Bar WC2 £27   Ⓐ ❌
47 Villiers St   7930 1408   3–4D
It's the "brilliant" atmosphere of this dingy "cave" of a wine bar, near Embankment, that makes it especially worth seeking out (and, for the summer, it has a huge terrace too); the food – cheese, "deli-style platters" and a barbecue – is incidental.
/ **Details:** www.gordonswinebar.com; 11 pm, Sun 10 pm; no booking.

The Goring Hotel SW1 £76   Ⓐ
15 Beeston Pl   7396 9000   1–4B
"For meeting elderly relatives 'in town'", this "dignified" bastion of "old-world courtesy and charm", near Victoria, is hard to beat; with its reassuringly "traditional" British menu, it's also "supremely reliable for business", or for breakfasts "just like nanny used to make". / **Details:** www.thegoring.com; 10 pm; closed Sat L.

Gourmet San E2 £18   ⭐⭐
261 Bethnal Green Rd   7613 1366   1–1D
"Amazing", "mouth-numbingly-hot" Sichuanese dishes are the whole point of a visit to this East End dive – "if you're fussy about ambience, don't bother!" / **Details:** www.oldplace.co.uk; 11 pm; D only.

The Gowlett SE15 £30   Ⓐ⭐
62 Gowlett Rd   7635 7048
"Top-quality pizza" – with "authentic bases and classic toppings" – delight regulars at this "proper neighbourhood pub" in Peckham; "sometimes slow, but worth the wait!"
/ **Details:** www.thegowlett.com; 10.30 pm, Sun 9 pm.

The Grapes E14 £42   Ⓐ⭐
76 Narrow St   7987 4396
"Hidden-away" in Docklands, this "olde worlde" riverside pub makes "a great find"; you can eat in the bar, or in the quirky upstairs dining room, which serves "fantastic, simply cooked fish". / **Details:** 9.30 pm; closed Sat L & Sun D.

Great Eastern Dining Room EC2 £40   Ⓐ⭐
54-56 Great Eastern St   7613 4545   1–1B
Will Ricker's perennially "cool" Shoreditch hang-out is an impressive all-rounder that's always "busy", thanks not least to its "really fresh and exciting" pan-Asian fare; "pricey" cocktails, though. / **Details:** www.rickerrestaurants.com; 10.30 pm; closed Sat L & Sun.

Great Queen Street WC2 £40   Ⓐ⭐
32 Great Queen St   7242 0622   3–1D
"Like the Anchor & Hope, but without the fight for a table" – on the fringe of Covent Garden, this "brilliant stablemate" of the famous pub serves up "wonderful" and "honest" dishes at "sensible" prices, in a "buzzy", "designer-grunge" dining room that "feels like a bar". / **Details:** 10.15 pm; closed Sun D; no Amex.

Green Papaya E8 £26   ⭐⭐
191 Mare St   8985 5486
"Ideal for a cheap bite", this "friendly" Hackney spot "stands out among the many Vietnamese places on the same street". /

The Greenhouse W1   **£98** 

27a Hays Mews   7499 3331   2–3B
Marlon Abela's "very discreet" operation in the backwoods of Mayfair wins acclaim for its "exceptional haute cuisine", "unbelievable" wine list, and "slick" style; prices verge on "mad", though, and the approach strikes some reporters as "fussy".
/ **Value tip:** *set weekday L £52 (FP).* **Details:** *www.greenhouserestaurant.co.uk; 11 pm; closed Sat L & Sun; booking: max 12.*

The Guinea Grill W1   **£47** ★

30 Bruton Pl   7499 1210   2–3B
"For a great steak 'n kidney, or a good rib-eye in Mayfair", this very "old-school" pub (plus adjacent dining room) perfectly fits the bill; "tucked-away" in a cute mews, it benefits from "charming" and "very professional" service.
/ **Details:** *www.theguinea.co.uk; 10.30 pm; closed Sat L & Sun; booking: max 8.*

Gung-Ho NW6   **£34**

328-332 West End Ln   7794 1444
A "classy" West Hampstead Chinese "stalwart", which still makes "a good choice for a family meal" – "consistent" food and "exceptionally friendly" service help it retain an impressive north London following. / **Details:** *www.stir-fry.co.uk; 11.30 pm; no Amex.*

Haché   **£31**

329-331 Fulham Rd, SW10   7823 3515   4–3B
24 Inverness St, NW1   7485 9100
"Every conceivable kind of burger" – usually realised to a high standard – win a big fan club for this "cramped and buzzy" bistro-style group; this year, though, its ratings overall dipped a bit. / **Details:** *www.hacheburgers.com; 10.30 pm, Sun 10 pm.*

Hakkasan   **£82** Ⓐ

17 Bruton St, W1   awaiting tel   2–2C
8 Hanway Pl, W1   7927 7000   3–1A

"Memorable" cooking and a "hedonistic" vibe have made this "sexy" and nightclubby West End basement London's best-known Chinese; prices are "eye-watering", though, and "arrogant" service and "merciless table-rotation" are beginning to set some nerves jangling; a branch opens in Mayfair in late-2010. / **Details:** *midnight, Sun 11 pm.*

Haozhan W1 £39 ⭐⭐
8 Gerrard St 7434 3838 3–3A
"Adventurous" Chinese cuisine makes this "very original" two-year-old "a surprise find in the heart of Chinatown", "IKEA"-esque decor notwithstanding. / *Value tip:* set dinner £23 (FP). **Details:** www.haozhan.co.uk; 11.30 pm, Fri & Sat midnight, Sun 11 pm.

Harwood Arms SW6 £45 ⭐
Walham Grove 7386 1847 4–3A
"Incredible food for a gastropub" – "earthy, rich and original British dishes", "superb game", and "the best Scotch eggs" – again won this "entertaining local", in a Fulham backstreet, huge acclaim from reporters. / **Details:** www.harwoodarms.com; 9.30 pm, Sun 9 pm; closed Mon L.

The Havelock Tavern W14 £39 Ⓐ⭐
57 Masbro Rd 7603 5374 6–1C
A change in ownership a couple of years ago, has been a mixed blessing for this "packed", "buzzy" backstreet Olympia local – the food "though still very good, has lost some zing", but its infamously snotty service is "much improved". / **Details:** www.thehavelocktavern.co.uk; 10 pm, Sun 9.30 pm; no Amex; no booking.

Hawksmoor £56 ⭐
11 Langley St, WC2 awaiting tel 3–2C
157 Commercial St, E1 7247 7392 1–2B
This "casual" – but rather "expensive" – hang-out near Spitalfields Market has a big name for "superb" steak and "ingenious" cocktails, that are (both) amongst "the best in town"; a large new branch opens in Covent Garden in late-2010. / **Details:** www.thehawksmoor.com; 10.30 pm; no Amex.

Hélène Darroze
The Connaught Hotel W1 £111
Carlos Pl 7499 7070 2–3B
"Given all the hype", it's easy to be "disappointed" by this "stuffy" Mayfair outpost of a celebrated Parisienne chef; it inspires far too many complaints of "unbalanced", "overcomplicated" or "passé" cuisine – and it's "so expensive" too. / *Value tip:* set weekday L £43 (FP). **Details:** www.the-connaught.co.uk; 10.30 pm; closed Mon & Sun; jacket & tie.

Hereford Road W2 £40 ⭐
3 Hereford Rd 7727 1144 5–1B
Tom Pemberton's "buzzy" Bayswater favourite offers "seasonal" school-of-St-John dishes that are "expertly executed" and "surprisingly good value"; the acoustics of the place, though, "still need sorting out". / **Details:** www.herefordroad.org; 10.30 pm, Sun 10 pm.

Hibiscus W1 £90
29 Maddox St   7629 2999   2–2C

Claude Bosi's style of haute cuisine is "experimental"
by West End standards, and fans find it "sublime" too;
his Mayfair restaurant is rather a "stuffy" place, though,
and there are many sceptics – citing "unmemorable" food
in "meagre portions", and "a credit card in meltdown" –
who just "don't 'get' the fuss". / *Value tip:* set weekday L £44
(FP). *Details:* www.hibiscusrestaurant.co.uk; 9 pm; closed Mon & Sun.

High Road Brasserie W4 £48
162-166 Chiswick High Rd   8742 7474   6–2A
Especially for "the ubiquitous blondes of Chiswick", this "buzzy"
brasserie makes a "great place to hang out" and "people-
watch", and it does a good "family-friendly" brunch too; culinary
speaking, though, there are "no fireworks". / *Value tip:* set weekday L
£29 (FP). *Details:* www.sohohouse.co.uk; 10.30 pm, Fri & Sat 11.30 pm,
Sun 9.30 pm.

Hilliard EC4 £27 ⭐
26a Tudor St   7353 8150
"Always full of lawyers", this "upmarket soup and sandwich
joint" – by a gateway to the Temple – also offers "imaginative"
hot dishes, an "abundance of cakes" and a "fairly extensive
wine list". / *Details:* www.hilliardfood.co.uk; 6 pm; L only, closed Sat & Sun;
no booking.

Holly Bush NW3 £39 Ⓐ
22 Holly Mount   7435 2892
A "lovely old pub", hidden-away in a "beautiful" Hampstead
Village location; thanks to its all-round appeal – including simple
but "well thought-out" grub – it "can get very crowded".
/ *Details:* www.hollybushhampstead.co.uk; 10 pm, Sun 9 pm.

Hot Stuff SW8 £22 Ⓐ⭐
19 Wilcox Rd   7720 1480
"An amicable owner" oversees this "wonderful, lively, BYO Indian
joint", "hidden-away" in deepest Vauxhall; thankfully a recent
revamp hasn't spoilt its "cheap" and "spicy" scoff that always
"hits the spot". / *Details:* www.eathotstuff.com; 9.30 pm; closed Sun;
no Amex.

Hummus Bros £17 ⭐

88 Wardour St, W1   7734 1311   2–2D
36-67 Southampton Row, WC1   7404 7079   1–1D
128 Cheapside, EC2   7726 8011

*"Who'd have thought you could base a whole restaurant on hummus?" – well, they have, and this "cheerful" mini-chain is universally hailed by reporters as a "great concept". / **Details:** www.hbros.co.uk; W1 10 pm, Thu-Sat 11 pm; WC1 9 pm; WC1 closed Sat & Sun; no booking.*

Hunan SW1 £50 ⭐⭐

51 Pimlico Rd   7730 5712   4–2D

*"Leave the menu choice to Mr Peng", then "sit back and enjoy" course after course of "genius" Taiwanese food at this "unassuming", "crowded" and "hectic" Pimlico stalwart – again the survey's highest-rated 'Chinese'. / **Details:** www.hunanlondon.com; 10.30 pm; closed Sun.*

Hush W1 £55

8 Lancashire Ct   7659 1500   2–2B

*"Hidden-away" off Bond Street, this potentially "delightful" bar/brasserie (with "fantastic outside tables in summer") has always seemed a bit "pretentious and full of itself"; it had a major revamp in mid-2010, so – to give it the benefit of any doubt – we've left it un-rated till next year. / **Value tip:** set weekday L £35 (FP). **Details:** www.hush.co.uk; 10.45 pm; closed Sun; booking: max 12.*

Ida W10 £30 Ⓐ

167 Fifth Ave   8969 9853

*It looks like a "'50s tea shop", but this North Kensington Italian is a "warm and friendly, family-run place" offering "hearty" food, and a "real buzz" too. / **Details:** www.idarestaurant.co.uk; 11 pm; closed Sat L & Sun D; no Amex.*

Ikeda W1 £78 ⭐⭐

30 Brook St   7629 2730   2–2B

*"London's best sushi" – still a claim occasionally made on behalf of this Mayfair veteran; it's "expensive", though, and the decor looks thoroughly "worn out". / **Details:** 10.20 pm; closed Sat L & Sun.*

Inaho W2 £37 ⭐⭐

4 Hereford Rd   7221 8495   5–1B

*A "tiny and delightful" Japanese shack, in Bayswater, where the miraculous sushi is second to none, and marvellous value too; the "charming" service, however, is so slow "it beggars belief". / **Value tip:** set weekday L £20 (FP). **Details:** 11 pm; closed Sat L & Sun; no Amex or Maestro.*

Indali Lounge W1 £34 ⭐

50 Baker St   7224 2232   1–1A

*A large and self-avowedly "health-conscious" contemporary Indian bar/café in Marylebone; an all-round crowd-pleaser, it offers "clean-flavoured" dishes that "aren't any less tasty in the absence of ghee". / **Details:** www.indalilounge.com; midnight; closed Sat L & Sun.*

Indian Rasoi N2 £33 ⭐⭐
7 Denmark Ter   8883 9093
"High-quality meals, served very elegantly, with plenty of fresh flavours" make this Muswell Hill Indian extremely popular – it's *"always packed, even during the week"*.
/ **Details:** www.indian-rasoi.co.uk; 11 pm.

Indian Zing W6 £41 ⭐⭐
236 King St   8748 5959   6–2B
"Zing by name, and zing zing zing by nature!"; Manoj Vasaikar's increasingly-acclaimed Hammersmith Indian inspires rapturous reports on its *"daring"* and *"wonderfully light"* dishes, its *"keen"* service, and its *"fresh and contemporary"* style.
/ **Details:** www.indianzing.co.uk; 11 pm, Sun 10.30 pm.

Inside SE10 £43 ⭐
19 Greenwich South St   8265 5060
"Still the best place in Greenwich" (perhaps *"a back-handed compliment!"*) – this *"proper"* local restaurant *"stands out"* with its *"serious"* and *"original"* cuisine; *"the only downside"* is a *"noisy"* interior that arguably *"could do with an uplift"*. / **Value tip:** set weekday L £25 (FP). **Details:** www.insiderestaurant.co.uk; 10.30 pm, Fri & Sat 11 pm; closed Mon & Sun D.

Isarn N1 £41
119 Upper St   7424 5153
"Enjoyable" food and *"very sweet"* and *"attentive"* service make this modern Thai establishment one of the surprisingly few destinations on Islington's main drag that's of any real note; despite the press of diners, though, the ambience of its *"corridor-like"* room can *"lack oomph"*.
/ **Details:** www.isarn.co.uk; 11 pm.

The Ivy WC2 £60 Ⓐ
1-5 West St   7836 4751   3–3B
"Not in the league it once was" – this famous Theatrelander offers *"comfort"* fare that can sometimes smack of the *"conveyor belt"* nowadays; if you can get a table, you're still *"pretty much guaranteed to see a celeb"*, though, and service – under maître d' Fernando Peire – is undoubtedly *"brilliant"*.
/ **Details:** www.the-ivy.co.uk; midnight, 11.30 pm; booking: max 6.

Izakaya Aki WC1 £32 ⭐
182 Gray's Inn Rd   7837 9281   1–1D
"A Japanese bistro of a good few years' standing" that's always been *"popular with oriental ex-pats"*; its *"excellent"* sushi and other *"reassuringly authentic"* dishes are served at *"good-value"* prices by staff who are *"entirely helpful and prompt"*.
/ **Details:** www.akidemae.com; 10.30 pm; closed Sat L & Sun.

Jin Kichi NW3 £38

73 Heath St   7794 6158

"As close to Tokyo as you get in London" – this *"tiny"* and *"cramped"* Hampstead café *"never fails"*, serving *"outstanding"* sushi and *"fantastic"* yakitori (skewers), and all at *"credit-crunch-sensitive"* prices. / **Details:** www.jinkichi.com; 11 pm, Sun 10 pm; closed Mon, Tue-Fri D only, Sat & Sun open L & D.

Julie's W11 £55

135 Portland Rd   7229 8331   5–2A

This *"warren of rooms"*, below a pretty Holland Park street, seduces many reporters with its *"faded Bohemian grandeur"*; even fans, though, can feel it's *"overpriced"*, or find themselves complaining of *"appalling"* service. / **Details:** www.juliesrestaurant.com; 11 pm.

JW Steakhouse
Grosvenor House Hotel W1 £70

86 Park Ln   7399 8460   2–3A

A large new steakhouse, on the former Mayfair site of Bord'Eaux (RIP), where – on our early-days visit – the meat (USDA) was excellent; incidentals were poor, though, and neither service (amateurish) nor ambience (soulless) helped justify the Rolls-Royce prices. / **Details:** www.jwsteakhouse.co.uk; 10.30 pm, Fri & Sat 11 pm.

Kaffeine W1 £ 8

66 Great Titchfield St   7580 6755   2–1C

With its *"fantastic coffee,"* *"sublime brownies"*, and *"innovative salads"*, this *"very friendly"* new Fitzrovian is *"quickly becoming a local institution"*. / **Details:** www.kaffeine.co.uk; L only, closed Sun; no Amex.

Kai Mayfair W1 £105

65 South Audley St   7493 8988   2–3A

"A great Chinese, but incredibly expensive" – this *"outstanding"* Mayfair joint is, for fans, *"the best oriental in town in terms of quality of ingredients and cuisine"*, but not everyone is convinced it lives up to the eye-popping prices. / **Details:** www.kaimayfair.com; 10.45 pm, Sun 10.15 pm.

Kaifeng NW4 £55

51 Church Rd   8203 7888

Chinese food *"as good as in the West End"* makes this *"expensive"* kosher spot Hendon's greatest culinary landmark. / **Details:** www.kaifeng.co.uk; 10.30 pm; closed Fri & Sat.

Karma W14 £32

44 Blythe Rd   7602 9333   6–1D

"Tucked-away behind Olympia but well worth winkling out", this slightly *"quiet"* Indian wins nothing but praise for its *"subtle"* and *"creative"* cuisine, and its *"charming and helpful"* staff. / **Details:** www.k-a-r-m-a.co.uk; 11.30 pm; no Amex.

Kastoori SW17 £28 ⊕⊛
188 Upper Tooting Rd   8767 7027
"A flavour sensation" that's "worth crossing town for!";
this "friendly" (if grungy-looking) family-run Tooting stalwart
is rightly renowned for its "wonderful delicacies" from a "wow"
of a menu (Gujarati/East African), and at "bargain-basement"
prices too. / *Details:* www.kastoorirestaurant.com; 10.30 pm; closed Mon L &
Tue L; no Amex or Maestro; booking: max 12.

Kazan £38 ⊛
93-94 Wilton Rd, SW1   7233 7100   1–4B
34-36 Houndsditch, EC3   7626 2222
"A great place for friends, family, or a quick bite" – these
"lively" Pimlico and City joints provide "vast" helpings of "tasty"
Turkish fare, with "helpful" staff, and a "bustling" setting too.
/ *Details:* www.kazan-restaurant.com; 10.45 pm; EC3 closed Sun.

Ken Lo's Memories SW1 £55
65-69 Ebury St   7730 7734   1–4B
It "won't knock your socks off with its originality", but this grand
Belgravia Chinese is still a "safe bet", and it offers a very
"decent" standard of cooking. / *Value tip:* set weekday L £29
(FP). *Details:* www.londonfinedininggroup.com; 11 pm.

Ken Lo's Memories of China W8 £52 ⊕⊛
353 Kensington High St   7603 6951   6–1D
"So professional all round", this "cosy" Chinese, on the
Kensington/Olympia borders, wins incredibly consistent praise
from reporters; even fans, though, can find it "pricey, given the
lack of innovation". / *Details:* www.memories-of-china.co.uk; 11 pm,
Sun 10 pm.

Kennington Tandoori SE11 £34 Ⓐ⊛
313 Kennington Rd   7735 9247
"It's had a total refit, but nothing has really changed!" at this
politicos'-favourite curry house – it's maybe a bit "swisher",
though, and the food has, if anything, "improved". / *Value tip:* set
weekday L £22 (FP). *Details:* www.kenningtontandoori.co.uk; midnight; no Amex.

Khoai £27 ⊛
362 Ballards Ln, N12   8445 2039
6 Topsfield Pde, N8   8341 2120
"Fresh and interesting" fare is helping make quite a name for
these "reasonably-priced" Vietnamese cafés, in Crouch End and
Finchley. / *Details:* 11.30 pm; N12 closed Mon; no booking Fri & Sat after
7.30 pm.

Kiku W1 £60 ⊛
17 Half Moon St   7499 4208   2–4B
"A real slice of Japan"; this little-known Mayfair spot serves
"wonderful" food – in particular, "faultless sushi and sashimi" –
and offers an "excellent-value" set lunch; no prizes, though,
for ambience. / *Details:* www.kikurestaurant.co.uk; 10.15 pm; closed Sun L.

Kiraku W5 £26 ⭐⭐
8 Station Pde 8992 2848

"Ealing Common's best kept secret"; this "superb" Japanese is "always packed with the local Asian community", presumably because it offers an "incredibly authentic" selection of dishes at "fantastic" prices. / *Details:* www.kiraku.co.uk; 10 pm; closed Mon; no Amex.

Kitchen W8 W8 £40 Ⓐ⭐⭐
11-13 Abingdon Road 7937 0120 4–1A

"A neighbourhood surprise!"; with the input of Philip Howard (of Square fame), this previously ho-hum outfit in a Kensington side street (formerly Bistrot Eleven, RIP) now "really hits the spot", offering "superb" and "reasonably-priced" food in a "fun" and "buzzy" environment. / *Details:* www.kitchenw8.com; 10.30 pm, Sun 9.30 pm.

Koba W1 £44 ⭐
11 Rathbone St 7580 8825 1–1C

"Staff are keen to help you decipher the menu", at this Fitzrovia Korean BBQ, which – despite its "authentic" dishes, "outstanding" service and "reasonable" prices – attracts remarkably little survey feedback. / *Details:* www.koba-london.com; 11 pm; closed Sun L.

Koffmann's
Berkeley Hotel SW1 £60
Berkeley Hotel, Wilton Pl 7107 8844 4–1D

As Pierre Koffmann was London's top chef in the '90s, his new venture near Hyde Park Corner (on the site of Boxwood Café, RIP) opens amidst high expectations; a very early-days visit found a plush (but bland) hotel basement, very ably overseen by maitre d' Eric Garnier, but an absence of fireworks – or the hearty robustness some advance PR had suggested – in the competent, classic dishes. / *Details:* www.the-berkeley.co.uk.

Kovalam NW6 £26 ⭐
12 Willesden Ln 7625 4761

It "doesn't look much" but this Kilburn spot wins praise for its "delicious and authentic" south Indian dishes. / *Details:* www.kovalamrestaurant.co.uk; 10.30 pm; no Amex.

The Ladbroke Arms W11   £43   Ⓐ⭐
54 Ladbroke Rd   7727 6648   5–2B
A brilliant "upmarket" boozer, off Ladbroke Grove, which offers "imaginative" cooking and attracts a good mix of people – "from families, to Notting Hill international types, to old English grannies"; arrive early for the "great terrace in summer".
/ **Details:** www.capitalpubcompany.com; 9.30 pm; no booking after 7.30 pm.

Lahore Karahi SW17   £12   ⭐⭐
1 Tooting Hill, London   8767 2477
This "super-busy" Tooting subcontinental is "all about value" – "you don't get great service, or great atmosphere, but for a cheap Pakistani meal, you won't find better"; BYO is a "bonus" too. / **Details:** www.lahorekarahi.co.uk; midnight; no Amex.

Lahore Kebab House E1   £22   ⭐⭐
2-10 Umberston St   7488 2551
"Even if you go early, there's a queue", at this legendary East End "landmark" – London's top-rated subcontinental – where the Pakistani grills and curries are "world-class" (but prices are "so low"); "ignore the decor"; BYO.
/ **Details:** www.lahore-kebabhouse.com; midnight; need 8+ to book.

Lamberts SW12   £45   Ⓐ⭐⭐
2 Station Pde   8675 2233
"A budget alternative to Chez Bruce!" – this "relaxed" Balham local gives its stellar (and more ambitious) rival a respectable "run for its money", with "impressive", "well thought-out" cuisine, "personal" service, and "ludicrously good-value prices".
/ **Details:** www.lambertsrestaurant.com; 10.30 pm, Sun 9 pm; closed Mon, Tue-Fri L & Sun D; no Amex.

The Landau
The Langham W1   £88   Ⓐ
1c, Portland Pl   7965 0165   1–1B
This "wonderfully elegant" dining room north of Oxford Circus has maintained a pretty even keel since Elisha Carter took over the reins from Andrew Turner in late-2009, offering food – albeit in a more "classic" idiom – which is notably "well-prepared".
/ **Value tip:** set pre-theatre £53 (FP). **Details:** www.thelandau.com; 10 pm; closed Sat L & Sun; no trainers.

(Winter Garden)
The Landmark NW1   £79   Ⓐ
222 Marylebone Rd   7631 8000
An "excellent Sunday brunch" (with jazz) and "the best afternoon tea in town" are the main reasons to seek out the "palm-filled" atrium of this "opulent" Marylebone hotel; its attractions at other times are severely limited.
/ **Details:** www.landmarklondon.co.uk; 10.30 pm; no trainers; booking: max 12.

Langan's Brasserie W1   £55   Ⓐ
Stratton St   7491 8822   2–3C
"No question, the most fun place in London", say diehard fans of this once-famous and still "really buzzy" Mayfair old-timer; the cooking is often no more than "workmanlike" nowadays, though, and the uninitiated can find the whole experience very "old hat". / **Details:** www.langansrestaurants.co.uk; 11 pm, Fri & Sat 11.30 pm; closed Sun.

La Lanterna SE1 £39
6-8 Mill St   7252 2420
*"A very good 'local' Italian", just over Tower Bridge,
with particularly "warm and attentive" service (and a nice
courtyard for the summer). / **Details:** www.pizzerialalanterna.co.uk;
11 pm; closed Sat L.*

Latium W1 £48
21 Berners St   7323 9123   2–1D
*A "serious" Italian, "tucked away north of Oxford Street", where
Maurizio Morelli's food is "as creative as it is mouthwatering",
and where "gracious" service enlivens the "stark" setting; house
speciality – "exquisite" ravioli. / **Details:** www.latiumrestaurant.com;
10.30 pm, Sat 11 pm; closed Sat L & Sun.*

Launceston Place W8 £72
1a Launceston Pl   7937 6912   4–1B
*"Onwards and upwards", at this "discreet" Kensington
backwater "gem"; thanks to Tristan Welch's "wonderfully
inventive" cuisine, which is served in a "sleek and beautiful"
town-house setting, this is now clearly "the jewel in the D&D
group's crown". / **Value tip:** set weekday L £30
(FP). **Details:** www.danddlondon.com; 10.30 pm; closed Mon L.*

The Ledbury W11 £90
127 Ledbury Rd   7792 9090   5–1B
*This "pretty much flawless" Notting Hill spot is now hailed
as one of the capital's "top-5" foodie destinations; Brett
Graham's "consistently innovative" and "superbly executed"
cuisine is key, of course, but the "sophisticated" interior,
"brilliant" service and "excellent" wine all rate mention. / **Value
tip:** set weekday L £48 (FP). **Details:** www.theledbury.com; 10.30 pm.*

Lemonia NW1 £40
89 Regent's Park Rd   7586 7454
*Primrose Hill's "quintessential" neighbourhood Greek taverna
remains as incredibly "popular", "friendly" and "noisy" as ever –
progressively, though, critics feel it "doesn't live up to its
reputation, or its prices". / **Details:** 11.30 pm; closed Sat L & Sun D;
no Amex.*

Leong's Legends £28
4 Macclesfield St, W1   7287 0288   3–3A
82 Queensway, W2   7221 2280   5–2C
*"Excellent xiao long bao" (soup dumplings) at "fantastic" prices
help establish these "unusual" and stylish Taiwanese spots
as "real Chinatown gems". / **Details:** www.leongslegend.com; 11 pm
Thu-Sat 11.30 pm; no bookings.*

Levant W1 £50
Jason Ct, 76 Wigmore St   7224 1111   2–1A
*"Excellent belly dancing" and "great cocktails" fuel a very
"lively" vibe at this souk-like Lebanese in Marylebone – "if food's
really your thing," though, "it's probably worth the five minute
walk to the Edgware Road…" / **Details:** www.levant.co.uk; 11 pm,
Sat 11.30 pm.*

Lisboa Pâtisserie W10 £ 6 ⭐

57 Golborne Rd   8968 5242   5–1A

Pasteis de nata (custards tarts) "as good as in Portugal" – plus other "good-value" pastries and "outstanding coffee" – make it worth seeking out this "authentic" North Kensington café. / **Details:** *7.30 pm; L & early evening only; no booking.*

LMNT E8 £31 🅐

316 Queensbridge Rd   7249 6727

"Crazy" decor and "very friendly" staff help make this Dalston pub-conversion "good for a party", or for a "cheap 'n' cheerful" date. / **Details:** *www.lmnt.co.uk; 10.45 pm; no Amex.*

Lobster Pot SE11 £56 ⭐

3 Kennington Ln   7582 5556

"Wonderfully kitsch" decor and the "entertaining" owner Hervé contribute to the splendidly "quirky" experience of visiting this "quaint" stalwart in the "gastronomic dessert of Kennington"; on the menu – "excellent", if "old-fashioned", Gallic fish and seafood. / **Details:** *www.lobsterpotrestaurant.co.uk; 10.30 pm; closed Mon & Sun; booking: max 8.*

Locanda Locatelli Churchill InterCont'l W1 £66 🅐⭐

8 Seymour St   7935 9088   1–2A

"Bravissimo!"; after a slight dip last year, Giorgio Locatelli's "luxurious" Marylebone dining room is back on "fabulous" form, and "at its best offers some of the top Italian food in London"; on the downside, though, prices can seem a bit "crazy".
/ **Details:** *www.locandalocatelli.com; 11 pm, Fri & Sat 11.30 pm, Sun 10.15 pm; booking: max 8.*

Locanda Ottomezzo W8 £69

2-4 Thackeray St   7937 2200   4–1B

This is "potentially a great neighbourhood Italian", but even fans say prices at this Kensington fixture are a "joke" – it would be "excellent... if it cost about 30% less"! / **Value tip:** *set weekday L £43 (FP).* **Details:** *www.locandaottoemezzo.co.uk; 10.30 pm, Fri & Sat 10.45 pm; closed Sat L & Sun.*

Lola Rojo £41 ⭐

140 Wandsworth Bridge Rd, SW6   7371 8396
78 Northcote Rd, SW11   7350 2262

An "excellent modern twist on tapas" makes these "stark" – but "buzzing" and "friendly" – Fulham and Clapham spots quite a 'rave'; there's a downside to being "inventive", though – "not everything always works". / **Details:** *www.lolarojo.net; SW11 11.30 pm; SW6 11 pm; SW6 Mon-Fri D only.*

Lucky Seven W2 £37 Ⓐ

127 Westbourne Park Rd 7727 6771 5–1B

"You constantly expect the Fonz to pop up", at Tom Conran's *"funky"* US-style diner, on the fringe of Notting Hill, where you sit in *"shared cramped booths"*; it's still often tipped for *"colossal"* breakfasts and *"burgers to die for"*, but ratings overall dipped a bit this year. / **Details:** www.tomconranrestaurants.com; 10.15 pm, Sun 10 pm; no Amex; no booking.

Ma Goa SW15 £35 ★

244 Upper Richmond Rd 8780 1767

"Exciting" Goan dishes – *"so different from usual Indian cuisine"* – make it *"well worth the excursion to Putney"*, to visit this *"charming"* family-run fixture. / **Details:** www.ma-goa.com; 11 pm, Sun 10 pm; closed Mon L, Tue & Sat L.

Made in Italy SW3 £35 Ⓐ★

249 King's Rd 7352 1880 4–3C

"The food is so good you forget about the service", at this *"little bit of Naples"*, in Chelsea, which serves up *"some of the best pizza in London"* (sold by the 1/2 metre) in *"fun"* but *"chaotic"* style; *"charming roof terrace"* too.

/ **Details:** www.madeinitalyrestaurant.co.uk; 11.30 pm, Sun 10.30 pm; closed weekday L; no Amex.

Magdalen SE1 £51 ★

152 Tooley St 7403 1342

"Superior" (and *"quite rich"*) Anglo-French cooking and *"knowledgeable and friendly"* service have made this *"cosy"* and *"lively"* spot the best-known foodie destination within easy reach of London Bridge station. / **Details:** www.magdalenrestaurant.co.uk; 10 pm; closed Sat L & Sun.

Maggie Jones's W8 £48 Ⓐ

6 Old Court Pl 7937 6462 4–1A

"A rustic escape in urban Kensington" – this *"lovely"* farmhouse-style veteran is particularly popular as a cold-weather destination, especially for those with romance in mind; the food – *"mostly British"* – is a bit incidental. / **Details:** 11 pm, Sun 10.30 pm.

Maison Bertaux W1 £13 Ⓐ★

28 Greek St 7437 6007 3–2A

"I've been going for all my 60 years – it's cramped and uncomfortable, but I love it!"; this *"eccentric"* institution (est 1871) may be one of the last bastions of 'old' Soho, but it still offers *"mouth-watering"* pâtisserie and croissants.

/ **Details:** 11 pm, Sun 8 pm; no credit cards; no booking.

Malabar W8 £38 ★

27 Uxbridge St 7727 8800 5–2B

For *"a smarter curry"*, many reporters still tip this rather *"different"* Indian stalwart, just off Notting Hill Gate, which has long been known for its *"interesting"* food and *"consistent"* standards; after a blip last year, ratings have improved.

/ **Details:** www.malabar-restaurant.co.uk; 11.15 pm, Sun 10.30 pm.

Mandarin Kitchen W2 £37 ⭐
14-16 Queensway   7727 9012   5–2C
"The lobster noodles are legendary and rightly so", at this "run-down" Bayswater veteran, whose "amazing" seafood – some of London's best – is in contrast to its "brusque" service, and decor that "seems to be falling apart". / *Details:* 11.30 pm.

Mangal 1 E8 £25 ⭐
10 Arcola St   7275 8981
"Plates piled high" with "hot quail", "lamb kebabs", and "home-baked breads" – all from a "crackling charcoal pit" – are the sort of "wonderful-value" fare that makes this BYO Turkish restaurant, in Dalston, very popular; they've recently expanded to accommodate the crush. / *Details:* www.mangal1.com; midnight, Sat-Sun 1 am; no credit cards.

Mango & Silk SW14 £31 ⭐
199 Upper Richmond Rd   8876 6220
"Udit Sarkhel conjures up some splendid delights", at his "high-end, high street Indian", in East Sheen; it is, however, still "not quite as good as when he was in Southfields".
/ *Details:* www.mangoandsilk.co.uk; 10 pm, Fri & Sat 10.30 pm; D only, ex Sun open L & D.

Manson SW6 £50 ⭐⭐
676 Fulham Rd   7384 9559
"Just what Fulham has been missing for so long" – this latest occupant of an "ill-fated" corner site may look and feel like an "understated" wine bar, but the "sensational" and "thoughtful" cooking of Ramsay-protégée Gemma Tuley makes it "a very refreshing addition to the area".
/ *Details:* www.balthazarrestaurant.co.uk; 10.30 pm, Sun 9 pm.

Marcus Wareing
The Berkeley SW1 £115 Ⓐ⭐⭐
Wilton Pl   7235 1200   4–1D

"Standing supreme as London's best restaurant"; Marcus Wareing's "formal" Knightsbridge dining room is again the survey's No. 1 – his food is a "tour de force", service "second to none", and the wine "exceptional"; perhaps owing to his Lancastrian roots, puddings are a particular highlight. / *Value tip:* set weekday L £67 (FP). *Details:* www.the-berkeley.co.uk; 10.30 pm; closed Sat L & Sun; no jeans or trainers; booking: max 10.

Market NW1 £44
43 Parkway 7267 9700
"A perfect local"; this admirably *"straightforward"* modern bistro, in Camden Town, offers *"honest"*, *"fresh"* and *"flavoursome"* food, *"charmingly"* served in an *"unflashy"* but *"buzzy"* setting.
/ **Details:** www.marketrestaurant.co.uk; 10.30 pm; closed Sun D.

Masters Super Fish SE1 £24
191 Waterloo Rd 7928 6924
"A million cabbies can't be wrong!"; this *"true chippy"*, near the Old Vic, offers *"no fuss"* – just *"the best fish 'n' chips within miles"*, and in *"vast portions"* too. / **Details:** 10.30 pm; closed Sun, Mon L; no Amex; no booking Fri D.

Matsuri SW1 £67
15 Bury St 7839 1101 2–3D
"Very good teppan-yaki" – *"great food-theatre"* – is the prime draw to this well-established (and *"pricey"*) St James's Japanese, but the sushi can be *"really fantastic"* too.
/ **Details:** www.matsuri-restaurant.com; 10.30 pm, Sun 10 pm.

maze W1 £72
10-13 Grosvenor Sq 7107 0000 2–2A
Even before Jason Atherton's recent departure (and then that of his successor!) this *"expensive"* and *"sterile"* Ramsay-group property in Mayfair – long acclaimed for its *"posh tapas"* formula – was *"losing it"*; the growing feeling among reporters: *"so what?"* / **Value tip:** set weekday L £39
(FP). **Details:** www.gordonramsay.com/maze; 10.30 pm.

maze Grill W1 £75
10-13 Grosvenor Sq 7495 2211 2–2A
A Ramsay-group Mayfair grill-house where the steak is typically *"excellent"*; unless you stick to the *"great-value"* lunch, though, it's often *"spoilt by the bill"*, and the ambience can be *"depressing"* too. / **Value tip:** set weekday L £47
(FP). **Details:** www.gordonramsay.com; 10.30 pm; no trainers.

Mennula W1 £45
10 Charlotte St 7636 2833 1–1C
"Oh-so-delicious" and *"refined"* Sicilian cooking and *"enthusiastic"*, *"professional"* staff have made this simple-looking newcomer (on the Fitzrovia site of Passione, RIP) a *"very welcome addition to London's Italians"*.
/ **Details:** www.mennula.com; 11 pm, Sun 9.30 pm; closed Sat & Sun L; no Amex.

Michael Nadra W4 £42
6-8 Elliott Rd 8742 0766 6–2A
"Well refurbished", renamed, and no longer serving just fish – this Chiswick newcomer (fka Fish Hook) wins acclaim for M. Nadra's *"even-more-impressive"* cuisine (it was already very good), and its *"great new buzz"*; it's still *"cramped"*, though.
/ **Details:** www.restaurant-michaelnadra.co.uk; 10 pm, Fri & Sat 10.30 pm.

Min Jiang
The Royal Garden Hotel W8   **£60**   Ⓐ ★
2-24 Kensington High St   7361 1988   4–1A
"Amazing views" and *"outstanding food"* don't often go hand
in hand, so this *"elegant"* 8th-floor Kensington Chinese is to
be congratulated – the dim sum is *"superb"*, but it's the
"stunning" Peking duck (pre-order) that people talk about most.
/ **Details:** www.minjiang.co.uk; 10 pm.

Minqala W1   **£28**   ★
9 Seymour Place   7724 5131   5–1D
*Near Marble Arch, a small, unglitzy and very welcoming Arabic
restaurant, where simple fare – lots of lamb, naturally – is done
well, and at reasonable cost; no booze.* / **Details:** 11.30 pm; no credit
cards.

Mint Leaf   **£63**
Suffolk Pl, Haymarket, SW1   7930 9020   1–2C
Angel Ct, Lothbury, EC2   7600 992

"Stunning" decor, *"great"* cocktails and *"beautifully-presented"*
dishes just about justify the toppish prices at these *"stylish"*
subcontinentals in Theatreland and the City; *"a bit more focus
on service, though, would really lift the overall experience"*.
/ **Value tip:** set weekday L £36 (FP). **Details:** www.mintleafrestaurant.com;
SW1 11 pm, Sun 10.30 pm; EC2 11 pm; SW1 closed Sat & Sun D; EC2 closed
Sat & Sun.

Miran Masala W14   **£20**   ★
3 Hammersmith Rd   7602 4555   6–1D
*"I lived in West Yorkshire for six years, so know a good curry
when I see one!"*; this *"budget"* caff by Olympia (now split from
the 'Mirch Masalas') serves *"wonderful"*, *"authentic"* Pakistani
dishes, many – including bread – from its tandoor oven.
/ **Details:** www.miranmasala.co.uk; midnight; D only; no Amex.

Mitsukoshi SW1   **£55**   ★
Dorland Hs, 14-20 Lower Regent St   7930 0317   2–3D
"Great food, shame about the atmosphere-free basement" –
the story's the same as ever at this *"drab"* Japanese, *"hidden-
away"* at the foot of a department store, near Piccadilly Circus,
where the sushi, in particular, is *"exceptional"*.
/ **Details:** www.mitsukoshi-restaurant.co.uk; 10 pm.

Miyama W1 £60
38 Clarges St   7499 2443   2–4B
The ambience is very "austere", at this "high-quality Japanese"
in Mayfair; the food, though, remains very "well-constructed"
and "reasonably-priced for what you get".
/ **Details:** *www.miyama.co.uk; 10.15 pm; closed Sat L & Sun L.*

Mohsen W14 £27
152 Warwick Rd   7602 9888   6–1D
"There's a good welcome from Mrs Mohsen", at this "low-key",
but "reliable" BYO Persian, by the Olympia Homebase, which
serves up "honest" portions of "down-to-earth" dishes
("excellent grills" and "fantastically fresh" mezze)
at "greatvalue" prices. / **Details:** *midnight; no credit cards.*

Momo W1 £62
25 Heddon St   7434 4040   2–2C

An "extraordinary Moroccan
ambience" – and a lovely terrace
too – bewitch fans of Mourad
Mazouz's seductive hang-out,
just off Regent Street; even some
reporters who find the place
"so beautiful", though, are not
blinded to the fact that the food
is "unexciting", and
very "overpriced".
/ **Value tip:** *set weekday L £32*
(FP). **Details:** *www.momoresto.com;*
11 pm; closed Sun L.

Monmouth Coffee Company £11
27 Monmouth St, WC2   7379 3516   3–2B
2 Park St, SE1   7645 3585
You get "by far the best coffee in London" ("no-one else comes
close"), say fans of this Borough Market phenomenon (which
also has a "tiny" Covent Garden branch); weekend breakfasts –
pastries, bread and jam – are a South Bank cult.
/ **Details:** *www.monmouthcoffee.co.uk; 6 pm-6.30 pm; SE1 2 pm; closed Sun,*
SE1 Sun-Fri; no Amex; no booking.

Montpeliano SW7 £68
13 Montpelier St   7589 0032   4–1C
A classic Knightsbridge trattoria that inspires little commentary
nowadays; it probably doesn't help that the food is both
"unremarkable" and "too pricey".
/ **Details:** *www.montpelianorestaurant.com; 11.45 pm, Sun 11.30 pm.*

Mooli's W1 £10
50 Frith St   7494 9075   3–2A
"Inventive" rotis that truly "rock" – "an interesting mix of spicy
meat and vibrantly fresh chutney in a slightly chewy wrap" –
have made a whopping hit of this "chilled" Soho newcomer;
the lunch for a fiver offers particularly brilliant value.
/ **Details:** *www.moolis.com; Mon-Wed 10 pm, Thu-Sat 11.30 pm.*

Morgan M N7 £64 ⭐⭐
489 Liverpool Rd 7609 3560
Morgan Meunier's "quirky" pub-conversion makes
an "incongruous" find in Holloway, but his "inspirational" cuisine
(amongst the top five French kitchens in London) well "justifies
the trek", and the service is "impeccable" too; so why
no Michelin star? – now, if he was on TV…
/ **Details:** www.morganm.com; 9 pm; closed Mon, Tue L, Sat L & Sun D;
no Amex; booking: max 8.

Moro EC1 £46 Ⓐ⭐⭐
34-36 Exmouth Mkt 7833 8336
"Love the food… love the atmosphere… love the integrity of the
place"; this "vibrant" ("so noisy"!) Exmouth Market fixture
is "many Londoners' favourite", thanks to its "easy-going" style,
its "incredible" Spanish/Moorish fare, and its "fantastic" Iberian
wines and sherries. / **Details:** www.moro.co.uk; 10.30 pm; closed Sun.

Moti Mahal WC2 £50 ⭐
45 Gt Queen St 7240 9329 3–2D
"An interesting take on Indian food" ("with a twist") is winning
a growing following for this "vibrant" Covent Garden outpost of a
Delhi-based group. / **Details:** www.motimahal-uk.com; 11 pm; closed
Sat L & Sun.

Mr Kong WC2 £31
21 Lisle St 7437 7341 3–3A
This "lively and bustling" Chinatown stalwart remains
a most "reliable haunt", presided over by its "great host", Edwin;
"you need to know what to order", though – "go for the out-of-
the-ordinary dishes", which are often "amazing".
/ **Details:** www.mrkongrestaurant.com; 2.45 am, Sun 12.45 am.

Mr Wing SW5 £45 Ⓐ
242-244 Old Brompton Rd 7370 4450 4–2A
"Jungle decor, with wall-sized fish-tanks" (in the basement),
"a cosy ground-floor", "terrific" service, and regular jazz confirm
that this Earl's Court veteran is "not your typical Chinese";
the food's pretty good too, making this a handy all-rounder,
especially for a party or romance. / **Details:** www.mrwing.com; midnight.

Mrs Marengos W1 £15 ⭐
53 Lexington St 7287 2544 2–2D
It's impossible not to warm to this "lovely" café/cake shop
(an offshoot of neighbouring Mildred's), which offers "fantastic-
quality food" (including "outstanding" baking), and "great value
for money" too. / **Details:** www.mrsmarengos.co.uk; L only, closed Sun;
no Amex; no booking.

Murano W1 £86 ⭐
20-22 Queen St 7495 1127 2–3B
"The best of Ramsay's places" – Angela Hartnett's "remarkably
skilful" cuisine ("more modern European than Italian") adds
considerably to the brio of this grand but "bland" Mayfair
yearling; there's no doubt, though, that – "after a great opening"
– it's "slipped a bit". / **Value tip:** set weekday L £49
(FP). **Details:** www.angela-hartnett.com; 10.15 pm; closed Sun.

My Old Place E1   £29 ⭐⭐
88-90 Middlesex St   7247 2200
"Extraordinary", "tongue-numbing" Sichuan dishes at "insanely cheap" prices (and in "large portions" too) inspire a hymn of praise to this "crowded" Chinese, near Liverpool Street; it's an "unexciting" room, though, and service is "perfunctory".
/ **Details:** 11 pm.

Nahm
Halkin Hotel SW1   £85
5 Halkin St   7333 1234   1–3A
Fans of David Thompson's long-running Belgravia Thai extol the "genius" of his cuisine, and feel the place is let down only by the "strangely barren and charmless" dining room; sceptics, though, say the prices are "absurd" too. / **Value tip:** set weekday L £55 (FP). **Details:** www.nahm.como.bz; 10.30 pm; closed Sat L & Sun L.

The National Dining Rooms
National Gallery WC2   £50
Sainsbury Wing, Trafalgar Sq   7747 2525   1–2C
"A great view over Trafalgar Square" is the chief draw to this gallery café – its "very average" food is a "disappointing" advertisement for our national cuisine.
/ **Details:** www.thenationaldiningrooms.co.uk; 7.15 pm; Sat-Thu closed D, Fri open L & D.

Nautilus NW6   £32 ⭐
27-29 Fortune Green Rd   7435 2532
Fans acclaim this West Hampstead institution for the "best fish 'n' chips in North West London"; "who cares about the ambience?" / **Details:** 10 pm; closed Sun; no Amex.

Needoo E1   £18 ⭐⭐
87 New Rd   7247 0648   1–2D
"As good as Tayyabs and, initially at least, without the queue" – this "fabulous" Pakistani newcomer has grills and curries to rival its legendary neighbour (the former employer of the boss here); it's a "small" room, though, and all that sizzling can make it seem "smoky". / **Details:** www.needoogrill.co.uk; 6 pm; closed Sun; no Amex.

New Tayyabs E1   £27 ⭐⭐
83 Fieldgate St   7247 9543
"A must do!" for curry-lovers; this "dirt cheap" Pakistani grill – known for its "absolutely fabulous" lamb chops – remains a major East End phenomenon; "the chaos and the long waits are well worth it", and "BYO is a bonus".
/ **Details:** www.tayyabs.co.uk; 11.30 pm.

19 Numara Bos Cirrik N16   £21 ⭐⭐
34 Stoke Newington Rd   7249 0400
"An unexpected star, by Hackney Central station" – a "friendly" Turkish charcoal grill-restaurant offering "amazing mezze" and "the most authentic kebabs this side of Istanbul", all at "terrific" prices. / **Details:** midnight; no Amex or Maestro.

Nobu
Metropolitan Hotel W1   **£88**   ⭐
19 Old Park Ln   7447 4747   2–4A
"The allure has faded a bit" ("it's much easier to get a table now"), and it's easy for guests to feel "processed", but this Japanese-fusion legend, in Mayfair, still churns out "fabulously adventurous" dishes; "just make sure someone else is paying".
/ **Details:** www.noburestaurants.com; 11 pm, Sun 9.30 pm.

Nobu W1   **£88**
15 Berkeley Street   7290 9222   2–3C
"More fun" (and "posier") than its Park Lane namesake, the younger Nobu serves "superb" sushi that's nearly as good, at prices that are equally "extravagant"; the noise level is "deafening" though, and – for such an expensive joint – a visit can seem a surprisingly "cramped" and "rushed" experience.
/ **Details:** www.noburestaura
nts.com; 11 pm, Thu-Sat midnight, Sun 9 pm.

Noor Jahan   **£36**   ⭐
2a Bina Gdns, SW5   7373 6522   4–2B
26 Sussex Pl, W2   7402 2332   5–1D
"Standard curry house fare" is prepared to a consistently "excellent" level at this well-known, "always-packed" South Kensington veteran; its W2 spin-off has yet to build a comparable following. / **Details:** 11.30 pm.

North China W3   **£34**   ⭐
305 Uxbridge Rd   8992 9183   6–1A
"Who'd have thought it, and in the heart of Acton too?" – this family-run (and "family-friendly") "old favourite" is a "classy" sort of place, offering "genuine" and "high-quality" Chinese cuisine. / **Details:** www.northchina.co.uk; 11 pm, Fri & Sat 11.30 pm.

Nozomi SW3   **£70**
15 Beauchamp Pl   7838 1500   4–1C
A "pretentious" Knightsbridge Japanese which is presumably sustained by its "good after-dinner bar scene"; judged by restaurant standards, the 'rapport prix/qualité' is "not good", with "atrocious" service a particular bugbear.
/ **Details:** www.nozomi.co.uk; 1 am, Sun 12.30; closed Mon L & Sun L.

Nuovi Sapori SW6   **£38**   ⭐
295 New King's Rd   7736 3363
All reports affirm the "authentic" and "very tasty" cooking at this Fulham Italian; shame, then, about the "serious lack of atmosphere". / **Details:** 11 pm; closed Sun.

O'Zon TW1 £30
33-35 London Rd 8891 3611
*A "favourite" Chinese in central Twickenham, hailed for its
"great value" and "good service", and which comes
recommended both "for families" and "for groups".
/ **Details:** 11 pm, Fri & Sat 11.30 pm.*

The Oak W2 £42 🅰⭐
137 Westbourne Park Rd 7221 3355 5–1B
*Thanks to the "ridiculously cool ambience" and the "crisp" and
"utterly amazing" wood-fired pizzas, it is "almost impossible
to get a table" at this "light and airy" former boozer, on the
fringe of Notting Hill. / **Details:** www.theoaklondon.com; 10.30 pm;
Sun 10 pm; closed weekday L; no booking.*

Odette's NW1 £57
130 Regent's Park Rd 7586 8569
*Bryn Williams's cuisine is "excellent and exquisitely presented"
(if rather "expensive") at this "romantic" Primrose Hill
landmark; "amateur" service can be a bugbear, though, and for
some old fans the place has never recovered from a (they think
"ghastly") revamp a few years ago. / **Value tip:** set weekday L £29
(FP). **Details:** www.odettesprimrosehill.com; 10.30 pm; closed Mon.*

Odin's W1 £56 🅰
27 Devonshire St 7935 7296 1–1A
*"Delightfully old-school, and with a delightful old-school
clientele"; this "quiet", "art-filled" and "so civilised" Marylebone
veteran still gratifies traditionalists, although its "cosseting"
service is a greater draw than the sometimes "bland" cuisine.
/ **Details:** www.langansrestaurants.co.uk; 11 pm; closed Sat L & Sun; booking:
max 12.*

Ye Olde Cheshire Cheese EC4 £33 🅰
145 Fleet St 7353 6170
*"Lots of history" makes this Fleet Street hostelry – rebuilt after
the Great Fire, and beloved of Dr Johnson et al – "a great place
to bring out-of-towners"; its "good"-to-"ordinary" English fodder
could be worse. / **Details:** 9.30 pm; closed Sun D; no booking, Sat & Sun.*

Oliveto SW1 £44 ⭐⭐
49 Elizabeth St 7730 0074 1–4A
*This Belgravia Sardinian may look unexciting, but "pizza
amongst the best in London" – with "thin" crusts and "creative"
toppings – ensures it's always "bustling".
/ **Details:** www.olivorestaurants.com; 11 pm, Sun 10.30 pm; booking: max 7
at D.*

Olivomare SW1 £54 ⭐⭐
10 Lower Belgrave St 7730 9022 1–4B
*"Really lovely seafood with a Sardinian slant" makes this smart
Belgravian well worth seeking out; take your sunnies, though –
the "cool" retro decor really is very white.
/ **Details:** www.olivorestaurants.com; 11 pm, Sun 10.30 pm; booking: max 10.*

Olley's SE24   **£37**   ★

65-67 Norwood Rd   8671 8259

Nowadays becoming a "South London institution" –
this "interesting" Brockwell Park chippy has won renown for its
"amazing fish 'n' chips"; it's "not cheap", though, and the decor
is "not to all tastes". / *Details:* www.olleys.info; 10.30 pm; closed Mon;
no Amex.

1 Lombard Street EC3   **£75**

1 Lombard St   7929 6611

Ratings are again heading south at this "impressive"-looking
former banking hall, which a few years ago was the City's top
spot for entertaining; its location by Bank is undeniably
"convenient", but too many reporters nowadays find it "sterile",
"noisy" and "overpriced"; the cheaper brasserie is probably the
better bet. / *Details:* www.1lombardstreet.com; 10 pm; closed Sat & Sun.

One-O-One

Sheraton Park Tower SW1   **£85**   ★★

101 Knightsbridge   7290 7101   4–1D

"Out-of-this-world" fish and seafood from Breton chef Pascal
Proyart – "London's finest" – makes it worth bearing the
"airport-lounge" styling of this Knightsbridge hotel dining room;
look out for 50%-off deals – they're an absolute "steal".
/ *Details:* www.oneoonerestaurant.com; 10 pm; booking: max 6.

The Orange SW1   **£47**   Ⓐ

37-39 Pimlico Rd   7881 9844   4–2D

"The latest SW1 pub to be bleached, limed and gastro-ed!" –
this "welcome addition" to Orange Square (fka Pimlico Green)
bears all the hallmarks of its Thos. Cubitt and Pantechnicon
siblings, such as "a really buzzy and comfy" interior and
"simple" food that's well realised, if no great bargain.
/ *Details:* www.theorange.co.uk; Mon-Thu 11.30 pm, Fri & Sat midnight,
Sun 10.30 pm.

L'Oranger SW1   **£85**

5 St James's St   7839 3774   2–4D

Fans say this "plush" St James's veteran is "very reliable"
("especially for the great set lunch menu") – there are
almost as many critics however, who say it has degenerated into
being a "ghetto for rich people", with cooking of no more than
"'hotel' standard". / *Details:* www.loranger.co.uk; 10.30 pm; closed Sat L &
Sun; no jeans or trainers; booking: max 8.

Orrery W1   **£68**   ★

55 Marylebone High St   7616 8000   1–1A

"First-class" cuisine and "polished" service make for
a "soothing" all-round experience at this "airy" (if "oddly-
shaped") first-floor dining room, "tucked-away" in Marylebone,
with "lovely views" (over a churchyard); for some reporters,
it's "the only really good 'Conran'" (as the D&D group was
formerly called). / *Details:* www.orreryrestaurant.co.uk; 10.30 pm, Fri-Sat
11 pm.

Oslo Court NW8 £54 A ⭐

Charlbert St, off Prince Albert Rd   7722 8795

"From the salmon-pink colour scheme to decrumbing with a mini-vacuum cleaner", this "'70s throwback", at the base of a Regent's Park apartment block, is "a total joy"; other highlights include the "fabulously retro" menu, staff who "really make you feel at home", and the irresistible sweet trolley. / **Details:** 11 pm; closed Sun; no jeans or trainers.

Osteria Dell'Angolo SW1 £45 ⭐

47 Marsham St   3268 1077   1–4C

A Westminster Italian, where the "authentic", "creative" and "well-executed" dishes are winning something of a following — if it weren't for the dull decor, we suspect it would be a much broader one. / **Details:** www.osteriadellangolo.co.uk; 10.30 pm; closed Sat L & Sun.

Ottolenghi £43 ⭐⭐

13 Motcomb St, SW1   7823 2707   4–1D
63 Ledbury Rd, W11   7727 1121   5–1B
1 Holland St, W8   7937 0003   4–1A
287 Upper St, N1   7288 1454

The "mouthwatering" pastries and "out-of-this-world" salads are "to die for", at these "zeitgeist-y" communal café/delis — a fine choice for an "epic" brunch; they're "frustratingly cramped", though, and the queues can be "ridiculous". / **Details:** www.ottolenghi.co.uk; 10.15 pm; W8 & W11 8 pm, Sat 7 pm, Sun 6 pm; N1 closed Sun D; Holland St takeaway only; W11 & SW1 no booking, N1 booking for D only.

(Restaurant)
Oxo Tower SE1 £77 ✕

Barge House St   7803 3888

"Still shamelessly trading off the admittedly wonderful view" — too often "you pay a fortune for mediocrity" in the grandest section of this sixth-floor South Bank landmark, and sometimes the results are simply "rubbish". / **Details:** www.harveynichols.com; 11 pm, Sun 10 pm.

(Brasserie)
Oxo Tower SE1 £67 ✕

Barge House St   7803 3888

"Pricing itself in the smart bracket, while offering mediocrity" — the "brisk" cheaper section of this South Bank landmark has a "lovely view", of course, but takes flak for "so so" food, and staff who "pack 'em in and ship 'em out". / **Details:** www.harveynichols.com; 11 pm, Sun 10 pm.

The Painted Heron SW10 £49 ⭐⭐

112 Cheyne Walk   7351 5232   4–3B

An Indian "gem", in an "out-of-the-way" corner of Chelsea, that's "a delight year after year", thanks not least to its "innovative" cuisine; the premises are "smart" enough too, but they can "lack atmosphere". / **Details:** www.thepaintedheron.com; 11 pm; closed Sat L.

The Palm SW1   **£80** ❌
1 Pont St   7201 0710   4–1D
"A let-down"; this "over-hyped" Belgravia outpost of a famous
NYC steakhouse is "definitely not up to US standards", and its
prices are "astronomical"; still, nothing succeeds like failure –
2011 will see new branches both in the West End and
at Heathrow! / **Details:** www.thepalm.com; 11 pm, Sun 10 pm; closed Mon L.

The Palmerston SE22   **£43** ⭐
91 Lordship Ln   8693 1629
"Honest but clever cooking" – plus a "great homely feel" –
maintain the high popularity of this East Dulwich "restaurant
in a pub". / **Value tip:** set weekday L £26
(FP). **Details:** www.thepalmerston.net; 10 pm, Sun 9.30 pm; no Amex.

Paolina Café WC1   **£18** ⭐
181 Kings Cross Rd   7278 8176
Looking for a bite near King's Cross? – this tiny BYO café
is "the best-value and most authentic Thai around"; no prizes
for interior design, though! / **Details:** 10 pm; closed Sat L & Sun; no credit
cards.

Paradise by Way of Kensal Green W10 **£38** 🅰⭐
19 Kilburn Ln   8969 0098

A "truly original" gastropub; this vast Victorian building –
combining bars, a dining room, club, roof terraces and pretty
garden – has long been a "funky" Kensal Green destination,
with a "fantastic" atmosphere, "first-rate" service and "assured"
food. / **Value tip:** set weekday L £22 (FP). **Details:** www.theparadise.co.uk;
10.30 pm, Sun 9 pm; closed Sat D.

El Parador NW1   **£31** 🅰⭐
245 Eversholt St   7387 2789
"In the desert near Mornington Crescent", an "unassuming"
tapas bar, worth truffling out for its notably "excellent" tapas;
in summer, it becomes "another place again", thanks to its
"wonderful" patio garden. / **Details:** www.elparadorlondon.com; 11 pm,
Fri-Sat 11.30 pm, Sun 9.30 pm; closed Sat L & Sun L; no Amex.

Patio W12   **£30** 🅰
5 Goldhawk Rd   8743 5194   6–1C
"Staff make you feel at home" at this "quaint" and "cosy" Pole
in Shepherd's Bush, and serve up "generous helpings"
of "hearty" stodge, plus "loads of different vodkas" – "a great
cheap eat". / **Details:** www.patiolondon.com; 11.30 pm; closed Sat L & Sun L.

Patogh W1   **£12**   ⭐⭐

8 Crawford Pl   7262 4015   5–1D

"The best kebabs", and "superb-quality" salads, "justify the wait" for this "packed" and "authentic" Marylebone Iranian; "shared tables, BYO". / **Details:** 11 pm; no credit cards.

Patterson's W1   **£68**

4 Mill St   7499 1308   2–2C

A "useful" Mayfair location (especially for business), plus "enterprising" cuisine and "attentive" service all win fans for this "discreetly charming, yet unfussy" restaurant, hidden-away near Savile Row. / **Value tip:** set weekday L £43 (FP). **Details:** www.pattersonsrestaurant.co.uk; 11 pm; closed Sat L & Sun.

Pearl WC1   **£85**

252 High Holborn   7829 7000   1–1D

With Jun Tanaka's "terrific" cuisine, this "imposing" Holborn dining room is, for fans, simply a "magical" all-rounder (and particularly a "pearl for a business meeting"); growing complaints of "excessive" prices and "lackadaisical" service, however, are beginning to undermine its appeal. / **Value tip:** set weekday L £47 (FP). **Details:** www.pearl-restaurant.com; 10 pm; closed Sat L & Sun.

Pearl Liang W2   **£42**   ⭐

8 Sheldon Sq   7289 7000   5–1C

The "bizarre, corporate-feeling location" – a basement, "hidden away" in "bleak" Paddington Basin – hasn't stopped reporters from being drawn to this "upmarket" Chinese; the attraction? – "superb dim sum", and other "gourmet" fare, all at "excellent prices". / **Details:** www.pearlliang.co.uk; 11 pm.

The Peasant EC1   **£41**   Ⓐ

240 St John St   7336 7726

A 'gastropub' since before that word was coined, this "welcoming" Farringdon fixture – in a fine Victorian building – has been on top form of late, serving up some "textbook" cooking. / **Details:** www.thepeasant.co.uk; 10.45 pm, Sun 9.30 pm.

E Pellicci E2   **£14**   Ⓐ

332 Bethnal Green Rd   7739 4873   1–1D

"It's hard to leave this famous Bethnal Green cafe without a full tummy and a smile on your face"; indeed, this Art Deco gem (the interior's listed), which is renowned for its breakfasts, inspired only one complaint this year – they "give you too much food!" / **Details:** 4.15 pm; L only, closed Sun; no credit cards.

Pescatori   **£50**   ⭐

11 Dover St, W1   7493 2652   2–3C

55-57 Charlotte St, W1   7580 3289   1–1C

The "superb selection of fish" at these rather "typical"-looking (but "cheerful") West End Italians can be a surprise, and its very "decent food and prices" win consistent praise. / **Details:** www.pescatori.co.uk; 11 pm; closed Sat L & Sun.

Petersham Hotel TW10 £58 Ⓐ
Nightingale Ln   8940 7471
"A classic hotel dining room", in Richmond, with *"stunning views"* over Petersham Meadows and the Thames; the style may be a little *"old-fashioned"* for some tastes, but the cuisine is consistently *"well-executed"*. / **Value tip:** set weekday L £37 (FP). **Details:** www.petershamhotel.co.uk; Mon-Fri 9.45 pm, 8.45 pm.

Petersham Nurseries TW10 £63 Ⓐ⭐
Church Ln, Off Petersham Rd   8605 3627
"Larcenous" prices do little to dent the popularity of this *"idiosyncratic"* garden-centre restaurant, which is located in a *"rickety old greenhouse"* (where *"waitresses wear wellies on wet days"*); the whole concept *"has great charm"*, helped not a little by Skye Gyngell's *"innovative"* and *"memorable"* cuisine. / **Details:** www.petershamnurseries.com; L only, closed Mon.

La Petite Maison W1 £77 Ⓐ⭐
54 Brooks Mews   7495 4774   2–2B
For the *"beautiful people"* of Mayfair, this *"glamorous"* and *"fun"* Gallic restaurant is a *"great all-rounder"* that just keeps getting better; OK, prices are *"crazy"*, but it's a *"gorgeous"* experience, in which *"light"* but *"memorable"* Mediterranean tapas play no small part. / **Details:** www.lpmlondon.co.uk; 10.30 pm, Sun 9 pm.

Pétrus SW1 £85
1 Kinnerton St   7592 1609   4–1D
"Marcus Wareing needn't fret yet about this rival on his doorstep"; though Ramsay's Belgravia newcomer did dazzle some reporters, others have found *"the bill more memorable than the food"* – it doesn't help that it's served in a luxuriously beige room that can seem *"overshadowed"* by its central *"wine Tardis"*. / **Details:** www.gordonramsay.com/petrus; 10.30 pm; closed Sun; no jeans or trainers.

Pham Sushi EC1 £29 ⭐⭐
159 Whitecross St   7251 6336   1–2A
"Forget the Formica tables and the haphazard service" – this *"stark"* and *"tiny"*, café, in an *"out-of-the-way"* location near the Barbican, serves up *"divine"* sushi at *"incredible"* prices. / **Details:** www.phamsushi.co.uk; 10 pm; closed Sat L & Sun.

Pho £29 ⭐
3 Great Titchfield St, W1   7436 0111   2–1C
Westfield, Ariel Way, W12   07824 662320   6–1C
86 St John St, EC1   7253 7624
Chains where the food gets better as they expand are as rare as hen's teeth, so hats off to these *"cramped"* but *"cheerful"* Vietnamese outfits, whose fare is not just *"super-fresh and healthy"*, but *"good value"* too. / **Details:** www.phocafe.co.uk; EC1 10 pm, Fri & Sat 10.30 pm; W1 10.30 pm; W12 9 pm, Sat 7 pm, Sun 6 pm; EC1 closed Sat L & Sun; W1 closed Sun; no Amex; no booking.

Pied à Terre W1 £93 ★

34 Charlotte St 7636 1178 1–1C

Shane Osborn's "sublime mixing of flavours" plus "a fantastic array of both New and Old World wines" put David Moore's "unassuming" Fitzrovia townhouse near the top of London's foodie premier league; the "oddly thin" dining room can seem "dull", but fans prefer to think of it as "cosy". / **Value tip:** set weekday L £38 (FP). **Details:** www.pied-a-terre.co.uk; 8.45 pm; closed Sat L & Sun; no Maestro; booking: max 7.

The Pigalle Club W1 £65 A X

215-217 Piccadilly 0800 988 5470 2–3D

Right by Piccadilly Circus, a cabaret venue where the food is decidedly "underwhelming" – you "don't go for the scoff", though, "but for the music and atmosphere". / **Details:** www.thepigalleclub.com; 11.30 pm; D only, closed Sun.

El Pirata de Tapas W2 £30 A ★

115 Westbourne Grove 7727 5000 5–1B

No wonder it's "lively" – this Bayswater yearling dishes up "dainty and inventive" tapas at "incredibly reasonable prices". / **Details:** www.elpiratadetapas.co.uk; 11 pm.

Pissarro's W4 £40 A

Corney Reach Way 8994 3111

"A lovely location on the river" ("super" views), makes this tucked-away spot – on the towpath, near Chiswick House – a classic "special occasion" destination; standards have continued to be rather up-and-down of late – maybe the new manager will inspire greater consistency? / **Details:** www.pissarro.co.uk; 10 pm; closed Sun D.

Pizza East E1 £37 A

56 Shoreditch High St 7729 1888 1–1B

"Just too cool for school!" – Nick Jones's "buzzy, industrial-NYC" Shoreditch newcomer – with its "achingly trendy" (if sometimes "dismissive") staff – is totally "hip" (especially for generation Y types); the "creative" pizzas? – they're "OK". / **Details:** www.pizzaeast.com; midnight, Thu 1 am, Fri & Sat 2 am.

Plateau E14 £67 X

Canada Pl 7715 7100

"Fabulous cityscape views" make this "light", elevated Canary Wharf dining room (run by the D&D group) a natural "business venue"; otherwise, though, its standards are "so average it hurts". / **Value tip:** set always available £45 (FP). **Details:** www.plateaurestaurant.co.uk; 10 pm; closed Sat L & Sun.

Polpo W1 £25 A

41 Beak St 7734 4479 2–2D

With its "NYC"-styling, "cool" staff and "vibrant" atmosphere, Russell Norman's "intimate" ("squashed") Venetian newcomer – on the Soho site of Aperitivo, long RIP – has been one of the smash hits of 2010; realisation of its "little-plates" menu may be a bit "hit-and-miss", but they do come at "bargain prices". / **Details:** www.polpo.co.uk; 11 pm, Sun 4 pm.

Popeseye   **£42** ⭐

108 Blythe Rd, W14   7610 4578   6–1C
277 Upper Richmond Rd, SW15   8788 7733
*The menu offers "nothing but steak" – fortunately "excellent",
and accompanied by "exceptional-value wines" – at these
"sparse" bistros, in Brook Green and Putney.*
/ **Details:** www.popeseye.com; 10.30 pm; D only, closed Sun; no credit cards.

Portal EC1   **£57** Ⓐ

88 St John St   7253 6950
*"Interestingly modernised" Portuguese food (with intriguing
wines and ports) wins many fans for Antonio Correia's smart but
"laid-back" Clerkenwell venture, which has a notably light and
pleasant conservatory; if only it were a tad more consistent...*
/ **Details:** www.portalrestaurant.com; 10.15 pm; closed Sat L & Sun.

Il Portico W8   **£41** Ⓐ

277 Kensington High St   7602 6262   6–1D
*A "cosy and warm" Kensington Italian, by the Odeon, that's
"been there practically for ever"; the menu holds "no surprises",
which is rather how the regulars seem to like it.*
/ **Details:** www.ilportico.co.uk; 11 pm; closed Sun.

**The Portrait
National Portrait Gallery WC2** **£46** Ⓐ

St Martin's Pl   7312 2490   3–4B

*For an "iconic" London view (best at sunset), you won't do better
than this top-floor venue, by Trafalgar Square; the food, though,
is only "average" (but they do a nice afternoon tea).*
/ **Details:** www.searcys.co.uk; Thu-Fri 8.30 pm; Sat-Wed closed D.

La Poule au Pot SW1   **£58** Ⓐ

231 Ebury St   7730 7763   4–2D
*With its "snugly nooks" and candlelight, Pimlico's "dark and
inviting" little "corner of France" is "an all-time winner for
romance" (topping this survey category for the 16th successive
year); classic "rustic" fare is served by staff who've refined Gallic
"shoulder-shrugging" to a fine art.* / **Value tip:** set always available £38
(FP). **Details:** 11 pm, Sun 10 pm.

Princess Garden W1   **£58** ⭐

8 North Audley St   7493 3223   2–2A
*"Always a civilised experience" – this "smart" and "spacious"
Mayfair Chinese wins particular acclaim for its "top-of-the-range
dim sum" at lunch, but it is a "pretty good all-rounder" at any
time.* / **Details:** www.princessgardenofmayfair.co.uk; 11.15 pm.

Princess Victoria W12 £37 Ⓐ★

217 Uxbridge Rd 8749 5886 6–1B

"A fabulous oasis in a desert!" – this "massive gin palace" looks "surprisingly stunning" for somewhere in the remote reaches of Shepherd's Bush, and also serves "excellent" food and "dazzling wine"; it even has a "knowledgeable sommelier" – "just how often do you find that in a pub?"
/ *Details:* www.princessvictoria.co.uk; 10.30 pm, Sun 9.30 pm; no Amex.

Princi W1 £20 Ⓐ★

135 Wardour St 7478 8888 2–2D

"Very flash" and "cool", but "chaotic", this large Soho snacketeria offers "magical" coffee, "fabulous" salads and "irresistible" pastries and pizza; shame about the sometimes "shoddy" service. / *Details:* www.princi.co.uk; midnight, Sun 10 pm; no booking.

The Providores W1 £61

109 Marylebone High St 7935 6175 1–1A

"You practically crawl over other diners" in this "crushed" space above the Tapa Room; even some fans of the "exciting" fusion cuisine say the "eye-watering" prices are unjustified, and to critics this is just an "awful" experience all-round, with "overcomplicated" food and "surly" service. / *Details:* www.theprovidores.co.uk; 10 pm.

Quadrato
Four Seasons Hotel E14 £74

Westferry Circus 7510 1857

A "fabulous Sunday brunch" remains the culinary highlight at this rather corporate dining hall, off the foyer of a grand Canary Wharf hotel; feedback otherwise is mixed.
/ *Details:* www.fourseasons.com; 10.30 pm.

Le Querce SE23 £35 Ⓐ★★

66-68 Brockley Rise 8690 3761

"It'll blow your socks off" – the "simple Sardinian cooking", that is – at this "exceptionally friendly" Brockley spot; culinary highlights include "always-delightful daily specials", "the best pizza", and ice creams "in an amazing array of unusual flavours". / **Value tip:** set Sun L £22 (FP). **Details:** www.lequercerestaurant.co.uk; 10 pm, Sun 9 pm; closed Mon & Tue L.

Quilon SW1 £55 ★★

41 Buckingham Gate 7821 1899 1–4B

"Exemplary" cuisine, "professional" service – what's not to like about this posh Indian near Buckingham Palace? unfortunately the answer is the "dull" decor, and "comatose" ambience.
/ *Details:* www.quilon.co.uk; 11 pm, Sun 10.30 pm; closed Sat L.

Quirinale SW1   **£57**   ⭐

North Ct, 1 Gt Peter St   7222 7080   1–4C

A "gem" in the Westminster mud – this "crisp" and "stylish"
basement Italian showcases "amazing home-made pasta" and
a wine list that's "beyond belief"; it makes "a great venue for
smaller business meetings". / **Value tip:** set weekday L £37
(FP). **Details:** www.quirinale.co.uk; 10.30 pm; closed Sat L & Sun.

Quo Vadis W1   **£58**

26-29 Dean St   7437 9585   3–2A

"Rejuvenated" by the Hart brothers, this Soho veteran
is undoubtedly "classy" and "elegant", but it "somehow lacks
fizz" – except as regards the rather "steep" pricing, the very
British virtue of "understatement" is too evident throughout.
/ **Details:** www.quovadissoho.co.uk; 10.30 pm, Sun 9.30 pm.

Racine SW3   **£51**   ⭐

239 Brompton Rd   7584 4477   4–2C

"Why go to France?", when you can zip along to this "little bit
of Paris", in Knightsbridge? – Henry Harris's "elegantly bustling"
bistro retains a huge fan club thanks to its "rustic" fare and its
"very professional" service. / **Value tip:** set always available £33
(FP). **Details:** 10.30 pm, Sun 10 pm.

Ragam W1   **£26**   ⭐⭐

57 Cleveland St   7636 9098   1–1B

"Don't be put off by the fact you're dining in a setting straight
out of a '70s sit-com" – it's the "amazing" Keralan food
("outstanding dosas") at "absurdly cheap" prices which justifies
the trip to this "dingy" dive, near the Telecom Tower; BYO.
/ **Details:** www.ragam.co.uk; 11 pm, Fri & Sat 11.30 pm, Sun 10.30 pm.

Randall & Aubin W1   **£42**   Ⓐ

16 Brewer St   7287 4447   2–2D

"Fun for people-watching!"; this "lovely and buzzy" gem –
an ex-butcher's shop in the sleazy heart of Soho – makes
a "handy" perch for "a glass of fizz and some great seafood".
/ **Details:** www.randallandaubin.co.uk; 11 pm, Sun 10 pm; closed Sun L;
no booking.

Rani N3   **£27**   ⭐

7 Long Ln   8349 4386

The "excellent-value" buffet – an "amazing selection of all kinds
of veggie Indian food" – still draws fans from all quarters
of London to this "slightly faded" Finchley veteran.
/ **Details:** www.raniuk.com; 10 pm; D only, ex Sun open L & D.

Rasa N16   **£27**   Ⓐ⭐⭐

55 Stoke Newington Church St   7249 0344

"A revelation in Indian food" – the "unassuming" Stoke
Newington crucible of this south Indian chain is even better than
its marvellous spin-offs, offering Keralan cooking which
"you have to taste to believe", and "attentive" service too.
/ **Details:** www.rasarestaurants.com; 10.45 pm, Fri & Sat 11.30 pm; closed
weekday L.

Rasa £36
5 Charlotte St, W1 7637 0222 1–1C
6 Dering St, W1 7629 1346 2–2B
Holiday Inn Hotel, 1 Kings Cross, WC1 7833 9787
56 Stoke Newington Church St, N16 7249 1340
715 High Rd, E11 8859 1700
"Vibrant, creative and unusual" Keralan dishes at "amazing
prices" make these "perennially superb" spin-offs from the N16
original very "hard to beat"; Dering Street and N16 offer meat
and veggie fare – in the "very pink" Charlotte Street branch the
focus is on "super-zippy" fish; in the new Leytonstone branch
it is Keralan Christian dishes, plus veggie fare, which are the
attractions. / **Details:** www.rasarestaurants.com; 10.45 pm; variable hours
especially on weekends.

Rasoi SW3 £88
10 Lincoln St 7225 1881 4–2D
"No one in India has ever eaten so well!", say fans of Vineet
Bhatia's "unique" and "exquisite" cuisine at this "opulent"
Chelsea townhouse; neither service nor ambience quite lives up,
though, and there are some critics for whom the food is "over-
rated", and prices "extortionate". / **Value tip:** set weekday L £41
(FP). **Details:** www.rasoirestaurant.co.uk; 10.30 pm; closed Sat L & Sun;
no trainers.

Rebato's SW8 £33
169 South Lambeth Rd 7735 6388
"For a great taste of Spain", it's hard to beat this "unchanging"
Lambeth tapas bar, with its "wonderfully warm" and comforting
atmosphere, and its "brilliant-value" dishes; the appeal of the
marvellously cheesy rear dining room is "more questionable".
/ **Details:** www.rebatos.com; 10.45 pm; closed Sat L & Sun.

Red Fort W1 £62
77 Dean St 7437 2525 3–2A
Revamped after a fire, this Soho veteran remains
an "old favourite" for some reporters, who say its Indian cooking
is "consistently brilliant"; it's really "not cheap", though, and can
be let down by "dour" service and an atmosphere that has,
um, still not caught fire. / **Value tip:** set pre-theatre £38
(FP). **Details:** www.redfort.co.uk; 11.30 pm; closed Sat L & Sun L.

(Restaurant, Level 7)
Tate Modern SE1 £43
Bankside 7887 8888
You undoubtedly get "one of the finest views in London" from
this famous gallery's elevated café; some reporters vaunt its
attractions all round, but others complain of "half-hearted"
service and "really ordinary" food. / **Details:** www.tate.org.uk; 9.30 pm;
Sun-Thu closed D, Fri & Sat open L & D.

Rhodes W1 Restaurant
Cumberland Hotel W1 £75

Gt Cumberland Pl 7616 5930 1–2A
*Gary R's luxurious (and slightly wacky) fine dining room near
Marble Arch has never set the world on fire, and inspires few
comments; reporters have little to relay that's bad – indeed,
the service is "especially good" – but often find the whole
experience "overpriced".* / **Value tip:** *set weekday L £38
(FP).* **Details:** *www.rhodesw1.com; 10.15 pm; closed Mon, Sat L & Sun;
no trainers.*

Rib Room
Jumeirah Carlton Tower Hotel SW1 £105

2 Cadogan Pl 7858 7250 4–1D
*The steaks (and roast beef) are some of "the best in town",
say fans of this grand (if perhaps rather "tired") dining room,
and service is "superb" too; prices are such, however, that its
clientele is dominated "by expense-accounters and
Knightsbridge rich kids".* / **Value tip:** *set always available £63
(FP).* **Details:** *www.jumeirah.com; 10.45 pm, Sun 10.15 pm.*

RIBA Café
Royal Ass'n of Brit' Architects W1 £46 Ⓐ

66 Portland Pl 7631 0467 1–1B
*"Stylish... architecturally and the diners!", the café at this fine
'30s HQ is something of a "well kept secret" for the
cognoscenti; it is mainly of note for its "lovely dimensions and
airiness", and its super summer terrace – the simple fare
is "secondary".* / **Details:** *www.riba-venues.com; L only, closed Sat & Sun.*

Rick's Café SW17 £34 Ⓐ⭐

122 Mitcham Rd 8767 5219
*"Rick really cares about his food and wine", at this Tooting
open-kitchen favourite – a "great local bistro".* / **Details:** *11 pm,
Sun 4 pm; closed Mon & Sun D; no Amex.*

El Rincón Latino SW4 £29 Ⓐ

148 Clapham Manor St 7622 0599
*"You're made to feel at home", at this "lovely" and "lively"
family-run Clapham bar, which serves "great" tapas at "cheap"
prices; "breakfasts are particularly wonderful".*
/ **Details:** *www.rinconlatino.co.uk; 11.30 pm; closed Mon, Tue-Fri L & Sun D.*

Rising Sun NW7 £29 ⭐

137 Marsh Ln, Highwood Hill 8959 1357
*"Packed and chaotic at times, but worth it" – this "family-run
pub" in Mill Hill serves "interesting" and "tasty" Mediterranean
cuisine.* / **Details:** *9.30 pm, Sun 8.30 pm; closed Mon.*

Ristorante Semplice W1 £61 ⭐

9-10 Blenheim St 7495 1509 2–2B
*"A haven just off Oxford Street" – with its "excellent" dishes,
"attentive" service and "sophisticated" style, this "lovely
modern Italian" has carved out a big reputation; for some
tastes, though, it can seem a little "claustrophobic".*
/ **Details:** *www.ristorantesemplice.com; 10.30 pm; closed Sat L & Sun; booking:
max 12.*

The Ritz Restaurant
The Ritz W1 £113
150 Piccadilly   7493 8181   2–4C
"One of the world's most beautiful dining chambers" – this Louis
XVI-style room, overlooking Green Park, has long traded on its
"fabulously opulent" and "romantic" decor; it's "outrageously
expensive", naturally, but both the service ("superb") and food
("passable") have perceptibly improved in recent times.
/ Details: www.theritzlondon.com; 10 pm; jacket & tie required.

Riva SW13 £55
169 Church Rd   8748 0434
Devotees of Andreas Riva's long-running Barnes Venetian adore
its "diligent" staff, and extol his "constantly innovative" cuisine;
even supporters may note the place "lacks any sense of fun",
though, and newbies can simply find it "dull" and "over-hyped".
/ Details: 10.30 pm, Sun 9.30 pm; closed Sat L.

The River Café W6 £78
Thames Wharf, Rainville Rd   7386 4200   6–2C
This "incredible" Hammersmith modern Italian – famous
worldwide for its cookbooks – offers "simple" but "phenomenal"
dishes that are amongst "the best in London"; as ever though,
even fans say its prices are just "silly"; (RIP co-founder Rose
Gray, 1939-2010). / Details: www.rivercafe.co.uk; 9 pm, Sat 9.15 pm;
closed Sun D.

Roast
The Floral Hall SE1 £63
Stoney St   034 7300

"Perched above Borough Market",
this "gorgeous"-looking British dining
room has "so much potential",
and some reporters do indeed find
it a "great all-rounder";
more striking, though – "fantastic"
breakfasts excepted – is the number
who say it "always disappoints".
/ Details: www.roast-restaurant.com;
10.15 pm, Sun 6 pm.

Rock & Sole Plaice WC2 £26
47 Endell St   7836 3785   3–1C
"Right in the heart of Covent Garden" a "wonderful old-
fashioned fish 'n' chip shop"; the fare is always "fresh", and it
tastes even better "on a summer evening", when you can sit
outside. / Details: 11 pm; no Amex.

Rock & Rose TW9 £43
106-108 Kew Rd   8948 8008
"Crazy" and "glamorous" decor ("Venetian bordello-meets-
French bistro") certainly distinguishes this Richmond spot as a
party or romantic destination; when it comes to the cuisine,
though, critics diagnose "style without substance".
/ Details: www.rockandroserestaurant.co.uk; 10 pm.

Roka **£70** Ⓐ✪✪

37 Charlotte St, W1   7580 6464   1–1C
Unit 4, Park Pavilion, 40 Canada Sq, E14   7636 5228
It may have "less attitude than its sibling Zuma", but this "very cool" Fitzrovia Japanese serves equally "amazing fusion fare", not least from the "fantastic" robata grill (and it has a "very sexy" basement bar too); the new E14 spin-off, almost as highly rated, is "a very welcome addition to Canary Wharf". / **Details:** www.rokarestaurant.com; 11.15 pm; booking: max 8.

Rosa's **£26** ✪

48 Dean St, W1   7494 1638   3–2A
12 Hanbury St, E1   7247 1093   1–2C
"Lip-smacking food at sensible prices" and "genuine" service win praise for this small and "buzzy" Thai café, near Brick Lane; its new Soho sibling is similarly highly rated.
/ **Details:** www.rosaslondon.com; 10.30 pm, Fri & Sat 11 pm; some booking restrictions apply.

Roussillon SW1 **£80** ✪

16 St Barnabas St   7730 5550   4–2D
This low-key but renowned Pimlico outfit recently suffered a major staff defection (to Gauthier Soho); despite the odd 'miss', our visit in the early days of the new régime suggested it will stay on London's foodie map, and the capital's grandest veggie menu is still a feature. / **Value tip:** set weekday L £39 (FP). **Details:** www.roussillon.co.uk; 11 pm; closed Sat L & Sun; no trainers.

**Roux At Parliament Square
RICS SW1** **£77** ✪

12 Great George St   7334 3737   1–3C
Just off Parliament Square, the newest Roux family outlet occupies elegant period chambers, which are not especially improved by their contemporary decor; the food, though, respects the family's Gallic classicism, and – on our early-days visit – rarely failed to impress. / **Value tip:** set weekday L £48 (FP). **Details:** www.rouxatparliamentsquare.co.uk; 10 pm.

Royal China Club W1 **£61** ✪

40-42 Baker St   7486 3898   1–1A
The upmarket manifestation of the Royal China brand is more "quiet" and "genteel" than its cousins; the food is "pricey", but fans say "worth every penny" (not least the "fabulous dim sum"). / **Details:** www.royalchinagroup.co.uk; 11 pm, Fri & Sat 11.30 pm, Sun 10.30 pm.

**The Royal Exchange Grand Café
The Royal Exchange EC3** **£48** Ⓐ

Bank   7618 2480
The "majestic atrium" of the Royal Exchange makes "a fun place for a quick and lively City lunch"; the food's a bit incidental, though, at this D&D-group operation – "great for those who eat architecture…" / **Value tip:** set always available £27 (FP). **Details:** www.danddlondon.com; 10 pm; closed Sat & Sun; no booking at L & D.

Royal Oak E2 £38 A ★
73 Columbia Rd   7729 2220   I–IC
"Be the envy of the crushed hoards at Columbia Road Flower
Market, and book for Sunday lunch!" – this "gold-standard"
East End boozer offers food that's "more than decent", and on
quite a scale too. / **Details:** www.royaloaklondon.com; 10 pm; closed Mon,
Tue-Fri closed L , Sat open L & D, closed Sun D.

Rules WC2 £65 A
35 Maiden Ln   7836 5314   3–3D
The "magnificent" Edwardian decor of London's
oldest restaurant (1798) is "unlikely to disappoint American
visitors", but this Covent Garden veteran still manages,
remarkably, not to be a tourist trap; "superb" game is a
highlight of the "hearty" English fare. / **Details:** www.rules.co.uk;
11.30 pm, Sun 10.30 pm; no shorts; booking: max 6.

Sabor N1 £39 A
108 Essex Rd   7226 5551
"Reliably tasty Latin American dishes" (and "nice cocktails" too)
win fans for this "fun" and "friendly" Islington spot.
/ **Details:** www.sabor.co.uk; 10.45 pm, Sat & Sun 11 pm; closed Mon,
Tue-Fri D only, Sat & Sun open L & D; no Amex.

Saf £42
Whole Foods, 63-97 High St Ken', W8   7368 4555   4–1A
152-154 Curtain Rd, EC2   7613 0007   I–IB
"What they can do without animal products is amazing" –
this Shoreditch two-year-old serves vegan "raw food" that carries
off the rare double act of being both "healthy" and "interesting";
a new in-store branch recently opened in Kensington.
/ **Details:** www.safrestaurant.co.uk; EC2 11 pm; W8 9 pm.

Saigon Saigon W6 £40 ★
313-317 King St   8748 6887   6–2B
A "garish" facade hides this great Hammersmith "all-rounder",
which dishes up "excellent" Vietnamese fare in quite a "refined"
setting; "prices are very reasonable too".
/ **Details:** www.saigon-saigon.co.uk; 11 pm, Sun & Mon 10 pm, Fri & Sat
11.30 pm; no Amex.

St John EC1 £60 ★
26 St John St   7251 0848

"Ground-breaking" British cooking – "offal and other simple
dishes, flawlessly executed" – regularly wins Fergus Henderson's
"post-industrial" Smithfield ex-smokehouse a slot in 'The World's
Top 50 Restaurants'; there's a hint in reports, however, that its
"confident buzz" risks turning to arrogance.
/ **Details:** www.stjohnrestaurant.com; 11 pm; closed Sat L & Sun D.

St John Bread & Wine E1　　　　**£43**　　　⊛⊛
94-96 Commercial St　7251 0848　1–2C
The setting is "Spartan", but for "powerful, hearty and simple"
seasonal British food that'll "knock your socks off",
this Shoreditch canteen even outscored its legendary Smithfield
parent this year; for breakfast, they do "the best bacon sarnie
in town". / Details: www.stjohnbreadandwine.com; 10.30 pm.

St John Hotel WC2
1 Leicester St　7734 0224　3–3A
On a site just north of Leicester Square, long famous as Manzi's
(RIP), this latest venture from Trevor Gulliver and Fergus
Henderson – the team behind the famous Smithfield legend –
aims to bring their uncompromising brand of 'nose-to-tail' eating
to the heart of the West End; opening October 2010. /

St Pancras Grand
St Pancras Int'l Station NW1　　**£50**
The Concourse　7870 9900
It's a truly "gorgeous" space, but the Eurostar terminal's grand
brasserie is something of a missed opportunity – the food "is not
up to the standard of the decor", and the front-of-house "needs
to be much stronger". / Details: www.stpancrasgrand.com; 10.30 pm.

Sale e Pepe SW1　　　　　**£50**　　　Ⓐ⊛
9-15 Pavilion Rd　7235 0098　4–1D
"Still going strong after all these years", a "cramped",
"boisterous" and "chaotic" '60s trattoria, hidden-away near
Harrods; the "very accommodating" staff "are nearly as noisy
as the customers!" / Details: www.saleepepe.co.uk; 11.30 pm; closed Sun;
no shorts.

Salt Yard W1　　　　　**£37**　　　⊛
54 Goodge St　7637 0657　1–1B
"Such a tempting array" of "amazing tapas-style dishes"
("creative fusions of Italian and Spanish flavours") has made
a smash hit of this "down-to-earth" hang-out, "hidden-away"
in Fitzrovia; if you can, go upstairs. / Details: www.saltyard.co.uk;
11 pm; closed Sat L & Sun.

San Lorenzo SW3　　　　**£62**
22 Beauchamp Pl　7584 1074　4–1C
This Knightsbridge trattoria – a byword for fashionability from
the '60s to the '80s – excited very few reports this year; it's as
"overpriced" as ever, but can nowadays appear rather
"rudderless". / Details: 11.30 pm; closed Sun.

Sands End SW6　　　　　**£42**　　　Ⓐ⊛
135 Stephendale Rd　7731 7823
Brave the "dodgy location off Wandsworth Bridge Road"
(and the "Prince Harry-style clientele"), and this "very friendly"
gastropub will reward you with some "delicious" food.
/ Details: www.thesandsend.co.uk; 10 pm, Sun 9 pm.

Santa Maria W5 £20 Ⓐ⭐
15 St Mary's Rd   8579 1462
"A great new find for pizza!"… and in Ealing!; this "vibrant" little new Neapolitan gaff wins dazzling reviews from far and wide for its "simple menu done brilliantly well".
/ **Details:** www.santamariapizzeria.com; 10.30 pm.

Santa Maria del Sur SW8 £42 Ⓐ⭐
129 Queenstown Rd   7622 2088
Has this "thriving" Argentinean 'parilla' in Battersea become "too popular" on the back of its Ramsay TV fame? – the occasional reporter feels celebrity has "gone to its head", but most remain dazzled by its "brilliant" steaks.
/ **Details:** www.santamariadelsur.co.uk; 11.30 pm; closed weekday L; no Amex.

Santini SW1 £69
29 Ebury St   7730 4094   1–4B
As usual, we had little – and mixed – commentary on this datedly-glamorous Belgravia Italian; fans praise its "accurate" service and "good" food ("even if it should be at the price!") – for critics, it just goes "from bad to awful".
/ **Details:** www.santini-restaurant.com; 11 pm, Sun 10 pm; closed Sat L & Sun L.

Sarastro WC2 £41 Ⓐ❌
126 Drury Ln   7836 0101   1–2D
"The decor is something else, and the entertainment is non-stop", at this "camp" Baroque-operatic venue in Covent Garden; the food, though? – yikes, it's "dreadful".
/ **Details:** www.sarastro-restaurant.com; 11.30 pm, Sun 10.30 pm.

Sargasso N21 £47 Ⓐ⭐
10 Station Rd   8360 0990
In Winchmore Hill, a "consistently well-run" spot with fans from far and wide; not everyone's happy with its change from being a pure fish restaurant, but the cooking's still generally "top-notch". / **Details:** www.sargassorestaurant.co.uk; 10.30 pm; closed Mon, Tue-Thu closed L, Fri open L & D, closed Sat L & Sun D; booking: max 9, Sat D.

Satsuma W1 £34 ⭐
56 Wardour St   7437 8338   2–2D
A "Wagamama-style restaurant" – but "with better food" – on the main crossroads of Soho; fans say "you can't beat it" for "fresh and tasty" sushi or noodles. / **Details:** www.osatsuma.com; 11 pm, Wed & Thu 11.30 pm, Fri & Sat midnight; no booking.

(Savoy Grill)
The Savoy Hotel WC2
Strand   7592 1600   3–3D
The long-awaited re-opening of the Savoy on 10-10-2010 will see the return of what was traditionally London's pre-eminent power dining room; the Ramsay group remains in charge, with the intention, it seems, of taking the establishment back over a century to the style of Escoffier.
/ **Details:** www.gordonramsay.com/thesavoygrill/; 11 pm; jacket required.

Scott's W1   £68   Ⓐ ⭐
20 Mount St   7495 7309   2–3A
"For once, the hype is justified!"; this A-list magnet in Mayfair may be London's "top celeb'-watching" haunt, but mortals love it too – "faultless" dishes of "sophisticatedly simple" fish and seafood are served in a "gorgeous" room, which exudes an "effortlessly grown-up buzz". / **Details:** www.scotts-restaurant.com; 10.30 pm, Sun 10 pm; booking: max 6.

Sedap EC1   £24   ⭐
102 Old St   7490 0200   1–1A
It may look "low-key", but this "homely", year-old café, in Shoreditch, has been an instant hit with its "spot-on" Nyonya (Chinese-Malaysian) dishes at "amazingly reasonable prices". / **Details:** www.sedap.co.uk; 10.30 pm; closed Sat L & Sun L; no Amex.

Seven Stars WC2   £32   Ⓐ
53 Carey St   7242 8521   1–2D
Behind the Royal Courts of Justice, a "wonderful and original" little pub – "packed with lawyers in the week, empty at weekends" – that serves "good home cooking". / **Details:** 11 pm, Sun 10.30 pm.

Shaka Zulu NW1
Stables Mkt   3376 9911
This vast new South African venue in Camden Town opened too late for survey feedback; it would seem all the more remarkable in its ambition and scale (it cost £5.5m!) were it not for the fact that it's just next to the similarly huge and lavish Gilgamesh… / **Details:** www.shaka-zulu.com; 2 am; D only.

Shampers W1   £40   Ⓐ
4 Kingly St   7437 1692   2–2D
"A '70s throwback" in a good way – fans "LOVE" this "stupendously popular" Soho wine bar, where Simon, the "knowledgeable owner", oversees the "cracking" wine list, "honest" food and "buzzing" vibe (to the point it can be "crazy"). / **Details:** www.shampers.net; 10.45 pm; closed Sun.

J Sheekey WC2   £64   Ⓐ ⭐⭐
28-32 St Martin's Ct   7240 2565   3–3B
"Pretty damn perfect", this Theatreland "classic" – yet again the survey's most-mentioned spot, and also top for fish – offers "simple" but "spectacular" seafood, and "swift" but "smooth" service, in a series of "snug" and "elegant" parlours (which can, admittedly, be a little "squashed"). / **Details:** www.j-sheekey.co.uk; midnight, Sun 11 pm; booking: max 6.

J Sheekey Oyster Bar WC2   £45   Ⓐ ⭐
St Martin's Ct   7240 2565   3–3B
"A pearl"; if you're looking for "a slice of the high life", at "very reasonable cost", seek out this "beautiful" (intimate and Deco-ish) annex to Theatreland's "old-school" fish favourite, where "divine" oysters head up a sophisticated light-bites menu. / **Details:** www.j-sheekey.co.uk; midnight, Sun 11 pm; booking: max 3.

Simpson's Tavern EC3 £34
38 1/2 Ball Ct, Cornhill   7626 9985
Being "wedged-in cheek-by-jowl" is all part of the timeless appeal of this ancient (1757) City chophouse; it's quite a "cheap" experience too, and the "solid English stodge" can be "unexpectedly good". / **Details:** *www.simpsonstavern.co.uk; L only, closed Sat & Sun.*

Simpsons-in-the-Strand WC2 £66
100 Strand   7836 9112   3–3D
This "quintessentially British" (but "touristy") temple to Roast Beef is a "substandard" operation nowadays – only the "show-stopper" of a cooked breakfast can really be recommended; the proprietors are the same as of the neighbouring Savoy – perhaps they could now turn their attention here? / **Details:** *www.simpsonsinthestrand.co.uk; 10.45 pm, Sun 9 pm; no trainers.*

Singapore Garden NW6 £41
83a Fairfax Rd   7624 8233
"A wonderful mix of Chinese and Singapore/Malay cuisines" comes "served with a smile" at this Swiss Cottage Veteran, where the decor is "quite high-end". / **Details:** *www.singaporegarden.co.uk; 11 pm, Fri & Sat 11.30 pm.*

(Lecture Room)
Sketch W1 £115
9 Conduit St   7659 4500   2–2C
It may be "poncy" and "pretentious", but this Mayfair dining room undoubtedly provides a very "enjoyable" experience... if you can forgive prices that are "just bonkers"; "great loos though!" / **Value tip:** *set always available £58 (FP).* **Details:** *www.sketch.uk.com; 10.30 pm; closed Mon, Sat L & Sun; jacket; booking: max 8.*

(Gallery)
Sketch W1 £62
9 Conduit St   7659 4500   2–2C
Got up "like a Lady Gaga video", this "style-over-substance" Mayfair brasserie can be "fun" ("if you can ignore the WAGs", that is); the food, though, is "pretentious rubbish", and comes at prices which "add insult to injury". / **Details:** *www.sketch.uk.com; 11 pm; D only, closed Sun; booking: max 12.*

Skipjacks HA3 £31
268-270 Streatfield Rd   8204 7554
A Harrow institution that's "just what a chippy should be", offering "top-quality fish, cooked to perfection" – "fried, steamed or grilled", it's all "excellent". / **Details:** *10.30 pm; closed Sun; no Amex or Maestro.*

Skylon
South Bank Centre SE1 **£59** Ⓐ

Southbank Centre, Belvedere Rd   7654 7800   1–3D
*"Truly magnificent" views and a "superb" (if rather
"cavernous"), "retro-chic" setting maintain the crush at this huge
D&D-group South Bank operation; in the light of the "hit-and-
miss" service and sometimes "woeful" food, though, a visit
just for a drink (or, if you must, a light brasserie meal)
is probably the best bet. / Value tip: set weekday L £40
(FP). Details: www.skylonrestaurant.co.uk; 10.45 pm, Sun 10.30 pm; no trainers.*

(Dining Room)
Smiths of Smithfield EC1 **£37**

67-77 Charterhouse St   7251 7950
*This "bustling and energetic" (read very noisy) second-floor
brasserie is still known as a "reliable" business venue; in recent
times, however, it has suffered from "pedestrian" food and "lax"
service. / Details: www.smithsofsmithfield.co.uk; 10.45 pm; closed Sat L & Sun;
booking: max 12.*

Sotheby's Café W1 **£46** Ⓐ⭐

34 New Bond St   7293 5077   2–2C
*"For serious people-watching", the café "delightfully tucked-
away" off the foyer of the famous Mayfair auction house
is "a real gem"; it's "reasonably priced" too, given its "faultless"
service and its range of "simple" but "classy" dishes.
/ Details: www.sothebys.com; L only, closed Sat & Sun; booking: max 6.*

Spianata & Co **£10** ⭐

41 Brushfield St, E1   7655 4411   1–2B
20 Holborn Viaduct, EC1   7236 3666
17 Blomfield St, EC2   awaiting tel
29-30 Leadenhall Mkt, EC3   7929 1339
73 Watling St, EC4   7236 3666
*"Lovely", "original" sarnies (using Roman-style spianata bread)
make a lunchtime treat at this "unfailingly cheerful" Italian
chain. / Details: www.spianata.com; 3.30 pm; EC3 11 pm; closed Sat & Sun;
E1 closed Sat; no credit cards; no booking.*

The Square W1 **£98** ⭐⭐

6-10 Bruton St   7495 7100   2–2C
*It's 20 this year, but Phil Howard's Mayfair dining room
"gets better all the time", and his "opulent" cuisine is on
"superlative" form as the anniversary approaches (and matched
by a "staggering" wine list too); as ever, non-suits can find the
setting a little "subdued". / Value tip: set weekday L £53
(FP). Details: www.squarerestaurant.com; 9.45 pm, Sat 10.15 pm, Sun 9.30 pm;
closed Sat L & Sun L; booking: max 8.*

Sufi W12 **£22** ⭐

70 Askew Rd   8834 4888   6–1B
*"One of the nicest Persian restaurants in west London" –
this homely venture in Shepherd's Bush has "very sweet" service,
and "fabulous" grills, plus "bread that's made in front of you"
at the oven by the window. / Details: www.sufirestaurant.com; 11 pm.*

Sukho Thai Cuisine SW6 £46 ⭐⭐

855 Fulham Rd   7371 7600

"Exemplary", "fresh-tasting" Thai fare and "charming" service again inspire reams of rave reviews for this "cramped" café in deepest Fulham – "reservations are essential". / **Value tip:** set weekday L £28 (FP). **Details:** www.sukhogroup.co.uk; 11 pm.

The Summerhouse W9 £40 Ⓐ

60 Blomfield Rd   7286 6752

This "New England-style" newcomer in Maida Vale – on the "delightful canalside site" once known as Jason's (long RIP) – is open only in summer; thanks to its "smart beach-side vibe", it's won instant popularity, but – sadly – "they don't actually seem to have thought much about the 'restaurant' side of the business!" / **Details:** www.summerhousebythewaterway.co.uk; Sat 10.30 pm, Sun 10 pm; Mon-Fri closed D, Sat & Sun open L & D; no Amex.

Sumosan W1 £75

26b Albemarle St   7495 5999   2–3C

"A less tarty version of Nobu!" – this lesser-known and rather "quiet" Mayfair spot is hailed by fans for Japanese fusion fare "to die for"; this year, however, its food rating slipped behind its in-crowd rival, and you can still expect a "big bill". / **Details:** www.sumosan.com; 11.30 pm; closed Sun L.

Sushi-Hiro W5 £40 ⭐⭐

1 Station Pde   8896 3175

"Probably the best sushi I'll have till I go to Japan!"; this "incredibly basic" outfit, near Ealing Common tube, has no atmosphere, but the sushi is some of "the best in the UK". / **Details:** 9 pm; closed Mon; no credit cards.

Sushi-Say NW2 £40 ⭐⭐

33b Walm Ln   8459 7512

"A world-class local!"... in Willesden Green; this "amazingly-friendly" family-run Japanese, near the tube, serves "the best sushi and sashimi outside of Tokyo" (well, nearly) and other "exquisite" dishes "at much lower prices than in the West End". / **Details:** 10 pm, Sat 10.30 pm, Sun 9.30; closed Mon, Tue-Fri D only, Sat & Sun open L & D; no Amex.

The Table SE1 £34 Ⓐ⭐

83 Southwark St   7401 2760

A South Bank "gem"; brunch at this "relaxing" café offers perhaps the best answer to the "pre-Tate Modern nightmare", and it also makes "a great place for a quick lunch" at any time. / **Details:** www.thetablecafe.com; 11 pm; Sat-Wed, closed D.

Taiwan Village SW6 £28 ⭐⭐

85 Lillie Rd   7381 2900   4–3A

An "excellent variety" of Chinese dishes at "amazing-value" prices again wins the highest praise for this "oddly-located" but "very friendly" spot, off the North End Road. / **Details:** www.taiwanvillage.com; 11.30 pm; closed weekday L; booking: max 20.

Tamarind W1 ★ £68

20 Queen St 7629 3561 2–3B

"Superb" Indian cuisine wins continued acclaim for this "civilised" Mayfair basement; while the decor strikes most reporters as "seductive", though, it can also seem a touch "drab". / **Details:** www.tamarindrestaurant.com; 11 pm, Sun 10.15 pm; closed Sat L.

Taqueria W11 £31

139-143 Westbourne Grove 7229 4734 5–1B

"Amazing tacos" – "the real thing, not pastiche-Mexican" – and other "street-style" dishes win fans for this "casual" Notting Hill cantina; "bland" results can take the edge off the experience, but "good margaritas" offer considerable consolation. / **Details:** www.coolchiletaqueria.co.uk; Mon-Thu 11 pm, Fri & Sat 11.30 pm, Sun 10.30 pm; no booking, Sat & Sun.

Tartufo Trattoria WC1 ★ £29

54 Red Lion St 7430 2880 1–1D

"A perfect place for a quick and reasonably-priced meal" – this "friendly" husband-and-wife-owned spot, in Bloomsbury, wins praise for its "really good, fresh and genuine" Italian dishes. / **Details:** 10 pm; closed Sat & Sun.

A Taste of McClements TW9 ★ £60

8 Station Approach 8940 6617

John McClements's foodie flagship, near Kew Gardens tube has won a small but dedicated fan club, who particularly laud its "beautiful tasting menu"; the "hard-surfaced" dining room (just 20 seats), however, can seem rather "dull". / **Details:** www.tasteofmcclements.com; 9.30 pm; closed Mon & Sun; no Amex.

(Rex Whistler) Tate Britain SW1 Ⓐ £48

Millbank 7887 8825 1–4C

Whistler's "thrilling" murals add much to the "charming" ambience of this Westminster dining room, which is also renowned for offering "daring" wine at "very fair" prices; fans say this guide "grossly under-rates" its "straightforward" British fare – the survey consensus, however, rates it no higher than "decent". / **Value tip:** set weekday L £30 (FP). **Details:** www.tate.org.uk; L & afternoon tea only.

Tendido Cero SW5 Ⓐ★ £37

174 Old Brompton Rd 7370 3685 4–2B

A "smart" and "very buzzy" South Kensington bar (opposite its parent, Cambio de Tercio) which offers some of "the best upmarket tapas in London" – only the "cramped" accommodation and "two-sittings booking policy" give any cause for complaint. / **Details:** www.cambiodetercio.co.uk; 11 pm.

Tendido Cuatro SW6   **£39**   ⭐

108-110 New King's Rd   7371 5147

"Superb tapas at the 'wrong' end of the King's Road" — that's the deal at this "buzzy" Parson's Green sibling to South Kensington's Cambio de Tercio. / *Details: www.cambiodetercio.co.uk; 11 pm.*

Tentazioni SE1   **£48**   ⭐

2 Mill St   7394 5248

"An Italian with finesse"; this tucked-away and "intimate" Bermondsey "gem" offers some "unusual", hearty dishes and a "warm" sense of "real customer care"; look out for deals (including the set lunch). / **Value tip:** set weekday L £24 (FP). *Details: www.tentazioni.co.uk; 10.45 pm; closed Sat L & Sun.*

The Terrace in the Fields WC2   **£41**   Ⓐ

Lincoln's Inn Fields   7430 1234   1–2D

"It feels like you're outside the city", at this modern 'shed', in the middle of Lincoln's Inn Fields, that's particularly "lovely outside in summer"; it serves "thoroughly enjoyable" cuisine with a slight Caribbean twist. / *Details: www.theterrace.info; 9 pm; L only, closed Sat & Sun.*

Terroirs WC2   **£41**   ⭐

5 William IV St   7036 0660   3–4C

"Who would guess that a wine bar near Trafalgar Square would be so good?"; well, however unlikely, this "so Gallic" two-year-old has become a smash hit thanks to to its "meaty" cuisine and its "adventurous" wines... with the "patchy" service and "crowded" setting just adding to the authenticity.
/ *Details: www.terroirswinebar.com; 11 pm; closed Sun.*

Texture W1   **£77**   ⭐

34 Portman St   7224 0028   1–2A

For a "delicious, contemporary dining experience", this Marylebone two-year-old is hard to beat, and it offers an "interesting" ("non-obvious") wine selection to match its "creative" fare; the decor can seem "weirdly bland", but the place's rising popularity makes this less of an issue than it was.
/ **Value tip:** set weekday L £43 (FP). *Details: www.texture-restaurant.co.uk; 11 pm; closed Mon & Sun.*

Theo Randall
InterContinental Hotel W1 **£75** ⭐
1 Hamilton Pl 7318 8747 2–4A
Few reporters doubt the "brilliant" quality of ex-River Café head chef Theo Randall's "wonderful, simple Italian food"; the "soulless" decor of the Mayfair dining room in which it is served, however, could hardly be more at odds with his rustic and generous cuisine. / **Value tip:** set always available £49 (FP). **Details:** www.theorandall.com; 11.15 pm; closed Sat L & Sun.

The Thomas Cubitt SW1 **£54** Ⓐ
44 Elizabeth St 7730 6060 1–4A
"Beloved of young Belgravians", this "superior" gastropub all-rounder "continues to thrive"; "it's perfect in summer when they open up the interior to the street" – for greater comfort and space, however, head for the dining room upstairs. / **Details:** www.thethomascubitt.co.uk; 10 pm; closed Sat L & Sun D; booking only in restaurant.

Tinello SW1
87 Pimlico Rd 7730 3663 4–2D
Set to open in late-2010 on the former Pimlico site of L'Incontro (RIP), this new Italian will be run by protégés of Giorgio Locatelli – given the standard of his main restaurant over the years, it should be 'one to watch'. / **Details:** www.tinello.co.uk; 10.30 pm; closed Sun.

Toff's N10 **£32** ⭐
38 Muswell Hill Broadway 8883 8656
"One of the best chippies in London" – this "always-packed" Muswell Hill veteran is highly prized for its "very fresh" fish in "superb" batter. / **Value tip:** set always available £21 (FP). **Details:** www.toffsfish.co.uk; 10 pm; closed Sun.

Tom Aikens SW3 **£114**
43 Elystan St 7584 2003 4–2C
"Phenomenal" dishes are often served up with "panache" at Tom Aikens's "cold" Chelsea HQ; the place also manages to inspire an awful lot of criticisms, though – of "silly" (over-elaborate) creations, of "charmless" service, and of "astronomical" mark-ups. / **Details:** www.tomaikens.co.uk; 11 pm; closed Sat L & Sun; jacket and/or tie; booking: max 8.

Tom's Kitchen SW3 **£59**
27 Cale St 7349 0202 4–2C
Thanks not least to its "good, honest food", Tom Aikens's "Chelsea neighbourhood favourite" is "always jammed"; critics, though, find it "ridiculously expensive", especially bearing in mind "the cramped surroundings, reminiscent of a white-tiled sanatorium". / **Details:** www.tomskitchen.co.uk; 11 pm.

Toto's SW1 **£58** Ⓐ
Lennox Gardens Mews 7589 0075 4–2C
A "really romantic" interior and "lovely garden" underpin the enduring appeal of this "charming" Italian, near Knightsbridge; its "old-school" style can seem "dated" or "over-priced", but for most reporters it's a "high-quality" experience. / **Details:** 11 pm, Sun 10.30 pm.

Tower Tandoori SE1 £26 ✪
74-76 Tower Bridge Rd   7237 2247
It's "nothing swish", but this "unprepossessing" South Bank Indian is "seriously overlooked", say fans, who laud its notably "attentive" service, and cooking which "punches well above its weight". / **Details:** www.towertandoori.co.uk; midnight; no Amex.

Trinity SW4 £56 Ⓐ✪✪
4 The Polygon   7622 1199
"A shining Clapham beacon of gastronomy!"; Adam Byatt's "fantastic" neighbourhood venture just "keeps improving"; his "exciting" cuisine – full of "subtle luxury" – is just part of an experience that's nowadays simply "great all round".
/ **Details:** www.trinityrestaurant.co.uk; 10.30 pm; closed Mon L & Sun D.

Trishna W1 £48 ✪✪
15-17 Blandford St   7935 5624   1–1A
"Masterful" dishes – with "perfectly spiced" seafood, served tapas-style the speciality – make this "trendy" Marylebone yearling "a worthy little sister to the great Mumbai original".
/ **Details:** www.trishnalondon.com; 10.45 pm.

Les Trois Garçons E1 £66 Ⓐ
1 Club Row   7613 1924   1–1C
"Crazy" and "glamorous" decor (with "stuffed animals in tiaras") makes a "feast for the eyes" at this "indulgent" East End pub-conversion – "perfect for a romantic tête-à-tête"; the Gallic cuisine "doesn't match the ambience", of course, but it really isn't bad at all. / **Details:** www.lestroisgarcons.com; 10.15 pm; D only, closed Sun.

La Trompette W4 £57 Ⓐ✪✪
5-7 Devonshire Rd   8747 1836   6–2A
"The best in the West!"; this "elegant" Chez Bruce sibling in Chiswick delivers a "totally rewarding experience" that's almost without equal, providing "fine food without frippery", and "fabulous" wine; the only real downside? – "the tables are a little too close together". / **Value tip:** set weekday L £36 (FP). **Details:** www.latrompette.co.uk; 10.30 pm, Sun 10 pm.

Troubadour SW5 £33 Ⓐ
263-267 Old Brompton Rd   7370 1434   4–3A
"Quirky", "wonderfully eccentric", "unique" – this veteran Earl's Court café may have had its ups and downs over its long life ("my mum came here in the '60s"), but it's currently on quite a high; "really great weekend fry-ups" – ideally "in the garden, on a sunny morning" – are the highlight.
/ **Details:** www.troubadour.co.uk; 11 pm.

Tsunami £42 ✪✪
93 Charlotte St, W1   7637 0050   1–1C
5-7 Voltaire Rd, SW4   7978 1610
"As good as Nobu, if not better!" (and at a fraction of the cost), this "buzzing" Japanese-fusion outfit punches well "above-weight for its location" (which is by Clapham High Street BR); the Fitzrovia offshoot, useful enough, is less of a destination.
/ **Value tip:** set always available £21 (FP). **Details:** www.tsunamirestaurant.co.uk; SW4 10.30 pm, Fri & Sat 11 pm, Sun 9.30 pm; W1 11 pm; W1 Mon - Fri D only; W1 closed Sun; no Amex.

28-50 EC4 £41 ⭐

140 Fetter Ln 7242 8877
Just off Fleet Street, a hidden-away basement wine bar from the team behind Texture; it's an unpromising site, but we enjoyed our early-days visit – the chef betrays his Ramsay HQ heritage in the good-quality renditions of bistro classics, but the establishment's heart seems to be in its wines.
/ Details: www.2850.co.uk; 10.30 pm; no Amex.

Two Brothers N3 £31 ⭐

297-303 Regent's Park Rd 8346 0469
"Expert fish 'n' chips" wins enduring acclaim for this "packed" and "homely" north London chippy; it changed hands a couple of years back, and most (if not quite all) reporters feel "the quality stays the same". / Details: www.twobrothers.co.uk; 10.15 pm; closed Mon & Sun; no booking at D.

Uli W11 £35 ⭐⭐

16 All Saints Rd 7727 7511 5–1B
A "delightful" pan-oriental favourite near Portobello Market, where "charming service from Michael and his family" vies with the "excellent", "un-gloopy" food for top billing; it's "reasonably priced" too, and has a "good summer terrace".
/ Details: www.uli-oriental.co.uk; 11 pm; D only; no Amex.

Umu W1 £80 Ⓐ

14-16 Bruton Pl 7499 8881 2–2C
"The best Japanese food in London, maybe even Europe" makes Marlon Abela's "serene" Kyoto-style venture, in Mayfair, of considerable note; the prices are equally "exceptional", of course, so it's perhaps no great surprise that not everyone thinks it's worth 'the damage'. / Details: www.umurestaurant.com; 11 pm; closed Sat L & Sun; no trainers; booking: max 14.

Upstairs Bar SW2 £44 Ⓐ⭐

89b Acre Ln (door on Branksome Rd) 7733 8855
Brixton's "worst-kept secret" – despite its "speakeasy"-style entrance – makes a "great place to surprise a date"; it's a "lovely, little, cosy, classic French restaurant and bar", with yummy cocktails and "delicious" cooking.
/ Details: www.upstairslondon.com; Tue-Thu 9.30 pm, Fri-Sat 10.30 pm; D only, closed Mon & Sun.

Vanilla W1 £50 Ⓐ⭐

131 Great Titchfield St 3008 7763 2–1C
"Über-chic" decor draws a "beautiful" crowd to this "intriguing" Fitzrovia basement (where the "private booths and nooks" add a romantic air); cocktails are "excellent" too, though the "competent" fare is arguably "pricey" for what it is.
/ Details: www.vanillalondon.com; 10 pm; closed Mon, Sat L & Sun; no trainers; booking: max 6.

Vasco & Piero's Pavilion W1   **£51**   ⭐

15 Poland St   7437 8774   2–1D

A "buzzy" and "cramped" 'old Soho' favourite that's currently back on top form; with its "good-quality" Italian food and its "welcoming" service, it could show many of the whippersnappers a thing or two! / **Details:** www.vascosfood.com; 10.30 pm; closed Sat L & Sun.

Veeraswamy W1   **£54**   🅐⭐

Victory Hs, 99-101 Regent St   7734 1401   2–3D

Reinvented after a "chic" and "exotic" facelift a few years ago, this is London's oldest curry house, near Piccadilly Circus; "very sophisticated" cuisine and "discreet" service keep it in the first rank. / **Details:** www.realindianfood.com; 10.30 pm, Sun 10 pm; booking: max 12.

El Vergel SE1   **£28**   🅐⭐

132 Webber St   7410 2308

Though "more mainstream" in its "bigger-and-better new site", this "exemplary" Borough operation still inspires enthusiastic acclaim for its "genuine", "vibrant" Latino food at "incredibly cheap" prices. / **Details:** www.elvergel.co.uk; Mon-Fri closed D, Sat open L & D, closed Sun.

Vertigo 42
Tower 42 EC2   **£64**   🅐❌

25 Old Broad St   7877 7842

"To stare into your loved one's eyes" – or, more prosaically, to entertain a client – this "classy", 42nd-floor City eyrie may be just the place; given the "breathtaking views", though, it's no great surprise that the food is "poor" and "overpriced" (stick to nibbles and champagne). / **Details:** www.vertigo42.co.uk; 11 pm; closed Sat L & Sun L; no shorts; booking essential.

Viajante E2   **£90**   🅐⭐⭐

Patriot Sq   7871 0461

RESTAURANT RÉMY
WINNER 2011
RÉMY MARTIN FINE CHAMPAGNE COGNAC

"Sheer pleasure all the way"; Nuno Mendes's brave, "off-the-beaten track" opening in Bethnal Green – a "lively" room with open kitchen – marks a "stupendous" return for the Portuguese chef; his "thoughtfully composed" small plates, featuring "amazing food combinations" are a total "wow".
/ **Details:** www.viajante.co.uk; 10.45 pm; closed Sun.

Viet Grill E2 £31 Ⓐ⭐
58 Kingsland Rd 7739 6686 1–1B
"The best of the Shoreditch Vietnamese restaurants";
this "vibrant" spot offer "classic" dishes – "with some real
stand-outs" – and "good wine" too (chosen by Malcolm Gluck).
/ Details: www.vietnamesekitchen.co.uk; 11 pm, Fri & Sat 11.30 pm,
Sun 10.30 pm.

Vijay NW6 £27 ⭐⭐
49 Willesden Ln 7328 1087
"Ignore the nondescript decor"; this Kilburn veteran
is consistently an "exceptional" performer, with "utterly
charming" staff and "stunning" south Indian food, and all
at very "economical" prices. / Details: www.vijayrestaurant.co.uk;
10.45 pm, Fri & Sat 11.45 pm.

Vincent Rooms
Westminster Kingsway College SW1 £27
Vincent Sq 7802 8391 1–4C
Service can be "awkward" and the food "variable", as the
students "learn the ropes" at this Westminster catering college;
"with such low prices one can't complain", though – staff can
be "wonderfully enthusiastic", and the cooking, on a good day,
"daring and experimental". / Details: www.thevincentrooms.com; 9 pm;
times vary; only term times; closed Mon D, Wed D, Fri D, Sat & Sun; no Amex.

Vinoteca EC1 £39 Ⓐ
7 St John St 7253 8786
"When a glass of wine and a good vibe are the order of the
evening", this "laid-back" wine bar is the place – its "helpful"
staff advise on a "superb" list ("a mile long and full
of novelties"), which comes with food that's "good enough".
/ Details: www.vinoteca.co.uk; 10 pm; closed Sun; no Amex; no booking
D, max 8 L.

Vrisaki N22 £30
73 Myddleton Rd 8889 8760
Hidden "behind a kebab shop" in Bounds Green, this upbeat
Greek veteran has long been known for its "very big" mezze
at "great prices"; one or two reporters are starting to find
it "tired", but most still feel it's "fantastic". / Details: 11.30 pm,
Sun 9 pm.

The Wallace
The Wallace Collection W1 £50 Ⓐ
Hertford Hs, Manchester Sq 7563 9505 2–1A
"A great place to escape" – the "stunning" atrium of this
"gracious" restaurant in a Marylebone palazzo is incredibly
"light and airy" for somewhere two minutes from Oxford Street;
there is a catch! – service is too often "clueless", and the food's
"very expensive". / Details: www.thewallacerestaurant.com; Fri & Sat
9.15 pm; Sun-Thu closed D; no Amex.

The Walmer Castle W11 £36 Ⓐ⭐
58 Ledbury Rd 7229 4620 5–1B
"A lovely and cosy dining room", "hidden-away" above
a "buzzy" Notting Hill pub, and serving "delicious" Thai fare.
/ Details: www.walmercastle.co.uk; 10.45 pm; D only.

Wapping Food E1 £48 Ⓐ
Wapping Power Station, Wapping Wall   7680 2080
*The (post-)"industrial" setting of a former hydraulic power
station (now part art-space, part restaurant) makes a visit
to this Wapping spot a "beautiful and surreal" experience;
its "seasonal" fare is "satisfying" too, but it's the "extensive"
Oz wine list that steals the show. / **Details:** www.thewappingproject.com;
midnight; Mon-Fri D only, Sat open L & D, closed Sun D.*

The Wells NW3 £43 Ⓐ
30 Well Walk   7794 3785
*A "stylish" and "sociable" boozer that's "well geared up for
dogs, walkers and kids"; with its "enjoyable" grub, it makes
"an ideal complement to a trip to Hampstead Heath".
/ **Details:** www.thewellshampstead.co.uk; 10 pm, Sun 9.30 pm; no Amex.*

Whits W8 £46 ★
21 Abingdon Rd   7938 1122   4–1A
*"Caring" service and "honest" food help create "a really good
overall experience", at this "unpretentious" bistro, in a
Kensington side street. / **Value tip:** set pre-theatre £27
(FP). **Details:** www.whits.co.uk; 10.30 pm; closed Mon, Tue L, Sat L & Sun.*

Wild Honey W1 £59 Ⓐ★
12 St George St   7758 9160   2–2C
*Arbutus's Mayfair sibling is likewise a "superb all-rounder",
serving "top-class" British dishes at "realistic" prices,
plus "fantastic wines by the bottle, carafe or glass";
its "attractive wood-panelled" premises are, however, "a bit
awkward" – the booths (for four) offer the best seating. / **Value
tip:** set pre-theatre £37 (FP). **Details:** www.wildhoneyrestaurant.co.uk; 10.30 pm,
Sun 9.30 pm.*

William Curley Dessert Bar SW1 £15 ★
198 Ebury St   7730 5522   4–2D
*"Not just a taste of perfection, but a visual treat as well" –
this new 'patissier chocolatier' overlooking Pimlico's Orange
Square serves "extravagant, luscious and positively
overindulgent" treats – "as good taken out as eaten in".
/ **Details:** www.williamcurley.co.uk; 6.30 pm; no Amex.*

Wiltons SW1 £97 Ⓐ
55 Jermyn St   7629 9955   2–3C
*New chef Andrew Turner is known for his inventive cuisine,
but London's "most plutocratic restaurant" seems to have tamed
him, and it still delights the "civilised" ("stuffy") denizens
of St James's with just the same "excellent" oyster-fish-and-game
formula as ever; "you don't ask for a bill here", though, "you ask
for an estimate!" / **Details:** www.wiltons.co.uk; 10.30 pm; closed Sat & Sun;
jacket required.*

The Wine Library EC3 £28 Ⓐ
43 Trinity Sq   7481 0415
*"One of the best wine-drinking experiences in town" –
an "amazing" array of vintages sold "at retail price,
plus modest corkage" – fuels a "really good atmosphere"
in these ancient City vaults; the "basic buffet" is very much
"secondary". / **Details:** www.winelibrary.co.uk; 8 pm, Mon 6 pm; closed
Mon D, Sat & Sun.*

Wódka W8   £43   Ⓐ
12 St Alban's Grove   7937 6513   4–1B
"Spectacular house vodkas" help fuel the "fun" and "romantic"
vibe at this "unpretentious" stalwart, in a cute Kensington
backstreet; supporters insist that its Polish cuisine is realised
"with flair" too. / **Details:** www.wodka.co.uk; 11.15 pm, Sun 10.30 pm;
Sat-Tue closed L.

The Wolseley W1   £57   Ⓐ
160 Piccadilly   7499 6996   2–3C
"A gloriously civilised Continental grand café" of "rare glamour";
Corbin & King's "wonderfully buzzy" linchpin, by the Ritz, is a
top venue for business, "celeb-spotting", or just about any
occasion (not least an "unbeatable power breakfast");
its "brasserie-style" fare is "good enough".
/ **Details:** www.thewolseley.com; midnight, Sun 11 pm.

Wong Kei W1   £22
41-43 Wardour St   7437 8408   3–3A
A legendary Chinatown "cheap eat", offering "fast and furious"
service of "filling", "no-nonsense" chow; "it's famous for its rude
waiters", but – sadly – "they don't seem to be quite so rude
nowadays". / **Details:** 11.30 pm, Fri & Sat 11.45 pm, Sun 10.30 pm;
no credit cards; no booking.

Wright Brothers   £42   Ⓐ⭐⭐
12-13 Kingly St, W1   awaiting tel   2–2D
11 Stoney St, SE1   7403 9554
"The best oysters in London, and a fish pie that's the 8th
wonder of the world" are the sort of "orgasmic" treats that keep
this "cosy" seafood bar in Borough Market humming along;
a larger offshoot opens in Soho in late-2010. / **Details:** 10.30 pm,
Sun 9 pm; booking: max 8.

Yalla Yalla W1   £25
1 Greens Ct   7287 7663   2–2D
"A cramped Soho shop-front" provides the setting for this
"tightly-packed" Lebanese yearling – it makes a great "cheap 'n'
cheerful" option, even if its "zingy" dishes aren't "always
as exotic as they sound". / **Details:** www.yalla-yalla.co.uk; 11 pm,
Sun 10 pm; no Amex.

Yauatcha W1   £60   ⭐⭐
Broadwick Hs, 15-17 Broadwick St   7494 8888   2–2D
"The best dim sum ever" and "awesome cocktails" still create
a heady recipe for success at this "glamorous", "crowded" and
"vibey" Soho spot; "it's a shame they don't have the pâtisserie
any more", though, and – with creator Alan Yau no longer
involved – service, in particular, is ever-more "patchy" and
"snooty". / **Details:** www.yauatcha.com; 11.30 pm, Sun 10.30 pm.

The Yellow House SE16   £35   ⭐
126 Lower Rd   7231 8777
"The best Rotherhithe/Surrey Quays local"; this "friendly" former
boozer makes a "surprise find", and it offers a "good variety
of well-cooked food" (with "fabulous" pizza the highlight).
/ **Details:** www.theyellowhouse.eu; 10.30 pm, Sun 9.30 pm; closed Mon, Tue–Sat
closed L, Sun open L & D.

Yming W1 £38 ⭐

35-36 Greek St   7734 2721   3–2A

Christine Lau's Soho "gem" has "such lovely staff", and – with its "cracking" cuisine – this "lounge-like" room has long been "a truly civilised option among the many mediocre Chinese places hereabouts". / **Value tip:** *set pre-theatre £22 (FP).* **Details:** *www.yminglondon.com; 11.45 pm.*

Yoshino W1 £39 ⭐

3 Piccadilly Pl   7287 6622   2–3D

"Spartan perhaps, but still a hidden treasure" – this "incredibly friendly" café, "tucked-away" off Piccadilly, offers "superb" sushi at "unbelievably good-value" prices; "some say the decor is contemporary – I say it's bleak". / **Details:** *www.yoshino.net; 9 pm; closed Sun.*

Zafferano SW1 £63

15 Lowndes St   7235 5800   4–1D

"It's lost some sparkle" since its days at the zenith of London's Italians, but this well-known Belgravian is "still a cut above most"... "even if the bill does make you wince". / **Details:** *www.zafferanorestaurant.com; 11 pm, Sun 10.30 pm.*

Zaika W8 £58 ⭐⭐

1 Kensington High St   7795 6533   4–1A

"Stunning" and "sophisticated" subcontinental cuisine contributes to a "fabulous" all-round experience at this "Raj-glam" former banking hall, in Kensington; if there is a reservation, it's that some reporters find the ambience a touch "flat". / **Details:** *www.zaika-restaurant.co.uk; 10.45 pm, Sun 9.45 pm; closed Mon L.*

Zucca SE1 £35 ⭐

184 Bermondsey St   7378 6809

No surprise this "genuine and personal" new Bermondsey Italian is "heaving"; with its "clean and simple flavours" it's already attracting comparisons with the early-days River Café – unlike in W6, though, a meal here is often "excellent value"! / **Details:** *www.zuccalondon.com; 10 pm; closed Mon & Sun D; no Amex.*

Zuma SW7 £74 🅰⭐⭐

5 Raphael St   7584 1010   4–1C

"WOW!"... and that's just the "eye-candy and the oligarchs" on view in the bar of this "super-slick" Knightsbridge scene; "amazing" sushi and "outstanding" Japanese fusion fare add considerable substance to all the style, though, albeit at "breathtaking" prices. / **Details:** *www.zumarestaurant.com; 10.45 pm, Sun 9.45 pm; booking: max 8.*

London Area
Overviews

CENTRAL

Soho, Covent Garden & Bloomsbury
(Parts of W1, all WC2 and WC1)

£90+	L'Atelier de Joel Robuchon	"	Ⓐ✪
£80+	Pearl	"	
	Asia de Cuba	Fusion	
£60+	The Ivy	British, Modern	Ⓐ
	Rules	British, Traditional	Ⓐ
	Simpsons-in-the-Strand	"	
	J Sheekey	Fish & seafood	Ⓐ✪✪
	Yauatcha	Chinese	✪✪
	Red Fort	Indian	✪
£50+	Arbutus	British, Modern	✪
	Quo Vadis	"	
	The National Dining Rms	British, Traditional	
	Clos Maggiore	French	Ⓐ✪
	Vasco & Piero's Pavilion	Italian	✪
	Hawksmoor	Steaks & grills	✪
	Moti Mahal	Indian	✪
£40+	Konstam	British, Modern	Ⓐ✪
	Dean Street Townhouse	"	Ⓐ
	The Portrait	"	Ⓐ
	Shampers	"	Ⓐ
	The Terrace	"	Ⓐ
	Le Deuxième	"	
	Great Queen Street	British, Traditional	Ⓐ✪
	Wright Brothers	Fish & seafood	Ⓐ✪✪
	J Sheekey Oyster Bar	"	Ⓐ✪
	Terroirs	French	✪
	Randall & Aubin	"	Ⓐ
	Sarastro	International	Ⓐ✪
	The Forge	"	
	Dehesa	Italian	Ⓐ✪
	Bocca Di Lupo	"	✪
	Barrafina	Spanish	Ⓐ✪✪
	Edokko	Japanese	✪
£35+	The Easton	British, Modern	Ⓐ✪
	Andrew Edmunds	"	Ⓐ
	The Giaconda	French	✪
	Yming	Chinese	✪
	Rasa Maricham	Indian, Southern	✪
	Abeno	Japanese	✪
	Haozhan	Pan-Asian	✪✪
£30+	Cork & Bottle	International	Ⓐ✪
	Seven Stars	"	Ⓐ
	Byron	Burgers, etc	
	Mr Kong	Chinese	
	Izakaya Aki	Japanese	✪
	Satsuma	"	✪
£25+	Gordon's Wine Bar	International	Ⓐ✪
	Tartufo Trattoria	Italian	✪
	Polpo	"	Ⓐ
	Rock & Sole Plaice	Fish & chips	
	Fernandez & Wells	Sandwiches, cakes, etc	Ⓐ✪✪

	Yalla Yalla	*Lebanese*	
	Leong's Legends	*Chinese, Dim sum*	✪
	Rosa's Soho	*Thai*	✪
£20+	Princi	*Italian*	Ⓐ✪
	Bar Italia	*Sandwiches, cakes, etc*	Ⓐ
	Wong Kei	*Chinese*	
£15+	Hummus Bros	*Mediterranean*	✪
	Food for Thought	*Vegetarian*	✪
	Mrs Marengos	*Sandwiches, cakes, etc*	✪
	Baozi Inn	*Chinese*	✪
	Paolina Café	*Thai*	✪
£10+	Caffé Vergnano	*Italian*	Ⓐ✪
	Monmouth Coffee Co	*Sandwiches, cakes, etc*	Ⓐ✪✪
	Maison Bertaux	*"*	Ⓐ✪
£5+	Flat White	*"*	Ⓐ✪

Mayfair & St James's (Parts of W1 and SW1)

£110+	Le Gavroche	*French*	Ⓐ✪✪
	Sketch (Lecture Rm)	*"*	✪
	The Ritz Restaurant	*"*	Ⓐ
	Hélène Darroze	*"*	
£100+	Alain Ducasse	*"*	
	G Ramsay at Claridges	*"*	
	Kai Mayfair	*Chinese*	
£90+	Wiltons	*British, Traditional*	Ⓐ
	The Square	*French*	✪✪
	The Greenhouse	*"*	Ⓐ
	Hibiscus	*"*	
£80+	Dorchester Grill	*British, Modern*	
	Galvin at Windows	*French*	Ⓐ
	L'Oranger	*"*	
	Murano	*Italian*	✪
	The Palm	*Steaks & grills*	✪
	Hakkasan	*Chinese*	Ⓐ
	Nobu	*Japanese*	✪
	Umu	*"*	Ⓐ
	Nobu Berkeley	*"*	
£70+	Roux At Parliament Square	*British, Modern*	✪
	Bellamy's	*"*	Ⓐ
	The Browns (Albemarle)	*British, Traditional*	
	La Petite Maison	*French*	Ⓐ✪
	maze	*"*	
	Cipriani	*Italian*	✪
	Theo Randall	*"*	✪
	Babbo	*"*	
	JW Steakhouse	*Steaks & grills*	
	maze Grill	*"*	
	China Tang	*Chinese*	
	Benares	*Indian*	Ⓐ✪
	Ikeda	*Japanese*	✪✪
	aqua kyoto	*"*	
	Sumosan	*"*	

£60+	Athenaeum	British, Modern	🅐✪
	The Pigalle Club	"	🅐✪
	Patterson's	"	
	Corrigan's Mayfair	British, Traditional	
	Scott's	Fish & seafood	🅐✪
	Bentley's	"	✪
	Sketch (Gallery)	French	✪
	The Caramel Room	International	
	Ristorante Semplice	Italian	✪
	Goodman	Steaks & grills	✪
	Momo	North African	🅐
	Tamarind	Indian	✪
	Mint Leaf	"	
	Kiku	Japanese	✪
	Miyama	"	✪
	Matsuri	"	
£50+	Automat	American	
	Le Caprice	British, Modern	🅐✪
	Wild Honey	"	🅐✪
	Langan's Brasserie	"	🅐
	The Wolseley	"	🅐
	Hush	"	
	Pescatori	Fish & seafood	✪
	Bar Boulud	French	✪
	Cecconi's	Italian	🅐
	Levant	Lebanese	🅐
	Princess Garden	Chinese	✪
	Veeraswamy	Indian	🅐✪
	Quilon	Indian, Southern	✪✪
	Mitsukoshi	Japanese	✪
£40+	Sotheby's Café	British, Modern	🅐✪
	Osteria Dell'Angolo	Italian	✪
	The Guinea Grill	Steaks & grills	✪
	Chor Bizarre	Indian	🅐✪
£35+	Rasa	Indian, Southern	✪
	Chisou	Japanese	✪
	Yoshino	"	✪
£25+	Minqala	Middle Eastern	✪
£10+	Mooli's	Indian	✪✪

Fitzrovia & Marylebone (Part of W1)

Price	Restaurant	Cuisine	
£90+	Pied à Terre	French	✪
£80+	The Landau	British, Modern	🅐
	Hakkasan	Chinese	🅐
£70+	Rhodes W1 Restaurant	British, Modern	
	Texture	Scandinavian	✪
	Roka	Japanese	🅐✪✪
£60+	L'Autre Pied	French	✪
	Orrery	"	✪
	The Providores	Fusion	
	Locanda Locatelli	Italian	🅐✪
	Royal China Club	Chinese	✪

£50+	Vanilla	British, Modern	Ⓐ✪
	Odin's	British, Traditional	Ⓐ
	Pescatori	Fish & seafood	✪
	The Wallace	French	Ⓐ
	Archipelago	Fusion	Ⓐ✪
	Fino	Spanish	Ⓐ✪
	Caleya Ibérica	"	✪
	Crazy Bear	Thai	Ⓐ
£40+	Café Luc	British, Modern	✪
	RIBA Café	"	Ⓐ
	Back to Basics	Fish & seafood	✪✪
	Galvin Bistrot de Luxe	French	Ⓐ✪✪
	Latium	Italian	✪
	Mennula	"	✪
	Trishna	Indian	✪✪
	Defune	Japanese	✪✪
	Tsunami	"	✪✪
	Koba	Korean	✪
	Bam-Bou	Vietnamese	Ⓐ✪
£35+	Salt Yard	Spanish	✪
	La Fromagerie Café	Sandwiches, cakes, etc	Ⓐ
	Rasa Samudra	Indian, Southern	✪
	Dinings	Japanese	✪✪
£30+	Indali Lounge	Indian	✪
£25+	Ragam	"	✪✪
	Pho	Vietnamese	✪
£20+	Golden Hind	Fish & chips	✪✪
£15+	Atari-Ya	Japanese	✪✪
£10+	Cocorino	Ice cream	✪
	Patogh	Middle Eastern	✪✪
£5+	Kaffeine	Sandwiches, cakes, etc	Ⓐ✪

Belgravia, Pimlico, Victoria & Westminster (SW1, except St James's)

£110+	Marcus Wareing	French	Ⓐ✪✪
£100+	Rib Room	British, Traditional	
£80+	One-O-One	Fish & seafood	✪✪
	Roussillon	French	✪
	Pétrus	"	
	Apsleys	Italian	
	Nahm	Thai	
£70+	The Goring Hotel	British, Modern	Ⓐ
£60+	Koffmann's	French	
	Santini	Italian	
	Zafferano	"	
	Amaya	Indian	Ⓐ✪✪
	The Cinnamon Club	"	Ⓐ✪
£50+	The Thomas Cubitt	British, Modern	Ⓐ

	Olivomare	Fish & seafood	✪✪
	La Poule au Pot	French	Ⓐ
	Sale e Pepe	Italian	Ⓐ✪
	Quirinale	"	✪
	Toto's	"	Ⓐ
	Hunan	Chinese	✪✪
	Ken Lo's Memories	"	
£40+	Tate Britain (Rex Whistler)	British, Modern	Ⓐ
	Le Cercle	French	Ⓐ✪
	Ottolenghi	Italian	✪✪
	Caraffini	"	Ⓐ
	About Thyme	Mediterranean	✪
	Oliveto	Pizza	✪✪
£35+	Kazan	Turkish	✪
£30+	Blue Jade	Thai	
£25+	Vincent Rooms	British, Modern	
	Cyprus Mangal	Turkish	✪✪
£15+	William Curley	Afternoon tea	✪

WEST

Chelsea, South Kensington, Kensington, Earl's Court & Fulham (SW3, SW5, SW6, SW7, SW10 & W8)

Price	Name	Cuisine	Awards
£120+	Gordon Ramsay	French	
£110+	Tom Aikens	British, Modern	
£100+	Blakes	International	Ⓐ
£90+	Aubergine	French	
£80+	The Capital Restaurant	"	
	Rasoi	Indian	✪
£70+	Launceston Place	British, Modern	Ⓐ✪
	Bibendum	French	Ⓐ
	Brunello	Italian	
	Zuma	Japanese	Ⓐ✪✪
	Nozomi	"	
£60+	Babylon	British, Modern	Ⓐ
	Cheyne Walk Bras'	French	
	Montpeliano	Italian	
	San Lorenzo	"	
	Locanda Ottomezzo	Mediterranean	
	Min Jiang	Chinese	Ⓐ✪
£50+	Clarke's	British, Modern	Ⓐ✪✪
	Manson	"	✪✪
	The Abingdon	"	Ⓐ✪
	Tom's Kitchen	"	
	Bibendum Oyster Bar	Fish & seafood	
	L'Etranger	French	✪
	Racine	"	✪
	Belvedere	"	Ⓐ
	Daphne's	Italian	Ⓐ
	Cambio de Tercio	Spanish	Ⓐ✪
	Ken Lo's Memories	Chinese	✪✪
	Good Earth	"	✪
	Zaika	Indian	✪✪
	Chutney Mary	"	Ⓐ✪
	Blue Elephant	Thai	Ⓐ✪
£40+	Kitchen W8	British, Modern	Ⓐ✪✪
	Sands End	"	Ⓐ✪
	Harwood Arms	"	✪
	Whits	"	✪
	Ffiona's	British, Traditional	Ⓐ
	Maggie Jones's	"	Ⓐ
	Ottolenghi	Italian	✪✪
	Il Portico	"	Ⓐ
	Wódka	Polish	Ⓐ
	Lola Rojo	Spanish	✪
	Saf	Vegetarian	
	Mr Wing	Chinese	Ⓐ
	The Painted Heron	Indian	✪✪
	Sukho Thai Cuisine	Thai	✪✪
£35+	Made in Italy	Italian	Ⓐ✪
	Aglio e Olio	"	✪

	Nuovi Sapori	"	★
	The Atlas	Mediterranean	A ★
	Tendido Cero	Spanish	A ★
	Tendido Cuatro	"	★
	Malabar	Indian	★
	Noor Jahan	"	★
£30+	Haché	Steaks & grills	
	Byron	Burgers, etc	
	Troubadour	Sandwiches, cakes, etc	A
£25+	Taiwan Village	Chinese	★★
	Addie's Thai Café	Thai	A★
£20+	Café 209	"	A

Notting Hill, Holland Park, Bayswater, North Kensington & Maida Vale (W2, W9, W10, W11)

£90+	The Ledbury	British, Modern	A A ★
£60+	Angelus	French	A ★
	Assaggi	Italian	★
£50+	Julie's	British, Modern	A
	Le Café Anglais	French	A
£40+	The Dock Kitchen	British, Modern	A★
	The Ladbroke Arms	"	A★
	First Floor	"	A
	Hereford Road	British, Traditional	★
	The Summerhouse	Fish & seafood	★
	Ottolenghi	Italian	★★
	The Oak	"	A★
	Pearl Liang	Chinese	★
	Bombay Palace	Indian	★
	E&O	Pan-Asian	A A ★
£35+	Lucky Seven	American	A
	Paradise, Kensal Green	British, Modern	A★
	Mandarin Kitchen	Chinese	★
	Noor Jahan	Indian	★
	Inaho	Japanese	★★
	Uli	Pan-Asian	★★
	The Walmer Castle	Thai	A★
£30+	Ida	Italian	A
	El Pirata de Tapas	Spanish	A★
	Taqueria	Mexican/TexMex	
	Al-Waha	Lebanese	★
£25+	Leong's Legends	Chinese, Dim sum	★
£5+	Lisboa Pâtisserie	Sandwiches, cakes, etc	★

Hammersmith, Shepherd's Bush, Olympia, Chiswick, Acton & Ealing (W4, W3, W5, W6, W12, W14)

£70+	The River Café	Italian	★

Price	Name	Cuisine	Rating
£50+	La Trompette	French	Ⓐ✪✪
£40+	The Anglesea Arms	British, Modern	Ⓐ✪✪
	Pissarro's	"	Ⓐ
	High Road Brasserie	"	
	Michael Nadra	International	✪
	Annie's	"	Ⓐ
	Popeseye	Steaks & grills	✪
	The Gate	Vegetarian	✪
	Indian Zing	Indian	✪✪
	Sushi-Hiro	Japanese	✪✪
	Saigon Saigon	Vietnamese	✪
£35+	The Havelock Tavern	British, Modern	Ⓐ✪
	Princess Victoria	"	Ⓐ✪
	Chella	Persian	✪
	Brilliant	Indian	Ⓐ✪✪
£30+	Patio	Polish	Ⓐ
	Byron	Burgers, etc	
	North China	Chinese	✪
	Karma	Indian	✪
£25+	Albertine	French	Ⓐ
	Adams Café	Moroccan	Ⓐ
	Chez Marcelle	Lebanese	✪✪
	Mohsen	Persian	✪
	Kiraku	Japanese	✪✪
	Pho	Vietnamese	✪
£20+	Santa Maria	Pizza	Ⓐ✪
	Sufi	Persian	✪
	Abu Zaad	Syrian	
	Gifto's	Pakistani	✪
	Miran Masala	"	✪
£15+	Franco Manca	Pizza	✪✪

NORTH

Hampstead, West Hampstead, St John's Wood, Regent's Park, Kilburn & Camden Town (NW postcodes)

£70+	Landmark (Winter Gdn)	British, Modern	Ⓐ
£50+	Odette's	"	
	St Pancras Grand	"	
	L'Aventure	French	Ⓐ✪
	Oslo Court	"	Ⓐ✪
	Good Earth	Chinese	✪
	Kaifeng	"	✪
£40+	Market	British, Modern	✪
	The Wells	"	Ⓐ
	Bull & Last	British, Traditional	Ⓐ✪✪
	Lemonia	Greek	Ⓐ
	Atma	Indian	✪
	Sushi-Say	Japanese	✪✪
	Singapore Garden	Malaysian	✪
£35+	Holly Bush	British, Traditional	Ⓐ
	Alisan	Chinese	✪
	Eriki	Indian	✪
	Jin Kichi	Japanese	✪✪
	Abeno	"	✪
£30+	Daphne	Greek	Ⓐ
	El Parador	Spanish	Ⓐ✪
	Haché	Steaks & grills	
	Skipjacks	Fish & chips	✪✪
	Nautilus	"	✪
	Gung-Ho	Chinese	
	Café Japan	Japanese	✪✪
£25+	Rising Sun	British, Modern	✪
	Vijay	Indian	✪✪
	Kovalam	"	✪
	Asakusa	Japanese	✪✪
£15+	Geeta	Indian	
	Atari-Ya	Japanese	✪✪
£5+	Ginger & White	Sandwiches, cakes, etc	✪

Hoxton, Islington, Highgate, Crouch End, Stoke Newington, Finsbury Park, Muswell Hill & Finchley (N postcodes)

£80+	Fifteen Restaurant	Italian	✪
£60+	Morgan M	French	✪✪
£40+	Sargasso	Fish & seafood	Ⓐ✪
	Ottolenghi	Italian	✪✪
	Isarn	Thai	
£35+	Chez Liline	Fish & seafood	✪✪
	Banners	International	Ⓐ
	Sabor	South American	Ⓐ

	Rasa Travancore	*Indian, Southern*	✪
£30+	Vrisaki	*Greek*	
	500	*Italian*	✪
	Byron	*Burgers, etc*	
	Toff's	*Fish & chips*	✪
	Two Brothers	*"*	✪
	Indian Rasoi	*Indian*	✪✪
£25+	Rani	*"*	✪
	Anglo Asian Tandoori	*"*	Ⓐ
	Rasa	*Indian, Southern*	Ⓐ✪✪
	Dotori	*Korean*	✪
	Khoai	*Vietnamese*	✪
	Khoai Cafe	*"*	✪
£20+	La Bota	*Spanish*	Ⓐ✪
	19 Numara Bos Cirrik	*Turkish*	✪✪
£15+	Café del Parc	*Spanish*	Ⓐ✪

SOUTH

South Bank (SE1)

Price	Name	Cuisine	
£70+	Oxo Tower (Rest')	British, Modern	●
£60+	Roast	British, Traditional	
	Oxo Tower (Brass')	Mediterranean	●
£50+	Magdalen	British, Modern	●
	Skylon	"	Ⓐ
£40+	Garrison	"	Ⓐ
	Wright Brothers	Fish & seafood	Ⓐ●●
	Champor-Champor	Fusion	Ⓐ●
	Tate Modern (Level 7)	International	●
	Tentazioni	Italian	●
£35+	The Anchor & Hope	British, Traditional	●●
	Zucca	Italian	●
	La Lanterna	"	
£30+	The Table	British, Modern	Ⓐ●
£25+	El Vergel	South American	Ⓐ●
	Tower Tandoori	Indian	●
£20+	Masters Super Fish	Fish & chips	●
£10+	Monmouth Coffee Co	Sandwiches, cakes, etc	Ⓐ●●
	Caffé Vergnano	"	Ⓐ●

Greenwich, Lewisham & Blackheath (All SE postcodes, except SE1)

Price	Name	Cuisine	
£50+	Lobster Pot	Fish & seafood	●
£40+	Inside	British, Modern	●
	The Palmerston	"	●
£35+	The Yellow House	International	●
	Le Querce	Italian	Ⓐ●●
	Olley's	Fish & chips	●
	Dragon Castle	Chinese	●●
	Babur	Indian	Ⓐ●●
£30+	Brasserie Toulouse-Lautrec	French	Ⓐ●
	The Gowlett	Pizza	Ⓐ●
	Ganapati	Indian	Ⓐ●●
	Kennington Tandoori	"	Ⓐ●
£25+	Angels & Gypsies	Cuban	Ⓐ●

Battersea, Brixton, Clapham, Wandsworth Barnes, Putney & Wimbledon (All SW postcodes south of the river)

Price	Name	Cuisine	
£60+	Chez Bruce	British, Modern	Ⓐ●●
£50+	Trinity	"	Ⓐ●●
	Enoteca Turi	Italian	●

	Riva	"	✪
£40+	Lambers	British, Modern	Ⓐ✪✪
	The Orange	"	Ⓐ
	Upstairs Bar	French	Ⓐ✪
	Annie's	International	Ⓐ
	Lola Rojo	Spanish	✪
	Popeseye	Steaks & grills	✪
	Santa Maria del Sur	Argentinian	Ⓐ✪
	Tsunami	Japanese	✪✪
£35+	Emile's	British, Modern	✪
	Bellevue Rendez-Vous	French	Ⓐ✪
	Donna Margherita	Italian	Ⓐ✪✪
	Ma Goa	Indian	✪
	Cho-San	Japanese	✪
£30+	Rick's Café	British, Modern	Ⓐ✪
	Canton Arms	British, Traditional	Ⓐ✪
	Rebato's	Spanish	Ⓐ
	Fish Club	Fish & chips	✪
	Mango & Silk	Indian	✪
	Cocum	Indian, Southern	✪
£25+	El Rincón Latino	Spanish	Ⓐ
	Brady's	Fish & chips	✪
	Kastoori	Indian	✪✪
	Chutney	"	✪
	Amaranth	Thai	✪
£20+	Doukan	Moroccan	Ⓐ✪
	Hot Stuff	Indian	Ⓐ✪
£15+	Franco Manca	Pizza	✪✪
£10+	Lahore Karahi	Pakistani	✪✪

Outer western suburbs
Kew, Richmond, Twickenham, Teddington

£70+	The Bingham	British, Modern	Ⓐ
£60+	Petersham Nurseries	"	Ⓐ✪
	A Taste of McClements	French	✪
£50+	The Glasshouse	British, Modern	✪✪
	Petersham Hotel	"	Ⓐ
£40+	Rock & Rose	"	Ⓐ
	Brula	French	Ⓐ✪
	A Cena	Italian	Ⓐ✪
£30+	O'Zon	Chinese	

EAST

Smithfield & Farringdon (EC1)

£70+	Club Gascon	French	Ⓐ✪
£60+	St John	British, Traditional	✪
	Dans le Noir	International	Ⓐ✪
£50+	Bleeding Heart	French	Ⓐ✪
	Café du Marché	"	Ⓐ✪
	Portal	Mediterranean	Ⓐ
£40+	The Peasant	British, Modern	Ⓐ
	Bistrot Bruno Loubet	French	Ⓐ✪✪
	Comptoir Gascon	"	Ⓐ✪
	Eastside Inn	"	✪
	$	International	✪
	Moro	Spanish	Ⓐ✪✪
£35+	Giant Robot	American	✪
	Caravan	British, Modern	Ⓐ✪
	Coach & Horses	"	✪
	Vinoteca	"	Ⓐ
	The Fox and Anchor	British, Traditional	Ⓐ
	Cellar Gascon	French	
	Fabrizio	Italian	✪✪
	Smiths (Dining Rm)	Steaks & grills	
£25+	The Eagle	Mediterranean	Ⓐ
	Pham Sushi	Japanese	✪✪
	Pho	Vietnamese	✪
£20+	Sedap	Malaysian	✪
£10+	Spianata & Co	Sandwiches, cakes, etc	✪
£5+	The Farm Collective	British, Traditional	✪
	Dose	Sandwiches, cakes, etc	✪

The City (EC2, EC3, EC4)

£70+	1 Lombard Street	British, Modern	
	Catch	Fish & seafood	
£60+	Vertigo 42	British, Modern	Ⓐ✪
	Coq d'Argent	French	
	L'Anima	Italian	✪
	Goodman City Restaurant	Steaks & grills	✪
	Bevis Marks	Kosher	
	Mint Leaf	Indian	
£50+	Chamberlain's	Fish & seafood	✪
	Cinnamon Kitchen	Indian	Ⓐ✪✪
£40+	The Don	British, Modern	✪
	28-50	French	✪
	The Royal Exchange	"	Ⓐ
	Saf	Vegetarian	
	Gt Eastern Dining Room	Pan-Asian	Ⓐ✪
£35+	Kazan	Turkish	✪

Price	Name	Cuisine	Rating
£30+	Ye Olde Cheshire Cheese	British, Traditional	Ⓐ
	Simpson's Tavern	"	Ⓐ
£25+	Hilliard	British, Modern	✪
	The Wine Library	International	Ⓐ
£15+	Hummus Bros	Mediterranean	✪
£10+	Spianata & Co	Sandwiches, cakes, etc	✪

East End & Docklands (All E postcodes)

Price	Name	Cuisine	Rating
£90+	Viajante	Fusion	Ⓐ✪✪
£70+	The Battery	British, Modern	
	Quadrato	Italian	
	Roka	Japanese	Ⓐ✪✪
£60+	Galvin La Chapelle	French	Ⓐ✪
	Plateau	"	✪
	Les Trois Garçons	"	Ⓐ
£50+	Brasserie Joël	"	
	Hawksmoor	Steaks & grills	✪
£40+	Bistrotheque	British, Modern	Ⓐ
	Wapping Food	"	Ⓐ
	St John Bread & Wine	British, Traditional	✪✪
	The Grapes	Fish & seafood	Ⓐ✪
	El Faro	Spanish	✪
	Ark Fish	Fish & chips	✪
	Buen Ayre	Argentinian	✪
	Café Spice Namaste	Indian	✪
£35+	Royal Oak	British, Modern	Ⓐ✪
	Il Bordello	Italian	Ⓐ✪
	La Figa	"	✪
	Pizza East	Pizza	Ⓐ
	Rasa Mudra	Indian	✪
£30+	LMNT	International	Ⓐ
	Byron	Burgers, etc	
	Viet Grill	Vietnamese	Ⓐ✪
£25+	Faulkner's	Fish & chips	✪
	Mangal 1	Turkish	✪
	My Old Place	Chinese	✪✪
	New Tayyabs	Pakistani	✪✪
	Rosa's	Thai	✪
	Green Papaya	Vietnamese	✪✪
£20+	Lahore Kebab House	Pakistani	✪✪
£15+	Gourmet San	Chinese	✪✪
	Needoo	Pakistani	✪✪
£10+	E Pellicci	Italian	Ⓐ
	Spianata & Co	Sandwiches, cakes, etc	✪
£5+	Brick Lane Beigel Bake	"	✪✪

London Index

INDEXES

RIBA Café
The Wolseley

West
The Abingdon
Annie's: *all branches*
Cheyne Walk Brasserie
First Floor
High Road Brasserie
Lucky Seven
The Oak
Ottolenghi: *all branches*
Taqueria
Tom's Kitchen
Troubadour
Zuma

North
Banners
Landmark (Winter Gdn)
Ottolenghi: *all branches*

South
Annie's: *all branches*
Bellevue Rendez-Vous
Garrison
Inside
Lamberts
Petersham Hotel
Roast
The Table
El Vergel

East
Bistrotheque
Caravan
Quadrato
Wapping Food

BUSINESS

Central
Alain Ducasse
Amaya
Apsleys
Athenaeum
Bar Boulud
Bellamy's
Benares
Bentley's
Le Caprice
Cecconi's
China Tang
The Cinnamon Club
Corrigan's Mayfair
Le Deuxième
Dorchester Grill
Fino
The Forge
Galvin at Windows
Galvin Bistrot de Luxe
Le Gavroche
Goodman: *all branches*
Gordon Ramsay at Claridge's
The Goring Hotel
The Greenhouse

The Guinea Grill
Hakkasan: *Hanway Pl W1*
Hélène Darroze
Hibiscus
Hush
The Ivy
JW Steakhouse
Kai Mayfair
Ken Lo's Memories
Koffmann's
The Landau
Langan's Brasserie
Locanda Locatelli
Marcus Wareing
Matsuri
maze Grill
Miyama
Murano
Nobu
Odin's
One-O-One
L'Oranger
Orrery
The Palm
Patterson's
Pearl
Pétrus
Pied à Terre
Quilon
Quirinale
Quo Vadis
Rhodes W1 Restaurant
Rib Room
Roka: *W1*
Roussillon
Roux At Parliament Square
Rules
Santini
Savoy Grill
Scott's
J Sheekey
Simpsons-in-the-Strand
The Square
Tamarind
Theo Randall
Veeraswamy
The Wallace
Wild Honey
Wiltons
The Wolseley
Zafferano

West
Aubergine
Bibendum
The Capital Restaurant
Gordon Ramsay
The Ledbury
Racine
Tom Aikens
La Trompette
Zuma

North
Landmark (Winter Gdn)
St Pancras Grand

INDEXES

BYO

(Bring your own wine at no or low – less than £3 – corkage. Note for £5-£15 per bottle, you can normally negotiate to take your own wine to many, if not most, places.)

CHILDREN

*(h – high or special chairs
m – children's menu
p – children's portions
e – weekend entertainments
o – other facilities)*

El Rincón Latino *(hp)*
Riva *(hp)*
Roast *(hm)*
Rock & Rose *(hm)*
Santa Maria del Sur *(h)*
Skylon *(hmp)*
The Table *(hp)*
Tate Modern (Level 7) *(hmo)*
Tentazioni *(hp)*
Tower Tandoori *(hp)*
Trinity *(hp)*
Tsunami: *SW4 (h)*
Upstairs Bar *(hp)*
El Vergel *(p)*
The Yellow House *(hm)*
Zucca *(h)*

East

L'Anima *(h)*
Ark Fish *(hm)*
Bistrot Bruno Loubet *(p)*
Bistrotheque *(h)*
Il Bordello *(hp)*
Brasserie Joël *(hm)*
Buen Ayre *(h)*
Café du Marché *(p)*
Café Spice Namaste *(hp)*
Caravan *(hm)*
Catch *(hp)*
Cinnamon Kitchen *(hp)*
Club Gascon *(hp)*
Coach & Horses *(hp)*
Comptoir Gascon *(h)*
Coq d'Argent *(h)*
$ *(p)*
Eastside Inn *(p)*
Fabrizio *(hp)*
Faulkner's *(hm)*
La Figa *(hp)*
The Fox and Anchor *(h)*
Giant Robot *(h)*
Gourmet San *(h)*
Great Eastern Dining Room *(em)*
Hilliard *(p)*
Kazan: *all branches (hp)*
Lahore Kebab House *(h)*
Mangal 1 *(m)*
Mint Leaf: *all branches (h)*
Moro *(h)*
Needoo *(h)*
New Tayyabs *(h)*
The Peasant *(hp)*
E Pellicci *(p)*
Pho: *EC1 (p)*
Plateau *(hp)*
Portal *(hp)*
Quadrato *(hm)*
Rosa's: *E1 (p)*
The Royal Exchange Grand
   Café *(p)*
Royal Oak *(h)*
Saf: *EC2 (hp)*
St John *(h)*
St John Bread & Wine *(hp)*
Sedap *(hp)*
Smiths (Dining Rm) *(hp)*

Viet Grill *(hop)*
Vinoteca *(p)*
Wapping Food *(h)*

ENTERTAINMENT
(Check times before you go)

Central
Bentley's
   (pianist, Wed-Sat)
Le Caprice
   (pianist, nightly)
Hakkasan: *Hanway Pl W1*
   (DJ, nightly)
Langan's Brasserie
   (jazz, Fri & Sat)
Levant
   (belly dancer, nightly)
Mint Leaf: *SW1*
   (DJ/jazz, Fri D)
Momo
   (live world music, Tue)
L'Oranger
   (pianist, Fri & Sat)
Pearl
   (pianist, Wed-Sat)
The Pigalle Club
   (live music, nightly)
Red Fort
   (DJ, Fri & Sat)
The Ritz Restaurant
   (live music, Fri & Sat)
Roka: *W1*
   (DJ, Thu-Sat)
Sarastro
   (opera, Sun & Mon D)
Savoy Grill
   (pianist, nightly)
Simpsons-in-the-Strand
   (pianist, nightly)
Sketch (Gallery)
   (DJ, Thu-Sat)

West
Babylon
   (nightclub Fri & Sat, magician Sun)
Belvedere
   (pianist, nightly Sat & Sun all day)
Le Café Anglais
   (magician, Sun L)
Chella
   (live music, Sun)
Cheyne Walk Brasserie
   (jazz, first Mon of month)
Harwood Arms
   (quiz night, Tue)
Mr Wing
   (jazz, Thu-Sat)
Nozomi
   (DJ, Tue-Sat)
Paradise by Way of Kensal
   Green
   *(live music and burlesque, Tue & Thu; comedy
   nights, Wed; DJ, Fri-Sun)*
Tendido Cuatro
   (Spanish guitar, Wed D)

INDEXES

Troubadour
(live music, most nights)

North
Bull & Last
(pub quiz, Sun)
Isarn
(live music)
Landmark (Winter Gdn)
(pianist & musicians, daily)

South
Brasserie Toulouse-Lautrec
(live music, nightly)
The Gowlett
(DJ, Sun; Lucky 7s, Thu)
La Lanterna
(live music occas)
Oxo Tower (Brass')
(live jazz, Sat & Sun L, Sun-Mon D)
Roast
(jazz, Sun)
Santa Maria del Sur
(live music, Mon)

East
Bistrotheque
(regular drag shows and cabarets, piano brunch)
Café du Marché
(pianist & bass, Mon-Thu, pianist, Fri & Sat)
Cinnamon Kitchen
(DJ, occasionally)
Coq d'Argent
(jazz, Sun L)
Great Eastern Dining Room
(DJs, Fri & Sat)
Kazan: EC3
(Turkish night, occasional)
Mint Leaf: EC2
(Jazz, Fri D; DJ, weekends)
The Royal Exchange Grand Café
(cocktail night, first Wed of month)

LATE
(open till midnight or later as shown; may be earlier Sunday)

Central
Asia de Cuba *(midnight, Thu-Sat 12.30 am)*
Automat
Bam-Bou
Bar Italia *(open 24 hours, Sun 3 am)*
Le Caprice
Cecconi's *(1am, Sun midnight)*
Cyprus Mangal *(Sun-Thu midnight, Fri & Sat 1 am)*
Le Deuxième
The Forge
Hakkasan: Hanway Pl W1 *(12.30 am)*
Haozhan *(Fri & Sat midnight)*
The Ivy
Mr Kong *(3 am, Sun midnight)*
Nobu Berkeley *(Thu-Sat 12.45 am)*

Princi
Satsuma *(Fri & Sat midnight)*
J Sheekey
J Sheekey Oyster Bar
The Wolseley

West
Brilliant *(Fri & Sat midnight)*
Chella
Mohsen
Mr Wing
Nozomi *(1 am, Sun 12.30)*

North
Banners *(Fri midnight)*
Shaka Zulu *(2 am)*

South
Kennington Tandoori
Lahore Karahi *(midnight)*

East
Brick Lane Beigel Bake *(24 hours)*
Buen Ayre
Cellar Gascon
Lahore Kebab House
Mangal 1 *(midnight, Sat-Sun 1 am)*
Pizza East *(midnight, Thu 1 am, Fri & Sat 2 am)*

OUTSIDE TABLES
(particularly recommended)*

Central
Andrew Edmunds
aqua kyoto*
Archipelago
Atari-Ya: W1
L'Autre Pied
Back to Basics
Bam-Bou
Bar Italia
Barrafina
Bentley's
Café Luc
Caraffini
Cecconi's
Chisou
Dean Street Townhouse
Dehesa
The Easton
Goodman: W1
Gordon's Wine Bar*
Hush
Indali Lounge
Kaffeine
Kazan: SW1
Levant
Maison Bertaux
Momo
Mooli's
Olivomare
L'Oranger
Orrery
Pescatori: Charlotte St W1
La Petite Maison

INDEXES

PRIVATE ROOMS

(for the most comprehensive
listing of venues for functions –
from palaces to pubs – visit
www.hardens.com/party, or buy
*Harden's London Party, Event
& Conference Guide*, available
in all good bookshops)
* particularly recommended

New Tayyabs *(35)*
Ye Olde Cheshire Cheese *(15,50)*
1 Lombard Street *(20)*
The Peasant *(18)*
Plateau *(24)*
Portal *(14)*
Rosa's: *E1 (40)*
The Royal Exchange Grand
   Café *(26)*
Saf: *EC2 (25)*
St John *(18)*
Les Trois Garçons *(10)*
28-50 *(12,6)*
Viajante *(20)*
Viet Grill *(100)*
Vinoteca *(30)*

ROMANTIC

Central
Andrew Edmunds
Archipelago
Bam-Bou
Le Caprice
Cecconi's
Le Cercle
Chor Bizarre
Clos Maggiore
Corrigan's Mayfair
Crazy Bear
Galvin at Windows
Le Gavroche
Gordon Ramsay at Claridge's
Gordon's Wine Bar
Hakkasan: *Hanway Pl W1*
Hush
The Ivy
Langan's Brasserie
Levant
Locanda Locatelli
Marcus Wareing
Momo
Odin's
L'Oranger
Orrery
Pied à Terre
The Pigalle Club
Polpo
La Poule au Pot
The Ritz Restaurant
Roussillon
Rules
Sarastro
J Sheekey
Toto's
Vanilla
The Wolseley
Zafferano

West
Albertine
Assaggi
Babylon
Belvedere
Bibendum
Blakes

Blue Elephant
Daphne's
E&O
Ffiona's
First Floor
Julie's
The Ledbury
Maggie Jones's
Mr Wing
Paradise by Way of Kensal
   Green
Patio
Pissarro's
Racine
The River Café
The Summerhouse
La Trompette
The Walmer Castle
Wódka
Zuma

North
Anglo Asian Tandoori
L'Aventure
Odette's
Oslo Court

South
A Cena
The Bingham
Brula
Le Cassoulet
Champor-Champor
Chez Bruce
Enoteca Turi
The Glasshouse
Lobster Pot
Petersham Hotel
Petersham Nurseries
Rock & Rose
Upstairs Bar

East
Bleeding Heart
Café du Marché
Club Gascon
Comptoir Gascon
LMNT
Moro
Pizza East
Les Trois Garçons
Vertigo 42
Wapping Food

ROOMS WITH A VIEW

Central
Galvin at Windows
The National Dining Rooms
Orrery
The Portrait
The Terrace in the Fields

West
Babylon
Belvedere

London Maps

MAP 1 - WEST END OVERVIEW

BAKER ST.

A

B

Archipelago

GT. PORTLAND ST.

Marylebone Road

REGENTS PARK

Vanilla •

Caleya Ibérica

Orrery

MARYLEBONE

Café Luc

• Odin's

• Ragam

• RIBA Cafe

Paddington St

Portland Place

Gloucester Place

Baker Street

Marylebone High

Great Portland Street

Back to Basics •

Barric

• Efes

Salt Y

Indali Lounge • Galvin

• Providores, Tapa Room

L'Autre Pied

Trishna

Golden Hind

• The Landau

Goodg

Stree

Royal China •

See Map 2

Wigmore Street

Locanda Locatelli •

Oxford Street

OXFORD CIRCUS

Rhodes W1 •

mour Street

Texture

Oxford Street

BOND ST.

New Bond Street

Regent Street

MARBLE ARCH

Grosvenor

2

Square

Berkeley

Square

Old Bond Street

MAYFAIR

Park Lane

Hyde Park

Piccadilly

St James's St

GREEN PARK

3

Green Park

See Map 4

Knightsbridge

HYDE PARK CORNER

Constitution Hill

Grosvenor Place

Buckingham Palace

KNIGHTSBRIDGE

• Nahm

Quilo

BELGRAVIA

Belgrave Square

• Goring Hotel

Sloane Street

Pont Street

Buckingham Palace Road

4

Olivomare •

Santini •

Eccleston St

Ken Lo's Memories •

Upton Square

VICTORIA

• dim T • Preto

Kazan,

About Thyme •

Thomas Cubitt •

• Oliveto

Vauxhall Bridge Road

Belgrave Road

Cyprus Mangal •

SLOANE SQ

• Blue Jade

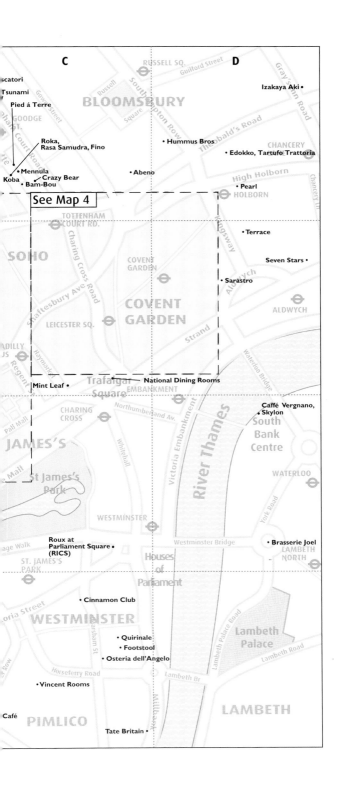

C

RUSSELL SQ.

Guilford Street

scatori

Tsunami

Pied á Terre

GOODGE
ST.

BLOOMSBURY

Russell
Square

Southampton Row

Gower Street

Charing Cross Road

D

Gray's Inn Road

Izakaya Aki •

Theobald's Road

• Hummus Bros

CHANCERY

• Edokko, Tartufo Trattoria

Roka,
Rasa Samudra, Fino

• Mennula
Koba ⁄ Crazy Bear
• Bam-Bou

• Abeno

High Holborn

• Pearl

HOLBORN

Chancery Ln.

See Map 4

TOTTENHAM
COURT RD.

SOHO

Charing Cross Road

COVENT
GARDEN

• Terrace

Kingsway

Seven Stars •

Shaftesbury Avenue

LEICESTER SQ.

**COVENT
GARDEN**

• Sarastro

Aldwych

ALDWYCH

Strand

ADILLY
US

Regent St.

Haymarket

Mint Leaf •

Trafalgar
Square

EMBANKMENT

National Dining Rooms

Waterloo Bridge

Pall Mall

CHARING
CROSS

Northumberland Av.

Victoria Embankment

River Thames

Caffé Vergnano,
• Skylon

**South
Bank
Centre**

JAMES'S

Whitehall

WATERLOO

e Mall

St James's
Park

WESTMINSTER

York Road

age Walk

ST. JAMES'S
PARK

Roux at
Parliament Square •
(RICS)

Westminster Bridge

Houses
of
Parliament

• Brasserie Joel
LAMBETH
NORTH

oria Street

• Cinnamon Club

WESTMINSTER

Marsham St.

• Quirinale
• Footstool
• Osteria dell'Angelo

Lambeth Palace Road

Lambeth
Palace

Lambeth Road

St Row

Horseferry Road

• Vincent Rooms

Lambeth Br

Millbank

Café

PIMLICO

Tate Britain •

LAMBETH

MAP 2 - MAYFAIR, ST JAMES'S & WEST SOHO

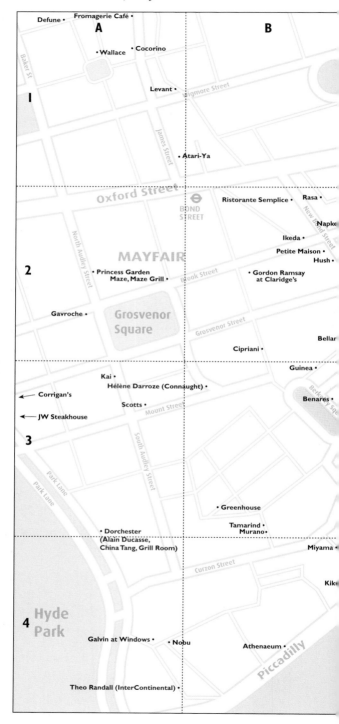

Defune •
Fromagerie Café •

A

B

Baker St

• Wallace   • Cocorino

Levant •

Wigmore Street

James Street

• Atari-Ya

1

Oxford Street

⊖ BOND STREET

Ristorante Semplice •   Rasa •

New Bond Street

Napke

North Audley Street

MAYFAIR

Ikeda •

Petite Maison •

Hush •

2

• Princess Garden
Maze, Maze Grill •

Brook Street

• Gordon Ramsay
at Claridge's

Gavroche •

**Grosvenor
Square**

Grosvenor Street

Bellar

Cipriani •

Guinea •

Kai •

Hélène Darroze (Connaught) •

Berke

Sq

← Corrigan's

Scotts •

Mount Street

Benares •

← JW Steakhouse

3

South Audley Street

Park Lane

Park Lane

• Greenhouse

Tamarind •

Murano•

• Dorchester
(Alain Ducasse,
China Tang, Grill Room)

Miyama •

Curzon Street

Kik

**Hyde
Park**

4

Galvin at Windows •   • Nobu

Athenaeum •

Piccadilly

Theo Randall (InterContinental) •

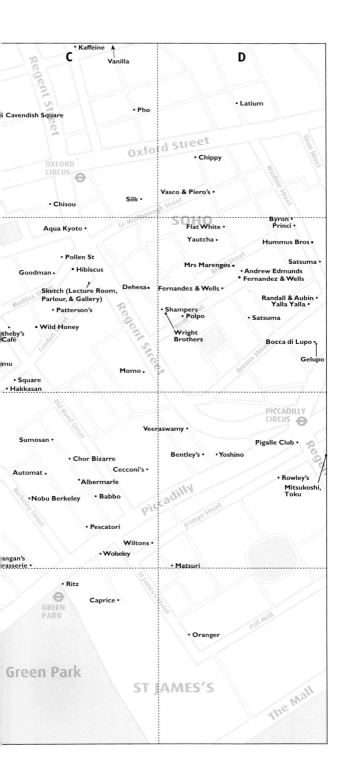

C

- Kaffeine
  Vanilla

Regent Street

§ Cavendish Square

- Pho

D

- Latium

OXFORD
CIRCUS

Oxford Street

- Chippy

Dean Street

Wardour Street

- Chisou

Silk •

Vasco & Piero's •

SOHO

Gt Marlborough Street

Byron •
Princi •

Aqua Kyoto •

Flat White •

Yautcha •

Hummus Bros •

Maddox Street

- Pollen St
- Hibiscus

Goodman •

Sketch (Lecture Room,
Parlour, & Gallery)

- Patterson's

theby's
Café

- Wild Honey

mu

Dehesa •

Mrs Marengos •

Beak Street

Fernandez & Wells •

Andrew Edmunds
Fernandez & Wells

Satsuma •

Randall & Aubin •
Yalla Yalla •

- Shampers
  • Polpo

Wright
Brothers

- Satsuma

Conduit Street

Regent Street

Berwick Street

- Square
- Hakkasan

Momo .

Brewer Street

Bocca di Lupo •

Gelupo

PICCADILLY
CIRCUS

Veeraswamy •

Regen

Sumosan •

Pigalle Club •

- Chor Bizarre

Cecconi's •

Bentley's • • Yoshino

Automat .

*Albermarle

•Nobu Berkeley

- Babbo

Berkeley Street

Piccadilly

- Rowley's
  Mitsukoshi,
  Toku

- Pescatori

Wiltons •

Jermyn Street

- Wolseley

angan's
rasserie •

- Matsuri

St James's Street

- Ritz

Caprice •

GREEN
PARK

Pall Mall

- Oranger

Green Park

ST JAMES'S

The Mall

MAP 3 - EAST SOHO, CHINATOWN & COVENT GARDEN

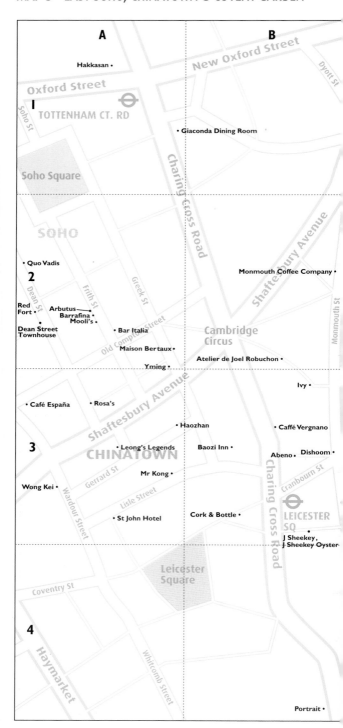

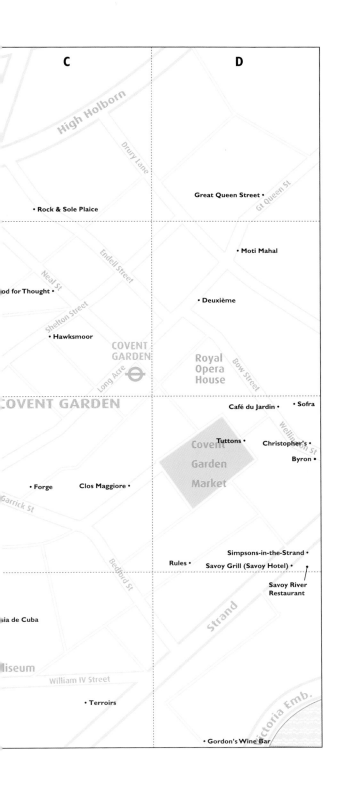

C

D

High Holborn

Drury Lane

Great Queen Street •

Gt Queen St

• Rock & Sole Plaice

Endell Street

Neal St

od for Thought •

Shelton Street

• Moti Mahal

• Deuxième

• Hawksmoor

**COVENT
GARDEN**

Long Acre

COVENT GARDEN

Royal
Opera
House

Bow Street

Café du Jardin •   • Sofra

Covent   Tuttons •   Christopher's •

Wellington St

Garden   Byron •

• Forge   Clos Maggiore •

Market

Garrick St

Bedford St

Simpsons-in-the-Strand •

Rules •   Savoy Grill (Savoy Hotel) •

Savoy River
Restaurant

sia de Cuba

Strand

liseum

William IV Street

• Terroirs

Victoria Emb.

• Gordon's Wine Bar

MAP 4 - KNIGHTSBRIDGE, CHELSEA & SOUTH KENSINGTON

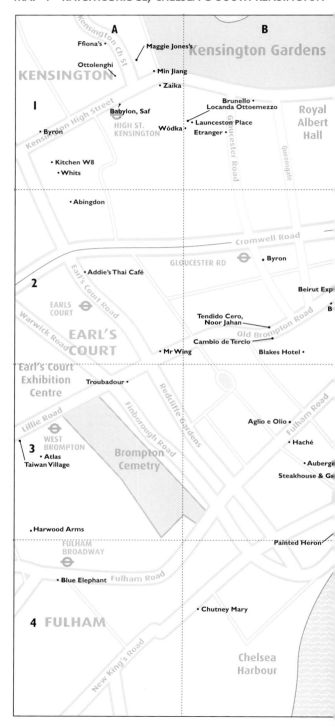

A

Ffiona's •

Maggie Jones's

Ottolenghi •

Kensington Gardens

B

KENSINGTON

Kensington Ch St

• Min Jiang

• Zaika

1

Babylon, Saf

Wódka •

Brunello •
Locanda Ottoemezzo
• Launceston Place
Etranger •

Royal
Albert
Hall

• Byron

Kensington High Street

HIGH ST.
KENSINGTON

Gloucester Road

Queensgate

• Kitchen W8
• Whits

• Abingdon

Cromwell Road

GLOUCESTER RD

• Byron

• Addie's Thai Café

2

Earl's Court Road

Beirut Exp

EARLS
COURT

Tendido Cero,
Noor Jahan

Old Brompton Road

B

Warwick Road

**EARL'S
COURT**

Cambio de Tercio

• Mr Wing

Blakes Hotel •

Earl's Court
Exhibition
Centre

Troubadour •

Redcliffe Gardens

Lillie Road

Finborough Road

Aglio e Olio •

Fulham Road

WEST
BROMPTON

3

• Atlas
Taiwan Village

**Brompton
Cemetery**

• Haché

• Aubergi

Steakhouse & Gr

• Harwood Arms

FULHAM
BROADWAY

Painted Heron

• Blue Elephant Fulham Road

• Chutney Mary

4 FULHAM

New King's Road

**Chelsea
Harbour**

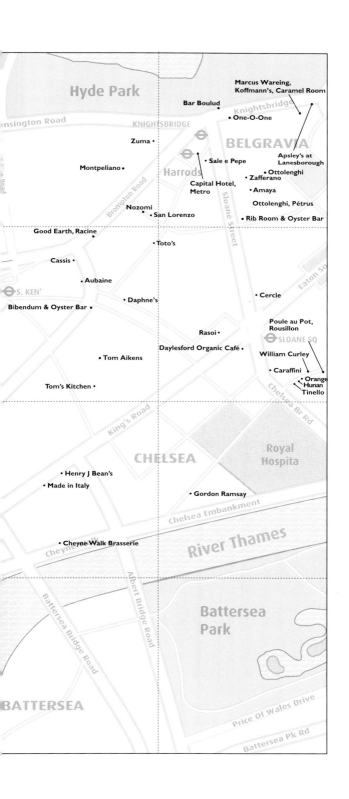

Hyde Park

Bar Boulud •

Knightsbridge

• One-O-One

KNIGHTSBRIDGE

Marcus Wareing,
Koffmann's, Caramel Room

ensington Road

Zuma •

BELGRAVIA

Apsley's at
Lanesborough

Montpeliano •

• Sale e Pepe

• Ottolenghi
• Zafferano

Harrods

Capital Hotel,
Metro

• Amaya

Ottolenghi, Pétrus

Nozomi •
• San Lorenzo

• Rib Room & Oyster Bar

Good Earth, Racine

•Toto's

Cassis •

• Aubaine

S. KEN'

• Daphne's

• Cercle

Bibendum & Oyster Bar •

Poule au Pot,
Rousillon

Rasoi •

SLOANE SQ

Daylesford Organic Café •

William Curley

• Tom Aikens

• Caraffini

• Orange
Hunan
Tinello

Tom's Kitchen •

CHELSEA

**Royal
Hospita**

King's Road

• Henry J Bean's
• Made in Italy

• Gordon Ramsay

Chelsea Embankment

• Cheyne Walk Brasserie

River Thames

**Battersea
Park**

Albert Bridge Road

Battersea Bridge Road

BATTERSEA

Price Of Wales Drive

Battersea Pk Rd

MAP 5 - NOTTING HILL & BAYSWATER

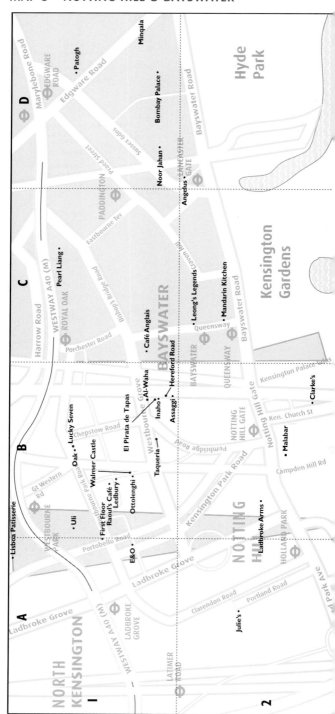

NORTH KENSINGTON

BAYSWATER

NOTTING HILL

Hyde Park

Kensington Gardens

- Lisboa Patisserie
- Pearl Liang •
- Oak •• Lucky Seven
- • Uli
- Walmer Castle
- First Floor
- Raoul's Café •
- Ledbury •
- • Ottolenghi
- Taqueria •
- El Pirata de Tapas
- E&O •
- • Al-Waha
- Inaho •
- Assaggi • • Hereford Road
- • Café Anglais
- • Leong's Legends
- • Mandarin Kitchen
- Noor Jahan •
- Angelus •
- Bombay Palace •
- • Patogh
- Minqala
- • Malabar
- • Clarke's
- Ladbroke Arms •
- Julie's •

Marylebone Road
EDGWARE ROAD
Edgware Road
LANCASTER GATE
Bayswater Road
Sussex Gdns
Praed Street
PADDINGTON
Eastbourne Ter
WESTWAY A40 (M)
Harrow Road
ROYAL OAK
Porchester Road
Bishop's Bridge Road
QUEENSWAY
Queensway
Bayswater Road
Westbourne Grove
Chepstow Road
Pembridge Road
Gt Western Rd
Eastbourne Park Road
WESTBOURNE PARK
Portobello Road
Ladbroke Grove
LADBROKE GROVE
Ladbroke Grove
LATIMER ROAD
WESTWAY A40 (M)
Kensington Park Road
Clarendon Road
Portland Road
Kensington Church St
Ken. Church St
NOTTING HILL GATE
Notting Hill Gate
Kensington Palace Gdns
Campden Hill Rd
HOLLAND PARK
Park Ave
Queen's ... Gate

A B C D
1
2

MAP 6 - HAMMERSMITH & CHISWICK

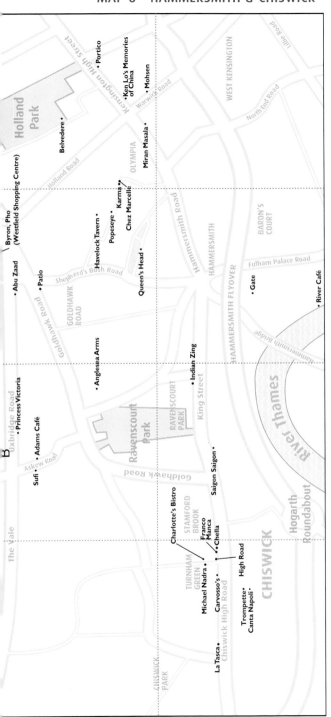

Holland Park

WEST KENSINGTON

Kensington High Street

• Byron, Pho
(Westfield Shopping Centre)

• Abu Zaad

• Portico

• Ken Lo's Memories
of China

• Mohsen

• Belvedere

Warwick Road

OLYMPIA

• Miran Masala

North End Road

Lillie Road

Holland Road

• Havelock Tavern

Popeseye • • Karma

• Chez Marcelle

Hammersmith Road

HAMMERSMITH

BARON'S
COURT

• Patio

Shepherd's Bush Road

• Queen's Head

Fulham Palace Road

GOLDHAWK
ROAD

Goldhawk Road

HAMMERSMITH FLYOVER

• Gate

• River Café

Hammersmith Bridge

River Thames

Uxbridge Road

• Princess Victoria

• Anglesea Arms

• Indian Zing

RAVENSCOURT
PARK

Sufi • • Adams Café

King Street

Askew Road

Ravenscourt
Park

Hogarth
Roundabout

The Vale

Goldhawk Road

STAMFORD
BROOK

Saigon Saigon •

Charlotte's Bistro

Franco
Manca

• Chella

CHISWICK

TURNHAM
GREEN

Michael Nadra •

• Carvosso's

• High Road

La Tasca •

Chiswick High Road

Trompette •
Canta Napoli •

CHISWICK
PARK

UK Survey Results
& Top Scorers

PLACES PEOPLE TALK ABOUT

These are the restaurants outside London that were mentioned most frequently by reporters (last year's position is shown in brackets). For the list of London's most mentioned restaurants, see page 33.

Waterside Inn

1. Fat Duck (1)
   Bray, Berks
2. Manoir aux Quat' Saisons (2)
   Great Milton, Oxon
3. Waterside Inn (3)
   Bray, Berks
4. Seafood Restaurant (5)
   Padstow, Cornwall
5. Hind's Head (4)
   Bray, Berks

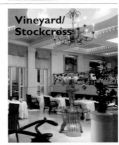

Star Inn

6. Northcote (10)
   Langho, Lancs
7= Star Inn (13=)
   Harome, N Yorks
7= Yang Sing (6)
   Manchester
9. Magpie (8)
   Whitby, N Yorks
10. Walnut Tree (-)
   Llandewi Skirrid, Monmouthshire

Vineyard/ Stockcross

11. Hix Oyster & Fish House (-)
   Lyme Regis, Dorset
12= Chapter One (9)
   Locksbottom, Kent
12= Vineyard/Stockcross (12)
   Stockcross, Berkshire
14= Gidleigh Park (13)
   Chagford, Devon
14= The Sportsman (-)
   Whitstable, Kent

Hambleton Hall

16= Kitchin (-)
   Edinburgh
16= Hambleton Hall (19=)
   Hambleton, Rutland
18. Champignon Sauvage (14)
   Cheltenham, Gloucs
19= The French Table (-)
   Surbiton, Surrey
19= Rick Stein's Café (14=)
   Padstow, Cornwall

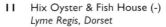

TOP SCORERS

All restaurants whose food rating is ✪✪; plus restaurants whose price is £50+ with a food rating of ✪.

£190+	The Fat Duck *(Bray)*	✪✪
£140+	Le Manoir aux Quat' Saisons *(Great Milton)*	✪✪Ⓐ
£130+	Waterside Inn *(Bray)*	✪✪
£120+	Gidleigh Park *(Chagford)*	✪✪Ⓐ
£100+	Lucknam Park *(Colerne)*	✪Ⓐ
	Andrew Fairlie *(Auchterarder)*	✪
	Midsummer House *(Cambridge)*	✪
£90+	Sharrow Bay *(Ullswater)*	✪✪Ⓐ
	Dining Room *(Easton Gray)*	✪✪
	Restaurant Sat Bains *(Nottingham)*	✪✪
	21212 *(Edinburgh)*	✪Ⓐ
	Restaurant Martin Wishart *(Edinburgh)*	✪
	Restaurant Nathan Outlaw *(Rock)*	✪
	Simon Radley *(Chester)*	✪
£80+	Hambleton Hall *(Hambleton)*	✪✪Ⓐ
	Summer Lodge *(Evershot)*	✪✪Ⓐ
	Bybrook Restaurant *(Castle Combe)*	✪✪
	L'Enclume *(Cartmel)*	✪✪
	Number One *(Edinburgh)*	✪✪
	Glenapp Castle *(Ballantrae)*	✪Ⓐ
	Colette's *(Chandler's Cross)*	✪
	Paris House *(Woburn)*	✪
£70+	Airds Hotel *(Port Appin)*	✪✪Ⓐ
	La Bécasse *(Ludlow)*	✪✪Ⓐ
	Northcote *(Langho)*	✪✪Ⓐ
	Seafood Restaurant *(Padstow)*	✪✪Ⓐ
	Simpsons *(Birmingham)*	✪✪Ⓐ
	The Albannach *(Lochinver)*	✪✪Ⓐ
	The Kitchin *(Edinburgh)*	✪✪Ⓐ
	The Three Chimneys *(Dunvegan)*	✪✪Ⓐ
	Yorke Arms *(Ramsgill-in-Nidderdale)*	✪✪Ⓐ
	36 on the Quay *(Emsworth)*	✪✪
	The Hambrough *(Ventnor)*	✪✪
	Bibury Court *(Bibury)*	✪Ⓐ
	Bohemia *(Jersey)*	✪Ⓐ
	Fawsley Hall *(Daventry)*	✪Ⓐ
	Gilpin Lodge *(Windermere)*	✪Ⓐ
	Lime Wood *(Lyndhurst)*	✪Ⓐ
	Ockenden Manor *(Cuckfield)*	✪Ⓐ
	Seafood Restaurant *(St Andrews)*	✪Ⓐ
	Summer Isles Hotel *(Achiltibuie)*	✪Ⓐ
	Harry's Place *(Great Gonerby)*	✪
	Holbeck Ghyll *(Windermere)*	✪
	Ocean Restaurant *(Jersey)*	✪
£60+	Braidwoods *(Dalry)*	✪✪Ⓐ
	Combe House *(Honiton)*	✪✪Ⓐ

TOP SCORERS

Hotel du Vin et Bistro *(Glasgow)*	★★★Ⓐ
Monachyle Mhor *(Balquhidder)*	★★★Ⓐ
Mr Underhill's *(Ludlow)*	★★★Ⓐ
Plas Bodegroes *(Pwllheli)*	★★★Ⓐ
The Box Tree *(Ilkley)*	★★★Ⓐ
Tyddyn Llan *(Llandrillo)*	★★★Ⓐ
5 North Street *(Winchcombe)*	★★
Anthony's *(Leeds)*	★★
Drakes *(Ripley)*	★★
Fischers at Baslow Hall *(Baslow)*	★★
Le Champignon Sauvage *(Cheltenham)*	★★
Plumed Horse *(Edinburgh)*	★★
Purnells *(Birmingham)*	★★
The Artichoke *(Amersham)*	★★
The Vanilla Pod *(Marlow)*	★★
Bluebells *(Sunningdale)*	★Ⓐ
Driftwood *(Rosevine)*	★Ⓐ
Green Inn *(Ballater)*	★Ⓐ
Hartwell House *(Aylesbury)*	★Ⓐ
Hipping Hall *(Kirkby Lonsdale)*	★Ⓐ
La Chouette *(Dinton)*	★Ⓐ
Little Barwick House *(Barwick)*	★Ⓐ
Samuel's *(Masham)*	★Ⓐ
The Castle Hotel *(Taunton)*	★Ⓐ
The Neptune *(Old Hunstanton)*	★Ⓐ
The Samling *(Windermere)*	★Ⓐ
Vintners Rooms *(Edinburgh)*	★Ⓐ
Darroch Learg *(Ballater)*	★
Michael Caines *(Exeter)*	★
Michael Caines *(Manchester)*	★
Moss Nook *(Manchester)*	★
Ramsons *(Ramsbottom)*	★
Thackeray's *(Tunbridge Wells)*	★
The Crown at Whitebrook *(Whitebrook)*	★
The Harrow at Little Bedwyn *(Marlborough)*	★
The Olive Tree *(Bath)*	★
Tony Tobin @ The Dining Room *(Reigate)*	★
Turners *(Birmingham)*	★
West Stoke House *(Chichester)*	★

£50+	Berwick Lodge *(Bristol)*	★★Ⓐ
	Feversham Arms *(Helmsley)*	★★Ⓐ
	Jeremy's at Borde Hill *(Haywards Heath)*	★★Ⓐ
	Lumière *(Cheltenham)*	★★Ⓐ
	The Old Passage Inn *(Arlingham)*	★★Ⓐ
	The Seafood Restaurant *(St Monans)*	★★Ⓐ
	The Wheatsheaf *(Bath)*	★★Ⓐ
	Tuscan Kitchen *(Rye)*	★★Ⓐ
	Fraiche *(Oxton)*	★★
	Gamba *(Glasgow)*	★★
	Goodfellows *(Wells)*	★★
	Gourmet Spot *(Durham)*	★★
	Ondine *(Edinburgh)*	★★
	Sienna *(Dorchester)*	★★
	The Fish House *(Chilgrove)*	★★
	The Seahorse *(Dartmouth)*	★★
	The Walnut Tree *(Llandewi Skirrid)*	★★

TOP SCORERS

West House *(Biddenden)*		✪✪
An Lochan *(Tighnabruaich)*		✪✪
Ardeonaig Hotel & Restaurant *(Killin)*		✪🅐
Brockencote Hall *(Chaddesley Corbett)*		✪🅐
Comme Ça *(Chichester)*		✪🅐
Crab & Lobster *(Asenby)*		✪🅐
Estbek House *(Sandsend)*		✪🅐
Grain Store *(Edinburgh)*		✪🅐
Hand & Flowers *(Marlow)*		✪🅐
Hix Oyster and Fish House *(Lyme Regis)*		✪🅐
Hotel Du Vin *(Newcastle upon Tyne)*		✪🅐
Hotel Tresanton *(St Mawes)*		✪🅐
Langar Hall *(Langar)*		✪🅐
Portmeirion Hotel *(Portmeirion)*		✪🅐
Restaurant Tristan *(Horsham)*		✪🅐
Russell's *(Broadway)*		✪🅐
Smiths Brasserie *(Ongar)*		✪🅐
Tanners Restaurant *(Plymouth)*		✪🅐
The Crab at Chieveley *(Newbury)*		✪🅐
The Loft Restaurant *(Beaumaris)*		✪🅐
The Sir Charles Napier *(Chinnor)*		✪🅐
The Star Inn *(Harome)*		✪🅐
Van Zeller *(Harrogate)*		✪🅐
Vatika *(Southampton)*		✪🅐
Whitstable Oyster Fishery Co. *(Whitstable)*		✪🅐
World Service *(Nottingham)*		✪🅐
60 Hope Street *(Liverpool)*		✪
Agaric *(Ashburton)*		✪
Allium *(Fairford)*		✪
Bosquet *(Kenilworth)*		✪
Calcot Manor (Gumstool Inn) *(Tetbury)*		✪
Cotto *(Cambridge)*		✪
Edmunds *(Birmingham)*		✪
Greens *(Whitby)*		✪
Jerichos *(Windermere)*		✪
La Potinière *(Gullane)*		✪
Lanterna *(Scarborough)*		✪
Miller Howe *(Bowness-on-Windermere)*		✪
Museum Inn *(Farnham)*		✪
Opus Restaurant *(Birmingham)*		✪
Restaurant Gilmore *(Uttoxeter)*		✪
Second Floor Restaurant *(Manchester)*		✪
Stock Hill House *(Gillingham)*		✪
Terravina *(Woodlands)*		✪
The Cellar *(Anstruther)*		✪
The Dining Room *(Ashbourne)*		✪
The Marquis *(Alkham)*		✪
The Restaurant At Drakes *(Brighton)*		✪
The Wensleydale Heifer *(West Witton)*		✪
Three Lions *(Stuckton)*		✪
Yew Tree Inn *(Newbury)*		✪
£40+	Chapter One *(Locksbottom)*	✪✪🅐
	Fat Olives *(Emsworth)*	✪✪🅐
	Gingerman *(Brighton)*	✪✪🅐
	Great House *(Lavenham)*	✪✪🅐
	Les Mirabelles *(Nomansland)*	✪✪🅐

TOP SCORERS

	Llys Meddyg (Newport)	✪✪Ⓐ
	No 7 Fish Bistro (Torquay)	✪✪Ⓐ
	Pebble Beach (Barton-on-Sea)	✪✪Ⓐ
	Porthminster Café (St Ives)	✪✪Ⓐ
	Sportsman (Whitstable)	✪✪Ⓐ
	Stagg Inn (Titley)	✪✪Ⓐ
	The Pipe & Glass Inn (Beverley)	✪✪Ⓐ
	Wheeler's Oyster Bar (Whitstable)	✪✪Ⓐ
	Wing's (Manchester)	✪✪Ⓐ
	Apicius (Cranbrook)	✪✪
	Culinaria (Bristol)	✪✪
	Dusit (Edinburgh)	✪✪
	J Baker's Bistro Moderne (York)	✪✪
	Loch Leven Seafood Cafe (Onich)	✪✪
	Maliks (Cookham)	✪✪
	Ostlers Close (Cupar)	✪✪
	Paul Ainsworth at No 6 (Padstow)	✪✪
	Roti (Edinburgh)	✪✪
	Royal Oak (White Waltham)	✪✪
	Simply Seafood (Leigh-on-Sea)	✪✪
	The Bildeston Crown (Bildeston)	✪✪
	The French Table (Surbiton)	✪✪
	The Westerly (Reigate)	✪✪
£30+	Aagrah (Bradford)	✪✪Ⓐ
	Aagrah (Leeds)	✪✪Ⓐ
	Anokaa (Salisbury)	✪✪Ⓐ
	Chiang Mai (Oxford)	✪✪Ⓐ
	El Gato Negro Tapas (Ripponden)	✪✪Ⓐ
	Michael's (Southport)	✪✪Ⓐ
	Quince & Medlar (Cockermouth)	✪✪Ⓐ
	Riverford Field Kitchen (Buckfastleigh)	✪✪Ⓐ
	Roz Ana (Kingston upon Thames)	✪✪Ⓐ
	The Art Kitchen (Warwick)	✪✪Ⓐ
	Aagrah (Shipley)	✪✪
	Baipo (Ipswich)	✪✪
	David Bann (Edinburgh)	✪✪
	Magpie Café (Whitby)	✪✪
	Mother India (Glasgow)	✪✪
	Punjab Tandoori (Manchester)	✪✪
	Rasa (Newcastle upon Tyne)	✪✪
	Terre à Terre (Brighton)	✪✪
	The Magdalen Arms (Oxford)	✪✪
	Vujon (Newcastle upon Tyne)	✪✪
£25+	Colman's (South Shields)	✪✪
	Hansa's (Leeds)	✪✪
£20+	Anstruther Fish Bar (Anstruther)	✪✪
	Bobby's (Leicester)	✪✪
	Mumtaz (Bradford)	✪✪
£15+	Cookies Crab Shop (Salthouse)	✪✪
	The Company Shed (West Mersea)	✪✪
£10+	Aldeburgh Fish And Chips (Aldeburgh)	✪✪
	This & That (Manchester)	✪✪

UK Directory

ABERAERON, CEREDIGION 4–3C

Harbourmaster £48
Quay Pde SA46 0BA (01545) 570755

"Superbly located on the waterfront of a beautiful town", this harbour-side inn "takes some beating" if you're looking for "fresh seafood and other quality local ingredients"; critics find it "pricey", though, and atmosphere can sometimes prove elusive.
/ **Details:** www.harbour-master.com; 9 pm; no Amex. **Accommodation:** 13 rooms, from £110.

The Hive On The Quay £36
Cadwgan Pl SA46 0BU (01545) 570445
A simple café, well-positioned near the water, that's tipped for its "big meaty sandwiches" and "hearty inventive soups".
/ **Details:** www.thehiveaberaeron.com; 9.00; closed Mon & Sun D; no Amex.

ABERDEEN, ABERDEENSHIRE 9–2D

Carmelite
Carmelite Hotel £38
Stirling St AB11 6JU (01224) 589101
"Good food and facilities" again win a tip for this city-centre hotel dining room. / **Details:** 10 pm; children: not under 5 afer 8pm. **Accommodation:** 50 rooms, from ££45.

Howies £33
50 Chapel St AB10 1SN (01224) 639500
A cosy city-centre bistro tipped for its sometimes "excellent" cuisine.
/ **Details:** www.howies.uk.com; 10 pm.

Silver Darling £59
Pocra Quay, North Pier AB11 5DQ (01224) 576229
"Fantastic views of ships going out from the harbour" only add to the experience of dining at this former lighthouse – the city's grandest restaurant, which serves "fresh, well-cooked fish".
/ **Details:** www.silverdarlingrestaurant.co.uk; beside harbour master's tower; 9 pm; closed Sat L & Sun; children: +16 after 8 pm.

ABERDYFI, GWYNEDD 4–3C

Penhelig Arms £37
LL35 0LT (01654) 767215
The nicely located estuarial inn has had the odd up and down since its take-over by Brains Brewery, but it's now "back on form"; it makes "a great place for a long weekend", with "excellent fresh seafood" a menu highlight. / **Details:** www.penheligarms.com; 9 pm; no Amex. **Accommodation:** 15 rooms, from £90.

Angel Hotel   £42   ⭐

15 Cross St NP7 5EN   (01873) 857121

"A real treat"; the attractively-updated dining room of this town-centre hotel offers some "serious" cooking, with highlights including "excellent" game and an "outstanding" cheeseboard (not to mention "the best afternoon tea anywhere").

/ **Details:** www.angelhotelabergavenny.com; 10 pm. **Accommodation:** 32 rooms, from £85.

The Hardwick   £42   ⭐

Old Raglan Rd NP7 9AA   (01873) 854220

Stephen Terry is establishing his "unpretentious" gastropub as one of South Wales's best-known destinations, thanks to its "quality" cuisine and "interesting wines"; ratings slipped across the board this year, though – perhaps adding the new 8-bedroom extension caused disruption? / **Details:** www.thehardwick.co.uk; 10 pm; closed Mon & Sun D; no Amex.

Duck's At Kilspindie   £41   🆃

East Lothian EH32 0RE   (01875) 870682

A "lovely old country house hotel" tipped for its "wonderful food, served with a smile". / **Details:** www.ducks.co.uk; Edinburgh 17 miles.
Accommodation: 23 rooms, from £150.

Gwesty Cymru   £43   ⭐

19 Marine Ter SY23 2AZ   (01970) 612252

"Especially worth knowing about in a poor area for food", this smart guesthouse is unanimously acclaimed for "excellent" food.
/ **Details:** www.gwestycymru.com; 9 pm; closed Tue L; no Amex; children: 8. **Accommodation:** 8 rooms, from £85.

Summer Isles Hotel   £72   🅰⭐

IV26 2YQ   (01854) 622282

"Marvellous fresh ingredients" are a particular strength of the dining room of this "remote" and "beautiful" waterside hotel; it's an "extremely well run" establishment all-round, with "superb breakfasts" a highlight. / **Details:** www.summerisleshotel.com; 25m N of Ullapool on A835; 8 pm; Closed from 1st Nov - 27 Mar; no Amex; children: 8+.
Accommodation: 13 rooms, from £145.

Moat House   £60   🅰

Lower Penkridge Rd ST17 0RJ   (01785) 712217

"A conservatory overlooking a canal" provides the "attractive" setting for this "great local" (which, thanks not least to its "useful" position near the M6, can sometimes get "horrendously busy"); "reliably good food" completes a "good-value" package.
/ **Details:** www.thelewispartnership.co.uk; Junction 13 off the M6, follow signs for A449; 9.30 pm. **Accommodation:** 41 rooms, from £150.

Planet Spice   £36   ⭐
88 Selsdon Park Rd CR2 8JT   (020) 8651 3300
*An "unlikely" but "happy" venue, offering a "contemporary and
surprising" subcontinental menu – there are some "fantastic" flavours
to be had, and at "very reasonable" prices too.*
/ **Details:** www.planet-spice.com; 11.30 pm.

ALBOURNE, WEST SUSSEX   3–4B

The Ginger Fox   £36
Henfield Rd BN6 9EA   (01273) 857 888

*An old petrol station converted a year ago
by Brighton's Gingerman group into
"a lovely gastropub", with a large garden
and "good, seasonal food"; early-days
results, though, have been a bit
"variable".*
/ **Details:** www.gingermanrestaurants.com;
10 pm, Sun 9 pm.

ALDEBURGH, SUFFOLK   3–1D

Aldeburgh Fish And Chips   £14   ⭐⭐
225 High St IP16 4BZ   (01728) 454685
*A legendary chippy, where the "spanking fresh fish" are "well worth the
queue" – "eat them on the sea wall, watching the anglers and the
passing ships".* / **Details:** 8 pm; no credit cards.

The Lighthouse   £37   Ⓐ
77 High St IP15 5AU   (01728) 453377
*Stick to the "wonderful fresh fish dishes", and you can eat well at this
"cheerful" seaside bistro – other dishes, however, can be "average".*
/ **Details:** www.thelighthouserestaurant.co.uk; 10 pm.

152   £38   Ⓐ
152 High St IP15 5AX   (01728) 454594
*A popular seaside restaurant that many reporters find a "wonderful"
destination for a "cosy" dinner; it's not entirely consistent, though,
and like last year, some meals of late have been positively
"disappointing".* / **Details:** www.152aldeburgh.co.uk; 10 pm.

Regatta   £38   Ⓐ
171-173 High St IP15 5AN   (01728) 452011
*"Possibly the best all-round local choice at the moment"; this long-
serving bistro offers a "largely unchanging" menu that's "mainly fish-
based and, if not hugely imaginative, always well-served".*
/ **Details:** www.regattaaldeburgh.com; 10 pm.

The Wentworth Hotel   £36   Ⓐ
Wentworth Rd IP15 5BD   (01728) 452312
*"Much better food that might be expected from a seaside hotel of this
type" – this "deceptively good" venue is tipped for its consistent
standards, and its "pleasant" surroundings.*
/ **Details:** www.wentworth-aldeburgh.com; 9 pm. **Accommodation:** 35 rooms,
from £139.

Konak £32 Ⓐ

27a London Rd SK9 7JT (01625) 581811

"In an area full of wine bars and grill-type eateries", this "small and welcoming" outfit "makes for an enjoyable change locally"; it proposes "Turkish staples with a bit more finesse than usual".
/ **Details:** www.konak.co.uk; 10 PM; D only, ex Sun open L & D; no Amex.

London Road £44 Ⓐ

46 London Rd SK9 7DZ (01625) 584163

"A busy place, with a nice buzz"; this popular brasserie is also almost invariably praised for its "good selection of interesting dishes"; a number of reporters, however, feel service is "a let down".
/ **Details:** www.heathcotes.co.uk; 10 pm, Fri & Sat 11 pm, Sun 9 pm; closed Mon.

The Grosvenor Arms £35 Ⓐ

Chester Rd CH3 6HJ (01244) 620228

"Picturesquely located" in a village on the edge of the Duke of Westminster's estate, this handsome and "comfortable" gastropub "gets all the basics right", including "a varied menu", "a good range of beers", and "helpful service"; beautiful garden too.
/ **Details:** www.grosvenorarms-aldford.co.uk; 6m S of Chester on B5130; 10 pm, Sun 9 pm.

The Marquis £56 ★

Alkham Valley Rd CT15 7DF (01304) 873410

This "minimalist" former pub in a "beautiful valley" is widely hailed as "a ray of brilliant sunshine in poorly-served south east Kent"; curiously, though, it's one of those places where even very favourable reports often come with an irritating 'niggle' – perhaps why critics many find the experience "over-hyped".
/ **Details:** www.themarquisatalkham.co.uk; 9.30 pm; closed Mon L & Sun D.
Accommodation: 5 rooms, from ££95.

The Tree House Ⓐ
The Alnwick Garden £38

Denwick Ln NE66 1YU (01665) 511852

"A ray of sunshine in what's otherwise a rather dismal dining area", this elegantly Disneyfied adjunct to the Duchess's new garden can make an "amazing" focal point to a "different day out"; "it's worth it for the arboreal experience", says one reporter, but the "standard" food is "pretty good" too, considering. / **Details:** www.alnwickgarden.com; 9.15 pm; closed Sun-Wed D; no Amex.

Dilli £32 Ⓐ

60 Stamford New Rd WA14 1EE (0161) 929 7484

"Excellent when on form, but the inconsistency is maddening"; this Altrincham restaurant is still hailed by some locals as "the best Indian restaurant in the North West of England" – to others, though, it's "resting on somewhat faded laurels".
/ **Details:** www.dilli.co.uk; on A538; 11 pm, Sun 10 pm.

(T)

Baraset Barn   £41
Pimlico Ln CV37 7RJ (01789) 295510
A "stunningly-converted" tithe barn, tipped for its "high quality gastropub-style food", and its "reasonable wine list".
/ **Details:** www.barasetbarn.co.uk; 9.30 pm; closed Sun D; no Amex.

(A)

Amberley Castle   £85
BN18 9LT (01798) 831992
"Drinks taken in the garden, amid the ruins" set the tone at this "magical" castle, which comes complete with peacocks, portcullis and "well-manicured grounds"; the fact that the food tends to "underwhelming" doesn't seem to prevent this from being a "superb" experience overall. / **Details:** www.amberleycastle.co.uk; N of Arundel on B2139; 9 pm; jacket or tie required; booking: max 8; children: 12+. **Accommodation:** 19 rooms, from £190.

(A) (★)

Britannia Inn   £38
Elterwater LA22 9HP (01539) 437210
A "quaint" (and "cramped") walker's pub in a "stunning" setting, where the food is "hearty" and "good value"; sit outside, and you get "great views" too. / **Details:** www.britinn.co.uk; 9.30 pm; no Amex; children: 18+ after 9 pm. **Accommodation:** 9 rooms, from £90.

(A)

Drunken Duck   £52
Barngates LA22 0NG (01539) 436347
A "perfect setting" with "beautiful views" (and "lovely rooms" too) contributes to the great popularity of this famous Lakeland inn-cum-microbrewery (which is, of course, particularly "busy at weekends"); the food has its fans too, but seems to play something of a supporting role. / **Details:** www.drunkenduckinn.co.uk; 3m from Ambleside, towards Hawkshead; 9 pm; no Amex; no trainers; booking: max 6. **Accommodation:** 17 rooms, from £95.

(X)

The Glass House   £39
Rydal Rd LA22 9AN (01539) 432137
"A terrific welcome" adds to the ambience of this "busy" converted mill; it's still something of a 'name' in these parts, but the food seems to have become "very variable" again of late – "come back Gordon, all is forgiven!". / **Details:** www.theglasshouserestaurant.co.uk; behind Little Bridge House; 9.30 pm, Sat 10 pm; no Amex; children: 5+ at D.

(A)

Lucy's on a Plate   £43
Church St LA22 0BU (01539) 431191
"Not quite as good as it was before the various expansions, but we keep coming back!"; this "personal and quirky" bistro is "as comforting as visiting a great aunt for tea", and serves up a "varied menu of good, local food" (including "puddings worth a 100-mile drive!").
/ **Details:** www.lucysofambleside.co.uk; centre of Ambleside; 9 pm.

(A)

Zeffirelli's   £35
Compston Rd LA22 9AD (01539) 433845
"With a 3-screen cinema and excellent jazz at weekends", this "slick" operation is "a great venue", serving "tasty" vegetarian food majoring in "excellent pizza and pasta". / **Details:** www.zeffirellis.com; 10 pm; no Amex.

The Artichoke £62 ⭐⭐
9 Market Sq HP7 0DF (01494) 726611
"Roaring back after the fire" – this *"tiny"* but ambitious restaurant
is back with a bang, offering *"perfectly judged"* Gallic cuisine from
a seasonal menu. / **Details:** www.theartichokerestaurant.co.uk; 10 pm; closed
Mon & Sun; no Amex; no shorts.

Gilbey's £48 Ⓐ
1 Market Sq HP7 0DF (01494) 727242
*This "cramped", "rustic-chic" bistro is invariably described as a
"pleasant" place to eat, thanks to its "wonderfully cheerful" staff,
"competent" fare and "fairly-priced" vino.* / **Details:** www.gilbeygroup.com;
in Old Amersham; 9.30 pm, Sat 9.45 pm.

Anstruther Fish Bar £23 ⭐⭐
42-44 Shore St KY10 3AQ (01333) 310518
"As fresh as it gets for fish and chips", this famous institution is a
"must-try"; *"don't eat in, though, but rather sit on a bench overlooking
the harbour"*. / **Details:** www.anstrutherfishbar.co.uk; 10 pm; no Amex;
no booking.

The Cellar £57 ⭐
24 East Grn KY10 3AA (01333) 310378

"Consistently first-class seafood" continues to inspire many rave reviews
for Peter & Susan Jukes's *"quirky"* family-run basement, near the
harbour; for the occasional critic, though, its appeal is becoming a little
"dated". / **Details:** www.cellaranstruther.co.uk; in the harbour area; 9 pm; closed
Mon & Sun.

Applecross Inn £32 ⭐
Shore St IV54 8LT (01520) 744262
"Worth the long drive", this *"remote"* inn is an *"efficient"* operation,
which has long been of note for its *"perfect"* seafood dishes.
/ **Details:** www.applecross.uk.com; off A896, S of Shieldaig; 9 pm; no Amex;
need 6+ to book. **Accommodation:** 7 rooms, from £90.

Kilberry Inn £45 Ⓐ⭐
Nr Tarbert PA29 6YD (01880) 770223
"On a single track road miles from anywhere", a *"friendly"* and
"professional" inn that's *"worth the long drive"* – its *"sensitive"* cuisine
"gives top-quality ingredients the chance to shine", and is
complemented by a wine list that's eclectic and *"reasonably-priced"*.
/ **Details:** www.kilberryinn.com; 9 pm; closed Mon; no Amex; no trainers;
children: 6+. **Accommodation:** 5 rooms, from £195.

Ⓐ ⭐⭐

The Old Passage Inn   £52
Passage Rd GL2 7JR (01452) 740547
*It's not just the "marvellous setting on the banks of the River Severn"
that makes it worth seeking out this "amazing" inn – its speciality,
seafood, is some of "the finest in the country".*
/ **Details:** www.theoldpassage.com; 9 pm; closed Mon & Sun D.
Accommodation: 3 rooms, from £80.

Ⓐ ⭐

Arundel House   £41
11 High St BN18 9AD (01903) 882136
*"A lovely, first-class restaurant in the heart of the town" – the dining
room at this small boutique hotel near the castle wins all-round praise
for its "wonderful" food and its "lovely" ambience, as well as service
that shows "impressive attention to detail".*
/ **Details:** www.arundelhouseonline.com; 9.30 pm; closed Sun; children: 12+
D. **Accommodation:** 5 rooms, from £80.

Ⓐ ⭐

The Town House   £41
65 High St BN18 9AJ (01903) 883847
*"A superb, small local restaurant", in a Regency townhouse overlooking
Arundel Castle; it is unanimously praised by reporters for its
"very accomplished food, delivered with great bonhomie".*
/ **Details:** www.thetownhouse.co.uk; 9.30 pm; closed Mon & Sun.
Accommodation: 4 rooms, from £85.

⭐

Ascot Oriental   £48
London Rd SL5 0PU (01344) 621877
*"A welcome surprise"; Konrad Liu's "absolute winner" of a venture
offers "superb, freshly-cooked" Chinese food; it is "served well" too,
and "with a minimum of fuss".* / **Details:** www.ascotoriental.com; 2m E
of Ascot on A329; 10.30 pm.

Ⓐ ⭐

Crab & Lobster   £53
Dishforth Rd YO7 3QL (01845) 577286
*"The totally wacky ambiance doesn't detract from the high-quality food"
– with "excellent" fish the highlight – at this knick-knack-stuffed
thatched pub.* / **Details:** www.crabandlobster.co.uk; at junction of Asenby Rd &
Topcliffe Rd; 9 pm, 9.30 pm Sat. **Accommodation:** 14 rooms, from £150.

⭐

The Dining Room   £55
33 St. John's St DE6 1GP (01335) 300666
*"A gastronomic tour de force" – this small restaurant in the heart
of the town generates only limited feedback, but all to the effect that
it's "the best place for miles around".*
/ **Details:** www.thediningroomashbourne.co.uk; D only, closed Mon & Sun;
no Amex; children: 12+.

ASHBURTON, DEVON   1–3D

Agaric   £55
30 North St TQ13 7QD   (01364) 654478
*"A small and cosy spot in a pretty village"; the menu may
be "straightforward", but most reporters highly recommend the
"fantastic seasonal food", from "excellent local ingredients".*
/ **Details:** www.agaricrestaurant.co.uk; 9.30 pm; closed Mon, Tue, Sat L & Sun;
no Amex. **Accommodation:** 5 rooms, from £110.

ASTON TIRROLD, OXFORDSHIRE   2–2D

Sweet Olive   £45
Baker St OX11 9DD   (01235) 851272
*"Well worth a detour"; this Gallic-run gastropub wins consistent praise
for its often-"excellent" cuisine.* / **Details:** www.sweet-olive.com; Half a mile
off the A417 between Streatley & Wantage; 9 pm; closed Feb.

AUCHTERARDER, PERTH AND KINROSS   9–3C

Andrew Fairlie
Gleneagles Hotel   £108
PH3 1NF (01764) 694267
*Andrew Fairlie's "extraordinary"
cooking ("with great use of local
produce") – complemented by a
"varied, global wine list" – makes a
visit to this darkly-decorated room,
in the bowels of the famous hotel, a
"perfect dining experience"; portions,
though, can sometimes seem a
tad "meagre".*

/ **Details:** www.andrewfairlie.com;
10 pm; L only, closed Sun; children:
12+. **Accommodation:** 273 rooms,
from £320.

AVIEMORE, INVERNESSHIRE   9–2C

Mountain Cafe   £18
111 Grampian Rd PH22 1RH   (01479) 812473
*"Obscurely located above a sports shop, but with amazing views over
the Cairngorms", this "popular little café" is tipped not only for its
"awesome breakfasts" and a "huge array of cakes", but also for its
"quirky" snacks ("in portions to feed an army").*
/ **Details:** www.mountaincafe-aviemore.co.uk; Village centre; L only; no Amex.

AXMINSTER, DEVON   2–4A

River Cottage Canteen   £36
Trinity Sq EX13 5AN   (01297) 631862
*The "homespun", "relaxed" and "family-friendly" canteen-annex
of Hugh Fearnley-Whittingstall's food store; it's decidedly nothing special
on the service or ambience fronts, but the "rustic" food is "honest",
and comes in "massive portions".* / **Details:** www.rivercottage.net; 9.30 pm;
closed Mon D, Tue D, Wed D & Sun D.

A ⭐

Hartwell House   £64
Oxford Rd HP17 8NR   (01296) 747444
For the full-blown "great country house experience", you won't do much better than Louis XVIII's one-time refuge in exile, which is nowadays owned by the National Trust – practically all reports attest to its dining room's "brilliant" all-round performance.
/ **Details:** www.hartwell-house.com; 2m W of Aylesbury on A418; 9.45 pm; no jeans or trainers; children: 4+. **Accommodation:** 49 rooms, from £260.

T

Hengist   £33
7-9 High St ME20 7AX   (01622) 719273
"Locally-sourced and well-cooked" Gallic dishes make this "stylish" Tudor-housed restaurant a top local tip; did YOU know this in "the oldest village in Britain"? / **Details:** www.hengistrestaurant.co.uk; 10.30 pm; closed Mon & Sun D.

A

Babington House   £55
BA11 3RW   (01373) 812266
"Still the contemporary country house hotel to beat"; this "exceptionally situated" outpost of the trendy Soho House empire may sometimes seem to be "more characterised by enthusiasm than talent", but the setting is "luxurious", and the overall formula almost invariably pleases.
/ **Details:** www.babingtonhouse.co.uk; 11 pm; open to residents & members only; children: 16+ in the Orangery. **Accommodation:** 32 rooms, from £260.

A

The Latymer
Pennyhill Park Hotel   £89
London Rd GU19 5EU   (01276) 471774
"The only really serious dining room in these parts", this "stylish" and "serene" country house hotel pleases most reporters, not least with its assured (if occasionally ""over-exuberant"") cuisine, and its "attentive" service. / **Details:** www.exclusivehotels.co.uk; 9.30 pm; closed Mon, Sat L & Sun; booking: max 8; children: 11. **Accommodation:** 123 rooms, from £195.

A

The Monsal Head Hotel   £39
DE45 1NL   (01629) 640250
"This beautifully-situated hotel/pub" has "peerless" views over a disued railway viaduct; its dining room (there's also a "fun" bar) serves an "eclectic" menu of "excellent-value" dishes, plus "a great selection of ales". / **Details:** www.monsalhead.com; Just up from Ashford in the Water on the B6465; 9.30 pm, Sat & Sun 9 pm; no Amex. **Accommodation:** 7 rooms, from £90.

A ⭐

Piedaniels   £36
Bath St DE45 1BX   (01629) 812687
"A delightful place hidden-away in one of the most beautiful villages in England"; this smart, Gallic-run newcomer comes strongly recommended for its "well-chosen menu using seasonal produce", and at "value-for-money" prices too.
/ **Details:** www.piedaniels-restaurant.com; 10.15 pm; closed Mon.

Glenapp Castle £83 🅐⭐
KA26 0NZ (01465) 831212

*A magnificent-looking castle with "top-flight" cuisine, "professional" service and "lovely reception and dining rooms"; feedback is limited – perhaps because diners are largely limited to those staying – but all very complimentary. / **Details:** www.glenappcastle.com; 9.30 pm; D only; children: 5+ after 7PM. **Accommodation:** 17 rooms, from £445.*

BALLATER, ABERDEENSHIRE 9–3C ⭐

Darroch Learg £65
Braemar Rd AB35 5UX (01339) 755443
*"Superb" food served in a "lovely peaceful atmosphere" is a combination which has long made this country house hotel a "favourite" for some reporters – it remains so, but the occasional critic can find the formula a little "dull" nonetheless. / **Details:** www.darrochlearg.co.uk; on A93 W of Ballater; 9 pm; D only, ex Sun open L & D; no Amex. **Accommodation:** 12 rooms, from £130.*

Green Inn £60 🅐⭐
9 Victoria Rd AB35 5QQ (01339) 755701
*The "beautiful" cooking at this "impressively professional" restaurant-with-rooms inspires the most positive reports; most (if not quite all) reporters really take to the ambience of the conservatory dining room too. / **Details:** www.green-inn.com; in centre of village, on the green; 9 pm; D only, closed Mon & Sun; no Amex; no shorts. **Accommodation:** 3 rooms, from £60.*

BALQUHIDDER, PERTH AND KINROSS 9–3C 🅐⭐⭐

Monachyle Mhor £66 🅐⭐⭐
FK19 8PQ (01877) 384622
*"Out-of-this-world"; Tom Lewis's "delightful" restaurant-with-rooms, in the Trossachs National Park, is "worth the long and tortuous loch-side drive"; the cuisine is "most inventive" in its approach, and outstanding in its execution. / **Details:** www.mhor.net; Take the Kings House turning off the A84; 8.45 pm; children: 12+ at D. **Accommodation:** 14 rooms, from £128.*

BANBURY, OXFORDSHIRE 2–1D

Sheesh Mahal £32 🅣
43 South Bar St OX16 9AB (01295) 266489
*A local curry house in a period building tipped for its "top-notch" Indian cooking. / **Details:** www.sheeshmahalbanbury.co.uk; midnight; D only.*

Thai Orchid £35 🅣
56 Northbar St OX16 0TL (01295) 270833
*A self-explanatory tip for those in search of a "solid and consistent eatery" in what's otherwise "a bit of a foodie desert". / **Details:** www.thaiorchidbanbury.co.uk; 10.30 pm.*

T

Glenskirlie House £32
Kilsyth Rd FK4 1UF (01324) 840201
"Hasn't been on the Harden's radar, but this is the best eating place within 15 miles of Glasgow!" – this small castle-boutique-hotel is tipped as a good-all-rounder; choose between 'fine dining' and the more relaxed Castle Grill. / *Details:* www.glenskirliehouse.com.

★

Emchai £29
78 High St EN5 5SN (020) 8364 9993
"A hidden gem", whose "sophisticated" oriental-fusion dishes, impress all who comment on it. / *Details:* 11 pm.

★

Savoro £38
206 High St EN5 5SZ (020) 8449 9888
It certainly doesn't have a glamorous location, but this "quiet" and "intimate" restaurant is "the best in this part of the world", attracting praise from most reporters for both its "lovely meat dishes" and its "excellent fresh fish, perfectly cooked". / *Details:* www.savoro.co.uk; 10.30 pm; closed Sun D. **Accommodation:** 11 rooms, from £75.

T

The Village Pub £41
GL7 5EF (01285) 740421
"If you don't mind the Cotswold Set", this posh gastropub – associated with nearby Barnsley House – is tipped for its "quality" cuisine. / *Details:* www.thevillagepub.co.uk; 9.30 pm. **Accommodation:** 6 rooms, from £95.

A ★

Barrasford Arms £38
NE48 4AA (01434) 681237
A departure from standard North Eastern pub fare! – "the very best is made of local produce", at this "unexpectedly good" gastropub, which is very much off the beaten track. / *Details:* www.barrasfordarms.co.uk; 9 pm; closed Mon L & Sun D; no Amex; children: 18 + in bar after 9.30pm. **Accommodation:** 7 rooms, from £85.

A ★ ★

Pebble Beach £48
Marine Drive BH25 7DZ (01425) 627777
Pierre Chevillard's "fantastically fresh" seafood dishes ("and good choice for meat-eaters too") make it hard to fault this notably "trustworthy" cliff-top all-rounder; it enjoys "lovely views of the Isle of Wight" too. / *Details:* www.pebblebeach-uk.com; 9 pm, Fri & Sat 9.30 pm; booking essential. **Accommodation:** 3, 1 penthouse rooms, from £89.95.

A ★

Little Barwick House £60
BA22 9TD (01935) 423902
"A beautiful Georgian dower house" provides the "delightful" setting for this "comfortable and well-run" restaurant-with-rooms – "a super place with wonderful food and tip-top service". / *Details:* www.littlebarwick.co.uk; Take the A37 Yeovil to Dorchester road, turn left at the brown sign for Little Barwick House; Tue-Fri 9 pm, Sat 9.30 pm; closed Mon, Tue L & Sun D; no Amex; children: 5+ . **Accommodation:** 6 rooms, from £69 pp.

Cavendish   £50

Church Ln DE45 1SP   (01246) 582311
This Chatsworth Estate hotel is still popular, not least for its "fantastic" views; its "country house style" can seem a little "dated" nowadays, however, to the extent that some long-term fans now find it "a little disappointing". / **Details:** *www.cavendish-hotel.net; J29 of the M1, follow tourist signs to Chatsworth; 10 pm; no jeans or shorts.* **Accommodation:** *24 rooms, from £163.*

Fischers at Baslow Hall   £68

Calver Rd DE45 1RR   (01246) 583259

A corner seems — finally — to have been turned, and there are once again many reports of "wonderful food", and "a real sense of occasion too", at this "beautiful country house hotel"; until a few years ago, it was among the the most celebrated in the UK — it now looks as if it may become so again. / **Details:** *www.fischers-baslowhall.co.uk; on the A623 ; 9 pm; closed Mon L & Sun D; no jeans or trainers; children: 9+ at D, L (except Sun).* **Accommodation:** *11 rooms, from £150.*

Rowley's   £42

Church Ln DE45 1RY   (01246) 583880
This "welcoming", "simple", and "understated" brasserie is still often praised for its "thoroughly enjoyable" cuisine; one or two regulars, however, sense a "lack of verve" of late.
/ **Details:** *www.rowleysrestaurant.co.uk; 9 pm, Fri & Sat 10 pm; closed Sun D; no Amex.*

Bath Priory Hotel   £93

Weston Rd BA1 2XT   (01225) 331922
Nowadays branded as an outpost of the Michael Caines empire, the dining room of this "tranquil and cosy" country house hotel is still "a real treat"; since Chris Horridge left last year, though, there has been a "slight decline" in standards, and the ambience has become more "formal". / **Details:** *www.thebathpriory.co.uk; 1m W of city centre, past Victoria Park; 9.30 pm; no jeans or trainers; children: 8+ D.*
Accommodation: *31 rooms, from £260.*

Casanis   £42

4 Saville Row BA1 2QP   (01225) 780055
"Simple", "elegant", "delicious", "refined" — these are the sort of adjectives reporters tend to apply to this "genuine" Gallic bistro, which almost all reporters agree is "well worth a visit".
/ **Details:** *www.casanis.co.uk; 10.30 pm; closed Mon & Sun; no Amex.*

The Circus £42 ⭐

34 Brock St BA1 2LN (01225) 466020

"Imaginative cooking served with a smile" makes this *"intimate"* yearling, near the Royal Crescent, *"well worth seeking out"*; a couple of 'dud' meals have been recorded of late, but the more prevalent impression is that *"early high standards have been maintained"*. / **Details:** www.thecircuscafeandrestaurant.co.uk; 10 pm; closed Sun; children: 7+ at D.

Demuths £41 Ⓐ

2 North Parade Pas BA1 1NX (01225) 446059

"Lovely veggie food" still makes this city-centre veteran a popular destination for many reporters; service can be *"slow"*, though, and – by its usual inspiring standards – the cooking has sometimes seemed rather *"nondescript"* of late. / **Details:** www.demuths.co.uk; 9 pm, Sat & Sun 10 pm; no Amex; booking: max 12.

The Dower House Royal Crescent Hotel £89 Ⓐ

16 Royal Cr BA1 2LS (01225) 823333

Sitting in view of the secluded gardens helps make it a "very civilised experience" to eat in this part-of-a-landmark hotel; "nothing matches up to the building in terms of quality", though, and critics can still find the experience "ridiculously overpriced". / **Details:** www.royalcrescent.co.uk; 9.30 pm; no jeans or trainers; booking: max 8. **Accommodation:** 45 rooms, from £235.

The Eastern Eye £34 Ⓣ

8a Quiet St BA1 2JS (01225) 422323

"Great after the rugby…", "good post-theatre…" – this handy Indian, in a grand Georgian chamber, attracts a very broad crowd, and is always *"buzzing"*. / **Details:** www.easterneye.co.uk; 11.30 pm.

Firehouse Rotisserie £42 Ⓣ

2 John St BA1 2JL (01225) 482070

"Great stone-fired pizza" wins a tip for this *"lively"* spot, handily located in the city-centre. / **Details:** www.firehouserotisserie.co.uk; 11 pm; closed Sun.

The Garrick's Head £38 Ⓐ

7-8 St. John's Pl BA1 1ET (01225) 318368

"A great place to relax", and with notably *"jolly"* staff – this city-centre gastropub scores hits and misses on the food front, but is particularly worth remembering for its *"good-value, pre-theatre menus"*. / **Details:** www.garricksheadpub.com; 10 pm; closed Sun D.

Hole in the Wall £43 Ⓐ

16 George St BA1 2EN (01225) 425242

"A few tweaks could restore this old-timer to its former glory" – so say fans of this quirky basement (made famous in the '50s by path-breaking chef George Perry-Smith); the cooking can be *"rather average"*, but this is a *"cosy"* place (*"with a lovely big fire"*), and it's *"always busy"*. / **Details:** www.theholeinthewall.co.uk; 10 pm, Sun 9.30 pm.

The Hop Pole £35 Ⓣ
7 Albion Buildings, Upper Bristol Rd BA1 3AR (01225) 446327
*Tipped for "imaginative food", and "good beer" too – this park-view boozer doesn't try too hard, but reporters invariably seem to leave pretty satisfied. / **Details:** www.bathales.com; opp Victoria Park; 9 pm, Sat 9.30 pm; closed Sun D.*

Jamie's Italian £38 Ⓐ
10 Milsom Pl BA1 1BZ (01225) 510051
*Jamie O's name over the door has made this "fun and buzzy" outpost of his growing chain the most reported-on place in town; its ratings are heading south, though – while fans say the "simple" Italian food is still "well above general chain standards", others are beginning to find it "lazy" and "overpriced". / **Details:** www.jamiesitalian.com; 11 pm, Sun 10.30 pm.*

King William £42 ★
36 London Rd BA1 5NN (01225) 428096
*"What a great find"; it's a "cramped" place that's "nothing fancy in the decor stakes", but this "truly wonderful traditional gastropub" serves "great food" made from "quality local foodstuffs", and "superb ales" too. / **Details:** www.kingwilliampub.com; 10 pm; closed Mon L.*

Moon & Sixpence £48 Ⓐ
27 Milsom Pl BA1 1BZ (01225) 320088
*"After a thorough make-over", this multi-level modern restaurant looks "lovely"; fans says it's "back on form" too, but even they may concede that the food is "standard", and it's certainly "not cheap". / **Details:** 10 pm, Fri & Sat10.30 pm; no Amex.*

The Olive Tree
Queensberry Hotel £62 ★
Russell St BA1 2QF (01225) 447928
*A "buzzy" and quite "stylish" boutique-hotel dining room, which lives up to its long-standing reputation for "talented" cooking; one or two reporters finds the culinary approach "fussy" though, and the "dark" basement location sometimes disappoints. / **Details:** www.thequeensberry.co.uk; 9.45 pm; closed Mon L.*
Accommodation: *29 rooms, from £125.*

The Pump Room £43 Ⓣ
Stall St BA1 1LZ (01225) 444477
*"Very average" and "expensive" food is served "rather amateurishly" in the space that's been at the heart of Bath's social life for over two centuries; why list it then? – the "spectacular" Georgian chamber itself is very much "worth the trip". / **Details:** www.searcys.co.uk; by the Abbey; L only; no booking, Sat & Sun.*

Rajpoot £36 Ⓐ
4 Argyle St BA2 4BA (01225) 466833
*"Staff are so sweet and obliging", and the food's good too, at this atmospheric Indian basement, intriguingly housed in a huge Georgian cellar. / **Details:** www.rajpoot.com; 11 pm.*

The Wheatsheaf £51 Ⓐ★★
Combe Hay BA2 7EG (01225) 833504
*In a glorious countryside ten minutes from the city-centre, this "trendy" but "relaxed" pub-with-rooms again wins impressively high ratings from reporters – the locally-sourced food is "spot-on", the wine list "fantastic" and the 18th century inn itself (with large gardens) "lovely". / **Details:** www.wheatsheafcombehay.com; 9.30 pm; closed Mon & Sun D; no Amex.* **Accommodation:** *4 rooms, from £105.*

The White Hart Inn   £37

Widcombe Hill BA2 6AA   (01225) 338053

"Peacefully located in a pleasant back street, tucked-away behind the railway station", this gastropub-with-rooms ("wooden tables and chairs, stripped floor") offers "straightforward" food at "reasonable prices".
/ **Details:** www.whitehartbath.co.uk; 10 pm; closed Sun D; no Amex.
Accommodation: 4 private, 24 dormitory beds rooms, from ££25.

Yen Sushi   £20

11 Bartlett St BA1 2QZ   (01225) 333313

"Very decent sushi" (from the conveyor) wins tips from locals for this "cheap and cheerful" Japanese café. / **Details:** www.yensushi.co.uk; 10.30 pm.

BAUGHURST, HAMPSHIRE   2–3D

The Wellington Arms   £44

Baughurst Rd RG26 5LP   (0118) 982 0110

![interior of the Wellington Arms restaurant]

"A friendly country restaurant with good rustic food and friendly service"; some of the sourcing is hyper-local, and even the sole reporter who didn't go a bundle on the place concedes that "the freshness of the food was memorable". / **Details:** www.thewellingtonarms.com; 9.30 pm; closed Sun D; no Amex.

BAWTRY, SOUTH YORKSHIRE   5–2D

China Rose   £34

16 South Pde DN10 6JH   (01302) 710461

"Great-quality food" wins consistently positive reports on this "surprisingly huge", but "pleasant", rural Chinese of long standing, which is still "the best of its type in the area".
/ **Details:** www.chinarose-bawtry.co.uk; 10 pm, Fri & Sat 10.30 pm; D only.

BEACONSFIELD, BUCKINGHAMSHIRE   3–3A

Crazy Bear   £50

HP9 1LX   (01494) 673086

It's the "weird" and "sexy" vibe of this bordello-style restaurant-with-rooms ("so dark we needed a torch!") which most makes this "amazing" venue worth seeking out; most reporters say the Thai cuisine is "excellent" too, but sceptics find it "hyped" and "overpriced".
/ **Details:** www.crazybeargroup.co.uk/beaconsfield; 10 pm; no Amex; children: Bar, not after 6pm. **Accommodation:** 10 rooms, from ££345.

Leigh House   £34

53 Wycombe End HP9 1LX   (01494) 676348

"Fabulous" food makes this elegantly-housed Chinese veteran popular with all who comment on it; service also attracts very favourable reports. / **Details:** www.leigh-house.co.uk; 10.30 pm.

Spice Merchant £45 **Ⓐ ✪**

33 London End HP9 2HW   (01494) 675474

"No flock wallpaper here!"; this "outstanding modern Indian" (which even has a "stunning" garden) wins rave reviews from the locals for its "sumptuous and imaginative food, and friendly service".

/ **Details:** www.spicemerchantgroup.com; opp Beaconsfield wine cellar; 11 pm, Sun 9.30 pm.

BEAMINSTER, DORSET   2–4B

The Wild Garlic £37 **Ⓐ**

4 The Sq DT8 3AS   (01308) 861446

As the name hints, there's a touch of the "rustic" at Mat Follas's "welcoming" restaurant in a "beautiful town"; most reporters find it "a great place to eat" with "superb" food, but a couple say it "can miss the mark", or "needs better front of house".

/ **Details:** www.thewildgarlic.co.uk.

BEARSTED, KENT   3–3C

Soufflé £46 **Ⓐ**

31 The Green ME14 4DN   (01622) 737065

Fans nominate this "relaxed" restaurant, "delightfully situated" on Bearstead Green as a "hidden treasure in the depths of Kent"; reports are polarised, though, and the place also attracts a fair degree of flak – for critics, it's "very expensive" and "losing its shine".

/ **Details:** www.soufflerestaurant.net; off M20; 9.30 pm; closed Mon, Sat L & Sun D.

BEAUMARIS, ISLE OF ANGLESEY   4–1C

The Loft Restaurant
Ye Olde Bull's Head £52 **Ⓐ ✪**

Castle St LL58 8AP   (01248) 810329

A "delightful", ancient and atmospheric coaching inn where the "consistently excellent food" can come as a surprise; there's also the handy option of a stylish (and cheaper) modern brasserie on the ground floor. / **Details:** www.bullsheadinn.co.uk; On the High Street, opposite the Spar shop; 9.30 pm; D only, closed Sun; no jeans; children: 7+ at D. **Accommodation:** 26 rooms, from £110.

BECKENHAM, KENT   3–3B

Mae Ping £39 **Ⓣ**

16 High St BR3 1AY   (020) 8650 7887

For a "hit to the taste-buds", many locals tip this popular Thai as a "reliable" option; even a reporter complaining of "tiny portions" admits the food's "tasty". / **Details:** www.maepingthai.co.uk; 10.30 pm.

BEELEY, DERBYSHIRE   5–2C

Devonshire Arms £40 **Ⓐ**

Devonshire Sq DE4 2NR   (01629) 733259

"Great location, incredible wines, hit-and-miss food" – one reporter neatly summarises feedback on this "atmospheric" Chatsworth Estate inn ("much revamped" by the Duchess in recent times, in "a melange of ancient and modern styles"); the service "sometimes isn't good at all". / **Details:** www.devonshirebeeley.co.uk; 9.30 pm. **Accommodation:** 8 rooms, from £120.

Aldens £39
229 Upper Newtownards Rd BT4 3JF   (028) 9065 0079
*Traditionally this contemporarily-designed operation is one of the best restaurants in the Province, and it continues to win praise for its "very good" cooking ("with a twist"), and an "interesting" wine list too. / **Details:** www.aldensrestaurant.com; 2m from Stormont Buildings; 10 pm, Fri & Sat 10.30 pm; closed Sun D.*

Deanes £61
36-40 Howard St BT1 6PF   (028) 9056 0000
*A "Belfast landmark" which wins praise for "exceptional food using local ingredients"; it also draws an awful lot of flak, though, for being "inconsistent" or "pretentious", and a high proportion of reporters feel that it is "overpriced" too. / **Details:** www.michaeldeane.co.uk; near Grand Opera House; 10 pm; closed Sun.*

Ginger £42
7-8 Hope St BT2 5EE   (0871) 426 7885
*The setting can seem a tad "clinical", but Simon McCance's "edgy" bistro continues to attract high praise from reporters for its often "excellent" cooking. / **Details:** www.gingerbistro.com; 9.30 pm, Mon 9 pm, Fri & Sat 10 pm; closed Mon L & Sun; no Amex.*

James Street South £48
21 James Street South BT2 7GA   (028) 9043 4310
*An "upscale central restaurant that never fails to deliver" on the food front; critics, though, can find the setting a bit "bland". / **Details:** www.jamesstreetsouth.co.uk; behind the City Hall, off Bedford Street ; 10.30 pm; closed Sun L.*

Soul Food Co £15
395 Ormeau Rd BT7 3GP   (028) 9064 6464
*A "great, little café", with a focus on "top-class ingredients", tipped for its house speciality – "a bacon butty of the highest order". / **Details:** www.soulfoodcaffe.co.uk; L only, closed Sun; no booking.*

Isle of Eriska £55
PA37 1SD   (01631) 720371
*"A favourite hide-away" for some reporters – this grand hotel is set on its own island, and its dining room is tipped as a "lovely" place, with "fabulous" food. / **Details:** www.eriska-hotel.co.uk; 9 pm; D only; no jeans or trainers; children: 6pm; high tea for resident's chldren. **Accommodation:** 25 rooms, from £325.*

Eat Fish £41
163-165 High St HP4 3HB   (01442) 879988
*A "reliable" restaurant, offering "good, simple fish dishes" and a "pleasant" overall dining experience; even a reporter who notes that it feels "a bit chain-like" concedes that it's "a good stand-by, with some interesting dishes". / **Details:** www.eatfish.co.uk; 10 pm, Sun 9 pm.*

The Gatsby £48
97 High St HP4 2DG   (01442) 870403
*A converted '30s cinema helps create a good "sense of occasion" at this "versatile" restaurant and piano bar, which is emerging as quite a success-story, thanks to its "imaginative" dishes and "great service". / **Details:** www.thegatsby.net; 10.30; booking: max 10.*

The Pipe & Glass Inn　　　　£46　　
West End　HU17 7PN
(01430) 810246

"Wow… a country pub where the cooking is so beyond pub level you can't believe it!"; James and Kate Mackenzie's "lovely" converted inn is "well worth a special trip", thanks to its "friendly, chatty staff" and "sublime" food that's the result of "lots of skill and imagination".
/ **Details:** www.pipeandglass.co.uk; 9.30 pm; closed Mon & Sun D; no Amex.

BIBURY, GLOUCESTERSHIRE　　　　　2–2C

Bibury Court
Bibury Court Hotel　　　　£70
GL7 5NT　(01285) 740337
A "beautiful" Jacobean manor house in a rural setting; reports suggest it's "going from strength to strength", offering "stylish cooking at dinner", and "excellent-quality set lunches" too.
/ **Details:** www.biburycourt.co.uk; 9 pm. **Accommodation:** 18 rooms, from ££170.

BIDDENDEN, KENT　　　　　3–4C

The Three Chimneys　　　　£44
Hareplain Rd　TN27 8LW　(01580) 291472
"Shame the fires are fake", but that's the only criticism reporters have of this "reliable" gastroboozer – which offers often-"excellent" food and service in a "delightful" setting, replete with "olde-worlde charm".
/ **Details:** www.thethreeechimneys.co.uk; A262 between Biddenden and Sissinghurst; 9.30 pm; no Amex.

West House　　　　£52
28 High St　TN27 8AH　(01580) 291341
"Simple and beautifully-prepared", the food at Graham Garrett's attractive old cottage is "pretty much faultless", say its fans; service is "friendly" too, adding spark to the rather "low-key" interior.
/ **Details:** www.thewesthouserestaurant.co.uk; 9.30 pm, Tue-Fri 8.45 pm; closed Mon, Sat L & Sun D; no Amex.

BIGBURY-ON-SEA, DEVON　　　　　1–4C

Burgh Island Hotel　　　　£78
TQ7 4BG　(01548) 810514
"Everyone should go once", to this "magical" Art Deco hotel, which makes you feel "just like being in an Agatha Christie novel"; "you go for the ambience", though – the "expensive" food is no more than "OK".
/ **Details:** www.burghisland.com; 8.30 pm; D only, ex Sun open L & D; no Amex; jacket & tie; children: 12+ at D. **Accommodation:** 25 rooms, from £390.

Oyster Shack £42

Millburn Orchard Farm, Stakes Hills TQ7 4BE (01548) 810876

"Slightly scruffy surroundings to not detract from the unique buzz" of this "beach shack", which has a big name for its "fantastic seafood"; let's hope a couple of let-downs this year aren't the beginning of a trend! / **Details:** www.oystershack.co.uk; 9 pm.

BILDESTON, SUFFOLK 3–1C

The Bildeston Crown
The Crown Hotel £44

High St IP7 7EB (01449) 740510
It may look "like a designer gastropub" in "a sleepy village an hour from London", but this restaurant-with-rooms (the brainchild of a local farmer) has "serious aspirations" when it comes to its cooking, and the execution is "top-class". / **Details:** www.thebildestoncrown.com; from the A14, take the B115 to Bildeston; 9.45 pm, Sun 9.30 pm. **Accommodation:** 12 rooms, from £150.

BILLERICAY, ESSEX 3–2C

The Magic Mushroom £46

Barleyland Rd CM11 2UD (01268) 289963
Darren Bennet runs "a great local restaurant", says a small local fan club, and he has delivered "consistently great food over many years" (15 at last count). / **Details:** www.magicmushroomrestaurant.co.uk; next to "Barleylands Farm"; midnight; closed Mon & Sun D; no shorts.

BIRCHOVER, DERBYSHIRE 5–2C

Druid Inn £39

Main St DE4 2BL (01629) 650302
"OK they can cook", at this "former walkers' pub in an isolated village"; "lax" or "stressed" service, though, can contribute to a curiously "soulless" ambience. / **Details:** www.thedruidinn.co.uk; SW of Bakewell off B5056; 9 pm, Fri & Sat 9.30 pm; closed Sun D; no Amex.

BIRMINGHAM, WEST MIDLANDS 5–4C

Asha's Indian Bar and Restaurant £38

12-22 Newhall St B3 3LX (0121) 200 2767
"If you want to be treated like a maharaja or maharani", the top tip locally is "one of the snug, pillow-lined alcoves" of this "quality" subcontinental; to those of less regal disposition, though, it can seem a little "pricey". / **Details:** www.ashasuk.co.uk; 10.30 pm; closed Sat L & Sun L; no shorts.

Bank £41

4 Brindleyplace B1 2JB (0121) 633 4466
This large '90s brasserie, overlooking the canal, often just seems rather "lost" nowadays (and "not cheap" either); for business and pre-theatre, however, it still has its uses. / **Details:** www.bankrestaurants.com; 10.30 pm, Fri & Sat 11 pm.

Buonissimo £32

1 Albany Rd B17 9JX (0121) 426 2444
In Harborne, a "friendly, local Italian that's always reliable"; it can
be "noisy", but service is "outstanding", and prices are
"very reasonable". / **Details:** www.buonissimouk.com; 10.15 pm; closed
Mon L & Sun; no Amex.

Café Ikon
Ikon Gallery £29

Oozells Sq, Brindley Place B1 2HS (0121) 248 3226
"Doing well under new management" ("if perhaps a bit chaotic"),
this "stylish" tapas bar makes a "funky" find – especially in "a city-
centre that's rather dominated by chains" – and remains a popular
rendezvous serving "acceptable" dishes. / **Details:** www.ikon-gallery.co.uk;
11 pm; closed Sun D; no Amex; children: 18+ after 9 pm.

Chez Jules £34

5a Ethel St, off New St B2 4BG (0121) 633 4664
Haute cuisine it ain't, but this "slightly Spartan" city-centre spot
is tipped for its "good range of classic French dishes at reasonable
prices". / **Details:** www.chezjules.co.uk; 11 pm; closed Sun D; no Amex.

Chung Ying Garden £32

17 Thorp St B5 4AT (0121) 666 6622
"An extensive range of good-value dim sum" helps underpin the appeal
of this Cantonese stalwart – the largest Chinese in the Midlands,
and boasting "many Asian customers". / **Details:** www.chungying.co.uk;
11 pm, Sun 10 pm.

Cielo £51

6 Oozells Sq B1 2JB (0121) 632 6882
This "handily-located" Brindleyplace Italian may look a bit "bling-y",
and the food may be no more than "competent", but it's
an "attractive" sort of place, with "attentive" service, and attracts
praise for its overall "good value". / **Details:** www.cielobirmingham.com;
11 pm, 10 pm Sun; Max booking: 20, Sat & Sun D.

Edmunds £55

6 Central Sq B1 2JB (0121) 633 4944
This "modern and relaxed" Brindleyplace venture is winning an ever
higher profile, thanks to its "top-quality" cuisine; no denying, though,
that the occasional sceptic finds realisation a little "jagged".
/ **Details:** www.edmundsbirmingham.com; 10 pm; closed Sat L & Sun.

Hotel du Vin et Bistro £50

25 Church St B3 2NR (0121) 200 0600
"The food is reliable and, besides, you're there for the wine", at this
"well-located" city-centre branch of this boutique-hotel chain, of which
this is one of the better representatives; it's a very popular business
destination. / **Details:** www.hotelduvin.co.uk; 10 pm, Fri & Sat 10.30 pm;
booking: max 12. **Accommodation:** 66 rooms, from £160.

Itihaas £42

18 Fleet St B3 1JL (0121) 212 3383
"Easily missed, but not to be underestimated"; this "elaborately
decorated" city-centre spot inspires the odd 'off' report, but for the
most part wins consistently high praise for its "cracking" cooking.
/ **Details:** www.itihaas.co.uk; 11, 10.30 Sun; closed Sat L & Sun L.

Jyoti £18

105 Stratford Rd B28 8AS (0121) 77855501
"Moved to a new site, and slightly the better for it" – this city-centre
spot continues to dish up often-"excellent" Gujarati (veggie) fare.
/ **Details:** www.jyotis.co.uk; 10 pm; closed Mon, Tue-Thu D only; no Amex.

Kinnaree Thai
The Mailbox, Holiday Wharf Building £33
22 Water Front Walk B1 ISN (0121) 665 6568
*"Warm", "relaxing" and "romantic", this canal-side Thai is tipped mainly for its location, but it's "reasonably-priced", and the food rarely disappoints. / **Details**: www.kinnaree.co.uk; 11 pm, 10.30 pm Sun.*

Lasan £40
3-4 Dakota Buildings, James St B3 ISD (0121) 212 3664
*"Puts all London's top Indians to shame!" – this "unique" and "ground-breaking" spot serves up dishes that are sometimes simply "astonishing"... "if you can get in", that is. / **Details**: www.lasan.co.uk; 11 pm; closed Sat L.*

Must £32
11-13 Newhall St B3 3NY (0121) 212 2266
*A "trendy cocktail bar-cum-Thai restaurant" serving "really fresh and tasty food in convivial surroundings" – "a must for snacks/drinks after work/lunch", and "very busy" for dinner too. / **Details**: www.mustgroup.co.uk; 10.30 pm; closed Sun.*

Opus Restaurant £52
54 Cornwall St B3 2DE (0121) 200 2323
*A "well-spaced" spot – "smack bang in the centre of the city" – with an "impressive" choice for anyone in search of "delicious, fresh and seasonal" fare; it's perhaps of particular note, though, as "a good bet for a quiet business lunch". / **Details**: www.opusrestaurant.co.uk; 9.30 pm; closed Sat L & Sun.*

Pascal's £50
1 Montague Rd B16 9HN (0121) 455 0999
*On a site some still remember from its days as Jessica's, this Edgbaston townhouse is tipped by loyal fans for its "charming maitre d'" (the "very Gallic" Pascal) and for its high standard of cuisine. / **Details**: www.pascalsrestaurant.co.uk; 10 pm; closed Mon, Tue, Sat L & Sun D; no Amex.*

Purnells £63
55 Cornwall St B3 2DH (0121) 212 9799
*Glyn Purnell's "imaginative" and "exceptionally well presented" cuisine wins the highest praise for his "professional" city-centre venture, especially as a business destination – perhaps why the style can sometimes seem a fraction "impersonal". / **Details**: www.purnellsrestaurant.com; 9.15 pm; closed Mon, Sat L & Sun; children: 6+.*

San Carlo £45
4 Temple St B2 5BN (0121) 633 0251
*Fans of this city-centre Italian of long standing acclaim its "stunning" food and "truly unique" ambience; even critics may concede the food's "OK", but find it "overshadowed" by the place's "rushed" and "noisy" style. / **Details**: www.sancarlo.co.uk; near St Philips Cathedral; 11 pm.*

Simpsons £71
20 Highfield Rd B15 3DU (0121) 454 3434
*"Now established as Birmingham's premier restaurant" (and "one of the best in the UK" too), Andreas Antona's "unfussy" dining room – part of a "lovely" Georgian house in leafy Edgbaston – offers "very polished" cuisine, as part of an "impressive" all-round performance. / **Details**: www.simpsonsrestaurant.co.uk; 9 pm, Fri & Sat 9.30 pm; closed Sun D. **Accommodation**: 4 rooms, from £160.*

Turners £63
69 High St B17 9NS   (0121) 426 4440
"Delicate" and "innovative" cuisine twinned with "professional" service
has made quite a name for this small Harborne restaurant; it inspires
the odd report, however, that it's "suffering from Michelinitis",
and ratings are less stellar than once they were.
/ Details: www.turnersofharborne.com; 9.30 pm; closed Mon, Sat L & Sun;
no Amex.

BISHOPS STORTFORD, HERTFORDSHIRE 3–2B

Baan Thitiya £35
102 London Rd CM23 3DS   (01279) 658575
"An old pub turned into a Thai restaurant"; it has become better
known than its older Hertford sibling, and serves "tasty" fare in a
manner that's always "friendly and attentive".
/ Details: www.baan-thitiya.com; 11 pm.

BISHOPS TACHBROOK, WARWICKSHIRE 5–4C

Mallory Court £74
Harbury Ln CV33 9QB   (01926) 330214

This "very attractive" Lutyens-designed country house hotel divides
opinion; fans – some of 25 years' standing – report "stunning flavours"
and "thoughtful" service, but critics find the style "increasingly
corporate", and complain of "snooty" service and "over-rated" food.
/ Details: www.mallory.co.uk; 2m S of Leamington Spa, off B4087; 8.30 pm;
closed Sat L. Accommodation: 30 rooms, from £139.

BISPHAM GREEN, LANCASHIRE 5–1A

Eagle & Child £37
Maltkiln Ln L40 3SG   (01257) 462297
"Cosy" and "convivial", this "traditional" inn has a big reputation as a
dining destination; it's "expensive", though, and critics have found the
menu "consistently more interesting than the food".
/ Details: www.ainscoughs.co.uk; M6, J27; 8.30 pm; no Amex.

BLACKPOOL, LANCASHIRE 5–1A

Kwizeen £40
47-49 King St FY1 3EJ   (01253) 290045
"A welcome relief in a culinary desert!"; this bastion of "very good food
at reasonable prices" – hidden-away in a back street, near the railway
station – is "well worth the effort of finding"; even a regular fan,
however, notes that results can vary widely.
/ Details: www.kwizeenrestaurant.co.uk; 100 yards inland from the Winter
Gardens; 9 pm; closed Sun; no Amex; no shorts.

BODIAM, EAST SUSSEX   3–4C

The Curlew   £47   Ⓐ⭐
Junction Rd TN32 5UY   (01580) 861 394
*Recently revamped, "this former pub-with-food is now a proper upscale restaurant", with a "cosy" ambience, and "top-notch" food and presentation; the proprietors are "passionate about wine" too, and the wine list is "always evolving". / **Details:** www.thecurlewrestaurant.co.uk; 9.30 pm; closed Mon & Tue; no Amex.*

BODSHAM, KENT   3–3C

Froggies @ The Timber Batts   £48   Ⓐ⭐
School Ln TN25 5JQ   (01233) 750237
*"A French restaurant in an olde-worlde Kentish pub", praised for its "well-cooked" food (albeit "from an unchanging menu"), its "charming" service and its "interesting" wine list. / **Details:** www.thetimberbatts.co.uk; 9 pm; closed Mon & Sun D; booking essential.*

BOLNHURST, BEDFORDSHIRE   3–1A

The Plough at Bolnhurst   £37   Ⓐ⭐
MK44 2EX (01234) 376274
*"An oasis in a desert of bad pub food"; in its "surprisingly out-of-the-way" setting, this "quiet" and "friendly" pub has made quite a name for its "fresh", "seasonal" and "locally-sourced" cuisine. / **Details:** www.bolnhurst.com; 9.30 pm; closed Mon & Sun D; no Amex.*

BOLTON ABBEY, NORTH YORKSHIRE   8–4B

The Devonshire Arms   £90   Ⓐ
BD23 6AJ (01756) 710441
*A "beautifully-situated, upmarket Dales hotel", where the wine list is of undoubted note – "you'll need to set aside a couple of hours to wade through it"; given the prices, though, the food isn't really much more than "passable". / **Details:** www.devonshirehotels.co.uk; on A59, 5m NE of Skipton; 9.30 pm; D only, closed Mon; no jeans or trainers.*
***Accommodation:** 40 rooms, from £238.*

BOSHAM, WEST SUSSEX   3–4A

Millstream Hotel   £45   Ⓐ⭐
PO18 8HL (01243) 573234
*With its "exceptional food for a small hotel", "professional service" and a "fantastic" location, reporters can find little fault with this traditional establishment, where "high standards are always maintained".
/ **Details:** www.millstream-hotel.co.uk; A259 from Chichister; 9.15 pm; no jeans or trainers. **Accommodation:** 35 rooms, from £145.*

BOUGHTON MONCHELSEA, KENT   3–3C

The Mulberry Tree   £30   Ⓐ
Hermitage Ln ME17 4DA   (01622) 749082
*Mixed reviews for this "hard-to-find", country restaurant (with pleasant courtyard garden); all agree it "tries" hard, but it seems to be a lucky dip whether the results are "excellent" or "uninspired".
/ **Details:** www.themulberrytreekent.co.uk; 9 pm, Fri & Sat 9.30 pm; closed Mon & Sun D; no Amex.*

BOURNEMOUTH, DORSET   2–4C

Chez Fred   £19
10 Seamoor Rd BH4 9AN   (01202) 761023
"The best fish 'n' chip shop for miles"; Peter & Fred Capel's "no-frills"
restaurant, which is lined with pictures of its celeb' fans, is a notably
"efficient" operation that wins praise from all who comment on it.
/ **Details:** www.chezfred.co.uk; 1m W of town centre; 9.45 pm, 9 Sun; closed
Sun L; no Amex; no booking.

Highcliff Grill
Highcliff Mariott Hotel   £48
St Micheal's Rd, West Cliff BH2 5DU   (01202) 557702
Marriott hotels may not be known as gastronomic redoubts, but this
newly-created dining room is already tipped as an "elegant" all-rounder
in "traditional" style; "ask for a window table".
/ **Details:** www.marriott.co.uk/hotels/travel/bohbm-bournemouth-highcliff-marriott-
hotel/; 9.30 fri & sat 10.00; no jeans or trainers. **Accommodation:** 160 rooms,
from £varies .

Ocean Palace   £31
8 Priory Rd BH2 5DG   (01202) 559127
This Chinese veteran may be a touch echoey, but it "gets all the basics
right", and "it's certainly very popular"; lunchtimes offer "terrific value".
/ **Details:** www.oceanpalace.co.uk; 11 pm.

West Beach   £48
Pier Approach BH2 5AA   (01202) 587785
"A bustling café on the town's main beach", with a "wonderful
ambience and excellent views of the sea"; the food is "usually very
good, but not always reliably so". / **Details:** www.west-beach.co.uk; 10 pm.

BOWNESS-ON-WINDERMERE, CUMBRIA   7–3D

Miller Howe   £57
Rayrigg Rd LA23 1EY   (01539) 442536
"Its' a long time since it buzzed as in John Tovey's day" (and still a bit
"trapped in the '80s"), but this once-famous country house hotel –
with "wonderful views of Windermere" – is "still worth a detour",
not least for the quality of the cuisine. / **Details:** www.millerhowe.com;
on A592 between Windermere & Bowness; 8.45 pm. **Accommodation:** 15
rooms, from £160.

BRADFORD, WEST YORKSHIRE   5–1C

Aagrah   £32
483 Bradford Rd LS28 8ED   (01274) 668818
The food "is up to the usual Aagrah
standards" – "the highest!" – at this
"warehouse-like" Indian; "big is not
always beautiful", however, and the
ambience can sometimes seem
a little "impersonal".
/ **Details:** www.aagrah.com; on A647;
11.30 pm; D only, ex Sun open L & D.

Akbar's Balti   £24
1276 Leeds Rd BD3 8LF   (01274) 773311
This "absolutely buzzing" curry house retains a big name for its
"tender, flavoursome and amazing-value curries"; there's also a "large
and exceedingly busy" café spin-off (unlicensed) down the road at 524
Leeds Road (tel 01274 737458), which similarly offers "excellent"
fare. / **Details:** www.akbars.co.uk; midnight; D only; no Amex.

195

Karachi   £12

15-17 Neal St BD5 0BX (01274) 732015

With its Formica tables and "basic" décor, the city's longest-established subcontinental "makes no effort to be aesthetically pleasing"; it's a "friendly" place, though, and "very good value-for-money for the standard of food". / **Details:** *I am, 2 am Fri & Sat; no credit cards.*

Mumtaz   £24

Great Horton Rd BD7 3HS (01274) 571861

It may be over 30 years old, but this "immensely popular" Indian is "all glass and chrome" nowadays; it's a "no-fuss" kind of place offering a "vast menu" of "home-style" dishes "that'll knock your socks off"; no alcohol. / **Details:** *www.mumtaz.com; midnight.*

BRAMPTON, CUMBRIA   7–2D

Farlam Hall   £55

CA8 2NG (01697) 746234

"The breakfast is excellent, and so is everything else", at this "personal and comfortable" country house hotel, which is strongly tipped by a small but very dedicated fan club. / **Details:** *www.farlamhall.co.uk; 2.5m S.E of Brampton on A689, not in Farlam Village; 8.30 pm; D only; no shorts; children: 5+.* **Accommodation:** *12 rooms, from £204.*

BRANCASTER STAITHE, NORFOLK   6–3B

The White Horse   £45

Main Rd PE31 8BY (01485) 210262

"A former pub that's now a lovely seaside hotel"; it "impresses with its sea view alone", but its "well prepared" seafood dishes also go down well. / **Details:** *www.whitehorsebrancaster.co.uk; 9 pm; no Amex.* **Accommodation:** *15 rooms, from £120.*

BRANSCOMBE, DEVON   2–4A

Masons Arms   £33

Main St EX12 3DJ (01297) 680300

An "idyllic" old boozer in a beautiful village, tipped as "a hidden gem at the southern end of the Lakes", which offers "great beers" and "delicious food". / **Details:** *www.masonsarms.co.uk; 9 pm; no Amex; children: 14+ in restaurant.* **Accommodation:** *21 rooms, from £80.*

BRAY, BERKSHIRE   3–3A

Caldesi In Campagna   £60

Old Mill Ln SL6 2BG (01628) 788500

Fans vaunt the "superb culinary skills" at this year-old Tuscan restaurant (which has a Marylebone sibling), and say it's a "delightful venue", where "nothing's too much trouble"; there is something of a feeling, though, that it is "not as good as when it opened". / **Details:** *www.campagna.caldesi.com; 10.30 pm; closed Mon & Sun D.*

Crown Inn   £39

High St SL6 2AH (01628) 621936

During our survey year, Heston Blumenthal added this romantic pub – just across from the Fat Duck – to his burgeoning 'Bray-menthal' empire; the aim is, apparently, to keep it more 'local' and less foodie than the Hind's Head. / **Details:** *www.crownatbray.co.uk; Opposite Town Hall; 930pm; no Amex; booking essential.*

The Fat Duck £196

High St SL6 2AQ   (01628) 580333

"Not a meal – a complete theatrical performance!"; Heston Blumenthal's "phenomenal" shrine to molecular gastronomy offers a "marvellously entertaining" dining experience, which includes some "unparalleled" taste sensations; the bill, though, can seem as "insane" as the cuisine. / **Details:** www.thefatduck.co.uk; 9 pm; closed Mon & Sun D.

The Hind's Head £49

High St SL6 2AB (01628) 626151
This is "the ultimate gastropub", say fans of Heston's "gorgeous" village inn – "all snugs and roaring fires" – over the road from the Fat Duck; its "strikingly good take on pub classics" offers "all the Blumenthal magic" (not least the "famous triple-cooked chips"), but "without the big prices". / **Details:** www.hindsheadbray.com; From the M4 take exit to Maidenhead Central, then go to Bray village; 9.30 pm; closed Sun D.

Riverside Brasserie £62

Monkey Island Ln, Bray Marina SL6 2EB   (01628) 780553
"Little more than a shed" – this "charming" waterside spot in hard-to-find Bray Marina is nonetheless "idyllic" on a summer evening; the food's good too, if not the 'main event'.
/ **Details:** www.riversidebrasserie.co.uk; follow signs for Bray Marina off A308; 9.30 pm.

Waterside Inn £130

Ferry Rd SL6 2AT   (01628) 620691
The bill may be "mind-boggling", but this Thames-side legend remains "the epitome of excellence" for most reporters, who are "totally blown away" by Alain Roux's "nigh-on perfect" cuisine; service is "immaculate" too, and the dining room ("old-fashioned" though it may be) enjoys an "idyllic setting". / **Details:** www.waterside-inn.co.uk; off A308 between Windsor & Maidenhead; 10 pm; closed Mon & Tue; no jeans or trainers; booking: max 10; children: 14+ D. **Accommodation:** 13 rooms, from £200.

BREARTON, NORTH YORKSHIRE   8–4B

The Malt Shovel £43

HG3 3BX   (01423) 862929
"A wonderful rustic family-run pub", whose "out-of-the-way" location most reporters think worth finding for its "very interesting" food (and "brilliant operatic evenings" too); the occasional off-evening, however, is not unknown. / **Details:** www.themaltshovelbrearton.co.uk; off A61, 6m N of Harrogate; 10 pm; closed Mon, Tue & Sun D; no Amex; need 8+ to book.

BRECON, POWYS   2–1A

Felin Fach Griffin   £49

Felin Fach LD3 0UB   (01874) 620111
This "mid-Wales charmer", in the Brecon Beacons, is a "cosy" and
"family-friendly" inn that impresses all reporters – "it's not a gourmet
experience, but delivers very good bistro food at very fair prices,
and with interesting wine too". / *Details: www.eatdrinksleep.ltd.uk; 20 mins
NW of Abergavenny on A470; 9 pm; no Amex.* **Accommodation:** *7 rooms,
from £110.*

BRENTFORD, GREATER LONDON   3–3B

Pappadums   £37

Ferry Quays, Ferry Ln TW8 0BT   (020) 8847 1123
"Making good use of a modern building in a riverside setting",
an Indian restaurant tipped for its consistently good standards.
/ *Details: www.pappadums.co.uk; 9 pm, Sat 11 pm, Sun 10.30 pm.*

BRIDGE OF ALLAN, STIRLING   9–4C

Clive Ramsay   £28

26 Henderson St FK9 4HR   (01786) 831616
Clive Ramsay's café/deli is tipped for its "welcoming style" and
"good variety of reasonably-priced dishes"… and, perhaps more
importantly, "there doesn't seem to be much else around in this part
of the world". / *Details: www.cliveramsay.com; 10 pm; no Amex.*

BRIDPORT, DORSET   2–4B

The Bull Hotel   £41

34 East St DT6 3LF   (01308) 422878
A former coaching inn tipped by supporters for cooking that's "always
reliable" (or, as a critic puts it "not mind-blowing").
/ *Details: www.thebullhotel.co.uk; 9.30 pm.* **Accommodation:** *19 rooms,
from £85.*

Hive Beach Cafe   £35

Beach Rd DT6 4RF   (01308) 897070

The style may be "shabby-chic", but there's nothing scruffy about the
"really excellent" fish on offer at this seaside café, which – in season –
is always "buzzing". / *Details: www.hivebeachcafe.co.uk; L only, varies
seasonally.*

Riverside   £45

West Bay DT6 4EZ   (01308) 422011
Celebrating 50 years in the hands of the Watson family, this popular
riverside café remains a favorite, thanks to its combination of "simple
but excellent" fish, "the nicest people" and its "light, bright and totally
unfussy setting". / *Details: www.thefishrestaurant-westbay.co.uk; 9 pm; closed
Mon & Sun D; no Amex.*

Brook's £43 Ⓣ
6 Bradford Rd HD6 1RW (01484) 715284
*"Worth a stop off the M62" – this "popular" Pennines eatery of over
20 years' standing is tipped for "good food at competitive prices".
/ **Details:** www.brooks-restaurant.co.uk; 11 pm; D only, closed Sun; no Amex.*

Aumthong Thai £31 Ⓐ
60 Western Rd BN3 1JD (01273) 773922
*"A long-standing Thai restaurant, serving varied dishes of good quality",
and at "reasonable prices" too. / **Details:** www.aumthong.com; 11 pm,
10 pm Sun; closed Mon L.*

Basketmakers Arms £18 Ⓐ
12 Gloucester Rd BN1 4AD (01273) 689006
*Looking for "really good pub food at non-gastro prices" (and "all locally-
sourced" too)? – head for this increasingly well-rated North Laine
boozer. / **Details:** 8.30 pm; no booking.*

Bill's at the Depot £34 Ⓐ
100 North Rd, The Depot BN1 1YE (01273) 692894
*This "pricey" but "fun" café in a large organic deli serves an "eclectic
range of dishes", and has a particular name for "Brighton's
best breakfast" – expect to queue; they've "crammed in far too many
tables", though, and critics are beginning to fear "style triumphing over
content". / **Details:** www.billsproducestore.co.uk; 10 pm; no Amex.*

Casa Don Carlos £28 Ⓐ
5 Union St BN1 1HA (01273) 327177
*"A lively tapas place that remains the best in the area for Spanish
food"; this "lovely" Lanes destination continues to please "locals and
tourists alike". / **Details:** 10.30 pm.*

The Chilli Pickle £36 ⒶⒶ
42 Meeting House Ln BN1 1HB (01273) 323 824
*"By far the best Indian in town"; this small Lanes bistro offers
"a contemporary take on regional subcontinental dishes" that's
"1000 miles away from the generic sticky-sweet sauces of usual local
curry houses". / **Details:** www.thechillipicklebistro.co.uk; 10.30 pm; closed
Mon & Tue; no Amex.*

China Garden £35 ★
88-91 Preston St BN1 2HG (01273) 325124
*"The best dim sum in town" ("you can tell by the number of Chinese
families!") is to be had at this "large and hectic" spot, on the
Hove/Brighton border. / **Details:** www.chinagarden.name; opp West Pier;
11.30 pm.*

Donatello £30 Ⓣ
1-3 Brighton Pl BN1 1HJ (01273) 775477
*A "busy, fun and cheap" option in the Lanes, tipped for decent pizza
and so on. / **Details:** www.donatello.co.uk; 11.30 pm.*

The Restaurant At Drakes
Drakes Hotel £56

44 Marine Pde BN2 1PE   (01273) 696934

"Standards seem to have improved over the last year", at this basement dining room (formerly part of the Gingerman empire); fans say it's again *"one of the best places in Brighton"*, and that the cooking is *"fantastic"*. / **Details:** www.therestaurantatdrakes.co.uk; 9.30 pm. **Accommodation:** 20 rooms, from £100.

Due South £40

139 King's Road Arches BN1 2FN   (01273) 821218

"Sitting outside on a sunny day, there's a real continental feel", at this *"Spartan"* but popular hang-out, which benefits from a *"wonderful beach-side setting"*; standards have drifted a bit of late, but most reporters still say the food's *"OK"*, with *"wonderful fresh fish"* a highlight. / **Details:** www.duesouth.co.uk; Brighton Beach, below the Odeon cinema; 9.45 pm.

English's £46

29-31 East St BN1 1HL   (01273) 327980

"Great oysters" head up a menu of *"first-class seafood"*, at this prominently-sited, Victorian veteran in the Lanes, which has been re-establishing itself in recent times; it has extensive al fresco seating. / **Details:** www.englishs.co.uk; 10 pm, Sun 9.30 pm.

Fishy Fishy £35

36 East St BN1 1HL   (01273) 723750

A cosy seafood bistro that's a local favourite for fans of its *"really fine, fresh seafood"*; it also has critics, though, for whom it's too *"highly priced"*. / **Details:** www.fishyfishy.co.uk; The Pavillion end of East Street; 9.30 week/10 weekends.

Food for Friends £36

17-18 Prince Albert St BN1 1HF   (01273) 202310

"Much improved under new ownership" – it doesn't yet have the same sort of following (or quite as dazzling ratings) as Terre–à-Terre, but this Lanes spot is praised by all who comment on it for its *"mouthwatering"* cooking from *"wonderful ingredients"*. / **Details:** www.foodforfriends.com; In the Lanes, South end; 10 pm, Fri & Sat 10.30 pm; no booking, Sat L & Sun L.

The Ginger Dog £39

12 College Pl BN2 1HN   (01273) 620 990

Despite its *"wonderful food, and excellent ethos when it comes to sourcing"*, this Lanes spot attracted surprisingly few reports this year, but it remains a pre-eminent restaurant locally – even the *"well-priced"* set lunch includes *"all the extras you'd expect in a top establishment"*. / **Details:** www.gingermanrestaurants.com; Off Eastern Road near Brighton College; 10 pm.

The Ginger Pig £36

3 Hove St BN3 2TR   (01273) 736123

This *"buzzy"* and *"efficient"* Hove gastropub, near the seafront, brings all the virtues of the acclaimed Gingerman empire to its *"imaginative"* and *"seasonal"* cuisine, and is a *"favourite stand-by"* for many local reporters. / **Details:** www.gingermanrestaurant.com; 10 pm; no trainers.

Gingerman £43

21a Norfolk Sq BN1 2PD   (01273) 326688

"A cosy restaurant serving food of exceptional quality"; this is the original venture of local food hero Ben McKellar, and many reports confirm that it is *"still the best"*; puddings find particular approval. / **Details:** www.gingermanrestaurants.com; off Norfolk Square; 9.15 pm; closed Mon.

Graze £46
42 Western Rd BN3 1JD (01273) 823707

This "friendly", if "tightly-packed", grazing (small plates) outfit in Hove is a "casual" favourite for many locals thanks to its flexible style and "quality" cooking. / **Details:** www.graze-restaurant.co.uk; 9.30 pm; closed Mon & Sun D.

Havana £50
32 Duke St BN1 1AG (01273) 773388
The décor is "more 'Raffles Hotel' than 'Castro'", but the light and "spaciousness" of this long-established restaurant makes a pleasant change from the cramped Lanes norm; a gourmet destination this ain't, but reporters enjoy many "fun" meals here nonetheless.
/ **Details:** www.havana.uk.com; By West Street and the Clock Tower; 10.30 pm, Fri & Sat 11 pm, Sun 10 pm; no shorts; children: 5+ at D.

Hotel du Vin et Bistro £50
Ship St BN1 1AD (01273) 718588
"The food has slipped from 'bistro' standard to simply poor, but prices remain high", at this still-popular outlet of the boutique-hotel chain, just off the seafront; "the main selling point is the wine list".
/ **Details:** www.hotelduvin.com; 9.45 pm; booking: max 10.
Accommodation: 49 rooms, from £170.

Indian Summer £36
69 East St BN1 1HQ (01273) 711001
"Fresh herbs and spices in fabulous and innovative combinations" make a big contribution to the "inventive", "fusion"-enriched dishes at this handily-located Indian. / **Details:** www.indian-summer.org.uk; 10.30 pm; closed Mon L.

Jamie's Italian £38
11 Black Lion St BN1 1ND (01273) 915480
"Queues are par the the course", at this mega-popular branch of Jamie O's chain-Italians, whose "vibe and general buzz" are key selling points; the food's "generally good", though – part of an experience that's generally "very enjoyable" all-round. / **Details:** www.jamiesitalian.com; 11 pm, Sun 10.30 pm.

Pomegranate £32
Kemp Town BN2 1TF (01273) 628386
On the edge of Kemp Town, this "friendly" Kurdish restaurant it tipped for its interesting range of dishes at "very reasonable prices".
/ **Details:** www.eatpomegranate.com; 11 pm.

Pub Du Vin
Hotel Du Vin £41
7 Ship St BN1 1AD (01273) 718588
Hotel du Vin's "quirky" take on the British pub is next door to its just-off-the-seafront hotel; all reporters give a big thumbs-up for its "well-executed British pub grub", its "charming" ambience and its "top ales".
/ **Details:** www.hotelduvin.co.uk/pub-du-vin; 10 pm; no shorts.
Accommodation: 49 rooms, from £.

Regency £26

131 Kings Rd BN1 2HH (01273) 325014

"Very good for plain fish and chips" – this "family-friendly" sea-front veteran continues to please all who comment on it; a "wide range" of other seafood is also available. / **Details:** www.theregencyrestaurant.co.uk; opp West Pier; 11 pm. **Accommodation: 30 rooms, from £60.**

Riddle & Finns £47 ★

12b, Meeting House Ln BN1 1HB (01273) 323008

Expect a "rapid turnaround, no booking and shared tables", but for "high-quality fish and seafood", this very popular champagne and oyster bar, in the Lanes, remains a hard act to beat. / **Details:** www.riddleandfinns.co.uk; 10 pm, Sat & Sun late.

Sam's Of Brighton £36

1 Paston Pl BN2 1HA (01273) 676222

Sam Metcalfe's "welcoming" Kemp Town yearling seems to be losing its way; the food is still tipped as being "good, for the area", but that's about as far as it goes. / **Details:** www.samsofbrighton.co.uk; Directly opposite County Hospital; 10 pm, Sun 9 pm.

Terre à Terre £39 ★★

71 East St BN1 1HQ (01273) 729051

 *"Still Britain's best vegetarian fine dining experience" – this "pleasant and professional" non-meat Lanes Mecca (Brighton's most reported-on restaurant) is just the place to "blow the minds of obstinate carnivores"; its "amazing taste sensations", say fans, are "worth travelling miles for".* / **Details:** www.terreaterre.co.uk; 10.30 pm; booking: max 8 at weekends.

BRINKWORTH, WILTSHIRE   2–2C

The Three Crowns £40 ★

The Street SN15 5AF (01666) 510366

"Still head and shoulders above anything else round here"; this "good gastropub" – a commendable all-rounder – is all the more worth knowing about in an area that's (surprisingly) "rather short on decent places to eat". / **Details:** www.threecrowns.co.uk; Opposite church in middle of village; 9.30 pm, Sun 9 pm.

BRISTOL, CITY OF BRISTOL   2–2B

The Albion £45 ★

Boyces Ave BS8 4AA (0117) 973 3522

"A firm favourite in Clifton Village" – this "very busy" gastropub serves a "delicious", "very British" and "unashamedly robust" menu, alongside "a good selection of real ales, ciders and decent wines". / **Details:** www.thealbionclifton.co.uk; 10 pm; closed Mon & Sun D.

Aqua £38

Welsh Back BS1 4RR (0117) 915 6060

"Wondrous pizza" and "good views over the water" are the highlights at this "attractive modern bar", in Clifton; more generally, however, the food offer can seem "formulaic". / **Details:** www.aqua-restaurant.com; Near the Bristol Bridge; two minutes walk; Sun-Thu 10 pm, Fri & Sat 10.30 pm.

Bell's Diner   **£43** ⭐

1 York Rd BS6 5QB (0117) 924 0357
Chris Wicks's "superior" cooking – which often demonstrate some
"seriously original" ideas – makes this "hard-to-find" Montpelier bistro
well worth seeking out. / **Details:** www.bellsdiner.co.uk; 10 pm; closed Mon L,
Sat L & Sun.

Berwick Lodge   **£59** Ⓐ⭐⭐

Berwick Drive BS10 7TD (0117) 9581590
"Potentially one of the best 'country house' dining rooms in the region";
this "exciting" newcomer occupies an "impressive" hotel, with kitchens
overseen by Chris Wicks of Bell's Diner fame; the food is "fantastic" -
all the more reason to sort out the sometimes "embarrassingly bad"
service! / **Details:** www.berwicklodge.co.uk; no Amex. **Accommodation:** 10
rooms, from £90.

7 Bordeaux Quay   **£45** Ⓐ

Canons Rd BS1 5UH (0117) 943 1200
"Great views" help make this "large and buzzy quayside brasserie"
(plus more ambitious restaurant upstairs) the most reported-on spot
in Bristol; even fans say the eco-friendly fare may "lack excitement",
but it's generally "competent". / **Details:** www.bordeaux-quay.co.uk; 10 pm;
closed Mon & Sun D.

Boston Tea Party   **£22** Ⓐ

75 Park St BS1 5PF (0117) 929 8601
A "comfy" places to hang out, this "quirky" café (part of a small local
group) has quite a name for "the best coffee" and "the best breakfasts
in town", and it has a nice small garden too; main meals are
"more average". / **Details:** www.bostonteaparty.co.uk; Very near Bristol
University; 8 pm; no Amex; no booking.

Brasserie Blanc   **£42** Ⓐ

Bakers And Cutlers Halls, The Friary Building BS1 3DF
(0117) 910 2410
A "tastefully converted old building", in the Cabot Circus shopping
centre, plays host to this year-old outpost of the Blanc empire; it mostly
wins praise for its "tasty" food (including an "excellent value set
lunch"), but some reporters do say standards are "slipping".
/ **Details:** www.brasserieblanc.com; Mon-Fri 10 pm, Sat 10.30 pm, Sun 9 pm.

Cafe Maitreya   **£36** Ⓣ

89 St Marks Rd BS5 6HY (0117) 951 0100
"Wonderfully imaginative vegetarian food", with "intriguing tastes and
textures" wins, for the most part, a hymn of praise from reporters for
this basic café. / **Details:** www.cafemaitreya.co.uk; 9.45pm; closed Mon, Tue &
Sun; no Amex.

Casamia   **£45** ⭐

38 High St BS9 3DZ (0117) 959 2884
It may feel "rather poky", but this family-run Italian pleases fans with
its "inspirational" and "experimental" cuisine; doubters find the
approach "fussy", though, and complain of "very small" portions and
"steep" prices. / **Details:** www.casamiarestaurant.co.uk; midnight; closed Mon,
Tue L, Wed L, Thu L, Fri L & Sun; no Amex.

Culinaria   £46   ⭐⭐
1 Chandos Rd BS6 6PG   (0117) 973 7999

Stephen Markwick has long been hailed as Bristol's top chef, and many reporters describe the food at his simple Redland dining room as simply "superb"; it's a shame, though, that the "canteen"-style decor can seem rather "sterile". / **Details:** www.culinariabristol.co.uk; 9.30 pm; closed Sun-Wed; no Amex.

Fishers   £38   Ⓐ
35 Princess Victoria St BS8 4BX   (0117) 974 7044
"Useful" is the word most used by reporters to describe this "reliable" fish bistro; it attracts particular praise for "good-value" menus at lunch and in the early evening. / **Details:** www.fishers-restaurant.com; 10.30 pm, Sun 10 pm.

Flinty Red   £42   ⭐
34 Cotham HIll BS6 6LA   (0117) 923 8755
"This newcomer on the Bristol scene is the place to go!", say early-days supporters; run by a local wine merchant, it offers "first-class" vino, plus a "superb mix of French and Spanish" small plates, which "vary from truly excellent to merely good". / **Details:** www.flintyred.co.uk; 10.15 pm; closed Mon L & Sun; booking essential.

The Glass Boat   £40   Ⓐ
Welsh Back BS1 4SB   (0117) 929 0704

With its "beautiful setting" by the river, this atmospheric moored barge makes "a perfect place for a celebration" or a date; those less swept away may feel that it's "a bit overpriced". / **Details:** www.glassboat.co.uk; below Bristol Bridge; 10.30 pm, Mon 10 pm; closed Mon L & Sun D; no Amex.

Goldbrick House   £40   Ⓐ
69 Park St BS1 5PB   (0117) 945 1950
This "stylish" and "buzzy" bar/restaurant it tipped mainly for its possibilities as a 'big-night-out' destination; it falls down on the food front, though, and critics consider it "a lost opportunity". / **Details:** www.goldbrickhouse.co.uk; 11 pm; closed Sun.

Green's Dining Room   **£40** ★

25 Zetland Rd BS6 7AH   (0117) 924 6437

"Imaginative" cooking has made quite a big name locally for this small local restaurant – plan ahead, as "getting a table can be tricky".
/ **Details:** www.greensdiningroom.com; 10.30 pm; closed Mon & Sun; no Amex.

Hotel du Vin et Bistro   **£50** Ⓐ

Sugar Hs, Narrow Lewins Mead BS1 2NU   (0117) 925 5577

An extremely popular branch of the boutique hotel chain, whose "unusual setting" – in an old sugar warehouse – is "full of atmosphere"; it is further buoyed not only by its trademark "amazing wine list", but also by "consistently decent" food.
/ **Details:** www.hotelduvin.com; 9.45 pm; booking: max 10.
Accommodation: 40 rooms, from £145.

Kathmandu   **£36** ★

Colston Tower, Colston St BS1 4XE   (0117) 929 4455

"A high-quality Indian/Nepalese", near the Colston Hall – a "very friendly" joint that's "always busy".
/ **Details:** www.kathmandu-curry.com; 11 pm, Sat 11.30 pm; D only.

The Kensington Arms   **£37** Ⓣ

35-37 Stanley Rd BS6 6NP   (0117) 944 6444

A Redland gastropub tipped for its "interesting" food; service, though, can't always keep up with the place's popularity.
/ **Details:** www.thekensingtonarms.co.uk; Near Redland Railway station; 10 pm; closed Sun D.

Krishna's Inn   **£26** ★

4 Byron Pl, Triangle South BS8 1JT   (0117) 927 6864

This café-style spot serves up "excellent south Indian food at remarkably low prices"; that, however, is its only obvious attraction.
/ **Details:** www.keralagroup.co.uk; 11 pm Fri & Sat midnight.

Lido   **£41** Ⓐ★

Oakfield Pl BS8 2BJ   (0117) 933 9533

How groovy is this for Clifton?; a "beautifully restored" Victorian lido ("engagingly lit at night") that's quickly established itself as "a Bristol 'in'-place" – just as surprising is the quality of its "fresh" and "interesting" Med-influenced fare, much of it from a wood-fired oven.
/ **Details:** www.lidobristol.com; On the edge of Clifton; 10 pm; closed Sun D; no Amex.

Loch Fyne   **£40** ★

51 Queen Charlotte St BS1 4HQ   (0117) 930 7160

A particularly successful branch of the national fish-specialist chain – "no surprises, but it's always very good". / **Details:** www.lochfyne.com; Near Bristol Temple Meads station, next to Queen's Square; 10 pm, Sat 10.30 pm.

Mud Dock Café
CycleWorks £36
40 The Grove BS1 4RB   (0117) 934 9734

"An excellent spot on a sunny day, with its terrace overlooking the quay"; this "laid-back, warehouse-style café" – over a bike store – it tipped for its "splendid views", and serves up some decent snacks too; "shame about the service". / **Details:** www.mud-dock.com; close to the Industrial Museum & Arnolfini Gallery; 10 pm; closed Mon D & Sun D.

Primrose Café £39
6 Boyces Ave BS8 4AA   (0117) 946 6577
A "charming" and "old-fashioned" ambience ("despite lots of students") adds to the appeal of this "really friendly" café – "a nice place to watch the world go by" over a "healthy" breakfast, or a bun; at night the food's more ambitious (with "expertly-cooked fish" the top recommendation). / **Details:** www.primrosecafe.co.uk; Right in Clifton Village; 10 pm; Sun D; no booking at L.

Prosecco £40
25 The Mall BS8 4JG   (0117) 973 4499
"An authentic family-fun Clifton Italian", decked out in a rather metropolitan style, that inspires almost unanimously positive reports; let's hope the "increased popularity after featuring in the Ramsay TV programme" doesn't wreck it! / **Details:** www.proseccoclifton.com; 11.30 pm; closed Mon & Sun, Tue-Thu L ; no Amex.

Rajpoot £39
52 Upper Belgrave Rd BS8 2XP   (0117) 973 3515
"A much nicer dining room than many Indians, very good food and friendly service" – what's not to like at this Clifton fixture? / **Details:** www.rajpootrestaurant.co.uk; 11 pm; D only, closed Sun.

riverstation £43
The Grove BS1 4RB   (0117) 914 4434
"Amazing views" add interest to a visit to this former river-police station, which has a "gem of a setting" on the docks; fans say the food is "simple and stylish", and say service is "perfect" too, but critics find performance "variable", especially on the food front. / **Details:** www.riverstation.co.uk; 10.30 pm, Fri & Sat 11 pm; closed Sat L & Sun D; no Amex.

Rockfish
Mitch Tonks £42
128-130 Whiteladies Rod BS8 2RS   (0117) 9737384
"Mitch Tonks is back!", with this "reincarnation of FishWorks" (the fishmonger/bistro chain he founded, of which this site was the Bristol branch); most reports suggest it's "better than its predecessor", and offers "superb fish, simply cooked" – they also observe, however, that it is "not cheap". / **Details:** www.rockfishgrill.co.uk; 10.30 pm; closed Mon & Sun.

San Carlo £46 Ⓐ

44 Corn St BS1 1HQ (0117) 922 6586

OK, it's never going to be a great foodie hot spot, but this "OTT" city-centre Italian has already — rather like its Manchester sibling — established itself as a "vibrant" destination, with standards "better than you might expect"; "fish and seafood are always good".
/ **Details:** www.sancarlo.co.uk; 11 pm.

Severnshed £41 Ⓐ

The Grove, Harbourside BS1 4RB (0117) 925 1212

You may feel rather as if "eating in a warehouse" (actually it's a converted boathouse), but the food at this large, waterside bar/brasserie is pretty consistently "OK" (as are the cocktails).
/ **Details:** www.severnshedrestaurants.co.uk; Sun-Thu 10.30 pm, Fri & Sat 11.30 pm.

Teohs £29 Ⓣ

26-34 Lower Ashley Rd BS2 9NP (0117) 907 1191

"Cavernous" and "echoey" it may be, but this "cheap and cheerful noodle bar" is tipped as a "great lunchtime rendezvous" nonetheless.
/ **Details:** www.teohs.net; 100 yds from M32, J3; 10.30 pm; closed Sun; no Amex.

The Thali Café £22 Ⓐ⭐

12 York Rd BS6 5QE (0117) 942 6687

"Very fresh-tasting food" at "low prices" — albeit "from a very limited menu" — makes this "delightfully bizarre" but "very enjoyable" Indian operation very popular; it's one of a four-strong chain, whose latest member recently opened in Clifton. / **Details:** www.thethalicafe.co.uk; 10 pm; D only, closed Mon; no Amex.

BROAD HAVEN, PEMBROKESHIRE 4–4B

Druidstone Hotel £40 Ⓐ

SA62 3NE (01437) 781221

"Engaging, if uneven"; this "tucked-away", "hippy-chic" restaurant-with-room wins over all reporters with its charm and its views; most of them like the food too, but — particularly in the bar — it can seem "overpriced". / **Details:** www.druidstone.co.uk; from B4341 at Broad Haven turn right, then left after 1.5m; 9.30 pm. **Accommodation:** 11 & 7 holiday cottages rooms, from £75.

BROADWAY, WORCESTERSHIRE 2–1C

Russell's £50 Ⓐ⭐

20 High St WR12 7DT (01386) 853555

"They make an extra effort" — on both the food and service fronts — at this "charming" restaurant in the heart of a chocolate-box Cotswold village; even fans tend to note it as an "expensive" destination, but it's also often tipped as a "a brilliant spot for a very good-value set lunch".
/ **Details:** www.russellsofbroadway.co.uk; 9.30 pm; closed Sun D. **Accommodation:** 7 rooms, from £95.

BROMLEY, KENT 3–3B

Saigon City £32 Ⓣ

38a East St BR1 1QU (020) 8464 2232

A new Vietnamese restaurant, already attracting uniformly positive reviews, and tipped for its "very tasty, flavoursome and beautifully-presented" dishes, and its "friendly" service; fish dishes are "particularly good". / **Details:** 11 pm.

Tamasha £44
131 Widmore Rd BR1 3AX (020) 8460 3240

*Done out in colonial style, this "very different" Indian has a big name hereabouts, and generally "lives up to the local hype"; even fans can find prices "on the high side", though, and sceptics found it "over-rated" or "too full of birthday parties". / **Details:** www.tamasha.co.uk; 10.30 pm; no shorts. **Accommodation:** 7 rooms, from £65.*

BROUGHTON, LANCASHIRE 5–1A

Italian Orchard £32 Ⓐ
96 Whittingham Ln PR3 5DB (01772) 861240
*"It may look unremarkable", but this large Italian restaurant – which imports many of its ingredients – is tipped for its "phenomenal stock of Italian wines"; there are some delights hidden-away in the menu too, if you "choose carefully"! / **Details:** www.italianorchard.com; 10.30 pm.*

BROUGHTON, NORTH YORKSHIRE 8–4B

Bull At Broughton £43 Ⓐ
BD23 3AE (01756) 792065
*Northcote's fourth gastropub offshoot (part of the fast-expanding Ribble Valley Inns chain) is smaller than its siblings and "appears to lack their 'wow'-factor" – it's a "reliable but unexciting dining pub"; time for a pause in the expansion programme, perhaps? / **Details:** www.thebullatbroughton.com; 9 pm.*

BRUNDALL, NORFOLK 6–4D

Lavender House £29 Ⓐ ★
39 The St NR13 5AA (01603) 712215
*Richard Hughes's "beautiful" thatched restaurant has a "pleasant centre-of-village location" and provides "an excellent standard of food, service and ambience". / **Details:** www.thelavenderhouse.co.uk; 9.30 pm; D only, closed Sun & Mon; no Amex.*

BRUTON, SOMERSET 2–3B

At The Chapel £39 Ⓐ
High St BA10 0AE (01749) 814070
*"Light, modern and spacious", this "attractively converted chapel" has become a "real community foodie focal point", offering "everything from coffee and croissants to excellent contemporary cuisine" (and good pizzas too). / **Details:** www.atthechapel.co.uk; 9.30 pm; closed Mon & Sun D; no Amex.*

Riverford Field Kitchen   £36   **Ⓐ ⭐ ⭐**
Wash Barn, Buckfast Leigh TQ11 0JU (01803) 762074
*"A mouth-watering selection of fabulous vegetable-based dishes straight
from the farm to the plate" is served up "bursting with flavour" at this
communal-tables farm dining room, which all reporters proclaim
an "absolute delight"; "you must book", though, "and do remember
to take a map". /* **Details:** *www.riverford.co.uk; closed Mon D & Sun D;
no Amex.*

The Stapleton Arms   £35   **Ⓐ**
Church Hill SP8 5HS (01963) 370396
*"A very welcoming pub" that's "charmingly decorated in rustic style",
serving "really interesting snacks and pub favourites" and "really good
ales" to match; something of an "oasis" locally, it has an impressive
reporter-following. /* **Details:** *www.thestapletonarms.com; 10 pm, 9.30 pm
Sun.* **Accommodation:** *4 rooms, from £90.*

The Trout
The Trout Inn   £44   **Ⓐ**
Tadpole Bridge SN7 8RF (01367) 870382
*"What could be nicer on a sunny day than to sit in a garden near the
Thames?"; this historic inn is also praised for its "innovative" fare,
and its "caring " service too. /* **Details:** *www.trout-inn.co.uk; 11 pm; closed
Sun D; no Mastercard.* **Accommodation:** *6 rooms, from £120.*

Queen's Head Inn   £40   **Ⓐ**
Main St NN17 3DY (01780) 450272
*This "genuinely olde-worlde" village pub had made quite a name under
its former owners, but changed hands as our survey for the year was
under way (so we've left it un-rated); the new owner successfully runs
a number of other pub/restaurants, so fingers crossed...
/* **Details:** *www.thequeensheadbulwick.co.uk; 9.30 pm; closed Mon & Sun D.*

The Dysart Arms   £37   **Ⓣ**
Bowes Gate Rd CW6 9PH (01829) 260183
*This church-side boozer has a "great setting" and is, typical of the
Brunning & Price chain of which it forms a part – it's a "friendly" place
with "good beer" and "dependable" food.
/* **Details:** *www.dysartarms-bunbury.co.uk; 9.30 pm, Sun 9 pm.*

Rancliffe Arms   £35   **Ⓐ**
139 Loughborough Rd NG11 6QT (0115) 98447276
*This "beautiful" and "relaxed" old inn is of particular renown for
offering "the best carvery for miles around"; this is not always available,
but fortunately "the range and quality of the food available on non-
carvery dates is very good too"! /* **Details:** *www.rancliffearms.co.uk; 9pm.*

Hoste Arms   £42

The Green PE31 8HD   (01328) 738777
"In the heart of a pretty village", this "lovely" old coaching inn is always "full of people 'up from town'" — drawn more by the *"amiable" atmosphere than by food that's been uneven in recent years; following the death of founder Paul Whittome (RIP 2010), it's now managed by his wife and daughters.* / **Details:** www.hostearms.co.uk; 6m W of Wells; 9 pm; no Amex. **Accommodation:** 36 rooms, from £112.

Devonshire Fell   £46

BD23 6BT   (01756) 729000
"Really one to watch"; this exceptional ducally-owned inn (sibling to the Devonshire Arms) is hailed by all reporters for its "beautiful" cuisine, and "wonderful" views across the valley too.
/ **Details:** www.devonshirefell.co.uk. **Accommodation:** 12 rooms, from £138.

Maison Bleue   £45

30-31 Churchgate St IP33 1RG   (01284) 760623
"A bit of a surprise, in Bury St Edmunds"; the Crépy family's "great-value" fish restaurant is, on most accounts, "an absolute delight" thanks not least to its "superb" cuisine; the occasional reporter does fear, however, that it's becoming "too popular".
/ **Details:** www.maisonbleue.co.uk; near the Cathedral; 9.30 pm; closed Mon & Sun; no Amex.

Pea Porridge   £41

28-29 Cannon St IP33 1JR   (01284) 700200

WINNER 2011
RÉMY MARTIN
FINE CHAMPAGNE COGNAC

"In a quiet part of the town", this "absolutely brilliant" new Gallic bistro enchants almost all who comment on it with its "wonderfully balanced and flavoured dishes", its "small but carefully-sourced wine list" and its "delightful" service. / **Details:** www.peaporridge.co.uk; 10 pm; closed Mon & Sun; no Amex.

The Alpine   £47

135 High Rd WD23 1JA   (020) 8950 2024
"Takes a lot of beating for a 'local'" — this Italian restaurant of four decades' standing *"maintains a consistently high standard".*
/ **Details:** www.thealpinerestaurant.co.uk; 10.30 pm; closed Mon; no shorts.

St James   £45   Ⓐ ⭐
30 High St WD23 3HL   (020) 8950 2480
*"A culinary oasis in the desert around Watford" – this "local gem" won
consistent praise this year for its "friendly welcome" and "high-class"
cooking; it's an "attractive" place, on most reports, but critics can find
it "noisy". / Details: www.stjamesrestaurant.co.uk; opp St James Church; 9 pm;
closed Sun; booking essential.*

Alimentum   £46   ⭐
152-154 Hills Rd CB2 8PB   (01223) 413000
*Despite its "grotty" location, "echoey and minimalist" decor,
and "slightly amateurish" service, this ambitious three-year old has
become the most reported-on place in town; it's all down to chef/patron
(and ex-Midsummer House chef) Mark Poynton, and the "flair and
imagination" of his cuisine. / Details: www.restaurantalimentum.co.uk;
10 pm; closed Sun D; booking essential.*

Backstreet Bistro   £39   Ⓣ
2 Sturton St CB1 2QA   (01223) 306306
*"They've managed to create a genuine community feel in most unlikely
premises, which were once a little-loved pub", at this descriptively-
named spot – a top tip for "neighbourhood casual dining".
/ Details: www.back-street.co.uk; 9.30 pm, Fri & Sat 10 pm; closed Mon.*

The Cambridge Chop House   £39   ✖
1 Kings Pde CB2 1SJ   (01223) 359506
*Fans praise the "genuine, if simple", cooking on offer at this city-centre
stand-by; too many critics for comfort, however, find this a "gloomy and
depressing" place – "Cambridge complacency strikes again!"
/ Details: 10.30 pm, Sat 11 pm, Sun 9.30 pm.*

Charlie Chan   £30   Ⓣ
14 Regent St CB2 1DB   (01223) 359336
*"Dim sum that's a great hit with the local Chinese community"
is possibly the best reason to seek out this much commented-on but
"fairly standard" spot; "avoid downstairs". / Details: 11 pm.*

Cotto   £55   ⭐
183 East Rd CB1 1BG   (01223) 302010
*This café/restaurant near Anglia Ruskin University "excels as a
lunchtime hang-out", when it offers "really good soups and sarnies";
its "fancy evening cuisine" is also pretty popular, though, and it's
complemented by a "short but interesting" wine list at "reasonable
prices". / Details: www.cottocambridge.co.uk; 8.45 pm; opening times vary
seasonally.*

D'Arrys   £36   Ⓐ
2-4 King St CB1 1LN   (01223) 505015
*One reporter did mention the food ("always well-executed, with some
Asian inspirations"), but it's the wines – the "eclectic" list of the
D'Arenberg vineyard – that figure most in feedback on this 'cookhouse
and wine shop'. / Details: www.darrys.co.uk; 10 pm; need 8+ to book.*

Dojo   £29   Ⓐ
1-2 Millers Yd, Mill Ln CB2 1RQ   (01223) 363471
*"Pan Asian fare delivered at speed in huge portions" – "and they were
doing it long before Wagamama hit town!" – has made this "student
joint" a veritable "Cambridge institution"; "pity there are so few tables".
/ Details: www.dojonoodlebar.co.uk; off Trumpington St; 11 pm; no Amex;
no booking.*

Graffiti

Hotel Felix £47

Whitehouse Ln CB3 0LX (01223) 277977

Fans of this designerish venture on the fringes of town extol it as an all-round "high-quality" experience; service can be "hit-and-miss", though – critics think "effort would be better spent on developing the menu than producing pretty looking food designed to impress guidebooks". / **Details:** www.hotelfelix.co.uk; 10 pm, Fri & Sat 10.30 pm, Sun 9.30 pm. **Accommodation:** 52 rooms, from £190.

Hotel Du Vin £50

15-19 Trumpington St CB2 1QA (01223) 227330

"By Cambridge standards", the food and service at this outpost of the boutique-hotel/bistro chain "are actually pretty good" – it has a notably "pleasant" atmosphere too, and the "cosmopolitan" wine list includes some "unexpected" choices. / **Details:** www.hotelduvin.com; 9.45 pm, Fri & Sat 10.30 pm. **Accommodation:** 41 rooms, from £180.

Jamie's Italian £38

The Old Library, Wheeler St CB2 3QJ (01223) 654094

Fans of J Oliver's "crowded" Italian newcomer tip this "atmospheric transformation" of a "beautiful building", and see it as "a needed addition" to the locality; up-and-down reports, however, tend to confirm fears that the fast-expanding chain may be "over-stretching itself". / **Details:** www.jamieoliver.com/italian/cambridge.

Loch Fyne £40

37 Trumpington St CB2 1QY (01223) 362433

"It feels like a chain" – indeed, it was one of the very first outlets – but this "reliable" branch of the seafood multiple makes "a useful stand-by", and remains one of the most reported-on eateries in this under-provided town. / **Details:** www.lochfyne.com; opp Fitzwilliam Museum; 10 pm.

Midsummer House £105

Midsummer Common CB4 1HA (01223) 369299

Daniel Clifford's "exciting" and "stunningly presented" cuisine wins many fans for this one-time pub, nicely located by the Cam; even fans can find the prices "monstrous", though, and critics complain of a "chilly" atmosphere, and staff who "need to lighten up". / **Details:** www.midsummerhouse.co.uk; On the river Cam, near Mitchams Corner and the boat sheds; 9.30 pm; closed Mon, Tue L & Sun.

Oak Bistro £35

6 Lensfield Rd CB2 1EG (01223) 323361

"On the way into town from the station", a "lovely little place" that "bucks the rule" that "Cambridge is a restaurant wasteland", according to most – if not quite all – reporters, who praise its "good modern British food at reasonable prices". / **Details:** www.theoakbistro.co.uk; 10.15 pm; closed Sun.

Peking Restaurant £34

Unit 3, The Belvedere, Homerton St CB2 8NX (01223) 245457

"Let the owner choose for you!", at this "friendly" and "good-quality" Chinese, which offers many "refreshingly different" Sichuanese dishes; it was formerly in another location and, its newish (two-year-old) site can seem "cold" by comparison. / **Details:** 10.30 pm; closed Mon L; no Amex.

Rainbow Café £28 **T**

9a King's Pde CB2 1SJ (01223) 321551

A "large choice of vegetarian food and excellent organic wines" –
generally of a "very high standard" – make this cellar-café worth
seeking out; the setting, though, can be rather "uncomfortable".
/ **Details:** www.rainbowcafe.co.uk; 9 pm; closed Mon & Sun D; no Amex;
no booking.

Sea Tree £27 **★**

13 The Broadway CB1 3AH (01223) 414349

A "brilliant" arrival – a "chippy, eat-in restaurant and wet fish counter"
already widely acclaimed for its "fresh" and "tasty" fare; "non-standard
fish are available, and you can have them grilled if you want".
/ **Details:** 9pm sun; closed Thu L, Fri L & Sat L.

22 Chesterton Road £43 **A★**

22 Chesterton Rd CB4 3AX (01223) 351880

The Tommasos' "lovely small restaurant", on the 'other' side of Victoria
Avenue Bridge, remains "an oasis" of very decent cuisine in the
"gastronomic desert" that is the Varsity. / **Details:** www.restaurant22.co.uk;
9.30 pm; D only, closed Mon & Sun; children: 12+.

CANTERBURY, KENT 3–3D

Café des Amis £35 **A**

95 St Dunstan's St CT2 8AD (01227) 464390

"Always enjoyable!"; this long-established Mexican, by Westgate Towers,
isn't aiming to set the world on fire, but its loyal local following say it's
a "solidly dependable" spot that's "buzzy", "friendly" and "good value".
/ **Details:** www.cafedez.com; by Westgate Towers; 10 pm, Fri & Sat 10.30 pm,
Sun 9.30 pm; booking: max 6 at D.

Goods Shed £39 **A**

Station Road West CT2 8AN (01227) 459153

Shame this "great restaurant in a former railway goods shed" –
overlooking a farmers' market, from which much produce is sourced –
continues to undercut its appeal with "unrealistic pricing"; otherwise,
it's a "buzzy" and "enjoyable" destination, near the West station.
/ **Details:** www.thegoodsshed.net; 9.30 pm; closed Mon & Sun D.

Michael Caines
ABode Canterbury £58 **A**

High St CT1 2RX (01227) 766266

A handily-located dining room hailed by fans as "a jewel in the centre
of a gourmet wasteland"; it's still the weakest member of the Caines
stable, though, with critics complaining of "small portions",
"poor service" and "high prices". / **Details:** www.ABodehotels.co.uk; 10 pm;
closed Sun D. **Accommodation:** 72 rooms, from £150.

Le Gallois Y Cymro   **£48**   Ⓐ
6-10 Romilly Cr CF11 9NR   (029) 2034 1264
*Slightly erratic reports this year on the Canton brasserie long known
as the Welsh capital's top place; still, feedback is mostly upbeat –
fans say "new chef Grady Atkins has brought it back to its former best,
if not better", and even a reporter who felt the food was "overpriced"
said it was "very good". /* **Details:** *www.legallois-ycymro.com; 1.5m W
of Cardiff Castle; 9.30 pm, Fri & Sat 10 pm; closed Mon & Sun; no Amex.*

Happy Gathering   **£33**   Ⓐ
233 Cowbridge Road East CF11 9AL   (029) 2039 7531
*The setting is "large and cavernous", but the food is "above-average,"
at this city-centre Chinese. /* **Details:** *www.happygathering.co.uk; 10.30 pm,
Sun 9 pm.*

Mint And Mustard   **£38**   ★
134 Whitchurch Rd CF14 3LZ   (02920) 620333
*"The best Indian food around Cardiff by a country mile"; this "superior
south Indian" offers "fascinating Keralan cuisine" that – certainly
by local standards – is just "magnificent".
/* **Details:** *www.mintandmustard.co.uk; 11 pm; no shorts.*

Le Monde   **£39**   ★
62 St Mary St CF10 1FE   (029) 2038 7376
*"Uncluttered fresh food" – chosen by each customer from the
refrigerated display – makes this city-centre veteran "a treat" for all
who comment on it; "it's great for fish, seafood and steak, and the
chips are good too". /* **Details:** *www.le-monde.co.uk; 11 pm; closed Sun;
need 10+ to book.*

Patagonia   **£42**   ★
11 Kings Rd CF11 9BZ   (029) 2019 0265
*The Riverside (capital R!) location "may not hint at the delights within",
but this Spanish-run restaurant and coffee house is, for some reporters,
"the best of Cardiff's bad bunch", thanks to its "inventive" menu,
and its "exceptional" steaks. /* **Details:** *www.patagonia-restaurant.co.uk;
10.30 pm, Sat 11 pm; D only, closed Mon & Sun; no Amex.*

Riverside Cantonese Restaurant   **£32**   ★
44 Tudor St CF11 6AH   (029) 2037 2163
*"As many Chinese as western diners" stand testimony to the quality
of the food at the longest-established Cantonese restaurant in town;
inevitably, it is not actually by the river – the menu, however, is of note
for the "good selection of seafood" on offer!
/* **Details:** *www.riversidecantonese.com; close to Millennium stadium; 11 pm.*

Thai House   **£40**   Ⓐ
3-5 Guiford Cr CF10 2HJ   (029) 2038 7404
*Near the International Arena, "the best Thai in town"; the food
is "excellent", says one fan, and the "traditionally-dressed" staff are
"very polite" too. /* **Details:** *www.thaihouse.biz; 10.30 pm; closed Sun.*

Woods Brasserie   **£45**   Ⓣ
Pilotage Building, Stuart St CF10 5BW   (029) 2049 2400
*Food that's of "a good standard" makes this Cardiff Bay spot worth
knowing about; however, it's "not quite up to the standard of its
heyday" (when it was one of the only outlets in the area).
/* **Details:** *www.woods-brasserie.com; next to the Mermaid Quay Complex;
10 pm; closed Sun D.*

L'Enclume   £85   ★★

Cavendish St LA11 6PZ   (01539) 536362

"Each dish is delivered like a magician unveiling his next trick", at Simon Rogan's *"inspirational"* restaurant-with-rooms in an old Lakeland smithy; for cuisine that *"pushes the boundaries"*, the ratio by which 'hits' exceed 'misses' is becoming ever more impressive – this is a place that *"deserves its accolades"*. / **Details:** www.lenclume.co.uk; Junction 36 from M6, down A590 towards Cartmel; 9 pm; closed Mon L & Tue L; children: no children at D.
Accommodation: 12 rooms, from £148.

Rogan & Co   £42   Ⓐ

Devonshire Sq LA11 6QD   (01539) 535917

It's still not hitting the heights with total consistency, but Simon Rogan's two-year-old bistro is generally acclaimed for its "interesting" cuisine (and "excellent" presentation too). / **Details:** www.roganandcompany.co.uk; 9 pm; no Amex.

★★

Bybrook Restaurant
Manor House Hotel   £83

SN14 7HR   (01249) 782206

This "very civilised" manor house "in a cinematically picturesque village" inspires surprisingly few reports, but all feedback continues to confirm that the food is simply "outstanding"; the dining room is "comfortable" and "elegant" too, but the odd critic finds it "soulless". / **Details:** www.exclusivehotels.co.uk; 9.30 pm; closed Sat L; no trainers.
Accommodation: 48 rooms, from £235.

Ⓣ

Caunton Beck   £40

Main St NG23 6AB   (01636) 636793

"A very pleasant rural pub", tipped for its *"long menu"* of *"good food"*, and at *"reasonable prices"* too. / **Details:** www.wigandmitre.com; 6m NW of Newark past British Sugar factory on A616; 10 pm, Sun 9.30 pm.

Ⓐ★

Brockencote Hall   £54

DY10 4PY   (01562) 777876

"Even better with the new chef" – this Frenchified country house hotel (run by the Petitjean family) is a *"relaxing"* place where the food is often *"faultless"*; only complaint? – *"maybe too many weddings"*. / **Details:** www.brockencotehall.com; on A448, just outside village; 9.30 pm; no trainers. **Accommodation:** 17 rooms, from £96

Gidleigh Park   £127
TQ13 8HH   (01647) 432367

WINNER 2011

🏇 RÉMY MARTIN
FINE CHAMPAGNE COGNAC

Michael Caines's "flawless" cuisine "just gets better", at this luxurious but "welcoming" Tudorbethan mansion – voted the best restaurant in the UK by reporters this year; it's part of a "wonderful" all-round experience, further boosted by the "gorgeous" location, on the fringe of Dartmoor. / Details: www.gidleigh.com; from village, right at Lloyds TSB, take right fork to end of lane; 9.30 pm; no jeans or shorts; children: 8+ at D. **Accommodation:** *24 rooms, from £310.*

The Clarendon   £43
Redhall Ln WD3 4LU   (01923) 270009
Offering both a bar and a "posh restaurant", this "lively" former boozer offers food that "has improved with a new chef", and is now much more "interesting" than it was; "it's nicer downstairs". / Details: www.theclarendon.co.uk; 10 pm.

Colette's
The Grove   £82
WD17 3NL   (01923) 296015
Firing on all cylinders at present – the traditionally-styled main dining room of this vast, swish country house hotel is naturally "a bit pricey", but offers a "good dining experience" across the board. / Details: www.thegrove.co.uk; J19 or 20 on M25; 9.30 pm; D only, closed Mon & Sun; jacket; children: 16+. **Accommodation:** *227 rooms, from £290.*

The Glasshouse
The Grove   £45
WD3 4TG   (01923) 296015
"Very expensive, for what's essentially a self-service restaurant" – the attractive, buffet-style dining room at this groovy-grand country house does have its fans, but "seems to be putting prices up without increasing quality". / Details: www.thegrove.co.uk; 9.30 pm, Sat 10.30 pm. **Accommodation:** *227 rooms, from £290.*

The Olive Press   £37
Landmark Hs, Station Rd SK8 7BS   (0161) 488 1180
A branch of Paul Heathcote's chain, sometimes tipped for its "brilliant" pizzas; service has sometimes seemed "chaotic", though, of late, leading to some "very ordinary" experiences overall. / Details: www.heathcotes.co.uk/olivepress/cheadle-hulme-restaurant.html; 10 pm; no shorts.

Brasserie Blanc
The Queen's Hotel   **£42**   Ⓐ
The Promenade GL50 1NN   (01242) 266800
Have they finally cracked it?; this perennially lacklustre operation has
emerged as "one of the better Blanc outposts" of late, and it is now
invariably reviewed as "a nice, light buzzy restaurant with efficient
friendly service, and reasonably-priced food".
/ **Details:** www.brasserieblanc.com; 10.30 pm, Sat 11 pm, Sun 10 pm.

Le Champignon Sauvage   **£69**   ✪✪
24-28 Suffolk Rd GL50 2AQ   (01242) 573449
"Foodie hero" David Everitt-Mathias again thrills reporters with the
"incredibly well-thought out" cooking at his city centre veteran
(est. 1987), while Mrs E-M is a "perfect hostess", and presides over
a "great-value" wine list; gripes? – "other staff occasionally slip up",
and the room is a touch "sterile".
/ **Details:** www.lechampignonsauvage.co.uk; near Cheltenham Boys College; 9 pm;
closed Mon & Sun.

Hotel Du Vin   **£50**   Ⓐ
Parabola Rd GL50 3AQ   (01242) 588450
Currently one of the steadier performers in the wine-led boutique-
hotel/bistro chain – no one rates the food less than "dependable",
and this "cleverly designed" space has a "good atmosphere" too.
/ **Details:** www.hotelduvin.com; 10 pm; no shorts. **Accommodation:** 49 rooms,
from £145.

Lumière   **£59**   Ⓐ✪✪
Clarence Pde GL50 3PA   (01242) 222200
"A consistently top-class experience"; new owners Jon Howe and Helen
Aubrey create some "fantastic" and "imaginative" dishes from
"unusual" ingredients, at this "friendly" townhouse-restaurant in the
city-centre, with which reporters find simply no fault.
/ **Details:** www.lumiere.cc; off the promenade on the inner ring; 9 pm; closed
Mon & Sun, Tue L; booking: max 10; children: 8+ D.

The Royal Well Tavern   **£38**   Ⓣ
5 Royal Well Pl GL50 3DN   (01242) 221212
An agreeable gastropub two-year-old tipped as "the kind of place you'd
love to have on your doorstop"; "the set menu is exceptional value".
/ **Details:** www.theroyalwelltavern.com; by the main bus station; 10 pm,
Sat 10.30 pm; closed Sun D.

Storyteller   **£35**   Ⓐ✪
11 North Pl GL50 4DW   (01242) 250343
An "excellent" format – featuring a walk-in wine room – distinguishes
this attractive and "very friendly" spot, two minutes' walk from the
town-centre, and the food is consistently highly-rated too.
/ **Details:** www.storyteller.co.uk; near the cinema; 10 pm; no Amex.

CHESTER, CHESHIRE   5–2A

Aqua-Vitus   **£42**   Ⓣ
58 Watergate St CH1 2LA   (01244) 313721
"An excellent lunch, and one that's very good value" is a particular
attraction of this Franco-Swedish venture, intriguingly located in an
ancient street. / **Details:** www.aquavitus.co.uk; 10.30 pm; closed Sun; no Amex.

La Brasserie
The Chester Grosvenor £54

Eastgate CH1 1LT (01244) 324024

It's undoubtedly "expensive", but this "smart" brasserie of an unusually upmarket city-centre hotel offers a surprisingly convincing pastiche of the classic Gallic brasserie experience – in fact, it's better than that, as breakfast here is a "class act" too! / **Details:** www.chestergrosvenor.com; 10 pm. **Accommodation:** 80 rooms, from £240.88.

Moules A Go Go £37

39 Watergate Row CH1 2LE (01244) 348818

"Fun and friendly, and the food's not bad either" – this "slightly crushed" bistro in the city's picturesque first-floor 'rows' may not set the world on fire, but it remains a "good-value" destination.
/ **Details:** www.moulesagogo.co.uk; 10 pm, Sun 9 pm.

Simon Radley
The Chester Grosvenor £93

Eastgate CH1 1LT (01244) 324024

Once known as 'Arkle', this plush city-centre hotel dining room continues to win praise for its "top-class food" and its "formal yet relaxed service"; even fans can find it "overpriced" though, so beware of seeking consolation in the "superb" wine list!
/ **Details:** www.chestergrosvenor.com; 9 pm; D only, closed Mon & Sun; no Amex; no trainers; children: 12+. **Accommodation:** 82 rooms, from £180.

Upstairs at the Grill £42

70 Watergate St CH1 2LA (01244) 344883

"They know their steaks", and offer a "good-value wine list" too, at this agreeable venture, whose stated aim is to bring some 'Manhattan style' to this originally Roman city-centre. / **Details:** www.upstairsatthegrill.co.uk; Mon-Thu D only, Fri-Sun open L & D.

CHETTLE, DORSET 2–3C

Castleman Hotel £35

DT11 8DB (01258) 830096

This small and traditional manor house hotel is tipped for its "excellent value" (and "fabulous breakfasts" too).
/ **Details:** www.castlemanhotel.co.uk; 1m off the A354, signposted; 9 pm; D only, ex Wed & Sun open L & D; no Amex. **Accommodation:** 8 rooms, from £80.

CHICHESTER, WEST SUSSEX 3–4A

Comme Ça £52

67 Broyle Rd PO19 6BD (01243) 788724

What's not to like? – this "really first-class French restaurant", is unanimously acclaimed for its "outstanding" cooking, its "courteous" staff and its "pleasant" location; it has a "delightful garden" too!
/ **Details:** www.commeca.co.uk; 0.5m N of city-centre; 9.30 pm, Fri & Sat 10.30 pm; closed Mon, Tue L & Sun D.

Field & Fork ⭐

Pallant House Gallery £44

9 North Pallant PO19 1TJ (01243) 770 827

*This "beautiful" gallery-café serves up some "imaginative" dishes which turn out "unexpectedly well"; "it can get busy, but an atmosphere of calm prevails". / **Details:** www.fieldandfork.co.uk; 10.30 pm; closed Mon, Tue D & Sun D.*

West Stoke House £66 ⭐

PO18 9BN (01243) 575226

*"Set in a lovely Georgian farmhouse", on the South Downs, this "refined" restaurant-with-rooms generally lives up to its high reputation for "cleverly cooked and wittily-presented cuisine"; on the downside, the interior is a bit "cavernous", and service doesn't always measure up. / **Details:** www.weststokehouse.co.uk; 9 pm; closed Mon & Tue; children: 12+ D. **Accommodation:** 8 rooms, from £150.*

CHIGWELL, ESSEX 3–2B

The Bluebell £45 🅣

117 High Rd IG7 6QQ (020) 8500 6282

*In an old cottage, a local restaurant frequently tipped for "good food and value". / **Details:** www.thebluebellrestaurant.co.uk; 10 pm, Sat 12.30 am; closed Mon.*

CHILGROVE, WEST SUSSEX 3–4A

The Fish House £59 ⭐⭐

High St PO18 9HX (01243) 519444

*On the edge of the South Downs, this year-old restaurant-with rooms has won instant acclaim for its "absolutely superb" fish and seafood; critics, though, can find it a little pricey for what it is. / **Details:** www.thefishhouse.co.uk; 9.30 pm, Fri & Sat 10 pm; no Amex. **Accommodation:** 15 rooms, from £100.*

CHILHAM, KENT 3–3C

White House £35 🅣

The Sq CT4 8BY (01227) 730355

*"A superb village location" adds to the appeal of this "very friendly" pub, tipped for its good-value selection of straightforward dishes, featuring "well-cooked local produce". / **Details:** www.thewhitehorsechilham.co.uk; 9 pm; closed Sun D; no Amex.*

CHILLESFORD, WOODBRIDGE, SUFFOLK 3–1D

The Froize Free House Restaurant £43 🅐

The St IP12 3PU (01394) 450282

*A "popular" inn, where catering comes carvery-style, and pleases most reporters; leave space for one of the "superb desserts". / **Details:** www.froize.co.uk; 8.30 pm but varies seasonally; closed Mon, Tue D, Wed D & Sun D.*

CHINNOR, OXFORDSHIRE 2–2D

The Sir Charles Napier £50 🅐⭐

Spriggs Alley OX39 4BX (01494) 483011

*"The most beautiful gardens" and a "delightful" Chilterns location make this "classy" pub particularly "hard to beat on a sunny day" (and it has long been celebrated as a day-out destination from the Smoke); the food's "wonderful" too, as are the "lovely wines". / **Details:** www.sircharlesnapier.co.uk; M40, J6 into Chinnor, turn right at roundabout, carry on straight up hill for 2 miles; 10 pm; closed Mon & Sun D.*

Gibbon Bridge   £46   **T**
Green Ln PR3 2TQ   (01995) 61456
*Tipped particularly for its "fantastic setting" in the Forest of Bowland
(complete with "beautiful gardens"), the dining room of this rural hotel
also wins praise for its "fantastic menu using local and seasonal
ingredients".* / **Details:** www.gibbon-bridge.co.uk; 8.30 pm; no shorts.
Accommodation: 30 rooms, from £130

CHOLMONDELEY, CHESHIRE   5–3A

Cholmondeley Arms   £33   **A**
SY14 8HN   (01829) 720300
*"Traditional pub-style dishes", with "everything home-made" and
"very decently done", make this "cheerful" boozer popular with all who
comment on it; beware, though – "popularity with huntin' and shootin'
types can make sittin' near the bar rather loud".*
/ **Details:** www.cholmondeleyarms.co.uk; on A49, 6m N of Whitchurch;
10.30 pm; no Amex. **Accommodation:** 6 rooms, from £80.

CHURCH CROOKNAM, HAMPSHIRE   3–3A

Foresters   £43   **T**
Aldershot Rd GU52 9EP   (01252) 616503
*"A lovely pub in lovely surroundings", in the New Forest, tipped for
"'good home cooking without frills".*
/ **Details:** www.foresters@churchcrookham.co.uk; 11.30 pm.

CHURCH STRETTON, SHROPSHIRE   5–4A

Berry's   £27   **T**
17 High St SY6 6BU   (01694) 724452
*"Delicious cakes and excellent coffee" are among the highlights of a
visit to this village-centre café; it's also tipped for an "interesting"
(if "not enormous") wine list, which includes "local vineyards".*
/ **Details:** www.berryscoffeehouse.co.uk; 10 pm; closed for D Mon-Thu & Sun D;
no credit cards.

CHURCHILL, OXFORDSHIRE   2–1C

Chequers   £38   ★
Church Ln OX7 6NJ   (01608) 659393
*A pub-restaurant in a cute Cotswold village acclaimed by all reporters
for food of a "very high standard", and "very friendly service" too;
no wonder you "need to book".* / **Details:** 9.30 pm, sun 9 pm; no Amex.

CLACHAN, ARGYLL AND BUTE   9–3B

Loch Fyne Oyster Bar   £40   **A**
PA26 8BL   (01499) 600236
*"Enchanting views over the eponymous loch" and the "freshness of the
fish" justify the trek to this remote smokehouse café (run separately
from the chain it spawned); the odd sceptic, though, does wonder
if fame hasn't made the operation a bit "blasé".*
/ **Details:** www.loch-fyne.com; 10m E of Inveraray on A83; 8 pm.

CLAVERING, ESSEX
3–2B

The Cricketers
£39

Wicken Rd CB11 4QT (01799) 550442
OK, it's most famous for being run by Jamie's mum and dad (who've owned it for over 30 years), but this pub on the village green is consistently praised for "delicious pub food" at "reasonable prices".
/ **Details:** www.thecricketers.co.uk; on B1038 between Newport & Buntingford; 9.30 pm. **Accommodation:** 14 rooms, from £110.

CLIFTON, CUMBRIA
8–3A

George & Dragon
£36

CA10 2ER (01768) 865381
"An excellent addition to the Cumbrian pub scene" (and "just off the M6" too); most reporters enjoy "good" and "hearty" fare here, using "genuinely local" ingredients (often from the neighbouring estate).
/ **Details:** www.georgeanddragonclifton.co.uk; 9.30 pm. **Accommodation:** 10 rooms, from £85.

CLIPSHAM, RUTLAND
6–4A

The Olive Branch
£48

Main St LE15 7SH (01780) 410355
"I didn't realise pubs could cook like this!"; this "beautiful" gastropub "hidden away in a tiny village, off the A1" has won a massive fan club over the years, due to its "attentive" service and "superb" food.
/ **Details:** www.theolivebranchpub.com; 2m E from A1 on B664; 9.30 pm, Sun 9 pm; no Amex. **Accommodation:** 6 rooms, from £120.

CLITHEROE, LANCASHIRE
5–1B

Inn at Whitewell
£45

Forest of Bowland BB7 3AT (01200) 448222

"A truly glorious setting with spectacular views up the Trough of Bowland really makes the experience", at this "lovely" and romantic inn; dishes – often "classical and meat-driven" – "use excellent produce to first-rate effect". / **Details:** www.innatwhitewell.com; 9.30 pm; D only; no Amex. **Accommodation:** 23 rooms, from £113.

CLYTHA, MONMOUTHSHIRE
2–1A

Clytha Arms
£42

NP7 9BW (01873) 840206
This well-known inn is worth knowing about on the any-port-in-a-storm principle, and is tipped for food that's sometimes "wonderful"; not ever meal is a success, though, and the decor is "crummy".
/ **Details:** www.clytha-arms.com; on Old Abergavenny to Raglan Rd; 9.30 pm; closed Mon L & Sun D. **Accommodation:** 4 rooms, from £80.

The Old Bear   £42   Ⓐ

Riverhill KT11 3DX   (01932) 862116

"Excellent food in leafy suburbia"; this former pub achieves "unexpectedly high standards", especially in an area that's something of a "gastronomic desert". / **Details:** www.theoldbearcobham.co.uk; 10 pm; closed Sun D.

Kirkstile Inn   £38   Ⓐ

Loweswater CA13 0RU   (01900) 85219

"A winter evening by the open fire is the best time to visit" this "gem" of an inn, in a "remote corner of the Lakes" – it serves up "good-value" food and "an excellent selection of locally-brewed beers". / **Details:** www.kirkstile.com; 9 pm; no Amex. **Accommodation:** 10 rooms, from £46.50.

Quince & Medlar   £39   Ⓐ★★

13 Castlegate CA13 9EU   (01900) 823579

"Can vegetarian food get any better?"; this elegant townhouse-restaurant has for over twenty years provided cooking "so good you won't miss the meat". / **Details:** www.quinceandmedlar.co.uk; next to Cockermouth Castle; 9.30 pm; D only, closed Mon & Sun; no Amex; children: 5+.

Baumann's Brasserie   £36   Ⓐ

4-6 Stoneham St CO6 1TT   (01376) 561453

Chef/patron Mark Baumann oversees "a skilled kitchen", at his popular local brasserie; reports were a bit up-and-down this year, but most reports were of "quality" fare, a "lively" atmosphere and "genuinely friendly" service. / **Details:** www.baumannsbrasserie.co.uk; 9.30 pm; closed Mon & Tue.

Green Room   Ⓐ
North Hill Hotel   £38

50-51 North Hill CO1 1PY   (01206) 574001

"A recent addition to the Colchester scene", this small-scale outfit enjoys "a growing reputation" for its "well thought-out and executed modern European cuisine". / **Details:** www.northhillhotel.com; 9.30 - 9.00 pm sun. **Accommodation:** 13 rooms, from £85.

COLERNE, WILTSHIRE

2–2B

Lucknam Park

£102

SN14 8AZ   (01225) 742777

For a top country retreat, many reporters would recommend this "beautiful old manor house" (with spa), where Hywel Jones's cuisine is often "brilliant", and service is "impeccable" too; offering less formality, and lower bills, there's now a brasserie option too.
/ **Details:** www.lucknampark.co.uk; 6m NE of Bath; 9.30 pm; no jeans or trainers; children: 5+ at D. **Accommodation:** 41 rooms, from £280.

COLNE, LANCASHIRE

5–1B

Banny's Restaurant

£26

1 Vivary Way   BB8 9NW   (01282) 856220
"Excellent fish and chips, always served hot" – the star menu item at this big (280-seat!) brasserie-style operation, which the locals say is "consistently excellent". / **Details:** www.bannys.co.uk.

CONGLETON, CHESHIRE

5–2B

Pecks

£45

Newcastle Rd   CW12 4SB   (01260) 275161
The "unique dining experience of 'dinner at eight'" – when a no-choice set menu is served, with pudding a highlight – continues to commend this "lively and novel" family-run veteran to all who comment on it; prices are lower earlier in the week. / **Details:** www.pecksrest.co.uk; off A34; 8 pm; closed Mon & Sun D; booking essential.

COOKHAM, BERKSHIRE

3–3A

Maliks

£42

High St   SL6 9SF   (01628) 520085
"Wonderful Indian food" – including "unusual dishes, with wonderful fresh spices" – makes this "cosy" former boozer – Heston Blumenthal's favourite place for a curry, apparently – an "outstanding" destination; the only problem is that it can sometimes be rather "crowded".
/ **Details:** www.maliks.co.uk; from the M4, Junction 7 for A4 for Maidenhead; 11.30 pm, Sun 10.30 pm.

CORSE LAWN, GLOUCESTERSHIRE

2–1B

Corse Lawn Hotel

£49

GL19 4LZ   (01452) 780771
"Off the beaten track", it may be, but this "super" destination – the Hine family's Queen Anne-style village house hotel – is worth seeking out for its "very good use of local ingredients", complemented by a "very long and reasonably-priced wine list".
/ **Details:** www.corselawn.com; 5m SW of Tewkesbury on B4211; 9.30 pm.
Accommodation: 19 rooms, from £150.

CORTON DENHAM, SOMERSET 2–3B

The Queen's Arms £37
DT9 4LR (01963) 220317
*An out-of-the-way "gem" of a boozer, tipped particularly for its "wonderful pork pies", and its "great selection of apple juices and ciders" too. / **Details:** www.thequeensarms.com; 10 pm, Sun 9.30 pm.*
Accommodation: *5 rooms, from £85.*

CRANBROOK, KENT 3–4C

Apicius £49 ★★
23 Stone St TN17 3HF (01580) 714666

"Continuing to delight" – Tim Johnson's "splendid small-scale high street operation" is a "calm, attractive, and spacious room", where the cuisine is "superb", and the service is "friendly and knowledgeable".
*/ **Details:** www.restaurant-apicius.co.uk; take the A21, turn left through Goudhurst, take the 3rd exit left on the roundabout; 9 pm; closed Mon, Tue, Sat & Sun D; no Amex; children: 8+.*

CRASTER, NORTHUMBERLAND 8–1B

Jolly Fisherman £20
NE66 3TR (01665) 576461
*"The sea view's great", at this waterside boozer, which is again tipped for its "superb crab sandwiches"; it's "so popular", though, and service can't always keep up. / **Details:** near Dunstanburgh Castle; 11 pm; L only; no credit cards; no booking.*

CRAYKE, NORTH YORKSHIRE 5–1D

Durham Ox £42 🅐★
Westway YO61 4TE (01347) 821506
This "fabulous" village gastropub – "lovely and cosy inside, and with a great garden" – "isn't trying to be a restaurant", but serves dishes that while "not posh, are a cut above regular pub food".
*/ **Details:** www.thedurhamox.com; 9.30 pm, Sat 10 pm, Sun 8.30 pm.*
Accommodation: *5 rooms, from £100.*

CREIGIAU, CARDIFF 2–2A

Caesars Arms £45 ★
Cardiff Rd CF15 9NN (029) 2089 0486
*"Fresh meat and fish, always simply cooked, but to a high standard" – from produce chosen at the counter – maintains continuing popularity for this "bustling" rural eatery, a "relaxed" place long on "Welsh bonhomie". / **Details:** beyond Creigiau, past golf club; 10 pm; closed Sun D.*

The Bear £36 **A**

High St NP8 1BW (01873) 810408
*This "intimate" inn ("as seen in many an 18th-century novel") has
quite a reputation, and it can be "phenomenally busy"; all reports
confirm that it offers "solid country cooking" – highlights include
"fine steaks of Welsh beef" and a "classic bread 'n' butter pudding".
/ Details: www.bearhotel.co.uk; 9.30 pm; D only, ex Sun open L only, closed Mon;
children: 7+. **Accommodation:** 34 rooms, from £90.*

Nantyffin Cider Mill £42 **A**

Brecon Rd NP8 1SG (01873) 810775
*"Reliable and locally-sourced food in a charming setting" makes this
"gem" – a gastropub since before the term was coined – "a great
discovery" for some reporters; overall, however, its ratings ebbed again
this year. / Details: www.cidermill.co.uk; on A40 between Brecon & Crickhowell;
9.30 pm; closed Mon; no Amex.*

Crinan Hotel £58 **T**

PA31 8SR (01546) 830261
*This remote and strikingly-located hotel is again tipped as an excellent
all-round destination for a meal... not that there are that many
alternatives in these parts. / Details: www.crinanhotel.com; 8.30 pm;
no Amex. **Accommodation:** 20 rooms, from £130.*

The Punch Bowl £42 **A ★**

LA8 8HR (01539) 568237
*"A great retreat from all the crowds" – this "remote" village inn makes
an excellent base for exploring the Lakes, not least because it offers
a "refined" cuisine "of restaurant quality".
/ Details: www.the-punchbowl.co.uk; off A5074 towards Bowness, turn right after
Lyth Hotel; 9.30 pm. **Accommodation:** 9 rooms, from £125.*

The Mark Cross Inn £36 **A**

Mark Cross TN6 3NP (01892) 852423
*Recently refurbished, this "pleasant" pub now has an atmosphere
rather "reminiscent of a library" (complete with a "lovely fire");
the "hearty" fare it offers is invariably rated as "solid", and sometimes
rather better. / Details: www.themarkcross.co.uk; 9.30 pm, Sun 9 pm;
no Amex.*

Albert's Table £44 **★**

49 South End CR0 1BF (020) 8680 2010
*"Surprisingly good" cooking, with "good use of seasonal produce",
has won lots of praise for this ambitious yearling; reports aren't entirely
consistent, though, and critics can find the whole "curiously less than
the sum of the parts". / Details: www.albertstable.co.uk; 10.30 pm; no Amex.*

Banana Leaf £30 **★**

7 Lower Addiscombe Rd CR0 6PQ (020) 8688 0297
*"Lovely food in a grotty restaurant in an awful area" – that's still the
deal at this stalwart South Indian in East Croydon, which – for those
who value food over other creature comforts – "still does the business".
/ Details: www.a222.co.uk/bananaleaf; near East Croydon station; 11.30 pm,
Sun 11 pm.*

Fish & Grill £42
48-50 South End CR0 1DP   (020) 8774 4060
"Awesome fish and some fabulous meat" win some rave reviews for
Malcolm John's neighbourhood newcomer; even fans, though, can find
its style *"a little formulaic".* / **Details:** www.fishandgrill.co.uk; 11.30 pm.

McDermotts Fish & Chips £23
5-7 The Forestdale Shopping Centre Featherbed Ln CR0 9AS
(020) 8651 1440
"Difficult to see what they could do better", say fans of this
"very superior chippy", which offers *"quality food"* at *"great prices"*;
"acceptable" wines too! / **Details:** www.mcdermottsfishandchips.co.uk;
9.30 pm, Sat 9 pm; closed Mon & Sun; no Amex.

CUCKFIELD, WEST SUSSEX 3–4B

Ockenden Manor £74
Ockenden Ln RH17 5LD   (01444) 416111
"A stunning panelled dining room" provides the setting in which to enjoy
some *"fine"* cuisine at this *"friendly"* country house hotel, which
attracted consistent praise from reporters this year.
/ **Details:** www.hshotels.co.uk; 9 pm; no jeans or trainers. **Accommodation:** 22
rooms, from £183.

CUPAR, FIFE 9–3D

Ostlers Close £40
25 Bonnygate KY15 4BU   (01334) 655574
"Hard to find", but worth seeking out, the Graham family's *"intimate"*
and *"quirky"* town-centre stalwart – *"a bit of a throwback to the '80s,
but none the worse for it"* – again wins praise for its *"brilliant"*,
traditional cooking. / **Details:** www.ostlersclose.co.uk; centrally situated in the
Howe of Fife; 9.30 pm; closed Sun & Mon, Tue-Fri D only, Sat L & D; children: 5+.

The Peat Inn £60
KY15 5LH   (01334) 840206
"Not cheap, but worth the money!"; the Smeddle family *"maintain
a very good level indeed"*, at this famous country inn – it remains
"full of atmosphere", and the menu delivers *"a brilliant gastronomic
experience".* / **Details:** www.thepeatinn.co.uk; at junction of B940 & B941,
SW of St Andrews; 9 pm; closed Mon & Sun. **Accommodation:** 8 rooms,
from £190.

DALRY, NORTH AYRSHIRE 9–4B

Braidwoods £64
Drumastle Mill Cottage KA24 4LN   (01294) 833544

*"A wee, converted cottage on a hillside, serving the best food
in Scotland"* (well, nearly) – all reports suggest that the food Keith and
Nicola Braidwood's *"tremendous"*, *"friendly"* restaurant simply *"never
disappoints".* / **Details:** www.braidwoods.co.uk; 9 pm; closed Mon, Tue L &
Sun D; children: 12+ at D.

T

Oven   £38
30 Duke St DL3 7AQ   (01325) 466668
*"No wonder they've expanded!"; "good food in huge portions" wins this
local restaurant a tip as a "real gem". / **Details:** www.ovenrestaurant.com;
9.30 pm, Sat 10 pm; closed Mon L & Sun D.*

DARTMOUTH, DEVON   1–4D

A

Angel   £65
2 South Embankment TQ6 9BH   (01803) 839425
*The year 2010 saw this famous harbourside restaurant lose both the
'New' in its name and its former chef/patron John Burton Race —
the site is being relaunched by the team behind the growing L'Ortolan
(Shinfield)- based empire, and should be 'one to watch'.
/ **Details:** www.thenewangel.co.uk; opp passenger ferry pontoon; 9.30 pm; closed
Mon & Sun; no Amex. **Accommodation:** 6 rooms, from £75.*

★ ★

The Seahorse   £53
5 South Embankment TQ6 9BH   (01803) 835147
*"Wonderful fresh fish properly cooked, and a lovely view too" – that's
the formula that's winning ever-greater renown for Mitch Tonks's
"sophisticated"-looking restaurant, by the River Dart; it's "not cheap,
but it delivers". / **Details:** www.seahorserestaurant.co.uk; 10 pm, Fri & Sat
10.30 pm; closed Mon, Tue L, Sat L & Sun.*

DAVENTRY, NORTHAMPTONSHIRE   2–1D

A ★

Fawsley Hall   £75
NN11 3BA   (01327) 892000
*An "impressive" setting the interior "feels like a castle") is twinned with
"highly competent" food at this Tudor country house hotel, which
is "a great venue for romance and special occasions"; poor service can
let the side down, however. / **Details:** www.fawsleyhall.com; on A361 between
Daventry & Banbury; 9.30 pm, Sun 9 pm. **Accommodation:** 59 rooms,
from £175.*

DEDHAM, ESSEX   3–2C

A

Milsoms   £42
Stratford Rd CO7 6HW   (01206) 322795
*This bar/brasserie offshoot of the famous Tolbooth (part of a small
country house hotel) is "an old favourite resting on its laurels" –
the food is "very average", and sometimes served with "attitude".
/ **Details:** www.milsomhotels.com; Just off the A12, the Stratford St Mary turning;
9.30 pm, Fri & Sat 10 pm; no booking. **Accommodation:** 15 rooms, from £115.*

A

The Sun Inn   £35
High St CO7 6DF   (01206) 323351
*This "beautiful old pub", in Constable Country, put in an uneven
performance this year; fans say it offers "excellent value", but others
are deeply unimpressed by its Mediterranean-influenced menu – "if this
is rustic Italian food, I'm a Dutchman!"
/ **Details:** www.thesuninndedham.com; opp church on the high street; Fri & Sat
10 pm, 9.30 pm. **Accommodation:** 5 rooms, from £75.*

A ✕

Le Talbooth   £58
Gun Hill CO7 6HP   (01206) 323150
*"Shame, because the setting is so beautiful…"; this "idyllic" riverside
veteran is not without fans praising its "high-quality" fare, but for too
many reporters it "promises a lot, but delivers little",
with "very disappointing food" at the centre of a "pompous" and
"dated" formula. / **Details:** www.milsomhotels.com; 5m N of Colchester
on A12, take B1029; 9.30 pm; closed Sun D; no jeans or trainers.*

DENHAM, BUCKINGHAMSHIRE 3–3A

Swan Inn £37 **A ⭐**
Village Rd UB9 5BH (01895) 832085
"Always busy" (and not just thanks to its location "close to the M40/M25"), this "friendly and buzzy" gastropub has a "great village location", and it offers sometimes "excellent" food too.
/ **Details:** www.swaninndenham.co.uk; 9.30 pm, Fri & Sat 10 pm.

DERBY, DERBYSHIRE 5–3C

Anoki £45 **A ⭐**
First Floor, 129 London Rd DE1 2QN (01332) 292888
"Such high standards are amazing, given the large scale of the operation", and this subcontinental in a former cinema is "so stylish" too: but wait – its "satellite" operation on the A38 is even better (Burton Road, Eggington, DE65 6GZ, tel 01283 704 888)!
/ **Details:** www.anoki.co.uk; 2m from town centre, opposite hospital; 11.30 pm; D only, closed Sun.

Le Bistrot Pierre £28 **A ⭐**
18 Friar Gate DE1 1BX (01332) 370470
For "French food, bistro-style", this "buzzy" and "good-value" spot almost invariably seems to satisfy – "it's often full, even when nearby places are empty". / **Details:** www.lebistrotpierre.co.uk; 10.30 pm, Sun & Mon 10 pm, Fri & Sat 11 pm; no Amex.

Darleys £47 **A**
Darley Abbey Mill DE22 1DZ (01332) 364987
This well-established, former mill by the river can seem "fussy" or "overpriced", but it attracts a fair number of reports, none of which suggest the food is less than good. / **Details:** www.darleys.com; 2m N of city centre by River Derwent; 9 pm; closed Sun D; no Amex.

Ebi Sushi £34 **T**
Abbey St DE22 3SJ (01332) 265656
"Impossibly tiny, but worth seeking out"; the proximity of a Toyota plant helps explain the otherwise implausible existence of this "stunning" city-fringe sushi and sashimi spot. / **Details:** 10.30 pm; D only, closed Mon & Sun; no Amex.

DINTON, BUCKINGHAMSHIRE 2–3C

La Chouette £62 **A ⭐**
Westlington Grn HP17 8UW (01296) 747422
Frederic, the Belgian chef/patron, may be "mad", but he is a "great" and "passionate" host, and "able in the kitchen" too; all reports agree that his restaurant — with its fantastic food and very interesting wine list — is "a hidden gem". / **Details:** off A418 between Aylesbury & Thame; 9 pm; closed Sat L & Sun; no Amex.

DODDISCOMBSLEIGH, DEVON 1–3D

Nobody Inn £38 **A**
EX6 7PS (01647) 252394
"A wonderful varied wine list, with options to suit all pockets" – not to mention a selection of 240 whiskies – is the stand-out attraction at this rural 16th-century inn; that said, its cooking was (in contrast to recent times) consistently well-rated this year. / **Details:** www.nobodyinn.co.uk; off A38 at Haldon Hill (signed Dunchidrock); 9 pm, Fri & Sat 9.30 pm; no Amex.
Accommodation: 5 rooms, from £60.

DONHEAD ST ANDREW, WILTSHIRE 2–3C

The Forester Inn £36 🅣
Lower St SP7 9EE   (01747) 828038
"More gastro than pub" – this cosy inn in a pretty village is tipped for
some *"excellent" food*. / **Details:** www.theforesterdonheasaintandrew.co.uk;
Off A30; 9 pm; closed Sun D.

DORCHESTER, DORSET 2–4B

Sienna £57 ✪✪
36 High West St DT1 1UP   (01305) 250022
"A most surprising tiny restaurant with excellent food" – all reporters
find a visit to Russell and Eléna Brown's venture a *"charming"* and
"personal" experience (*"if perhaps a little cramped"!*).
/ **Details:** www.siennarestaurant.co.uk; 9 pm; closed Mon & Sun; no Amex;
children: 12+.

Yalbury Cottage £48 🅐✪
DT2 8PZ   (01305) 262382

"A lovely cottage interior" and *"welcoming"* service set a cosy tone
at this small, part-thatched village hotel, which serves *"pleasing cooking
at reasonable prices"*. / **Details:** www.yalburycottage.com; 9 pm; D only,
closed Mon & Sun. **Accommodation:** 8 rooms, from £110.

DORE, SOUTH YORKSHIRE 5–2C

Moran's £43 ✪
289 Abbeydale Road South S17 3LB   (01142) 350101
A *"consistently good"* menu (with *"some creative choices"*) wins praise
for Brian and Sarah Moran's small local restaurant; not everyone
is wowed by the interior, but fans insist there's *"always a buzz"*.
/ **Details:** www.moranssheffield.co.uk; 9 pm; closed Mon, Tue L & Sun D;
no Amex.

DORKING, SURREY 3–3A

Little Dudley House £46 ✪
77 South St RH4 2JU   (01306) 885550
"A good addition to Dorking" – this venture in an imaginatively-
revamped Georgian building seems *"keen to impress"*, and early-days
reports suggest it is developing into an impressive all-rounder.
/ **Details:** www.littledudleyhouse.co.uk; 11pm.

DOVER, KENT 3–4D

The Allotment £38 ✪
9 High St CT16 1DP   (01304) 214467
"A real find", opposite the town hall of this culinarily benighted town –
"part coffee shop, part restaurant", it has a *"charming"* proprietor,
and offers *"honest"* cooking and *"interesting"* English wine at *"excellent
prices"*. / **Details:** www.theallotmentdover.co.uk; closed Mon & Sun; no Amex.

The Three Chimneys £71 ⒶⒶⒶ

Colbost IV55 8ZT (01470) 511258

"Finding your way is part of the treat!", when visiting Eddie and Shirley Spear's famous loch-side crofter's cottage – *"an unbeatable all-round experience"*, where *"truly superb"* cuisine (and an *"extensive"* wine selection too) are served in a location as *"stunning"* as it is remote. / **Details:** www.threechimneys.co.uk; 5m from Dunvegan Castle on B884 to Glendale; 9.45 pm; closed Sun L; children: 8+. **Accommodation:** 6 rooms, from £285.

Bistro 21 £47 Ⓐ

Aykley Heads Hs DH1 5TS (0191) 384 4354

This "quaint little restaurant", located "just outside the city-centre", has long been one of the best bets in the area, thanks to its "consistently good food" and its "friendly and competent" service. / **Details:** www.bistrotwentyone.co.uk; near Durham Trinity School; 10 pm; closed Sun.

ⒶⒶ

Gourmet Spot
Farnley Tower Hotel £53

The Ave DH1 4DX (0191) 384 6655

This "chic and contemporary" venture is somewhat "unexpected in an otherwise residential street"; "despite having having changed chef" (to Stephen Hardy) the (few) reports it inspires tend to confirm that it still offers food of "very high quality". / **Details:** www.gourmet-spot.co.uk; 9.30 pm; D only, closed Mon & Sun. **Accommodation:** 13 rooms, from £80.

Oldfields £38 Ⓐ

18 Claypath DH1 1RH (0191) 370 9595

As "a nice change from Durham's proliferating chains", this all-day brasserie wins strong praise for "good wholesome British food from great, local ingredients"; a couple of former fans this year, however, found the cuisine somewhat "uninspiring". / **Details:** www.oldfieldsrestaurants.com; 10 pm, Sun 9 pm.

Jolly Sportsman £44 Ⓐ

Chapel Ln BN7 3BA (01273) 890400

"Not really a pub any more", this "beautiful country restaurant" attracts an impressive number of reports, all of which suggest its "quality, classic cuisine" is "worth a detour". / **Details:** www.thejollysportsman.com; NW of Lewes; 9.15 pm, Sat 10 pm; no Amex.

ⒶⒶ

Star & Garter £41

PO18 0JG (01243) 811318

A "lovely" South Downs gastropub, which receives impressively consistent praise, not least for "a great selection of local meat and fresh fish, all well cooked". / **Details:** www.thestarandgarter.co.uk; 10 pm, Sun 9.30 pm; no Amex. **Accommodation:** 6 rooms, from £90.

Gravetye Manor   £77   Ⓐ
Vowels Ln RH19 4LJ   (01342) 810567

Unsurprisingly, the year which saw the business collapse into administration saw terrible reports on this potentially "splendid" country house hotel, long famous as a dining destination; no point in rating it, we feel, till it's clearer what the new régime can achieve.
*/ **Details:** www.gravetyemanor.co.uk; 2m outside Turner's Hill; 9.30 pm; jacket & tie; booking: max 8; children: 7+. **Accommodation:** 18 rooms, from £180.*

The Eyston Arms   £44   Ⓐ⭐
High St OX12 8JY   (01235) 833320
"An ideal bolthole from Oxford or Newbury", this "charming pub in a charming village" pleases all reporters with its "guaranteed good food".
*/ **Details:** www.eystons.co.uk; 9 pm; closed Sun D.*

The Royal Oak   £41   Ⓣ
Pook Ln PO18 0AX   (01243) 527 434
A "lovely old-worlde inn", tipped by reporters for its all-round charms, which include "jovial" service and food that's "improved" of late; even supporters, though, may find it "slightly pricey" for what it is.
*/ **Details:** www.royaloakeastlavant.co.uk; 9.30 pm; no shorts.*
***Accommodation:** 8 rooms, from £90.*

Trawlers   £42   Ⓣ
On The Quay PL13 1AH   (01503) 263593
This "busy" and "unfussy" restaurant, right on the dock, it tipped – as you might hope – for its "very fresh fish".
*/ **Details:** www.trawlersrestaurant.co.uk; 9.30 pm.*

Crown Inn   £39   Ⓐ
The Grn PE31 8RD   (01485) 528530
Part of a new group of Aussie-backed pubs in Norfolk, this is a gastropub consistently well-rated for its "very reliable and tasty" cooking and its "sympathetically-refurbished" interior.
*/ **Details:** www.crowninneastrudham.co.uk; 930; no Amex. **Accommodation:** 6 rooms, from £100.*

EAST TYTHERLEY, HAMPSHIRE 2–3C

Star Inn £34 ⭐
Romsey S051 0LW (01794) 340225
"Unexpectedly brilliant food in a cosy (but fairly standard) pub setting"
wins a big thumbs-up for this *"friendly"* gastropub, in the Test Valley.
/ **Details:** www.starinn.co.uk; 9 pm; closed Mon & Sun D. **Accommodation:** 3
rooms, from £80.

EAST WITTON, NORTH YORKSHIRE 8–4B

The Blue Lion £44 Ⓐ
DL8 4SN (01969) 624273
For *"marvellous food in God's own county"*, this *"solidly performing
Dales inn"* – with its *"cosy and old-fashioned"* style – has long been
a *"stalwart"* destination; critics, though, can find it a little *"overpriced"*.
/ **Details:** www.thebluelion.co.uk; between Masham & Leyburn on A6108;
9.15 pm; D only, ex Sun open L & D; no Amex. **Accommodation:** 15 rooms,
from £79.

EASTBOURNE, EAST SUSSEX 3–4B

Ⓐ
The Mirabelle
The Grand Hotel £62
King Edwards Pde BN21 4EQ (01323) 412345
A piano often accompanies dinner at what's perhaps the UK's
grandest seaside dining room, where the style is *"old-fashioned,
but pleasant nonetheless"*; it's a *"pricey"* treat, though, and, critics
suggest, *"not as good as it thinks"*. / **Details:** www.grandeastbourne.com;
9.45 pm; closed Mon & Sun; jacket or tie required at D. **Accommodation:** 152
rooms, from £190.

EASTON GRAY, WILTSHIRE 2–2C

⭐⭐
Dining Room
Whatley Manor £94
SN16 0RB (01666) 822888

*"Best dining experience I've had
in theUK for years"*; *"Martin
Burge is an exceptional chef"*,
and hecreates some *"excitingly
different"* dishes – the 'amuses'
rate special mention – at this
"beguilingly romantic" country
house hotel.
/ **Details:** www.whatleymanor.com;
10 pm; D only, closed Mon-Tue;
children: 12+. **Accommodation:** 23
rooms, from £295.

EDINBURGH, CITY OF EDINBURGH 9–4C

Ⓣ
Atrium £44
10 Cambridge St EH1 2ED (0131) 228 8882
This once über-trendy space inside the Traverse Theatre inspires little
feedback nowadays; it's better rated than its glory days, though,
and also tipped for its selection of wine.
/ **Details:** www.atriumrestaurant.co.uk; by the Usher Hall; 10 pm; closed Sat L &
Sun (ex during Festival).

blue bar café £42 Ⓣ
10 Cambridge St EH1 2ED (0131) 221 1222
It's *"trendy"*, *"noisy"* and *"a bit hit-and-miss"*, but this *"style-over-
substance"* West End brasserie is still tipped as a *"great pre-/post-
theatre destination"*. / **Details:** www.bluescotland.co.uk; by the Usher Hall;
10.30 pm, Fri & Sat 11 pm; closed Sun (except during Festival).

Cafe Marlayne £32 Ⓐ
7 Old Fishmarket Close EH1 1RW (0131) 225 3838
"Well-priced, imaginative, French-influenced food" makes this
"cramped" New Town bistro popular with some reporters; "poor"
service, though, sometimes takes the edge off the experience.
/ **Details:** www.cafemarlayne.com; 10 pm; closed Mon & Sun; no Amex.

Café Royal Oyster Bar £39 Ⓐ
19 West Register St EH2 2AA (0131) 556 4124
"Wonderful 19th century décor" is the high point at this "marvellous
olde-worlde" veteran in the New Town – a "beautiful" and "cosy" spot
with a "lovely dining room and buzzy bar"; food-wise it is "past its
best", but it remains very popular. / **Details:** www.thespiritgroup.com;
opp Balmoral Hotel; 10 pm.

Le Café St-Honoré £48 Ⓐ
34 NW Thistle Street Ln EH2 1EA (0131) 226 2211
"Hidden-away in the middle of the New Town", this "traditional" Gallic
bistro is, say fans, "well worth seeking out"; sometimes "disinterested"
service leads sceptics to conclude it's "slipped a bit", but it's typically
"packed" nonetheless. / **Details:** www.cafesthonore.com; 10 pm.

Calistoga Central £35 ★
70 Rose St EH2 3DX (01312) 251233
"A good budget choice for pre-theatre, or with friends", this New Town
bistro offers "consistently good food"; "good value" too, especially
on the (Californian) wine front, with no bottle marked up by more than
a fiver. / **Details:** www.calistoga.co.uk; 10 pm; closed Sun.

Centotre £42 Ⓐ
103 George St EH2 3ES (0131) 225 1550
"Best left for the tourists"; this "wonderfully-situated" grand Italian has
its fans, but reports of "high expectations, disappointed at every
course" are too frequent to make this a safe recommendation.
/ **Details:** www.centotre.com; 10 pm, Fri & Sat 11 pm, Sun 8 pm.

Chop Chop £28 ★
248 Morrison St EH3 8DT (0131) 221 1155
Can't be the "Formica tables and strip lighting" or the sometimes
"hilariously bad" service which ensure that this Haymarket Chinese
is "packed every night" – must have something to do, then, with the
"authentic" cuisine (of which the highlight is the "amazing
list of dumplings"); also in Leith. / **Details:** www.chopchop.co.uk; 10.30 pm;
closed Mon.

Creelers £39 Ⓐ
3 Hunter Sq EH1 1QW (0131) 220 4447
Just off the Royal Mile, this small fish restaurant of long standing
is tipped as "a lucky find", offering "fresh and simple seafood properly
cooked"; the main niggle is its "uppish prices", especially as it's
arguable the interior "could use an update". / **Details:** www.creelers.co.uk;
10.30 pm.

Daniel's £35 Ⓐ
88 Commercial St EH6 6LX (0131) 553 5933
"Simple" and "hearty" Alsatian cuisine at "reasonable prices" helps
maintain an agreeable "buzz" at Daniel Vencker's Leith veteran –
a "café-like place on the docks". / **Details:** www.daniels-bistro.co.uk; 10 pm.

David Bann   £35 ⭐⭐

56-58 St Marys St EH1 1SX (0131) 556 5888

*"Even non-veggies will love this"; David Bann's Old Town no-meat
stalwart is now getting back on top form, winning renewed acclaim this
year for its "unusually interesting" cooking at "reasonable prices",
and "knowledgeable service" too. /* **Details:** *www.davidbann.com; 10 pm,
Fri & Sat 10.30 pm.*

The Dogs   £33 🅐⭐

110 Hanover St EH2 1DR (0131) 220 1208

*"Basic" and "hearty" food at "great prices" has quickly made this "laid-
back", canine-themed gastropub (with its "barking" décor) hugely
popular, and it already has a couple of spin-offs – this may explain the
occasionally up-and-down performance. /* **Details:** *www.thedogsonline.co.uk;
10 pm.*

Dusit   £41 ⭐⭐

49a Thistle St EH2 1DY (0131) 220 6846

*"Fabulous food, not much atmosphere" – the story at this "terrific" and
"reasonably priced", but "noisy", New Town Thai is very much the
same as ever; NB "when they say dishes are hot, they mean it!"
/* **Details:** *www.dusit.co.uk; 11 pm.*

Favorita   £38 🅐⭐

325 Leith Walk EH6 8JA (0131) 554 2430

*"Very busy and bustling", this "bright" Italian lives up to its name –
"superb pizzas" (in particular), "great service" and "good wines by the
glass". /* **Details:** *www.la-favorita.com; 11 pm; no Amex.*

Fishers Bistro   £36 🅐

1 The Shore EH6 6QW (0131) 554 5666

*With its "nautical" theming and "cheery" staff, this "busy" fish bistro,
near the Leith waterfront, makes a relaxed destination; the cooking
does not convince all reporters, but fans find it "simple" and
"well presented". /* **Details:** *www.fishersbistros.co.uk; 10.30 pm.*

Fishers in the City   £40 🅐

58 Thistle St EH2 1EN (0131) 225 5109

*For "an efficient but relaxed meal" in a "great central location",
this New Town warehouse-conversion still has a lot going for it,
not least its "solidly-produced fish staples".
/* **Details:** *www.fishersbistros.co.uk; 10.30 pm.*

Forth Floor
Harvey Nichols   £64 🅐

30-34 St Andrew Sq EH2 2AD (0131) 524 8350

*With its impressive view, the location of this in-store venue is "as good
as ever"; prices can seem excessive, though, and critics dismiss this
as the classic "all-fur-coat-and-no-designer-undergarments" destination.
/* **Details:** *www.harveynichols.com; 10 pm; closed Mon D & Sun D.*

La Garrigue £42 Ⓐ
31 Jeffrey St EH1 1DH   (0131) 557 3032
Still many reports on this "authentic southern French bistro", in the Old Town; even a reporter who finds the food "technically excellent" complains of a "lack of flavour", though, and the impression that the place is "resting on its laurels" is becoming inescapable. / Details: www.lagarrigue.co.uk; 9.30 pm; closed Sun.

Glass & Thompson £27 Ⓣ
2 Dundas St EH3 6HZ   (0131) 557 0909
"The best place to have a light lunch, whether at the week or over the weekend" – an elegant café/deli in the New Town. / Details: L only.

Grain Store £52 Ⓐ⭐
30 Victoria St EH1 2JW   (0131) 225 7635
"Quirky", "low-profile" and "charming" – this veteran Old Town spot offers "solid" Scottish fare and "thoughtful" service; the "imaginative" and "good-value" lunch is especially worth seeking out. / Details: www.grainstore-restaurant.co.uk; 10 pm.

Henderson's £28 Ⓐ
94 Hanover St EH2 1DR   (0131) 225 2131
Fifty years old next year, this venerable veggie basement remains a perennially popular and "often crowded" New Town destination, thanks to its "yummy" food, and its "relaxed" style. / Details: www.hendersonsofedinburgh.co.uk; 10 pm; closed Sun; no Amex.

Kalpna £33 Ⓣ
2-3 St Patrick Sq EH8 9EZ   (0131) 667 9890
Few reports of late on this long-established Gujarati canteen near the University; it's still tipped for "lovely" food, though, that's "remarkably inexpensive". / Details: www.kalpnarestaurant.com; 10.30 pm; closed Sun; no Amex; no booking at L.

The Kitchin £79 Ⓐ⭐⭐
78 Commercial Quay EH6 6LX   (0131) 555 1755
"Such a laid-back and pleasant dining experience"; Tom Kitchin takes "high-quality raw materials" and turns them into "spectacular" and "inventive" dishes, at this "outstanding" Leith warehouse-conversion – it no doubt helps that le patron is "always there". / Details: www.thekitchin.com; 10 pm; closed Mon & Sun.

Kweilin £35 Ⓣ
19-21 Dundas St EH3 6QG   (0131) 557 1875
A "good and authentic" New Town Cantonese of long standing, tipped in particular for its fish specialities. / Details: www.kweilin.co.uk; 11 pm; closed Mon & Sun L.

Loch Fyne £40 Ⓣ
25 Pier Pl EH6 4LP   (0131) 559 3900
"I know it's part of a chain but this particular outlet has a perfect location overlooking the harbour"; it has "great views", and offers fish dishes that are "straightforward" and "well-executed". / Details: www.lochfyne.com; 10 pm, Sat 10.30 pm.

Mother India's Cafe £32 Ⓐ⭐
3-5 Infirmary St EH1 1LT   (0131) 524 9801
In the Old Town, a year-old offshoot from Glasgow's Mother India, offering "brilliant", "light and tasty" dishes – "the tapas-style presentation allows more of a choice of flavours". / Details: www.motherindiaglasgow.co.uk; 10 pm, Fri & Sat 10.30 pm; no Amex.

Mussel Inn £38 ⭐

61-65 Rose St EH2 2NH (0131) 225 5979

"Very crowded and crushed", this New Town seafood specialist is *"not the place for a relaxing meal"*, but it's a *"fun"* place, and *"great value"* too — be ready to queue if you have not booked. / **Details:** www.mussel-inn.com; 10 pm.

Number One
Balmoral Hotel £82 ⭐⭐

1 Princes St EH2 2EQ (0131) 557 6727

"Superb all the way"; the fine dining room of the city's grandest hotel offers Jeff Bland's *"outstanding"*, *"Scottish-creative"* cuisine and impressively *"understated"* service; for some tastes, though, the basement setting feels a little *"quiet"*. / **Details:** www.roccofortehotels.com; 10 pm; D only; no jeans or trainers. **Accommodation:** 188 rooms, from £360.

Oloroso £57 Ⓐ

33 Castle St EH2 3DN (0131) 226 7614

It's primarily the *"stunning rooftop location"* which makes this once-fashionable, but increasingly *"tired"*, operation of interest — *"indifferent"* service contributes to an overwhelming impression that it is *"massively over-rated and overpriced"*. / **Details:** www.oloroso.co.uk; 10.30 pm, Sun 10 pm; no Amex.

Ondine £50 ⭐⭐

2 George IV Bridge EH1 1AD (0131) 2261888

"A really good addition to the city's dining options" — Roy Brett's first-floor newcomer, near the Royal Mile (featuring good views, and a crustacea bar) offers *"cracking fresh produce"* — highlights include a *"fabulous oyster selection"* and a *"superb-value assiette de fruits-de-mer"*. / **Details:** www.ondinerestaurant.co.uk; 10 pm; booking: max 12.

Outsider £39 Ⓐ

15-16 George IV Bridge EH1 1EE (0131) 226 3131

One of the *"coolest"*-looking restaurants in town — a busy modern bistro with spectacular views of the castle; the cuisine is quite *"plain"*, but dishes are consistently *"well-cooked"*. / **Details:** 11 pm; no Amex; booking: max 10.

Papoli £22 ⭐

244a Morrison St EH3 8DT (0131) 4777047

An *"unassuming"* newcomer offering some *"excellent Middle Eastern-influenced Italian food"* that's *"really creative and tasty"*, and *"all at reasonable prices"* too. / **Details:** www.papoli.co.uk; 10.30 pm; closed Sun.

Le Petit Paris £38 Ⓐ

38-40 Grassmarket EH1 2JU (0131) 226 2442

"Like a little bit of France in Edinburgh" — this *"cramped"* little bistro is *"a good find at the price"*, serving *"standard dishes"* of a *"solid standard"*; for *"very good value"*, seek out the pre-theatre and lunch menus. / **Details:** www.petitparis-restaurant.co.uk; near the Castle; 11 pm; children: - .

Plumed Horse £64 ⭐⭐

50-54 Henderson St EH6 6DE (0131) 554 5556

A *"very smart"* (but *"tiny"*) Leith eatery which is *"somewhat reminiscent of a top London joint"*, and *"charges accordingly"* — fortunately the food invariably seems to measure up. / **Details:** www.plumedhorse.co.uk; 9 pm; closed Mon & Sun.

Restaurant Martin Wishart £90

54 The Shore EH6 6RA (0131) 553 3557

"A real sensory treat for the adventurous" – Martin Wishart's "stylish" Leith dining room has won renown for the pure "genius" of his "uncompromising, complex and exciting" cuisine; even some reporters with "no complaints" about the food, however, feel you "pay through the nose for it". / **Details:** www.martin-wishart.co.uk; near Royal Yacht Britannia; 9.30 pm; closed Mon & Sun; no trainers.

Rhubarb
Prestonfield Hotel £67

Priestfield Rd EH16 5UT (0131) 225 1333

With its "amazing" OTT decor, the "magnificent" dining room of this country house hotel, just outside the city, is "perfect for romance"; the cooking is usually "very good" too, but, on some reports, the place has been "failing on the basics" of late. / **Details:** www.prestonfield.com; 10 pm, Fri & Sat 11 pm; children: 12+ at D, none after 7pm.
Accommodation: 23 rooms, from £225.

Roti £40

73 Morrison St EH3 8BU (0131) 221 9998

"A delicious and well-presented fine dining interpretation on Indian cookery at reasonable cost" – this rather cavernous New Town joint presents an "amazing contrast" to your standard subcontinental, and continues to impress all who comment on it.
/ **Details:** www.roti.uk.com; midnight; no Amex.

The Shore £37

3-4 The Shore EH6 6QW (0131) 553 5080

A handy stand-by, on the Leith waterfront, tipped for its "quirky" atmosphere – if you visit, "make time for a drink in the bar first".
/ **Details:** www.theshore.biz; 10.30 pm.

Skippers £37

1a Dock Pl EH6 6LU (0131) 554 1018

"A trusty old establishment" in a former dock building near the Leith waterfront – a "cosy", "cramped" and "busy" place with "reliable" fish, and "where staff take pride in what they do". / **Details:** 10 pm.

The Stockbridge £50

54 St Stephen's St EH3 5AL (0131) 226 6766

This "small", "intimate", and quite strikingly-decorated basement restaurant, hidden-away in the New Town, wins nothing but upbeat reports for its "lovely food, great wine list, and attentive service".
/ **Details:** www.thestockbridgerestaurant.co.uk; 9.30 pm; closed Mon, Tue-Fri D only, Sat & Sun open L & D; children: 18+ after 8 pm.

Sweet Melindas   £38 ⭐

11 Roseneath St EH9 1JH (0131) 229 7953

"A lovely neighbourhood place" in Marchmont, offering food that's consistently *"interesting, well-cooked and tasty"*.

/ **Details:** www.sweetmelindas.co.uk; 10 pm; closed Mon L & Sun; children: Not allowed .

The Tower   Ⓐ

Museum of Scotland   £53

Chambers St EH1 1JF (0131) 225 3003

This elevated dining room benefits from *"amazing views"* of the Castle (if you sit in the right area); fans insist *"it's much-maligned but offers excellent food and service"* – to critics, however, it's *"too expensive, given the indifferent overall experience"*.

/ **Details:** www.tower-restaurant.com; 11 pm.

21212   £94 Ⓐ⭐

3 Royal Ter EH7 5AB (0845) 222 1212

Paul Kitching's *"perfect synthesis of complex tastes"* is winning higher acclaim at this *"grand"* Calton townhouse than his Manchester operation ever did; inevitably some of his *"exciting"* dishes *"try too hard"* (*"too many flavours"*), but most reporters acclaim a visit as a *"thoroughly enjoyable"* experience all-round.

/ **Details:** www.21212restaurant.co.uk; 9.30 pm; closed Mon & Sun; no shorts; children: 5 +. **Accommodation:** 4 rooms, from £250.

Urban Angel   £33 Ⓐ

121 Hanover St EH2 1DJ (0131) 225 6215

An *"upmarket basement café"* in the New Town; its *"sweet"* service and *"good if not spectacular food"* (burgers, sarnies, cakes) make it a handy option for a satisfying bite. / **Details:** www.urban-angel.co.uk; 10 pm; closed Sun D.

Valvona & Crolla   £37 Ⓐ

19 Elm Row EH7 4AA (0131) 556 6066

Though *"always busy"*, it's hard to avoid the impression that the café annex to this famous Italian deli/food importers, on the way to Leith, is *"resting on its legendary laurels"* – too often the food is *"rather ordinary"*, and can seem *"massively overpriced"* too.

/ **Details:** www.valvonacrolla.com; at top of Leith Walk, near Playhouse Theatre; L only.

Vintners Rooms   £61 Ⓐ⭐

87a Giles St EH6 6BZ (0131) 554 6767

It's *"a delightful and memorable experience"* to dine at this ancient candlelit whisky warehouse, on the way to Leith; remarkably, though, both food and service generally live up to the setting!

/ **Details:** www.thevintnersrooms.com; 10 pm; closed Mon & Sun.

Wedgwood   £46 ⭐

267 Canongate EH8 8BQ (0131) 558 8737

Paul Wedgwood's *"friendly"* (but quite *"posh"*) New Town outfit – which won our 'best newcomer' award last year – is, on most accounts, a *"really wonderful restaurant"* with *"novel"* cuisine; bizarrely, though, roughly one reporter in five has precisely the opposite impression – is it a case of *"chef's night off"*? / **Details:** www.wedgwoodtherestaurant.co.uk; 10 pm.

The Witchery by the Castle £50

Castlehill, The Royal Mile EH1 2NF (0131) 225 5613

A "magical" Gothic dining room
(plus 'Secret Garden') and a
wine list that's famously
"of Biblical proportions" make this
"memorable" Castle-side veteran a
classic "special occasion"
destination; of late, however,
the minority of reporters who find
the cooking "expensive and poor"
has found renewed voice.
/ **Details:** www.thewitchery.com; 11.30 pm.
Accommodation: 7 rooms, from £295

EGHAM, SURREY 3–3A

The Oak Room
Great Fosters Hotel £65

Stroude Rd TW20 9UR (01784) 433822

"Consistently good" (and "quite exciting") cooking is on offer at this
"beautiful" country house hotel; it benefits from a "really fantastic"
garden, so a visit for the "snip" of a lunch menu is a 'no-brainer' – à la
carte and wine prices, however, are "very high", making dinner a less
compelling proposition. / **Details:** www.greatfosters.co.uk; 9.15 pm; closed
Sat L; no jeans or trainers; booking: max 12. **Accommodation:** 44 rooms,
from £155.

ELLAND, WEST YORKSHIRE 5–1C

La Cachette £30

31 Huddersfield Rd HX5 9AW (01422) 378833

"From a light lunch to a family celebration", this long-running brasserie
is again tipped for its "consistently-good" cooking.
/ **Details:** www.lacachette-elland.com; 9.30 pm, Fri & Sat 10 pm; closed Sun;
no Amex.

ELY, CAMBRIDGESHIRE 3–1B

The Boathouse £40

5-5A, Annesdale CB7 4BN (01353) 664388

It's "always a nice experience" to visit this "quiet" and "discreet" water-
sider – a place with "wonderful views", "friendly" service and "great
food at cheap prices". / **Details:** www.cambscuisine.com/theboathouse;
9.30 pm ; no Amex.

Old Fire Engine House £44

25 St Mary's St CB7 4ER (01353) 662582

It can seem "a bit too old-fashioned nowadays", but this "very old and
dear friend" (well into the fifth decade), in the centre of the city, is still
tipped for its "traditional", "homely" and "seasonal" fare.
/ **Details:** www.theoldfireenginehouse.co.uk; 9 pm; closed Sun D; no Amex.

EMSWORTH, HAMPSHIRE 2–4D

Driftwood Cafe £29

44 The High St PO10 7AW (01243) 37 73 73

Tipped "for a light lunch in a pretty seaside town", this "great little local
place" – "prettily decorated in pale blue and cream" – attracts
consistent praise for its "excellent quiches, salads, cakes and puddings".
/ **Details:** www.driftwood-cafe.co.uk; L only, closed Sun.

Fat Olives £42 ⒶⒶⒶ✪

30 South St PO10 7EH (01243) 377914

*"A small and simple restaurant, where the food is always excellent" –
one reporter speaks for all on this former cottage, a short walk up the
hill from the waterfront; "just a shame it can't accommodate more
people". / **Details:** www.fatolives.co.uk; 9.15 pm; closed Mon & Sun; no Amex;
children: 8+, unless Sat L.*

36 on the Quay £70 ✪✪

47 South St PO10 7EG (01243) 375592

*"Pricey, but worth it"; Ramon Farthing's "romantic hide-away
overlooking the harbour" has been much more consistent of late,
pleasing almost all reporters with cooking "of the highest quality";
service, though, is still sometimes "slow".
/ **Details:** www.36onthequay.co.uk; off A27 between Portsmouth & Chichester;
9.45 pm; closed Mon & Sun; no Amex. **Accommodation:** 5 (plus cottage)
rooms, from £95.*

EPSOM, SURREY 3–3B

Le Raj £32 Ⓐ

211 Fir Tree Rd KT17 3LB (01737) 371371

*A "sophisticated" culinary approach has won a big name locally for this
well-established suburban subcontinental; both food and service,
though, can be a bit "hit-and-miss". / **Details:** www.lerajrestaurant.co.uk;
next to Derby race course; 11 pm; no jeans or trainers.*

ESHER, SURREY 3–3A

Good Earth £48 Ⓐ✪

14-18 High St KT10 9RT (01372) 462489

*"Expensive for a Chinese, but always good" – this "slick" suburban
veteran maintains the high standards that have kept it in business for
over 30 years; "it's usually very busy". / **Details:** www.goodearthgroup.co.uk;
11.15 pm, Sun 10.45 pm; booking: max 12, Fri & Sat.*

Sherpa £29 Ⓣ

132 High St KT10 9QJ (01372) 470777

*A "lovely" subcontinental, tipped for its "good interpretation
of Nepalese cuisine", its "friendly" service and its "attractive" decor.
/ **Details:** www.sherpakitchen.co.uk; 11 pm; no Amex.*

Siam Food Gallery £42 Ⓣ

95-97 High St KT10 9QE (01372) 477139

*An upmarket suburban spot, tipped as "a lovely Thai restaurant".
/ **Details:** www.siamfoodgallery.co.uk; 11 pm; closed Mon.*

ETON, BERKSHIRE 3–3A

Gilbey's £43 Ⓣ

82-83 High St SL4 6AF (01753) 854921

*"A nice conservatory, excellent wine list and open fire in winter" all
contribute to the "enjoyable" charms of this long-established bistro,
near the College – we're not entirely sure, though, that the recent
refurb has added to its attractions. / **Details:** www.gilbeygroup.com; 5 min
walk from Windsor Castle; 9.30 pm, Fri & Sat 10 pm.*

EVERSHOT, DORSET
2–4B

Summer Lodge
Country House Hotel & Restaurant   £85
Summer Lodge DT2 0JR   (01935) 482000

"Utterly sublime" for traditionalists; this "sumptuous" (in a "chintzy" way) Hardy Country manor house not only has a "wonderful" setting, but also offers "excellent" cooking and "elegant" service; even the wine list is a "masterpiece". / *Details:* www.summerlodgehotel.co.uk; 12m NW of Dorchester on A37; 9.30 pm; no shorts. **Accommodation:** 24 rooms, from £200.

EVESHAM, WORCESTERSHIRE
2–1C

Evesham Hotel   £42
Coopers Ln WR11 1DA   (01386) 765566
"Basil Fawlty on a good day" (also known as John Jenkinson) runs this Cotswolds-fringe hotel with "sheer originality and oddball quirkiness"; the food is "nothing to write home about", but the "idiosyncratic" wine list – three volumes, but no French or German vintages! – is amazing, and "well-priced too". / *Details:* www.eveshamhotel.com; 9.30 pm; booking: max 12. **Accommodation:** 40 rooms, from £120.

EXETER, DEVON
1–3D

Michael Caines
Royal Clarence Hotel   £64
Cathedral Yd EX1 1HD   (01392) 223 638
Gidleigh Park's famous chef helps oversee this "stylish and civilised" dining room, "conveniently located" in a hotel by the cathedral; most feedback praises the "excellent" food you'd hope for, but not all reporters are quite convinced. / *Details:* www.abodehotels.co.uk; 9.30 pm; closed Sun; booking essential. **Accommodation:** 53 rooms, from £115.

EXTON, RUTLAND
5–3D

The Fox And Hounds   £39
19 The Grn LE15 8AP   (01572) 812403
This "friendly" ivy-clad coaching inn is not just of note for its "delightful village setting", but also its "excellent roasts, and home-made pizza too!" / *Details:* www.foxandhoundsrutland.co.uk; 9 pm; closed Mon & Sun D; no Amex. **Accommodation:** 4 rooms, from £70.

FAIRFORD, GLOUCESTERSHIRE
2–2C

Allium   £58
1 London St GL7 4AH   (01285) 712200
James Graham's "innovative cooking with good use of ingredients" – twinned with his wife Erica's "pleasant" service – makes this small country restaurant an almost invariable hit with reporters; surprise feature: "a great and unusual selection of wines".
/ *Details:* www.allium.uk.net; 9 pm; closed Mon, Tue L, Sun D; no Amex; booking: max 10.

Bistro de la Mer   £44
⭐

28 Arwenack St TR11 3JB (01326) 316509
"A tiny bistro" with a *"very intimate"* ambience and – say fans –
offering *"perfectly-cooked fish"*; there is the odd quibble, though –
the approach can seem *"stuck in the past"*, or *"relatively expensive"* for
what it is. / **Details:** www.bistrodelamer.com; 9.30 pm, Fri & Sat 10 pm; closed
Mon L & Sun L; no Amex.

Rick Stein's Fish & Chips   £32
Ⓐ

Discovery Quay TR11 3AX (01841) 532700
"Don't miss Rick's new chippy", say fans of this big new branch of the
famous Padstow chef's expanding empire, praised in most – if not quite
all – early reports for *"the fish 'n' chips of dreams"*.
/ **Details:** www.rickstein.com; 9 pm.

Museum Inn   £50
⭐

DT11 8DE (01725) 516261
"An excellent example of what a country pub should be" – the cuisine
is invariably *"well-cooked and presented"* at this posh village inn.
/ **Details:** www.museuminn.co.uk; Off the A354, signposted to Farnham; 9.30 pm,
9 pm Sun; no Amex. **Accommodation:** 8 rooms, from £110.

Read's   £69
Ⓐ

Macknade Manor, Canterbury Rd ME13 8XE (01795) 535344
This veteran restaurant-with-rooms, in a Georgian building, is often
acclaimed for *"country house-style dining at its best"*; some reporters
are beginning to find the food rather *"unimaginative"*, though,
or complain of meals that are *"disappointing, given the rave reviews"*.
/ **Details:** www.reads.com; 9.30 pm; closed Mon & Sun. **Accommodation:** 6
rooms, from £165.

Fence Gate Inn & Banqueting Centre   £42
Ⓐ

Wheatley Lane Rd BB12 9EE (01282) 618101
"Don't be put off by the name", say fans, this large enterprise –
comprising a fantastic pub and a *"lovely"* brasserie – is *"probably the
best place in East Lincs"*; even so, service can sometimes be *"poor"*,
and the occasional critic complains of a *"general lack of attention
to detail"*. / **Details:** www.fencegate.co.uk; 9 pm, Fri 9.30 pm, Sat 10 pm,
Sun 8 pm.

General Tarleton   £42
Ⓐ⭐

Boroughbridge Rd HG5 0PZ (01423) 340284
"The welcome is warm", and the food *"first-rate"*, at this well-known
gastropub near the A1, which is decked out in *"attractive"* style;
the dinner experience, it is sometimes suggested, is more consistent
than lunch. / **Details:** www.generaltarleton.co.uk; 2m from A1, J48 towards
Knaresborough; 9.15 pm. **Accommodation:** 14 rooms, from £129.

Radhuni   £29
Ⓣ

Straightbit HP10 9LS (01628) 530614
"A good new Indian restaurant", tipped for consistently good food,
and *"efficient and friendly service"*. / **Details:** www.radhunirestaurant.co.uk;
10.15 pm; no Amex.

A

The Bricklayers Arms   £47
Hogpits Bottom HP3 0PH   (01442) 833322
*Numerous fans say this "out-of-the-way" but "always busy" country pub
is "well worth the trip" – "a hidden treasure" that's "quite pricey but
worth it"; it does have its critics, though, who find its performance
"rather predictable and tired". / **Details:** www.bricklayersarms; J18 off
the M25, past Chorleywood; 9.30 pm, Sun 8.30 pm.*

FLETCHING, EAST SUSSEX   3–4B

A **★**

The Griffin Inn   £46
TN22 3SS   (01825) 722890
*A village pub, that's typically "very busy", on account of its "very good"
food, "top beer garden" (where there's an excellent BBQ), "great
beer" and "surprisingly good wine list"; prices are "on the high side',
though and service can be "patchy". / **Details:** www.thegriffininn.co.uk;
off A272; 9.30 pm. **Accommodation:** 13 rooms, from £85.*

FONTHILL GIFFORD, WILTSHIRE   2–3C

A

Beckford Arms   £36
SP3 6PX   (01747) 870 385
*A "jolly atmosphere and great food" win strong praise for this recently-
revamped traditional country pub off the A303; it is set to re-open
in mid-2011, after a fire. / **Details:** www.thebeckfordarms.co.uk; 9.30 pm,
Sun 9 pm. **Accommodation:** 8 rooms, from £80.*

FOREST GREEN, SURREY   3–3A

A

The Parrot Inn   £41
RH5 5RZ   (01306) 621339

*The "high-quality" meat "comes from the landlord's own farm", at the
Gotto family's "pretty rural pub", which has a "lovely setting on a village
green", in the heart of the Surrey Hills. / **Details:** www.theparrot.co.uk;
10 pm; closed Sun D; no Amex.*

FOREST ROW, WEST SUSSEX   3–4B

T

Anderida Restaurant
Ashdown Park Hotel   £61
Wych Cross RH18 5JR   (01342) 824988
*It may be "very large", but the dining room of this country-house resort-
hotel is tipped as a "relaxing" venue nonetheless; portions can be on
the small side, but they generally hit the spot.
/ **Details:** www.ashdownpark.com; 9.30 pm, Fri & Sat 10 pm; jacket and/or tie.
Accommodation: 106 rooms, from £170.*

Crannog   £43   **T**
Town Pier PH33 6DB   (01397) 705589
*On the pier, a seafood restaurant tipped for fish "straight from the
Loch", treated "with care and served without fuss"; there's also
something of a feeling, though, that it's "resting on its reputation".
/ Details: www.crannog.net/restaurant.asp; 9.30 pm; no Amex.*

Inverlochy Castle   £93   **T**
Torlundy PH33 6SN   (01397) 702177
*Visiting this famously grand Baronial loch-side hotel can seem
a "bizarre" experience, complete with "bedroom-size tables", a "big-
cheese pianist" and a "comically high-class tourist clientele"; if you have
"a taste for aristocratic theatre", however, it's tipped for a "really
refined" cuisine that rarely disappoints.
/ Details: www.inverlochycastlehotel.com; off A82, 4 m N of Ft. William; 10 pm;
jacket & tie required at D; children: 8+ at D.* **Accommodation:** *17 & gate lodge
rooms, from £300.*

Sam's   £35   **A**
20 Fore St PL23 1AQ   (01726) 832273
*"Fun, friendly and well-priced", this seaside bistro has made quite
a name with holidaymakers, and not just for its "great seafood" –
they also do a "top burger"! / Details: www.samsfowey.co.uk; 10 pm;
no Amex; no booking.*

The Chequers at Fowlmere   £45   **T**
SG8 7SR   (01763) 208369
*Attracting more limited feedback nowadays, this country inn – a classic
day-out-from-Cambridge destination – is still tipped for all-round good
standards, and in particular for its "excellent and varied choice
of specials". / Details: www.thechequersfowlmere.co.uk; on B1368 between
Royston & Cambridge; 9.30 pm; children: 14+ in bar.*

The Fox & Goose   £41   **A ☆**
Church Rd IP21 5PB   (01379) 586247
*"Well worth a visit", this "terrific" country inn is a notably "slick" and
"efficient" operation, which consistently delivers very good food
at decent prices. / Details: www.foxandgoose.net; off A143; 8.45 pm, Fri & Sat
9 pm, Sun 8.15 pm; closed Mon; no Amex; children: 9+ for D.*

Pot Kiln   £39   **☆**
RG18 0XX   (01635) 201366
*"Excellent game" is the menu highlight at this "gem of a pub in the
middle of nowhere"; set amidst "great walking country", it is
"well worth the drive". / Details: www.potkiln.org; between J12 and J13 of the
M4; 11 pm, Sun 10 pm; closed Tue.*

The Alford Arms £41
HP1 3DD (01442) 864480

"Consistently good-quality food", a "decent wine list" and "excellent ales" are among the attractions which have built up a huge reporter following for this "cosy" and "tucked-away" boozer.
/ **Details:** www.alfordarmsfrithsden.co.uk; near Ashridge College and vineyard; 9.30 pm, Fri & Sat 10 pm; booking: max 12.

Eslington Villa Hotel £40
8 Station Rd NE9 6DR (0191) 487 6017
Even those with criticisms of this "pleasant" hotel in a Victorian building say it "does many things right", and the overall verdict is that it's "a welcoming place, with food of a consistently-good standard".
/ **Details:** www.eslingtonvilla.co.uk; A1 exit for Team Valley Trading Estate, then left off Eastern Avenue; 9.30 pm; closed Sat L & Sun D.
Accommodation: 18 rooms, from £89.50.

Raval £42
Church St, Gateshead Quays NE8 2AT (0191) 4771700
"Authentic" and "delicate" cuisine wins a tip for this "contemporary" and "very popular" Gateshead Indian. / **Details:** www.ravalrestaurant.com; 11 pm; D only, closed Sun; no shorts.

Apple Tree £35
Oxford Rd SL9 7AH (01753) 887335
"A converted boozer, with a good and imaginative menu"; even a reporter who says it's "nothing outstanding" praises it as "a good stand-by, with food that's well-presented and tasty".
/ **Details:** www.appletreegerrardscross.co.uk; 10 pm.

Maliks £42
14 Oak End Way SL9 8BR (01753) 880888
An offshoot of the acclaimed Cookham curry house, this "great Indian (aimed at the affluent local market)" may not be quite as highly-rated as the original, but wins solid praise for its "excellent" cooking, even if service can be "overwhelmed" at peak times. / **Details:** www.maliks.co.uk.

Stock Hill House £59
SP8 5NR (01747) 823626
"The Austrian influences of chef Peter Hauser's homeland" contribute to some "very interesting" dishes, at this "comfortable" country house hotel – a "formal" sort of place but, say fans, but still "very relaxed".
/ **Details:** www.stockhillhouse.co.uk; 8.30 pm; closed Mon L; no Amex; no jeans; children: 8+ at D in dining room. **Accommodation:** 10 rooms, from £260.

Gamba £57
225a West George St G2 2ND   (0141) 572 0899
*Derek Marshall's "mouthwatering" fish and seafood dishes,
plus "brilliant" service, earn this "smart" but "unassuming" city-centre
basement the highest food (and all-round) ratings in Scotland's
largest metropolis. / Details: www.gamba.co.uk; 10.30 pm; closed Sun L.*

Hotel du Vin et Bistro £65
1 Devonshire Gdns G12 0UX   (0141) 339 2001
*After a "chequered history" in recent years, the former
'One Devonshire Gardens' "seems to be finding its feet" under Hotel
du Vin – thanks to its "beautiful" dining room and often "exquisite"
cuisine, some reporters now tip this as being once again the city's top
address; "bar meals are very good too".
/ Details: www.onedevonshiregardens.com; 9.45 pm; closed Sat L.*
Accommodation: *49 rooms, from £140.*

Michael Caines
ABode Hotel £45
The Arthouse. 129 Bath St G2 2SZ   (0141) 572 6011
*Still attracting surprisingly little comment from reporters, this city-centre
outpost of the Gidleigh Park chef (see Chagford) is nonetheless tipped
as "heaven" for those who like grazing – some menus are "amazing",
and they offer "value-for-money" too. / Details: www.michaelcaines.com;
10 pm; closed Mon & Sun; no jeans or trainers.* **Accommodation:** *59 rooms,
from £130.*

Mother India £34
28 Westminster Ter G3 7RU   (0141) 221 1663
*"Exceptional food" that's "different from your normal Indian" has won
long won a massive following for this "busy" and "buzzy"
subcontinental near Kelvingrove Park; even the odd reporter who feels
that "standards have dropped a little" of late says "it's still very good".
/ Details: www.motherindiaglasgow.co.uk; beside Kelvingrove Hotel; Mon-Thu
10.30 pm, Fri & Sat 11 pm, Sun 10.30 pm; Mon-Thu D only, Fri-Sun open L & D.*

Rogano Seafood Bar & Restaurant £57
11 Exchange Pl G1 3AN   (0141) 248 4055
*It's "stunning" to look at, but this Art Deco seafood "institution" finally
seems to be offering more than "a piece of history"; most reporters
now compliment its "fresh" produce, that's "always well-prepared and
presented". / Details: www.roganoglasgow.com; 10.30 pm; no Amex.*

Stravaigin £40
28 Gibson St G12 8NX   (0141) 334 2665
*"Clever" – some would say "over-elaborate" – "modern Scottish
cooking" has made a big name for Colin Clydesdale's well-established
venue in a West End basement; there's also a no-bookings ground floor
bar, whose 'grazing' menu includes all-day breakfasts.
/ Details: www.stravaigin.com; 11 pm; Mon-Thu D only, Fri-Sun open L & D.*

Two Fat Ladies £29
88 Dumbarton Rd G11 6NX   (0141) 339 1944
*This "tiny" West End fish-specialist – the long-standing original of a
small local chain – has long had a name for its "fantastic seafood",
and its "cramped but interesting" style; the other spin-offs are in the
city-centre, as well as at the Buttery.
/ Details: www.twofatladiesrestaurant.com; 10.30 pm, Sun 9 pm.*

(Two Fat Ladies at) The Buttery £48
652 Argyle St G3 8UF (0141) 221 8188
*Seemingly "randomly located" in an "unpromising part of town"
(near the SECC), this "ornate" Victorian "oasis" is a notably
"comfortable" and "friendly" destination, whose well-spaced tables are
suited to either business or romance; "fantastic fish dishes" are the
menu highlight. / **Details:** www.twofatladiesrestaurant.com; 10 pm.*

Ubiquitous Chip £58
12 Ashton Ln G12 8SJ (0141) 334 5007

*"Age doesn't dim the charm" of this celebrated and "beautiful" local
institution (whose founder, Ronnie Clydesdale, died this year); the food
has long played second fiddle to the "fantastic global wine list",
but recent ratings suggest a "slight improvement"; "get a table in the
courtyard if you can". / **Details:** www.ubiquitouschip.co.uk; behind Hillhead
station; 11 pm.*

Wee Curry Shop £28
Buccleuch St G3 6SJ (0141) 353 0777
*Service can be "amateur", so the press of customers at this "tiny"
Byres Road offshoot of Mother India (one of three) must be testament
to the often "outstanding" quality of the food and "excellent prices".
/ **Details:** www.motherindiaglasgow.co.uk; 10.30 pm; closed Sun L; no credit
cards.*

GODALMING, SURREY 3–3A

Bel & The Dragon £38
Bridge St GU7 18Y (01483) 527333
*"Few, if any local alternatives, rival the setting of this impressive-
converted church", which trades as a "loud and crowded" gastropub;
it's too early to tell what changes new owners (mid-2010) may bring.
/ **Details:** www.belandthedragon-godalming.co.uk; at the bottom of Godalming
High St, directly opposite Waitrose; 10 pm, Sun 9 pm; no Amex.*

La Luna £44
10-14 Wharf St GU7 1NN (01483) 414155
*"Improved by a recent revamp", this "thoughtful, local modern Italian"
has been a notably "more consistent" performer of late – all reporters
agree that it's a "high-class" joint that's definitely "worth a visit".
/ **Details:** www.lalunarestaurant.co.uk; Between the High Street and Flambard
Way; 10 pm.*

GOLDSBOROUGH, NORTH YORKSHIRE 8–3D

The Fox And Hounds Inn £44
YO21 3RX (01947) 893372
*"Less really can be more!"; "great local ingredients" are "prepared with
restraint and a wonderful feel for balance", at this "charming" and
"personal" small inn. / **Details:** www.foxandhoundsgoldsborough.co.uk;
8.30 pm; D only, closed Sun-Tue; no Amex.*

GORING-ON-THAMES, BERKSHIRE   2–2D

A

Leatherne Bottel   £59
Bridleway RG8 0HS (01491) 872667
A popular Thames-sider of particular note for its "unbeatable al fresco summer dining"; as ever, though, there are a few sceptics, who find the food "unable to live up to its pretensions".
*/ **Details:** www.leathernebottel.co.uk; 0.5m outside Goring on B4009; 9 pm; closed Sun D; children: 10+ for D.*

GRASMERE, CUMBRIA   7–3D

A ⭐

The Jumble Room   £44
Langdale Rd LA22 9SU (01539) 435188
*"A great find in such a touristy spot"; this "quirky" and "totally laid-back" operation offers "freshly made" and "well cooked" fare – "like home cooking but nicer and with less washing up" – and a "warm and friendly" style. / **Details:** www.thejumbleroom.co.uk; Halfway along the Langdale road, between two hotels; midnight; closed Mon L, Tue, Wed L, Thu L & Fri L; no Amex. **Accommodation:** 2 rooms, from £180.*

A ⭐

Lancrigg Country House Hotel   £39
Easedale Rd LA22 9QN (01539) 435317
*"In a fabulous landscape", a country house hotel dining room where – unusually – the cuisine is vegetarian (and often organic); feedback (albeit limited) is all positive. / **Details:** www.lancrigg.co.uk; 1/2 mile up the Easedale road from the centre of Grasmere; 8 pm; no Amex. **Accommodation:** 12 rooms, from £140.*

T

Rothay Garden Hotel   £48
Broadgate LA22 9RJ (01539 435334) 435334
*"Newly refurbished in contemporary style", this Lakeland hotel is strongly tipped for its "faultless food" and "varied" wine; residential food-and-wine-matching courses a speciality.
/ **Details:** www.rothaygarden.com; 930pm; no Amex. **Accommodation:** 30 rooms, from £120.*

GREAT DUNMOW, ESSEX   3–2C

A

Starr   £50
Market Pl CM6 1AX (01371) 874321
*Opinions divide on this large town-centre inn inn-conversion, which has been in its current guise for the last three decades; for fans, the food's "exquisite" – for sceptics, this is "an establishment which aims to offer fine dining, but the cooking doesn't match up".
/ **Details:** www.the-starr.co.uk; 8m E of M11, J8 on A120; 9.30 pm; closed Mon & Sun D; no jeans or trainers. **Accommodation:** 8 rooms, from £130.*

GREAT GONERBY, LINCOLNSHIRE   5–3D

⭐

Harry's Place   £78
17 High St NG31 8JS (01476) 561780
*"Brilliant ingredients and the alchemy of Harry's sublime cooking" win a resounding "Bravo!" from most reporters for the Hallams' tiny (10 seats!) venture, presided over by wife Caroline; perhaps inevitably, given the scale of operations, critics can find prices on the high side.
/ **Details:** on B1174 1m N of Grantham; 9.30 pm; closed Mon & Sun; no Amex; booking essential; children: 5+.*

GREAT MALVERN, WORCESTERSHIRE   2–1B

⭐

Anupam Restaurant   £32
85 Church St WR14 2AE (01684) 573814
*Impressively consistent reports on this "affordable" Indian, where the food is "interesting, without being pretentious", and the service is "always friendly". / **Details:** www.anupam.co.uk; midnight.*

GREAT MILTON, OXFORDSHIRE 2–2D

Le Manoir aux Quat' Saisons £140
Church Rd OX44 7PD (01844) 278881

WINNER 2011
RÉMY MARTIN
FINE CHAMPAGNE COGNAC

«Magnifique!»; Raymond Blanc's "enchanting" manor house hotel
is "not just a restaurant but a total experience" – "amazing" cuisine,
a "to-die-for" wine list ("allow an hour"), "effortless" service and "chic"
accommodation, with a stroll in the "beautiful" gardens thrown in;
"don't forget the deeds to your house for when the bill comes".
/ **Details:** www.manoir.com; from M40, J7 take A329 towards Wallingford;
9.30 pm; booking: max 8. **Accommodation:** 32 rooms, from £460.

GREAT MISSENDEN, BUCKINGHAMSHIRE 3–2A

The Nags Head £44
London Rd HP16 0DG (01494) 862200
Numerous reports on this country inn, but they're bizarrely mixed;
on most accounts, this is a "charming" spot with "excellent" cooking
and a "welcoming" attitude – to a vocal minority, however, it's a
"clumsy" mix of "school-leaver-style" service and "unappetising" fare.
/ **Details:** www.nagsheadbucks.com; Off the A413; 9.30 pm, Sun 8.30 pm.
Accommodation: 5 rooms, from £90.

GREAT TEW, OXFORDSHIRE 2–1D

Falkland Arms £35
The Green OX7 4DB (01608) 683653
All reports agree that this "bustling" inn has "a great atmosphere inside
and out"; the food is generally hailed as at least "good" too
(with "great" ales), but critics do feel that this is a place that "trades
on its location". / **Details:** www.falklandarms.org.uk; A361 between Banbury &
Chipping Norton; 9.30 pm. **Accommodation:** 5 rooms, from £85.

GRETA BRIDGE, COUNTY DURHAM 8–3B

Morrit Arms Hotel £41
DL12 9SE (01833) 627232
A grand village-centre coaching inn that's been elegantly updated
in recent times; it's tipped for its "very good home-cooked locally-
produced food", and "excellent wine list", and all in a "wonderful
country setting" too. / **Details:** www.themorritt.co.uk.

GUERNSEY, CHANNEL ISLANDS

Da Nello £38
46 Lower Pollet St GY1 1WF (01481) 721552
"Always reliable", this long-established Italian St Peter Port has
a notably "warm" and "friendly" ambience; it impresses all reporters
with "family food at its best", and "good value" too. / **Details:** 10 pm.

Jamie's Italian   £38

A

13 Friary St GU1 4EH   (01483) 600 920
"Simple, tasty dishes, speedily prepared" inspire much enthusiasm for this new output of J Oliver's chain – a "nice buzzy place for a cheap 'n' cheerful get-together with friends".
/ **Details:** www.jamieoliver.com/italian/guildford; 11.00 mon/thu 11.30 sat 10.30 sun.

Rumwong   £36

A ★

18-20 London Rd GU1 2AF   (01483) 536092
"The best Thai restaurant in Surrey" – this "reliable" and "good-value" spot has won a most impressive following with its "authentic", "varied" and "stimulating" cuisine; unsurprisingly, it can be "crowded" at weekends. / **Details:** www.rumwong.co.uk; 10.30 pm; closed Mon; no Amex.

The Thai Terrace   £40

A

Castle Car Pk, Sydenham Rd GU1 3RT   (01483) 503350
"Perched on top of a multiple storey car park, this is not exactly a location you'd look for"; the views are "stunning", though, and this very popular – if sometimes "noisy" and "rushed" – Thai venue has quite a following for its "elegant" (though sometimes "variable") Thai cuisine. / **Details:** opposite Guildford Castle in town centre; 11 pm; closed Sun.

La Potinière   £54

★

Main St EH31 2AA   (01620) 843214

Keith Marley and Mary Runciman's traditionally-styled restaurant, half an hour from Edinburgh, doesn't attract quite the same attention as it did under its former ownership; the cooking, though, can still be "excellent". / **Details:** www.la-potiniere.co.uk; 20m E of Edinburgh, off A198; 8.30 pm; closed Mon, Tue & Sun D; no jeans or trainers; booking essential.

Horn of Plenty   £67

A

PL19 8JD   (01822) 832528
Peter Gorton sold this long-established restaurant-with-rooms – which has a "beautiful, peaceful setting", with "wonderful views" of the Tamar Valley – in mid 2010; we don't think a rating appropriate at this early stage, but we hope the chef (unchanged) continues to produce his "lovely" locally-sourced cuisine. / **Details:** www.thehornofplenty.co.uk; 3m W of Tavistock on A390; 9 pm; no jeans or trainers; children: 10+ at D.
Accommodation: 10 rooms, from £120.

GUNTHORPE, NOTTINGHAMSHIRE 5–3D

Tom Browns Brasserie £44 Ⓐ✪
The Old School Hs NG14 7FB (0115) 966 3642
*"Surprisingly good nosh in a riverside location near the banks of the River Trent"; this "large, airy, and consistently reliable" modern brasserie pleases all who comment on it. / **Details:** www.tombrowns.co.uk; 10 pm.*

HALE, CHESHIRE 5–2B

Earle £41 Ⓐ✪
4 Cecil Rd WA15 9PA (0161) 929 8869
*Don't let the fact it's backed by footballers put you off!; this Hale restaurant, run by Simon Rimmer of Green's fame, offers everything "from pub-style grub to fine dining", and reporters are unanimous that it's "a great little place". / **Details:** www.earlerestaurant.co.uk; 10.30 pm, Sun 9.30 pm; closed Mon.*

HALIFAX, WEST YORKSHIRE 5–1C

1885 The Restaurant £36 Ⓣ
Recreation Ground HX4 9AJ (01422) 373030
*A converted Victorian cottage, overlooking the Pennines, houses this cosy venture, tipped for its "excellent" food; other aspects of the experience don't always live up. / **Details:** www.1885therestaurant.co.uk; 9.30 pm; closed Mon, Tue–Sat D only, closed Sun D; no Amex.*

HAMBLETON, RUTLAND 5–4D

Finch's Arms £34 Ⓐ
Oakham Rd LE15 8TL (01572) 756575
*"Overlooking Rutland Water", this "very atmospheric gastropub"-with-rooms ("wish the bar was larger, it's mostly restaurant") serves "interesting and well-cooked" food "with charm"; the pricing, though, can seem a tad "ungenerous". / **Details:** www.finchsarms.co.uk; 9.30 pm, Sun 8 pm. **Accommodation:** 6 rooms, from £95.*

Hambleton Hall £87 Ⓐ✪✪
LE15 8TH (01572) 756991
*For "perfect country house dining", it's hard to beat Tim Hart's "cosseting", "old-school" establishment, in a one-time hunting lodge, which has a "wonderful location" overlooking Rutland Water; Aaron Patterson's "brilliant, ingredient-led cooking" is bang "up-to-date" too ("without being unduly modish"). / **Details:** www.hambletonhall.com; near Rutland Water; 9.30 pm. **Accommodation:** 17 rooms, from £205.*

HAROME, NORTH YORKSHIRE 8–4C

The Pheasant Hotel £37 Ⓐ
YO62 5JG (01439) 771241
*Under the same ownership as the legendary Star Inn, this "lovely" rural hotel is praised by (nearly) all reporters for "simply-presented food of the highest quality", and an "overall enjoyable experience" too. / **Details:** www.thepheasanthotel.com; 9 pm; no Amex. **Accommodation:** 14 rooms, from £150.*

The Star Inn £55
YO62 5JE (01439) 770397

Most reporters remain "endlessly charmed" by Andrew and Jacquie
Pern's "archetypal" thatched inn, not least due to its "well thought-out,
sublimely English" cooking, served "with gusto"; but is it becoming
"victim to its own success"? – the odd suggestion that it's "not exactly
poor, but lacking heart" are an unwelcome novelty.
/ **Details:** www.thestaratharome.co.uk; 3m SE of Helmsley off A170; 9.30 pm,
Sun 6 pm; closed Mon L & Sun D; no Amex. **Accommodation:** 14 rooms,
from £140.

HARPENDEN, HERTFORDSHIRE 3–2A

The Fox £35
469 Luton Rd AL5 3QE (01582) 713817
"In a gastronomic desert", a "dependable gastropub" whose "solid"
standards are "as good as it gets" in these parts.
/ **Details:** www.thefoxharpenden.co.uk; 10 pm.

HARROGATE, NORTH YORKSHIRE 5–1C

Bettys £30
1 Parliament St HG1 2QU (01423) 814070
"Every single visit is a delight, whether for a sandwich or just a coffee
and a cake" (or a "fabulous breakfast"), at this famously "old-
fashioned" Yorkshire "institution" – it's certainly "not cheap" but its
"unique charm" continues to satisfy reporters; "expect to queue".
/ **Details:** www.bettysandtaylors.co.uk; 9 pm; no Amex; no booking.

The Boar's Head £45
Ripley Castle Estate HG3 3AY (01423) 771888
A comfortable and rather grand village inn tipped for "good food in a
good location"; "both bistro and restaurant are friendly and reliable".
/ **Details:** www.boarsheadripley.co.uk; off A61 between Ripon & Harrogate; 9 pm.
Accommodation: 25 rooms, from £125.

Brio £33
Hornbeam Pk, The Lenz HG2 8RE (01423) 870005
"They've done a good job to avoid that canteen feeling", at this
"always-busy" Italian "on the ground floor of an office building";
it's tipped for "great pizza", and is "very child-friendly" too.
/ **Details:** www.brios.co.uk; 10 pm; closed Sun; no Amex.

Clock Tower
Rudding Park £41
Follifoot HG3 1JH (01423) 871350
If you're looking for a country house experience on the (relatively)
cheap, this "stunningly located" and "welcoming" all-day brasserie
is worth seeking out; after lunch, have a stroll in the "lovely gardens".
/ **Details:** www.ruddingpark.com; 10 pm. **Accommodation:** 49 rooms,
from £170.

Drum & Monkey   **£38**   Ⓐ

5 Montpellier Gdns HG1 2TF (01423) 502650
*This "tiny" and "tightly-packed" institution is renowned for its "fun"
atmosphere and "old-fashioned but satisfying seafood"; there are still
gripes, though, that it's "not as good as it was".*
/ **Details:** www.drumandmonkey.co.uk; 10 pm; closed Sun D; no Amex; booking:
max 10.

Graveley's Fish & Chip Restaurant   **£37**   ★

8-12 Cheltenham Pde HG1 1DB (01423) 507093
*"The best fish and chips in town" (and some more ambitious fare)
again wins praise for this eminent central chippy; "lovely premises" too.*
/ **Details:** www.graveleysofharrogate.com; 9 pm, Fri & Sat 10 pm, Sun 8 pm.

Hotel du Vin et Bistro   **£50**   Ⓐ

Prospect Pl HG1 1LB (01423) 856800
*After a poor showing in last year's survey, this branch of the boutique
hotel chain has put in a much stronger performance of late; there was
still the odd gripe, but it was widely praised for its "good atmosphere"
and "excellent" wine.* / **Details:** www.hotelduvin.com; 9.45 pm, Fri & Sat
10.15 pm. **Accommodation:** 48 rooms, from £95.

Orchid   **£44**   ★

28 Swan Rd HG1 2SE (01423) 560425
*"Interesting" dishes – with a "superb-value Sunday buffet" a highlight –
win high praise for this "very noisy and busy, high-quality pan-Pacific
eating house".* / **Details:** www.orchidrestaurant.co.uk; 10 pm; closed Sat L.
Accommodation: 28 rooms, from £104.

Quantro   **£40**   Ⓐ

3 Royal Pde HG1 2SZ (01423) 503034
*This "high-quality eatery" in the city-centre has a feeling rather
"reminiscent of a smart London chain"; thanks to its "good local food,
tastefully presented", and its "impeccable" service, it is often
"very busy".* / **Details:** www.quantro.co.uk; 10 pm, Sat 10.30 pm; closed Sun;
children: no under 4's in evening.

Timble Inn
The Timble Inn   **£35**   Ⓣ

Timble LS21 2NN (01943) 880530
*A "wonderful" refurbishment has done nothing to diminish the
"warm and cosy" charms of this old coaching inn, which is tipped for its
"small but impressive menu".* / **Details:** www.thetimbleinn.com; 9.30 pm;
closed Mon & Tue; no shorts.

Van Zeller   **£53**   Ⓐ★

8 Montpellier St HG1 2TQ (01423) 508762
*Tom Van Z is backed by David Moore (of London Pied à Terre fame),
and this "compact" and "contemporary" yearling has quickly become
"Harrogate's top place to eat"; supporters say the cuisine – "European
with a few Yorkshire elements!" – is "superb".*
/ **Details:** www.vanzellerrestaurants.co.uk; 10 pm; closed Mon & Sun D.
Accommodation: 3 rooms, from £.

William & Victoria   **£38**   Ⓐ

6 Cold Bath Rd HG2 0NA (01423) 521510
*British classics come in "generous" portions at this "rustic"-feeling
restaurant-cum-wine bar, which has been in the ownership of the same
family for over two decades; the only real problem seems to be that
it can get "a bit crowded and noisy".* / **Details:** www.willamandvictoria.com;
10 pm; no Mastercard; booking: max 12.

The Pier at Harwich   £51   (A)

The Quay CO12 3HH (01255) 241212
*The style can seem a little "old-fashioned", but this waterside hotel
(with both restaurant and bistro) is consistently praised as offering
a "very good overall experience", inlucding a menu which features
"a good choice of fish and shellfish". / **Details:** www.milsomhotels.com;
9.30 pm; no jeans. **Accommodation:** 14 rooms, from £105.*

Hassop Hall   £49   (A)(★)

DE45 1NS (01629) 640488
*"Stunning" but "not at all pretentious" – the Chapman family's
"beautiful" country house hotel continues to win praise for its "well-
mannered" service, and "quality food at easy prices".
/ **Details:** www.hassophall.co.uk; on the B6001 Bakewell - Hathersage Road,
Junction 29 of M1; 9 pm; closed Mon L, Sat L & Sun D. **Accommodation:** 13
rooms, from £95.*

Webbes Rock A Nore   £38   (★)

1 Rock a Nore Rd TN34 3DW (01424) 721650
*"A very welcome and popular addition to the town" – this year-old
operation uses "superb fish direct from the fishing boats right across
the street"; if you eat outside, "beware of the seagulls!"
/ **Details:** www.webbesrestaurant.co.uk; 9.30 pm.*

The Blue Strawberry   £41   (★)

The Street CM3 2DW (01245) 381333
*A real "local favourite for a classy night out" – this well-established
village-restaurant is a notably "friendly" destination with
a "high standard" of cooking, and "good-value wines" to match.
/ **Details:** www.bluestrawberrybistro.co.uk; 3m E of Chelmsford; 10 pm; closed
Sat L & Sun D.*

The Plough Inn   £39   (A)

Leadmill Bridge S32 1BA (01433) 650319
*"An absolute treasure a stone's throw from Winchester" by the River
Derwent – not really a gastropub, but "more a proper pub with great
food, and an atmosphere that's always welcoming".
/ **Details:** www.theploughinn-hathersage.co.uk; 9 pm, Sat 9.30 pm; no Amex;
booking: max 10. **Accommodation:** 9 rooms, from £95.*

The Great House   £37   (T)

Gills Grn TN18 5EJ (01580) 753119
*This 16th century inn is a fave rave for the locals, who acclaim its
"lovely" ambience, "unfailingly cheerful" staff and "delicious" food;
not all reporters, however, are quite convinced.
/ **Details:** www.elitepubs.com/the_greathouse/; 9.30 pm; no Amex.*

Weaver's   £40
15 West Ln BD22 8DU   (01535) 643822

By the the Bronte Parsonage Museum, the Rushworth family's restaurant-with-rooms, is tipped as "worth a detour".
/ **Details:** www.weaversmallhotel.co.uk; 1.5m W on B6142 from A629, near Parsonage; 9 pm; closed Mon, Sat L & Sun D; children: 5+ on Sat. **Accommodation:** 3 rooms, from £110.

The Half Moon   £38
The St RH17 5TR   (01444) 461227
Tipped as a "great option after a day on the South Coast", a pleasant village pub, offering "reliably good food" and "well-kept ales"; avoid the new extension, though, which "lacks atmosphere".
/ **Details:** www.thehalfmoonwarninglid.co.uk; 9.30 pm; closed Sun D; no Amex; children: 14+.

Jeremy's at Borde Hill   £50
Balcombe Rd RH16 1XP   (01444) 441102
Jeremy Ashpool "strikes a good balance between clever technique, and allowing quality ingredients to shine through", at his "long-standing favourite" – a "cheerful and bright" country restaurant, which is "best on the terrace, when weather allows".
/ **Details:** www.jeremysrestaurant.com; Exit 10A from the A23; 10 pm; closed Mon & Sun D.

Sky Apple Cafe   £25
182 Heaton Rd NE6 5HP   (01912) 092571
Perhaps it could do with "fancier accommodation" – the place feels like a "chaotic", "student" café – but this BYO veggie inspires enthusiastic support for the "delicious concoctions" from its "frequently-changing" menu. / **Details:** www.skyapple.co.uk; 10 pm; closed Sun; no credit cards.

Moyles   £48
New St HX7 8AD   (01422) 845272
"A town as small as Hebden Bridge is lucky to have a place as good as this!" – the bar ("usually abuzz at weekends") and restaurant of a small hotel, it is tipped for "everything from light snacks to fine dining dishes". / **Details:** www.moyles.com. **Accommodation:** 12 rooms, from £80.

Rim Nam Thai Restaurant   £38
New road HX7 8AD   (0871) 9624351
"Delicate" Thai food and "delightful" service make this "tiny" restaurant popular with all who comment on it; use your imagination, and perhaps the Rochdale Canal basin, which it overlooks, could double for the Chao Phraya? / **Details:** midnight; closed Mon.

Stubbing Wharf   £28   🅣

West Riding of Yorkshire HX7 6NW   (01422) 844107
"Good solid food and real ales" win a tip for this traditional pub, which
enjoys a picturesque location between the Rochdale Canal and the
River Calder. / **Details:** *www.stubbingwharf.co.uk; 9.30 pm, Sun 8 pm
; no Amex.*

HEDDON ON THE WALL, TYNE AND WEAR   8–2B

Close House   £50   🅣

NE15 0HT   (01661) 852255
"A beautiful Georgian house overlooking the Tyne Valley" with a *"lovely"*
dining room, tipped for its *"contemporary cuisine served with care"*.
/ **Details:** *www.closehouse.co.uk; St Andrews Church;
9pm.* **Accommodation:** *19 rooms, from £130.*

HEDLEY ON THE HILL, NORTHUMBERLAND   8–2B

The Feathers Inn   £35   ⭐

Hedley-on-the-Hill NE43 7SW   (01661) 843607
This *"proper pub"* is one of Northumbria's best-known culinary
destinations, thanks to cooking that's *"a real cut above"*; beware
"crowds". / **Details:** *www.thefeathers.net; 8.30 pm; closed Mon L; no Amex.*

HELMSLEY, NORTH YORKSHIRE   8–4C

Feversham Arms   £56   🅐⭐⭐

1-8 High St YO62 5AG   (01439) 770766
This *"very comfortable"* hotel and spa (a 'Small Luxury Hotel of the
World') is *"an excellent all-rounder"*, with *"exceptional"* cuisine and
"very friendly" service; let's hope new chef Chris Staines (ex-Foliage,
London) keeps up the standards! / **Details:** *www.fevershamarmshotel.com;
9.30 pm; no trainers; children: 12+ after 8 pm.* **Accommodation:** *33 rooms,
from £225.*

HEMEL HEMPSTEAD, HERTFORDSHIRE   3–2A

Cochin   £28   🅣

61 High St HP1 3AF   (01442) 233777
"Different from run-of-the-mill curry houses"; the *"subtle"* south Indian
food of this *"good-value"* spot is tipped by some reporters, despite
what's sometimes seen as a *"lack of atmosphere"*.
/ **Details:** *www.thecochincuisine.com; 10.45 pm, Fri & Sat 11.30 pm.*

HEMINGFORD GREY, CAMBRIDGESHIRE   3–1B

The Cock   £38   🅐

High St PE28 9BJ   (01480) 463609
In a *"calm"* location near the banks of the Ouse, this is an attractive
inn generally, but by no means invariably, hailed as offering
an *"excellent example of British pub food"*.
/ **Details:** *www.thecockhemingford.co.uk; 9 pm, Fri & Sat 9.30 pm, Sun 8.30 pm;
children: 5+ at D.*

HENLEY ON THAMES, OXFORDSHIRE   3–3A

Cherry Tree Inn   £38   🅐

RG9 5QA   (01491) 680430
It's *"a real off-the-beaten-track gem"*, say fans of this *"unpretentious"*
village hostelry *"poised between gastropub and plain country inn"*;
sceptics, though, say *"I've head people rave, but I found the food
mediocre"*. / **Details:** *www.thecherrytreeinn.com; 10 pm; closed Sun D.*
Accommodation: *4 rooms, from £95.*

Hotel du Vin et Bistro £50

New St RG9 2BP (01491) 848400

"Bizarre how the Henley HdV can't get it right"; the old riverside brewery is potentially a "lovely venue", but service is "so-so" and the food "like going back to the '70s" – "I've been several times", says one of a number of disappointed reporters, "and never had anything remotely acceptable!" / **Details:** www.hotelduvin.com; 10 pm, Fri & Sat 10.30 pm. **Accommodation:** 43 rooms, from £145.

Luscombes at the Golden Ball £48

Lower Assendon RG9 6AH (01491) 574157

"Assured" service and "competent" food have won much local acclaim for this "quietly-located" inn; increasingly, though, the prices "seem to assume everyone in Henley has deep pockets", leading a number of reporters to dismiss it as "over-hyped". / **Details:** www.luscombes.co.uk; 10.30 pm, Sun 9 pm; no Amex.

HEPWORTH, WEST YORKSHIRE 5–2C

The Butchers Arms £42

38 Towngate HD9 1TE (01484) 682361

"Unusual" cooking (not least "Yorkshire tapas") has won acclaim for this popular gastropub, picturesquely set high in the Pennines; critics find it "over-hyped", though – "too crowded", and offering "unfocussed" service and "mediocre" food.
/ **Details:** www.thebutchersarmshepworth.co.uk; 10 pm, Sun 9 pm; no Amex.

HEREFORD, HEREFORDSHIRE 2–1B

Café at All Saints £22

All Saints Church, High St HR4 9AA (01432) 370415

"Unusually-located in the middle of a church", a good lunch stop tipped for some "quite adventurous" dishes. / **Details:** www.cafeatallsaints.co.uk; near Cathedral; L only; closed Sun; no Amex; no booking; children: 6+ upstairs.

HERNE BAY, KENT 3–3D

Le Petit Poisson £36

Pier Approach, Central Parade CT6 5JN (01227) 361199

Recently trendified, a sea-view restaurant tipped for its "fresh and well-cooked fish", and seemingly at "half the price of places up the road in Whitstable"! / **Details:** www.lepetitpoisson.co.uk; 9.30 pm; closed Mon & Sun D; no Amex.

HERSHAM, SURREY 3–3A

The Dining Room £37

10 Queens Rd KT12 5LS (01932) 231686

"Friendly" and "unpretentious" – a veteran local restaurant in a series of cottage rooms, tipped for its "proper old-fashioned cooking".
/ **Details:** www.thediningroom.co.uk; 10.30 pm; closed Sat L & Sun D.

The Angel £45 A ★

BD23 6LT (01756) 730263

*This famous inn (with rooms) "copes admirably with its popularity" and continues to inspire an impressive number of "superb" reports; highlights include not just the food ("always good and well-presented, especially fish") and wine list ("strong", and "continuing to develop"), but also the "very professional" service. / **Details:** www.angelhetton.co.uk; 5m N of Skipton off B6265 at Rylstone; 9 pm; D only, ex Sun open L only. **Accommodation:** 5 rooms, from £145.*

Bouchon Bistrot £38 A

4-6 Gilesgate NE46 3NJ (01434) 609943

*Has "success in that Ramsay TV programme" led to a degree of "complacency" at this "relaxed" bistro? – no doubt it's a "lovely place to eat", which on most accounts offers "a good Gallic experience", but there were more reports of the "just OK" variety this year. / **Details:** www.bouchonbistrot.co.uk; 9.30 pm; closed Mon & Sun.*

The Old Queens Head £38 A

Hammersley Ln HP10 8EY (01494) 813371

*Fans are full of praise for this "excellent gastropub in a half-timbered Tudor barn" (and which benefits from a "quiet garden" too); even they, however, can sometimes find that the experience is "let down by the service". / **Details:** www.oldqueensheadpenn.co.uk; 9.30 pm, Fri & Sat 10 pm.*

Barnacles £44 T

Watling St LE10 3JA (01455) 633220

*Overlooking a private lake, a well-established restaurant tipped for the consistent quality of its fish-centric cuisine. / **Details:** www.barnaclesrestaurant.co.uk; 9.30 pm; closed Mon L, Sat L & Sun D; no Amex.*

Hintlesham Hall £66 T

Duke St IP8 3NS (01473) 652334

*This once-famous country house hotel is little commented-on nowadays; for those in search of "lovely and old-fashioned" style, it still has its attractions, but the food is, by contemporary standards, "nothing special". / **Details:** www.hintleshamhall.com; 4m W of Ipswich on A1071; 9.30 pm; jacket at D; children: 12. **Accommodation:** 33 rooms, from £150.*

Lord Poulett Arms   £43   Ⓐ⭐

TA17 8SE   (01460) 73149

"A delightful old village pub" in a *"picturesque location"*, with a *"lovely garden"*, and where *"quality local ingredients are used to create excellent dishes"*; it inspires an impressive amount of positive feedback. / **Details:** www.lordpoulettarms.com; 9 pm; no Amex. **Accommodation:** 4 rooms, from £85.

Phoenix   £28   Ⓐ

20 The Green CB4 4JA   (01223) 233766

On good form of late, this veteran Chinese serves food that's "very good", and "totally consistent" too. / **Details:** 10.30 pm; no Amex.

Victoria at Holkham   £47   Ⓐ

Park Rd NR23 1RG   (01328) 711008

A stone's throw from Holkham Beach, this "lovely country hotel" is well positioned for a post-prandial stroll; it's particularly acclaimed for its "excellent Sunday lunch", but reports on dinner are upbeat too. / **Details:** www.victoriaatholkham.co.uk; on the main coast road, between Wells-next-the Sea and Burnham Overy Staithe ; 9 pm; no Amex; booking essential. **Accommodation:** 10 rooms, from £125.

The Pigs   £36   Ⓐ

Norwich Rd NR24 2RL   (01263) 587634

"As befits the name, there is much focus on pork" at this *"spacious, airy, relaxed and friendly"* country pub, which makes *"a great local eatery"*; attractions include 'iffits' (Norfolk tapas). / **Details:** www.thepigs.org.uk; 9 pm; no Amex. **Accommodation:** 3 rooms, from £110.

Combe House   £65   Ⓐ⭐⭐

EX14 3AD   (01404) 540400

This "small, privately-owned country house hotel in its own grounds" (an Elizabethan manor house) pulls off an impressive hat trick, with its "interesting" food, "outstanding" service and "magical" location. / **Details:** www.combehousedevon.com; off A30, 20 minutes from Exeter; 9.15 pm. **Accommodation:** 16 rooms, from £179.

The Holt   £40   Ⓐ

178 High St EX14 1LA   (01404) 47707

"It looks like an ordinary (fairly uninspiring) pub on the outside", but almost all reporters really warm to this "very welcoming" boozer, thanks to its "delicious" food and "capable" service. / **Details:** www.theholt-honiton.com; 9 pm, Fri & Sat 9.30 pm; closed Mon & Sun; booking: max 8.

Ⓐ

Oak Room Restaurant
Tylney Hall £60
Rotherwick RG27 9AZ (01256) 764881
Settings don't come much more "stately" than the "traditional" dining room of this "beautiful" country house hotel; it's a "friendly" place too, but – though generally given the thumbs up – its overall style can seem to "lack the sophistication of similar places". / Details: www.tylneyhall.com; 10 pm, Sun 9.30 pm. Accommodation: 112 rooms, from £170.

Ⓐ⭐

The Bell Inn £41
High Rd SS17 8LD (01375) 642463
"A great find in an area not known for its cooking!"; this "well-kept former coaching inn" was arguably "one of the original gastropubs", and it is still almost universally hailed by reporters for its "interesting" and "tasty" cuisine from an "ever-changing" menu. / Details: www.bell-inn.co.uk; signposted off B1007, off A13; 9.45 pm; booking: max 12. Accommodation: 15 rooms, from £50.

Ⓐ⭐

Restaurant Tristan £53
3 Stans Way, East St RH12 1HU (01403) 255688
This "nice beamed space" can come as something of a surprise "among all the ring roads and shiny corporate palaces"; it's "definitely worth seeking out", though, thanks to Tristan Mason's "fabulous" cuisine, and in particular the "absolute steal" of a set lunch. / Details: www.restauranttristan.co.uk; 9.30 pm; closed Mon & Sun.

Ⓐ

Brownlow Arms £44
High Rd NG32 2AZ (01400) 250234
"Situated in a gastronomic wilderness", this village pub is "quintessentially English" and "pulls in crowds from far afield"; fans praise its "good, traditional fare", but others report disappointment of late with cooking that's "no better than average". / Details: www.brownlowarms.com; 9.15 pm; closed Mon, Tue–Sat D only, closed Sun D; no Amex; children: 12+. Accommodation: 5 rooms, from £96 in.

Ⓐ

Lino's £35
122 Market St CH47 3BH (0151) 632 1408
The occasional off-day is not unknown, but this "cosy" and "genteel" family-run veteran impresses most reporters with its "interesting" cuisine; it comes in "large portions" too. / Details: www.linosrestaurant.co.uk; 3m from M53, J2; 10 pm; closed Sun, Mon and Sat L; no Amex.

Ⓣ

Bradley's £38
84 Fitzwilliam St HD1 5BB (01484) 516773
"Not gastronomic, but honest"; this local bistro is consistently tipped for its "high standards" and its "value-for-money" (especially at lunch). / Details: www.bradleys-restaurant.co.uk; 10 pm; closed Sat L & Sun; no Amex.

HUNSDON, HERTFORDSHIRE 3–2B

The Fox And Hounds £39 Ⓐ⭐
2 High St SG12 8NH (01279) 843999
"Top-class cooking in a cosy setting" wins rave reviews for this "lovely country pub", in the Hertfordshire Hills.
/ *Details:* www.foxandhounds-hunsdon.co.uk; situated just off the A414, 10 min from Hertford; 10 pm.

HUNTINGDON, CAMBRIDGESHIRE 3–1B

Old Bridge Hotel £47 Ⓐ
1 High St PE29 3TQ (01480) 424300

An ivy-clad riverside hotel, where "well-trained" staff and "consistently good" food play honourable supporting roles; the proprietor, John Hoskin, is a Master of Wine, and the list is "remarkable" – "very interesting and reasonably-priced too".
/ *Details:* www.huntsbridge.com; off A1, off A14; 10 pm. **Accommodation:** 24 rooms, from £145.

HURLEY, BERKSHIRE 3–3A

Black Boys Inn £46 ⭐
Henley Rd SL6 5NQ (01628) 824212
"A great family-friendly country pub and restaurant", hailed by many reporters as a "relaxed gem", and offering an "imaginative" menu that's invariably "well-executed". / *Details:* www.blackboysinn.co.uk; 9 pm; closed Sun D; no Amex; children: 12+. **Accommodation:** 8 rooms, from £87.50.

HYTHE, KENT 3–4D

Hythe Bay £38 Ⓐ
Marine Pde CT21 6AW (01303) 267024
"Book ahead to get a table in the conservatory overlooking the sea", at this seafront stalwart; results can be "varied", but at best you get "an amazing range of well-prepared seafood" prepared with "no pretensions". / *Details:* www.thehythebay.co.uk; 9.30 pm.

ILFRACOMBE, DEVON 1–2C

The Quay £48 ⭐
11 The Quay EX34 9EQ (01271) 868090
With its "fabulous location", looking down on the harbour, you might think that Damien Hirst's restaurant would attract more feedback; such as it is, however, confirms that it's something of an "oasis" in this bit of the world, with "good-value" lunches a particular feature.
/ *Details:* www.11thequay.co.uk; 9 pm; closed Mon, Tue & Wed.

(A)(★)

Bettys   £36
32-34 The Grove LS29 9EE   (01943) 608029
*"Edwardian gentility is taken very seriously", at this famous café –
"part of the fabric of the town" and always "such a treat"; prices may
"seem high for what you get", but this does nothing to diminish the
perpetual queue. / Details: www.bettysandtaylors.com; 5.30 pm; no Amex;
no booking.*

(A)(★)(★)

The Box Tree   £64
35-37 Church St LS29 9DR   (01943) 608484
*"Getting better every time!"; with Simon Gueller in the kitchen,
this famous restaurant is – for perhaps the first time in a decade! –
offering "exceptional" food and "effortless" service commensurate with
its long-standing reputation; and then, in mid-2010, they bizarrely
decide to go and involve MPW... / Details: www.theboxtree.co.uk; on A65
near town centre; 9.30 pm; closed Mon & Sun D; no Amex; children: 10+ at D.*

(A)

The Far Syde   £38
1-3 New Brook St LS29 8DQ   (01943) 602030
*Sheer "consistency" makes this "decent-value" city-centre spot popular
with all who comment on it; "try to get a seat by the window".
/ Details: www.thefarsyde.co.uk; 10 pm; closed Mon & Sun; no Amex.*

(A)

Ilkley Moor Vaults   £32
Stockeld Rd LS29 9HD   (01943) 607012
*"A genuine Yorkshire gastropub", offering "good simple cooking with
fresh, often locally-grown ingredients". / Details: www.ilkleymoorvaults.co.uk;
9 pm, 9.30 pm Fri & Sat; closed Mon & Sun D.*

(A)

The Howard Arms   £39
Lower Grn CV36 4LT   (01608) 682226
*An "enjoyable" gastropub, with a "lovely" setting in the heart a pretty
North Cotswolds village; reports all suggest it remains a notably steady
performer. / Details: www.howardarms.com; 8m SW of Stratford-upon-Avon off
A4300; 9.30 pm, Fri & Sat 10 pm, Sun 9 pm; no Amex. **Accommodation:** 8
rooms, from £115.*

(T)

Kitchen   £35
15 Huntley St IV3 5PR   (01463) 259119
*"A very classy and welcoming restaurant", on the River Ness; it sadly
attracts too few reports for a proper rating, but all feedback is notably
positive. / Details: www.kitchenrestaurant.co.uk; 10 pm; no shorts.*

(A)

Mustard Seed   £35
16 Fraser St IV1 1DW   (01463) 220220
*In a "cosy" Georgian church overlooking the River Ness, a "lively" and
"friendly" restaurant consistently praised for its "great hospitality and
lovely food" – not least an "extremely good-value set lunch".
/ Details: www.themustardseedrestaurant.co.uk; On the bank of the Ness river,
30 yards from steeple; 9.45 pm.*

(A)(★)

Rocpool   £43
1 Ness Walk IV3 5NE   (01463) 717274
*This "buzzy" fish restaurant has a "wonderful" riverside location
(and "in the middle of the city" too); it's a really impressive all-rounder,
with attractions including "beautifully cooked" dishes, and a wine
list that's both "varied" and "well-priced".
/ Details: www.rocpoolrestaurant.com; 10 pm; closed Sun L , open Sun evenings
June-Sept only.; no Amex.*

Baipo   £34   ⭐⭐
63 Upper Orwell St IP4 1HP   (01473) 218402
*"If you can shut your eyes to the rather tired surroundings, the food
is incredible"*, at this veteran Thai, which all reports continue
to suggest *"is worth travelling for"*. / **Details:** www.baipo.co.uk; 10.45 pm;
closed Mon L & Sun; no Amex.

Bistro on the Quay   £34   🅣
3 Wherry Quay IP4 1AS   (01473) 286677
"Nothing fancy, but I've had nothing but good, fresh seafood here" –
a typical report tipping this *"very pleasant"* bistro by the waterfront,
which is *"probably the best-value eatery in the area"*.
/ **Details:** www.bistroonthequay.co.uk; 9.30 pm; closed Sun D.

Mariners at Il Punto   £40   🅐
Neptune Quay IP4 1AX   (01473) 289748

It's *"a consistently reliable slice of France"*, but this *"wonderfully-
situated"* restaurant – on a Victorian boat moored in the marina –
is *"a bit overpriced"* and not as outstanding as other Francis Crépy
ventures; perhaps the recent renaming (it was formerly called Il Punto)
suggests he intends to bring it up to scratch?
/ **Details:** www.marinersipswich.co.uk; 9.30 pm; closed Mon & Sun; no Amex.

Salthouse Harbour Hotel   £42   🅐
1 Neptune Quay IP4 1AS   (01473) 226789
In a trendily-revamped former warehouse, a waterside hotel where the
food is never rated less than *"competent"*, and is sometimes said
to offer *"excellent value"*; on occasions, however, the service can seem
to verge on *"chaotic"*. / **Details:** www.salthouseharbour.co.uk; 9.30 pm.
Accommodation: 70 rooms, from £130.

Trongs   £32   ⭐
23 St Nicholas St IP1 1TW   (01473) 256833
"The welcome is always friendly and bright", at this family-run
Vietnamese/Chinese; it *"goes from strength to strength"*, thanks to food
that's *"light, fresh and different from the norm"*, and *"well priced"* too.
/ **Details:** 10.30 pm; closed Sun; booking essential.

ITTERINGHAM, NORFOLK   6–4C

The Walpole Arms   £38   🅣
The Common, Itteringham NR11 7AR   (01263) 587258
"A good place for a summer lunch"; this *"enjoyable"* inn is tipped by a
number of reporters as an *"enjoyable"* all-rounder, and with
"good wines" too. / **Details:** www.thewalpolearms.co.uk; from Norwich take
A140, through Aylesham towards Blickling, 1m after Blickling Hall take first right
to Itteringham; 9 pm; closed Sun D; no Amex.

Bohemia
The Club Hotel & Spa   £70
Green St, St Helier JE2 4UH (01534) 876550
*"Shaun Rankin goes from strength to strength", say fans of his "sublime" ("stylish, but not too effortful") cuisine at this small contemporary hotel, near the business heart of St Helier; sceptics, unconvinced, find it "overpriced". / **Details:** www.bohemiajersey.com; 10 pm; closed Sun; no trainers. **Accommodation:** 46 rooms, from £215.*

Longueville Manor   £78
Longueville Rd, St Saviour JE2 7WF (01534) 725501
*The island's grandest traditional place to stay has a "wonderful manor house setting", on the fringe of St Helier; it's tipped for "good" food too ("if perhaps not quite as good as it should be for the money!"). / **Details:** www.longuevillemanor.com; Head from St. Helier on the A3 towards Gorey; less than 1 mile from St. Helier; 10 pm; no jeans or trainers. **Accommodation:** 31 rooms, from £220.*

Ocean Restaurant
Atlantic Hotel   £72
Le Mont de la Pulente, St Brelade JE3 8HE (01534) 744101
*"You look straight out at the ocean through palm trees", at this very popular hotel dining room (whose somewhat '30s vibe "Hercule Poirot would love"); local produce is prepared "to a very high standard" and delivered by "polished and friendly" staff. / **Details:** www.theatlantichotel.com; 10 pm. **Accommodation:** 50 rooms, from £150 - 250.*

Suma's   £37
Gorey Hill, Gorey JE3 6ET (01534) 853291
*The food at this first-floor establishment is "light and well executed" too – "what could be better on a sunny day than a table on the balcony here, overlooking Gorey Harbour?" / **Details:** www.sumasrestaurant.com; underneath castle in Gorey Harbour; 9.30 pm; closed Sun D; booking: max 12.*

Bosquet   £50
97a, Warwick Rd CV8 1HP (01926) 852463
*The food at Bernard and Jane Lignier's local landmark (which turns 30 this year) is "a lot better than in many places in France", and the service to go with it is notably "friendly" and "correct" too; on the downside, though, even fans can find the place "a little tired". / **Details:** www.restaurantbosquet.co.uk; on the main road through Kenilworth; 9 pm; closed Mon, Sat L & Sun; closed Aug.*

Loch Fyne   £40
6 High Street Clarendon Hs CV8 1LZ (01926) 515450
*One of the best-rated outlets of the commendable fish chain, praised for its "great food"… and "good prices" too. / **Details:** www.lochfyne.com; 10 pm. **Accommodation:** 31 rooms, from £95.*

Petit Gourmand   £44
101-103 Warwick Rd CV8 1HP (01926) 864567
*"Kenilworth's star turn" lives nicely up to its name, and almost all reporters praise its "well-prepared, traditional dishes"; particular highlight – "the best desserts ever". / **Details:** www.petit-gourmand.co.uk; 9.45 pm; closed Sun D.*

KETTLESHULME, CHESHIRE   5–2B

The Swan Inn   £36   ⭐
Macclesfield Rd SK23 7QU   (01663) 732943
*An "unpretentious" 15th-century inn in the Cheshire Peak District,
whose "delicious" food – from "well sourced ingredients" – is praised
by all who comment on it. / **Details:** www.swankettleshulme.com; 8.30 pm,
Thu-Fri 7 pm, Sat 9 pm, Sun 4 pm; closed Mon L; no Amex.*

KEYSTON, CAMBRIDGESHIRE   3–1A

The Pheasant   £48   Ⓐ
Loop Rd PE28 0RE   (01832) 710241
*Slightly mixed reviews on this "good-value gastropub", which has long
had quite a name locally; for some reporters it's "much improved
of late, and a favourite", but for others it's become "soulless, since it's f-
word success". / **Details:** www.thepheasant-keyston.co.uk; 1m S of A14
between Huntingdon & Kettering, J15; 9.30 pm; closed Sun D; booking essential.*

KIBWORTH BEAUCHAMP, LEICESTERSHIRE   5–4D

Firenze   £47   ⒶⒺ
9 Station St LE8 0LN   (0116) 279 6260

*"A little piece of Italy in the Leicestershire countryside" – the Poli family
run their attractive venture with practised charm, and the all-round
appeal of their formula includes a "great wine list" too.
/ **Details:** www.firenze.co.uk; 10 pm; closed Sun; no Amex.*

KILLIN, PERTH AND KINROSS   9–3C

Ardeonaig Hotel & Restaurant   £50   ⒶⒺ
South Loch Tay Rd FK21 8SU   (01567) 820400
*"A wonderful hotel in an exquisite location"; this (oddly) South African-
themed restaurant can sometimes seem "overpriced", but most reports
extol its "secluded" location on the south of Loch Tay, its "helpful" staff,
its "out-of-this-world" food, and its "splendid" wine.
/ **Details:** www.ardeonaighotel.co.uk; 8.30 pm; no Amex; children: 12+.
Accommodation: 27 rooms, from £100.*

KINGHAM, OXFORDSHIRE   2–1C

                                                        Ⓐ
The Kingham Plough   £44
The Grn OX7 6YD   (01608) 658327
*"A gem, with beautiful food", or a "shambolic" triumph of "style over
substance"? – fans are in the majority, but both schools of thought are
well represented in the copious feedback on this "Hoorays'-favourite"
Cotswolds gastro-boozer. / **Details:** www.thekinghamplough.co.uk; 8.45 pm,
Sun 8 pm; no Amex. **Accommodation:** 7 rooms, from £85.*

Byron   £30

4 Jerome Pl KT1 1HX   (020) 8541 4757

*An outlying branch of the "high end" diner chain that's taking the
capital by storm; it wins consistent praise for its "spacious" interior,
"super-helpful" service and "perfectly cooked, great-quality burgers".*
/ ***Details:*** *www.byronhamburgers.com; 10 pm.*

The Canbury Arms   £38

49 Canbury Park Rd KT2 6LQ   (020) 8255 9129

*"Wouldn't it be great if everyone could have a local pub just like this?"
– a "consistent", "friendly" and "welcoming" gastroboozer, serving
"fantastic food at decent prices" alongside "well kept real ales and
an interesting wine list".* / ***Details:*** *www.thecanburyarms.com; 10 pm,
Sun 9 pm.*

Frère Jacques   £42

10-12 Riverside Walk KT1 1QN   (020) 8546 1332

*"A beautiful setting overlooking the Thames" and "professional" service
underpin the attractions of this "busy" Gallic brasserie veteran,
by Kingston Bridge; it's "not cheap", though, and even some fans
concede the food is "not brilliant".* / ***Details:*** *www.frerejacques.co.uk; next to
Kingston Bridge and market place; 10 pm; no Amex.*

Jamie's Italian   £38

19-23 High St KT1 1LL   (020) 8912 0110

*"Surprisingly enjoyable for such a frenetic place" – this branch of Jamie
O's, no-reservation rustic-Italian chain continues to impress
most reporters with its "fresh and well-presented" food; it's hard not
to observe, however, that standards have already slipped a bit…*
/ ***Details:*** *www.jamiesitalian.com; 11 pm, Sun 10.30 pm.*

Norbiton Dragon   £32

16 Clifton Rd KT2 6PW   (0208) 546 1951

*A great pub with a "really good neighbourhood Thai restaurant
attached"; with its "terrace and large garden", it makes a "lovely
summer venue".* / ***Details:*** *www.norbitonanddragon.co.uk; 10.30 pm.*

Riverside Vegetaria   £38

64 High St KT1 1HN   (020) 8546 7992

*"The full and varied vegetarian and vegan menu covers most cooking
styles", at this "closely-packed" riverside café, much praised by fans for
its "tasty and wholesome" dishes.* / ***Details:*** *www.rsveg.plus.com; 10 mins
walk from Kingston BR; 11 pm; no Amex; children: 18+ ex L.*

Roz Ana   £39

4-8 Kingston Hill KT2 7NH   (020) 8546 6388

*"A really authentic, yet 'different', experience" – local reporters are
knocked out by this "great modern Indian" (with cocktail bar), where
the "interesting range" of "delicate" dishes is prepared to an
"exquisite" standard.* / ***Details:*** *www.roz-ana.com; 10.30 pm.*

Hipping Hall   £66

Cowan Bridge LA6 2JJ   (01524) 271187

*An "atmospheric, high-ceilinged hall" (15th century) provides
a positively "baronial" setting for a meal at this country house hotel;
its ratings have slipped a fraction in recent times, but most reporters
remain full of praise for its "first-class" food and its "friendly and
unpretentious" service.* / ***Details:*** *www.hippinghall.com; 9.30 pm;
Mon-Thu D only, Fri-Sun open L & D; no Amex; children: 10+.*
Accommodation: *9 rooms rooms, from £200.*

KNOWSTONE, DEVON   1–2D

The Mason's Arms   £55
EX36 4RY   (01398) 341231
*Mark Dodson's "lovely" thatched inn is a "surprising gourmet
experience on Exmoor", offering "top-notch cooking in comfortably
pubby surroundings"; even fans, though, can find the experience
a touch "overpriced" nowadays. / Details: www.masonsarmsdevon.co.uk;
9 pm; closed Mon & Sun D; no Amex or Maestro; children: 18+ after 6pm.*

KNUTSFORD, CHESHIRE   5–2B

Belle Époque   £48
60 King St WA16 6DT   (01565) 633060
*With its "stylishly decadent" decor, this (genuine and rare) Art Nouveau
landmark provides a "stunning" backdrop to a meal; improving
feedback supports those reporters who feel the food – from a very low
base, admittedly – "has moved up a gear" in recent times.
/ Details: www.thebelleepoque.com; 1.5m from M6, J19; 9.30 pm; closed
Sat L & Sun D; booking: max 6, Sat. Accommodation: 7 rooms, from £100.*

Piccolino   £46
95 King St WA16 6EQ   (01565) 751402
*This smart outlet of a NW-based chain makes a handy stand-by, tipped
for its "friendly staff", and its "unpretentious" cuisine.
/ Details: www.individualrestaurants.co.uk; 11.30 pm.*

LANCASTER, LANCASHIRE   5–1A

The Bay Horse   £38
Bay Horse Ln LA2 0HR   (01524) 791204
*"A great stop-off on the way north" (just off the M6); it's "no great
shakes" on the décor or service fronts, but the "wholesome" and tasty
fare almost invariably satisfies. / Details: www.bayhorseinn.com; 0.75m S of
A6, J33 M6; 9 pm; closed Mon & Sun D. Accommodation: 2 rooms, from £89.*

The Borough   £36
3 Dalton Sq LA1 1PP   (01524) 64170
*"A lively and welcoming city-centre pub", tipped as worth seeking out
for its atmosphere; the food can be "variable".
/ Details: www.theboroughlancaster.co.uk; 9 pm.*

Pizza Margherita   £30
2 Moor Ln LA1 1QD   (01524) 36333
*Founded three decades ago by the sister of the founder
of PizzaExpress, this "always-welcoming and buzzy" veteran is still
tipped for its "superb" pizza. / Details: www.pizza-margherita.co.uk;
10.30 pm.*

Simply French   £37
27a St Georges Quay LA1 1RD   (01524) 843199
*"Lovely atmosphere, lovely food" – reports on this city-centre bistro are
impressively consistent. / Details: www.quitesimplyfrench.co.uk; 9.30 pm,
Sun & Mon 9 pm; D only, ex Sun open L & D; no Amex.*

Sultan of Lancaster   £32
Old Church, Brock St LA1 1UU   (01524) 61188
*"The quality of the cooking continues to be unfailingly good", say fans
of this intriguingly-converted church, which nowadays houses an Indian
café, restaurant and gallery; no boozing, though.
/ Details: www.sultanoflancaster.com; 11 pm; D only; no Amex.*

267

LANGAR, NOTTINGHAMSHIRE 5–3D

Langar Hall £53
Church Ln NG13 9HG (01949) 860559
*"Exuding eccentric charm", this "fabulous" country house hotel – presided over by "interesting" patronne Imogen Skiving – has "recently had some much-needed sprucing up"; it remains a "classy" destination, offering a "fantastic" cuisine (which, if anything, has "improved" of late). / **Details:** www.langarhall.com; off A52 between Nottingham & Grantham; 9.30 pm; no Amex; no trainers. **Accommodation:** 12 rooms, from £14.*

LANGHO, LANCASHIRE 5–1B

Northcote £75
Northcote Rd BB6 8BE (01254) 240555

*"Best in the North West!"; Messrs Haworth and Bancroft's "welcoming" restaurant-with-rooms has built its reputation on its "excellent use of local high-quality meat, home garden vegetables and herbs" – a huge local fan club says the results are regularly "perfect". / **Details:** www.northcote.com; M6, J31 then A59; 9.30 pm. **Accommodation:** 14 rooms, from £210.*

LAVENHAM, SUFFOLK 3–1C

The Angel £36
Market Pl CO10 9QZ (01787) 247388
*"A lovely pub in a delightful village", where the food is "imaginative" and "delicious", and comes at "reasonable prices" too. / **Details:** www.maypolehotels.com; on A1141 6m NE of Sudbury; 9.15 pm; no Amex. **Accommodation:** 8 rooms, from £95.*

Great House £46
Market Pl CO10 9QZ (01787) 247431
*The Crépy family's "totally French" market square restaurant-with-rooms has it all – "terrific" cooking (with "a cheeseboard to die for"), a "superb" wine list, "efficient" service and "a wonderful village setting"; "I've been going for nearly 30 years", says one reporter, "and never left less than delighted". / **Details:** www.greathouse.co.uk; follow directions to Guildhall; 9.30 pm; closed Mon & Sun D; closed Jan; no Amex. **Accommodation:** 5 rooms, from £96.*

LEAMINGTON SPA, WARWICKSHIRE 5–4C

La Copola £36
86 Regent St CV32 4NS (01926) 888873
*"An authentic Italian, where you can have a truly romantic meal" – this charming establishment serves some "tasty" fare (including some "good seafood dishes"), and has quite a following, thanks not least to its "fantastic" atmosphere. / **Details:** www.lacopola.co.uk; 10pm sat 1030pm; no Amex.*

Aagrah £32 🅐⭐
St Peter's Sq LS9 8AH (0113) 2455667
This "very classy" city-centre subcontinental – which offers
a "huge menu" of "very tasty" and "well prepared" fare – remains
"a cut above" (like others in the chain) and is "always busy".
/ **Details:** www.aagrah.com; midnight, Sun 11 pm.

Aagrah £32 🅐⭐⭐
Aberford Rd LS25 2HF (0113) 287 6606
"Even in this area of excellent Asian restaurants, the food
is outstanding" – almost all reporters find this outpost of the prominent
NE subcontinental chain "never disappoints". / **Details:** www.aagrah.com;
from A1 take A642 Aberford Rd to Garforth; 11.30 pm, 11 pm Sun; D only.

Akbar's £29 🅐⭐
16 Greek St LS1 5RU (0113) 242 5426
"Take a trip to India", at this "always-buzzing" city-centre outfit, often
recommended for its "amazing value"; for the very best deal, though,
seek out the "large and extremely busy" 'Café' offshoot, nearby (where
a no-alcohol rule ensures even greater authenticity).
/ **Details:** www.akbars.co.uk; midnight; D only.

Anthony's £66 ⭐⭐
19 Boar Ln LS1 6EA (0113) 245 5922
Thanks to his "sublime" and "so creative" flavour combinations (in the
style of 'molecular gastronomy'), Anthony Flinn remains Leeds's leading
culinary light; arguably, though, his "calm and comfortable" basement
dining room – little changed since opening – is now "due for
redecoration". / **Details:** www.anthonysrestaurant.co.uk; 9.30 pm; closed
Mon & Sun; no Amex.

Anthony's at Flannels £36 🅐
68-78 Vicar Ln LS1 7JH (0113) 242 8732
"Not an obvious choice, being on the top floor of a fashion store" –
this outpost of the local Flinn empire is commended as a venue for
a "smart lunch" (or for business); while the menu "never disappoints",
however, some reporters feel it "never excels" either.
/ **Details:** www.anthonysrestaurant.co.uk; closed Mon, L only; no Amex.

Art's £35 🅐
42 Call Ln LS1 6DT (0113) 243 8243
"Hidden away in the Calls", a "lovely, little place" with a "cosy" and
"rather cosmopolitan" ambience; it has long been "a useful pit stop",
whether for a "cheap and cheerful" meal or a coffee.
/ **Details:** www.artscafebar.com; near Corn Exchange; 10 pm, 2 am Sat;
no booking, Sat L.

Bibis Italianissimo £42 ❌
Criterion Pl, Swinegate LS1 4AG (0113) 243 0905
"Buzzy, to the point you can't hear yourself think", this "massive" and
"glitzy" Art Deco-style Italian, on the fringe of the city-centre, often
strikes reporters as "pretentious", and "outrageously overpriced" too.
/ **Details:** www.bibisrestaurant.com; 11.30 pm; no shorts; no booking, Sat.

Blackhouse Restaurant & Bar £40 🅣
31-33 East Parade LS1 5PS (0870) 401 2119
Aa "lively" two-year old grill in the city-centre tipped – "although it's
a chain" – for its "good-quality" steak 'n' seafood.
/ **Details:** www.blackhouse.uk.com; 10.30 pm; no Amex.

Brasserie Forty 4   £41

44 The Calls LS2 7EW   (0113) 234 3232

"Classy and convenient", this long-established canal-side brasserie has re-established itself as a notably *"dependable"* destination, for dishes *"both classic and contemporary"*. / **Details:** www.brasserie44.com; 10 pm, Sat 10.30 pm; closed Sun. **Accommodation:** 41 rooms, from £140.

Casa Mia Grande   £42

33-37 Harrogate Rd LS7 3PD   (0845) 688 3030

Sometimes touted by fans as *"the city's best Italian"* (and for its *"fantastic fish selection"* too), this *"busy"* city-centre spot also has quite a few foes – *"bills mount"*, they say, and the experience can be plain *"disappointing"*. / **Details:** www.casamiaonline.co.uk; 10.30 pm, Fri & Sat 11 pm, Sun 9.30 pm; D only.

Casa Mia Millenium   £38

Millenium Sq, Great George St LS2 3AD   (0845) 688 3030

A *"very convenient location"* wins this this city-centre Italian a tip as a *"perfect place for a business lunch"* (or breakfast meeting); it features a *"wide-ranging"* menu. / **Details:** www.casamiaonline.com; 10.30 pm, Thu-Sat 11.30 pm, Sun 11 pm.

Chaophraya   £34

20a, First Floor, Blayds Ct LS2 4AG   (0113) 244 9339

Offering *"quality food"* at *"competitive prices"*, this *"very popular"* and *"buzzy"* city-centre operation has proved *"a welcome addition to Leeds's Asian options"*. / **Details:** www.chaophraya.co.uk; in Swingate; 10.30 pm.

Engine House Cafe   £37

2 Foundry Sq LS11 5DL   (0113) 391 2980

In the new 'Holbeck Urban Village', an *"enjoyable café/bistro"*, which derives *"lots of character"* from its location in a former brick foundry; it is particularly tipped as *"a good lunch spot"*. / **Details:** www.theenginehouse.co.uk; closed Sat L & Sun; no Amex.

Flying Pizza   £36

60 Street Ln LS8 2DQ   (0113) 266 6501

It's still *"stuffed to the gills with the see-and-be-seen crowd"*, but this stalwart Roundhay Italian now trades *"on past glories"* to a dispiriting extent. / **Details:** www.theflyingpizza.co.uk; just off A61, 3m N of city centre; 11 pm, Sun 10 pm; no shorts.

Fourth Floor Café
Harvey Nichols   £40

107-111 Briggate LS1 6AZ   (0113) 204 8000

This elevated department store dining room (and terrace) has quite a name locally as a top lunch spot (at which time it's *"very busy"*), and is tipped as a *"surprisingly good experience"* all-round. / **Details:** www.harveynichols.com; 10 pm; L only, ex Thu-Sat open L & D.

Fuji Hiro   £23

45 Wade Ln LS2 8NJ   (0113) 243 9184

"It may not be pretty", but many aficionados of this *"wonderfully consistent"* city-centre-fringe Japanese are more than willing to overlook the *"transport-caff-stye décor"* to enjoy *"the best noodles in the North of England"*, and at *"great-value"* prices too. / **Details:** 10 pm, Fri & Sat 11 pm; no Amex; need 5+ to book.

La Grillade £39 Ⓐ
Wellington St LS1 4HJ (0113) 245 9707
"It feels more French than France", at this "underground bistro", which comes complete with "whitewashed walls and lots of nooks" – a great choice for "a confidential business conversation over a fine steak and wine". / Details: www.lagrillade.co.uk; 10 pm, Sat 10.30 pm; closed Sat L & Sun.

Hansa's £26 ✪✪
72-74 North St LS2 7PN (0113) 244 4408
"Light and fresh Indian food" that's "wonderfully-spiced" and "full of intricate flavours" – the cuisine that creates some "exciting" experiences at Mrs Handa-Dabhi's "courteous" city-centre stalwart. / Details: www.hansasrestaurant.com; 10 pm, Mon-Sat 11 pm; D only, ex Sun L only; no Amex.

Kendells Bistro £42 Ⓐ
St Peters square LS9 8AH (0113) 243 6553
There's an appealing "simplicity" to the Gallic bistro formula at this "vast" and "loud" – but "really friendly" – city-centre spot, where staples are realised to a "very good" standard; "a great pre-theatre stop". / Details: www.kendellsbistro.co.uk; 10.30 pm; closed Mon, Sat L & Sun; no Amex; booking essential.

Little Tokyo £30 Ⓐ
24 Central Rd LS1 6DE (0113) 243 9090
Japanese food that's "always of a high standard" wins quite a fan club for this "well-priced" outfit, behind Debenhams; it's a "relaxing" place too, with "friendly" staff. / Details: 10 pm, Fri & Sat 11 pm; need 8+ to book.

The Piazza By Anthony
The Corn Exchange £38 Ⓐ
Corn Exchange, Call Ln LS1 7BR (0113) 247 0995
Its immense Victorian setting certainly has quite a "wow-factor", and Anthony Flinn's budget operation has become Leeds's most reported-on restaurant; of late, however, the food has seemed "none too exciting" rather too often for comfort; wrap up for winter visits. / Details: www.anthonysrestaurant.co.uk; 10 pm; no Amex.

Pickles & Potter £19 Ⓣ
18 -20 Queens Arc LS1 6LF (0113) 242 7702
"An idiosyncratic and slightly chaotic venue", tipped for its "hearty", "good-value" deli food (featuring "fantastic" sandwiches) and "cheerful" service; "it's so popular that getting a seat can be quite difficult". / Details: www.picklesandpotter.co.uk; L only; no credit cards.

Rajas £27 Ⓣ
186 Roundhay Rd LS8 5PL (0113) 248 0411
A small fan club tip this somewhat inauspicious-looking Gledhow veteran for its top-quality Punjabi cooking. / Details: www.rajasleeds.co.uk; close to Roundhay Park; 10.30 pm; no Amex.

The Reliance £36 Ⓣ
76-78 North St LS2 7PN (0113) 295 6060
A "shabby-chic" bar and dining room near the city-centre, with a "cosy" and "easy-going" vibe, and food that's "a cut above traditional pub-grub". / Details: www.the-reliance.co.uk; 10, Thu-Sat 10.30 pm, Sun 9.30 pm; no booking.

Salvo's £45
115 Otley Rd LS6 3PX (0113) 275 5017
With its "great buzz, authentic pizzas and efficient service", this mega-popular '70s veteran, in Headingley, is a local institution; "no bookings, so you can expect to queue". / Details: www.salvos.co.uk; 2m N of University on A660; 10.30 pm, Fri & Sat 11 pm, Sun 9 pm; no booking at D.

Sous le Nez en Ville £43
Quebec Hs, Quebec St LS1 2HA (0113) 244 0108
Bistro fare that's "reliably on the good side of OK", plus staff who "go out of their way to be helpful" help make a continuing success of this "quirky" Gallic basement, in the city-centre (where the early-evening prix-fixe is prized by locals for its "great value"). / Details: www.souslenez.com; 10 pm, Sat 11 pm; closed Sun.

Sukhothai £33
8 Regent St LS7 4PE (0113) 237 0141

"Wonderful" service adds further to the appeal of this "lovely" Chapel Allerton Thai, which is highly praised for "consistent" dishes with "authentic and precise" flavours; there is also a branch in Headingley. / Details: www.thaifood4u.co.uk; 11 pm; closed Mon L; no Amex.

LEICESTER, LEICESTERSHIRE 5–4D

Barceloneta £36
54 Queens Rd LE2 1TU (0116) 2708408
This "friendly and bustling tapas bar" – "a good neighbourhood restaurant that deserves its popularity" – wins praise as an "always-enjoyable, fun, cheap 'n' cheerful" destination. / Details: www.barceloneta.co.uk; Sun-Wed 9 pm, Fri & Sat 10.30 pm; D only.

Bobby's £23
154-156 Belgrave Rd LE4 5AT (0116) 266 0106
"The sweets are worth a visit on their own", say fans of this grungy-looking fixture of the Golden Mile; its dining room "lacks ambience" but offers an "exciting" menu – "it's unusual to find so much veggie fare of such a high standard". / Details: www.eatatbobbys.com; 10 pm; no Amex.

The Case £44
4-6 Hotel St LE1 5AW (0116) 251 7675
"It's not perfect, but you can tell they care", at this attractive factory-conversion in St Martins – something of "a haven" of "enjoyable" food in this under-served city, and one that's "stood the test of time" too; there's also a champagne bar. / Details: www.thecase.co.uk; near the Cathedral, and St Martins Square; 9.45 pm; closed Sun.

Kayal £35
153 Granby St LE1 6FE (0116) 255 4667
An "always-friendly" subcontinental, of particular note for its "vibrant" Keralan menu, from which the dishes are "fresh and very well-balanced"; also branches in Leamington Spa and Nottingham. / Details: www.kayalrestaurant.com; 11 pm, Sun 10 pm.

Simply Seafood　　　　　　£46　　　　○○

High St SS9 2ER　(01702 716645) 716645
*A seaside venture that makes "a great find" – there's "no fuss",
just "imaginative dishes made with fresh locally-caught fish";
"good views over the estuary" too. / Details: www.simplyseafood.co.uk;
9 pm; closed Mon.*

Jolly Frog　　　　　　　　£46　　　　Ａ○

The Todden　SY7 0LX　(01547) 540298
*"A good fish-based bistro" – the worst criticism anyone can come
up with is that it's "shockingly French for an establishment deep in the
British countryside!" / Details: www.jollyfrogpub.co.uk; 9.30 pm; closed Mon.*

Kings Head　　　　　　　£39　　　　Ｔ

Holt Rd　NR25 7AR　(01263) 712691
*"In a beautiful north Norfolk village", this old inn (with large garden)
"morphed into a gastropub" a couple of years ago (under the
wonderfully-named Flying Kiwi group), and is consistently tipped
as "a good eating venue". / Details: www.letheringsettkingshead.co.uk;
930; no Amex.*

The Ship Inn　　　　　　　£38　　　　○

Church Ln　IP10 0LQ　(01473) 659573
*In a village outside Ipswich (amid "beautiful country with loads
of walks"), this "very busy" hostelry is commended for its "excellent
choice" of "reliable upmarket pub grub". / Details: 9.30 pm, Sun 9 pm;
no Amex; children: 14+.*

Bill's Produce Store　　　　£32　　　　Ａ

56 Cliffe High St　BN7 2AN　(01273) 476918
*This "entertaining" deli/café has won quite a name for its "excellent
breakfasts" and other "quality" snacks; it's arguably "too popular for its
own good", though, as its "very lively" interior can sometimes seem
"too cramped and noisy". / Details: www.billsproducestore.co.uk; 6 pm;
no Amex.*

Star Inn　　　　　　　　　£42　　　　Ａ

The Street　CB8 9PP　(01638) 500275
*It may look like your classic "olde worlde pub", but the cuisine here
is Catalan, and – say fans – "fabulous" too; it's "starting to get a bit
pricey", though, to the extent that critics feel it's "completely resting
on its laurels". / Details: on B1063 6m SE of Newmarket; 10 pm; closed
Mon & Sun D.*

Browns Pie Shop　　　　　£33　　　　Ｔ

33 Steep Hill　LN2 1LU　(01522) 527330
*The food may be "more homely than special", but this "olde-worlde"
spot near the cathedral is still sometimes tipped for its "rustic" English
charms. / Details: www.brownspieshop.co.uk; near the Cathedral; 10 pm,
Sun 8 pm; no Amex.*

The Old Bakery   £42
26-28 Burton Rd LN1 3LB (01522) 576057
Near the cathedral, this "gem" of a restaurant-with-rooms wins high praise for its "obliging" service and its "interesting" menu, which "makes the best of seasonal and local produce".
/ **Details:** www.theold-bakery.co.uk; 9 pm; closed Mon; no jeans.
Accommodation: 4 rooms, from £63.

The Wig & Mitre   £32
30-32 Steep Hill LN2 1TL (01522) 535190
This large inn occupying a "beautiful" ancient building near the cathedral is still "not what it was" – it can be "very good", say fans, but there are still too many reports of "poor" or "uninspiring" meals.
/ **Details:** www.wigandmitre.com; between Cathedral & Castle; 10.30 pm.

LINLITHGOW, WEST LOTHIAN   9–4C

Champany Inn   £88
EH49 7LU (01506) 834532
*Renowned for "amazing steaks at eye-watering prices", this luxurioius and "old-fashioned" inn is also known for its wine list – "so interesting it may take you half an hour to read!" / **Details:** www.champany.com; 2m NE of Linlithgow on junction of A904 & A803; 10 pm; closed Sat L & Sun; no jeans or trainers; children: 8+. **Accommodation:** 16 rooms, from £125.*

LITTLE BUDWORTH, CHESHIRE   5–2B

Cabbage Hall   £39
Forest Rd CW6 9ES (01829) 760292
Eminent local chef Robert Kisby has landed on his feet at this "rather out-of-the-way pub/restaurant, in a part of the world starved of good gastropubs"; there's an "interesting" ("confusing") array of menus, and "his classical training shines through" to "superb" effect.
/ **Details:** www.cabbagehallrestaurant.com; 9.30, Sun 8 pm; no Amex.

LITTLE WILBRAHAM, CAMBRIDGESHIRE   3–1B

The Hole In The Wall   £39
2 High St CB21 5JY (01223) 812282
This may be a "modest-looking" dining pub, but its "good, modern take on some hearty British classics" (from a protégé of Michael Caines) and "welcoming" service recommend it to all who comment.
/ **Details:** www.the-holeinthewall.com; 9 pm; closed Mon & Sun D; no Amex.

LITTLEHAMPTON, WEST SUSSEX   3–4A

East Beach Cafe   £39
Sea Rd, The Promenade BN17 5GB (01903) 731903
"A stunning setting" and "great views" only enhance the "vibey" atmosphere of this "superior" modern "beach caff", where "excellent fish" is the top culinary attraction; sit outside, though – "the interior has all the charm of the interior of a microwave oven".
/ **Details:** www.eastbeachcafe.co.uk; 8.30 pm.

LIVERPOOL, MERSEYSIDE   5–2A

Alma De Cuba
St Peter's Church   £40
Seel St L1 4bh (0151) 702 7394
It's the setting – a "fabulous conversion of a church in the up-and-coming city-centre" – that makes this South American-themed outfit of note; the "ordinary" and "overpriced" food is incidental.
/ **Details:** www.alma-de-cuba.com; 11 pm, Fri & Sat midnight; no shorts; children: 18+ in bar.

Chaophraya £38

5-6 Kenyon Steps L1 3DF (0151) 7076323
An "excellent" Thai in the new Liverpool 1 shopping centre, which
"stands out" thanks to its "elegant" styling and the consistently high
standard of its cuisine. / *Details:* www.chaophraya.co.uk.

Delifonseca £32

12 Stanley St L1 6AF (0151) 255 0808

"A small, friendly city-centre dining room above a fine delicatessen";
"keenly-priced", it offers an "excellent" range of dishes.
/ *Details:* www.delifonseca.co.uk; 9 pm, Fri & Sat 9.30 pm; closed Sun; no Amex.

Etsu £35

25 The Strand L2 0XJ (0151) 236 7530
A three-year-old café tipped by a number of locals as a "great
Japanese". / *Details:* www.etsu-restaurant.co.uk; Off Brunswick street; 10 pm;
closed Mon, Wed L & Sat L.

Everyman Bistro £26

5-9 Hope St L1 9BH (0151) 708 9545
"A Liverpool institution of decades' standing", this "self-service
basement bistro" is "as cheap as chips", but still manages to use
"plenty of local produce" in its "home-style cuisine"; leave space for
pudding. / *Details:* www.everyman.co.uk; midnight, Fri & Sat 2 am; closed Sun.

Host £31

31 Hope St L1 9HX (0151) 708 5831
"Beats Wagamama hands down!"; this "lively" noodle bar – part of the
"60 Hope Street empire" – is pretty much unanimously praised for its
"innovative", "fresh" and "tasty" Asian-fusion fare.
/ *Details:* www.ho-st.co.uk; 11 pm.

Italian Club fish £36

128 Bold St L1 4JA (0151) 707 2110
"A real find"; this Italo-Scottish café/restaurant – a venture
of Edinburgh's 'Valvona & Crolla' family – attracts consistent praise for
its fish-centric menu, and "the best chips in the city" too!
/ *Details:* www.theitalianclubliverpool.co.uk; 10 pm, Sun 9 pm; no Amex.

The London Carriage Works
Hope Street Hotel £50

40 Hope St L1 9DA (0151) 705 2222
Once the hottest place in town, this rather "sterile and echo-y"
boutique hotel dining room continues to put in a mystifyingly erratic
performance; there's a distinct feeling nowadays that it's "living on its
former reputation". / *Details:* www.tlcw.co.uk; opp Philharmonic Hall; 10 pm,
Sun 9 pm; no shorts. *Accommodation:* 89 rooms, from £150.

Malmaison £54
William Jessop Way, Princes Dock L3 1QW   (0151) 229 5000

The food may tend to "functional", but this recent dockside outpost of the trendy hotel chain is tipped by a number of reporters, not least as "good for business meetings".
/ **Details:** www.malmaison-liverpool.com; 10.30 pm. **Accommodation:** 130 rooms, from £99.

Mayur £32
130 Duke St L1 5AG   (0151) 709 9955
"Intense and authentic dishes" win high praise for this "classy" contemporary Indian, in the city-centre; "very popular, so avoid at busy times". / **Details:** www.mayurrestaurant.co.uk; 10.30 pm, Fri & Sat 11.30 pm.

The Monro £38
92-94 Duke St L1 5AG   (0151) 707 9933
"A stylishly refurbished pub serving good standard gastropub fare"; it's a "busy" sort of place, generally hailed for offering "reliable food at a reasonable price". / **Details:** www.themonro.com; 9.45 pm, Sun 7.30 pm.

Panoramic
Beetham West Tower £56
Brook St L3 9PJ   (0151) 236 5534
"Feast your eyes on the view, but ignore the food", should you visit this "spectacular" 34th-floor dining room – the cuisine is too often "fussy", and it comes at "inflated" prices. / **Details:** www.panoramicliverpool.com; 9.30 pm; no trainers.

Puschka £44
16 Rodney St L1 2TE   (0151) 708 8698
"Lovely modern British food, and a lively vibe" – that's the combo that makes this "intimate" and "reliable" restaurant popular with almost all who comment on it. / **Details:** www.puschka.co.uk; 10 pm, Sun 9 pm; D only, closed Mon.

The Quarter £33
7-11 Falkner St L8 7PU   (0151) 707 1965
A "Bohemian café, just around the corner from the Phil", serving salads, pizza 'n' pasta; owned by the 60 Hope Street people, it's a good "cheap and cheerful" bet (so long as you don't mind drinking your wine in glass tumblers, which some reporters do).
/ **Details:** www.thequarteruk.com; 11 pm.

San Carlo £45
41 Castle St L2 9SH   (0151) 236 0073
"The best new restaurant in Liverpool" – this former bank, near the Town Hall, is now an outpost of a successful Italian chain – a "stunning"-looking place, with "brisk" service, and serving "undoubtedly the best seafood in town" (in particular).
/ **Details:** www.sancarlo.co.uk; 11 pm.

60 Hope Street £50 ⭐

60 Hope St L1 9BZ (0151) 707 6060
"Getting back on track" – this townhouse-restaurant (with brasserie
in the basement) *"had a dip"* a few years ago, but is once again
acclaimed by many reporters as *"Liverpool's most reliable and polished
fine dining experience"*. / **Details:** www.60hopestreet.com; 10.30 pm; closed
Sat L & Sun.

Spire £36 Ⓐ

1 Church Rd L15 9EA (0151) 734 5040
*If you should find yourself in Wavertree ("quite far from the centre"),
this "welcoming" local restaurant is undoubtedly the top tip locally.*
/ **Details:** www.spirerestaurant.co.uk; Mon-Thu 9 pm, Fri & Sat 9.30 pm; closed
Mon L, Sat L & Sun.

Tai Pan £28 ⭐

WH Lung Bdg., Great Howard St L5 9TZ (0151) 207 3888
*"Go for dim sum, or one of the hot-pot dishes", and you're unlikely
to go far wrong at this vast, "warehouse-type" Chinese, above
an oriental supermarket.* / **Details:** 11.30 pm, Sun 9.30 pm.

Yuet Ben £30 Ⓐ

1 Upper Duke St L1 9DU (0151) 709 5772
*Long the Chinese of choice "for Liverpool's middle-aged middle classes",
this Chinatown institution treats its regulars as "honoured guests"
("which is what the name means", apparently) – its "always reliable
and welcoming".* / **Details:** www.yuetben.co.uk; 11 pm; D only, closed Mon.

LLANARMON DC, DENBIGHSHIRE   5–3A

The Hand At Llanarmonn £35 Ⓐ

Ceiriog Valley LL20 7LD (01691) 600666
*"Big hearty meals and flavours from locally-sourced ingredients"
(with "particularly good lamb", obviously) enthuse reporters on this
Ceiriog Valley inn – "an enjoyable, rather than polished, place".*
/ **Details:** www.thehandhotel.co.uk; 9.00; no Amex. **Accommodation:** 13
rooms, from £105.

LLANDENNY, MONMOUTHSHIRE   2–2A

Raglan Arms £42 Ⓣ

NP15 1DL (01291) 690800
*Our top tip in these parts, a "comfy" gastropub, offering "freshly-
cooked" fare from a "sensibly limited" menu.*
/ **Details:** www.raglanarms.com; 9.30 pm; closed Mon & Sun D.

LLANDEWI SKIRRID, MONMOUTHSHIRE   2–1A

The Walnut Tree £51 ⭐⭐

NP7 8AW (01873) 852797
*Shaun Hill's "immaculate" cooking – "simple ingredients, amazingly
cooked", in a style that's "unfussy" but "inventive" – has now restored
this surprisingly "plain and simple" rural pub to "its former glory"; it is
now, rightly, re-established as Wales's best-known culinary destination.*
/ **Details:** www.thewalnuttreeinn.com; 3m NE of Abergavenny on B4521; 10 pm;
closed Mon & Sun. **Accommodation:** 2 rooms, from £160.

A ⭐⭐

Tyddyn Llan £67
LL21 0ST   (01490) 440264
An "idyllic" setting sets the scene at Bryan & Susan Webb's "lovely"
rural restaurant-with-rooms, where "fantastic food is simply presented
to focus on the ingredients rather than fancy presentation".
/ **Details:** www.tyddynllan.co.uk; on B4401 between Corwen and Bala; 9 pm;
closed Mon (Tue-Thu L by prior arrangement only); no Amex; booking essential
Tue L-Thu L. **Accommodation:** 13 rooms, from £140.

LLANDUDNO, CONWY 4–1D

A

Bodysgallen Hall £52
LL30 1RS   (01492) 584466
The setting is undoubtedly "delightful" ("with wonderful mountain views
from the dining room"), but reports on the food at this country house
hotel – whose origins go back to the 13th century – have become
rather too mixed for comfort; perhaps it can find renewed vigour under
its new owners, the National Trust? / **Details:** www.bodysgallen.com; 2m off
A55 on A470; 9.15 pm, Fri 9.30 pm; closed Mon; no jeans or trainers; booking:
max 10; children: 6+. **Accommodation:** 31 rooms, from £165.

A

St Tudno Hotel £47
Promenade LL30 2LP   (01492) 874411

"Staff really try and make you feel comfortable, without too much
formality or pomposity", at this comfortable – if quite old-fashioned –
hotel, right by the pier; the food is "very well-prepared",
and complemented by a "fantastic" wine list.
/ **Details:** www.st-tudno.co.uk; 9.30 pm; no shorts; children: 6+ after 6.30 pm.
Accommodation: 18 rooms, from £100.

LLANDWROG, GWYNEDD 4–2C

A ⭐

Rhiwaf Allen £48
Caernarfon LL54 5SW   (01286) 830172
"An excellent find" – this "small", "intimate" and "elegant" restaurant-
with-rooms, on the Lleyn Peninsula, seems to be a very good all-
rounder; it's tipped for its "creative dishes from local ingredients",
and its "enthusiastic" and "sincere" service.
/ **Details:** www.rhiwafallen.co.uk; 9 pm; D only, closed Mon & Sun; booking
essential; children: 12 +. **Accommodation:** 3 rooms, from £100.

LLANFRYNACH, POWYS 2–1A

T

White Swan £39
Brecon LD3 7BZ   (01874) 665276
"A good pub in a nice village", in the heart of the Brecon Beacons,
tipped for its "honest" cooking. / **Details:** www.the-white-swan.co.uk; 9 pm;
closed Mon & Tue; no Amex; booking essential.

LLANGAMMARCH WELLS, POWYS 4–4D

Lake Country House £56 Ⓣ
LD4 4BS (01591) 620202
"Everything is competent and they're trying hard", at this country house hotel, where a *"huge wine list"* is a particular feature.
/ **Details:** www.lakecountryhouse.co.uk; off A483 at Garth, follow signs; 9.15 pm; no jeans or trainers; children: 8+ at D. **Accommodation:** 31 rooms, from £185.

LLANGOLLEN, DENBIGHSHIRE 5–3A

Corn Mill £38 Ⓐ
Dee Ln LL20 8PN (01978) 869555
"Above the raging River Dee", and *"with views of the steam railway, a ruined castle and surrounding hills"*, this *"tastefully-converted"*, three-story mill (part of the Brunning & Price chain) certainly has a *"stunning setting"*; no great surprise, then, that food and service are *"fairly ordinary"*. / **Details:** www.cornmill-llangollen.co.uk; 9.30 pm, Sun 9 pm.

LLANWRTYD WELLS, POWYS 4–4D

Carlton Riverside £52 Ⓐ
Irfon Cr LD5 4SP (01591) 610248
"Worth a visit, even if it is in the back of beyond"; the style of this riverside restaurant-with-rooms can seem *"a little old-fashioned"* nowadays, but its *"unusual"* dishes still impress most reporters.
/ **Details:** www.carltonriverside.com; 8.30 pm; D only, closed Sun; no Amex. **Accommodation:** 5 rooms, from £75.

LLYSWEN, POWYS 2–1A

Llangoed Hall £64 Ⓐ
LD3 0YP (01874) 754525
"The very model of a proper country house restaurant" – this *"tranquil"* and imposing hotel is a supremely *"elegant"* destination, also often praised for its *"outstanding"* cuisine; a couple of reports, though, hint at a blip in standards this year.
/ **Details:** www.llangoedhall.com; 11m NW of Brecon on A470; 8.45 pm; no Amex; jacket required at D. **Accommodation:** 23 rooms, from £210.

LOCHINVER, HIGHLAND 9–1B

The Albannach £71 Ⓐ✪✪
IV27 4LP (01571) 844407
"A sublime experience"; the *"atmospheric"* dining rooms of this small and remote hotel evokes a hymn of praise for its *"superb locally-sourced seafood, meat and vegetables"*, the *"extensive and interesting"* wine list and the *"friendly and knowledgeable"* service.
/ **Details:** www.thealbannach.co.uk; one sitting; D only, closed Mon; no Amex; children: 12+. **Accommodation:** 5 rooms, from £260.

LOCKSBOTTOM, KENT 3–3B

Chapter One £49 Ⓐ✪✪
Farnborough Common BR6 8NF (01689) 854848
"Top-notch food without having to make a journey up to town" – the concept that's won a gigantic following for this *"fabulous"* Bromley stalwart, one of the very best restaurants on the fringes of the capital.
/ **Details:** www.chaptersrestaurants.com; just before Princess Royal Hospital; 10.30 pm; booking: max 12.

LONG CRENDON, BUCKINGHAMSHIRE　　　2–2D

The Mole & Chicken　　　£40
Easington HP18 9EY   (01844) 208387
This "cheerful" place may look like like a "typical country pub", but its cuisine is "above-average", and "well presented" too.
/ Details: www.themoleandchicken.co.uk; follow signs from B4011 at Long Crendon; 9.30 pm, Sun 9 pm. Accommodation: 5 rooms, from £95.

LONGRIDGE, LANCASHIRE　　　5–1B

The Longridge Restaurant　　　£56
104-106 Higher Rd PR3 3SY   (01772) 784969
It's been an up-and-down year at the cottage restaurant where leading NW chef Paul Heathcote originally forged his reputation – some "sublime" meals have been recorded, but some "nowhere near past best standards" too. / Details: www.heathcotes.co.uk; follow signs for Jeffrey Hill; 9.30 pm, Sun 7.45 pm; closed Mon & Tue.

LOUGHBOROUGH, LEICESTERSHIRE　　　5–3D

The Hammer And Pincers　　　£50
5 East Rd LE12 6ST   (01509) 880735
A "quiet" and "friendly" rural restaurant, tipped by locals for cuisine that "imaginative", and "competently realised" too.
/ Details: www.hammerandpincers.co.uk; 9.30 pm, Sun 6 pm; closed Sun D; no Amex.

LOWER FROYLE, HAMPSHIRE　　　2–4C

The Anchor Inn　　　£41
GU34 4NA   (01420) 23261
A classic country inn tipped for its "excellent" setting, "high-quality" food and "great beer". / Details: www.anchorinnatlowerfroyle.co.uk; 9.30 pm.
Accommodation: *5 rooms, from £110.*

LOWER ODDINGTON, GLOUCESTERSHIRE　　　2–1C

The Fox Inn　　　£38
GL56 0UR   (01451) 870555
"A lovely rambling candlelit pub" in "a super-pretty Cotswold village"; its "sturdy" food and "friendly" service inspire many, invariably positive, reports. / Details: www.foxinn.net; on A436 near Stow-on-the-Wold; 10 pm, Sun 9.30 pm; no Amex. Accommodation: 3 rooms, from £75.

LOWER SLAUGHTER, GLOUCESTERSHIRE　　　2–1C

Lower Slaughter Manor
Von Essen　　　£68
GL54 2HP   (01451) 820456
A "stunningly beautiful" Cotswold hotel, part of the Von Essen group, tipped as an "elegant" destination for a special occasion; reports (few) record some "slight faults" on the food front (and service too), but these don't manage to disturb an overall impression that's often "superb". / Details: www.lowerslaughter.co.uk; 2m from Burton-on-the-Water on A429; 9 pm; no jeans or trainers. Accommodation: 19 rooms, from £310.

La Bécasse £77 Ⓐ ⭐⭐
17 Corve St SY8 1DA (01584) 872325
The "genius" of Will Holland's cuisine – "creative, yet so comfortingly classic" – wins the highest praise for the "stylish" panelled dining room of this northerly offshoot of L'Ortolan at Shinfield; it's a "comfy" destination too, though the atmosphere can sometimes seem "a little formal" and "hushed". / **Details:** www.labecasse.co.uk; 9 pm; closed Mon, Tue L & Sun D; no Amex.

Fishmore Hall £62 Ⓣ
Fishmore Rd SY8 3DP (01584) 875148
"The food is amazing, and so is the service!"; this country house hotel – occupying a Georgian manor house just outside the foodie town – is tipped as a "great dining experience"; it makes "a good place to stay" too.. / **Details:** www.fishmorehall.co.uk; 9.30 pm; booking essential.
Accommodation: 15 rooms, from £140.

Koo £35 Ⓐ
127 Old St SY8 1NU (01584) 878462
Discard your Ludlow preconceptions – the "fresh" and "imaginative" cooking that makes this well-established restaurant "popular with locals and visitors alike" is resolutely Japanese. / **Details:** www.koo-ook.co.uk; Off the A49; 9 pm; D only, closed Mon & Sun.

Mr Underhill's £68 Ⓐ ⭐⭐
Dinham Wier SY8 1EH (01584) 874431
"Just a great experience" – reporters can find almost nothing to fault at Chris & Judy Bradley's restaurant-with-rooms, "beautifully located" by a weir; it offers an "amazing mix" of "outstanding" food and "relaxed but thoughtful" service – the "interesting, well-priced wine list" is the icing on the cake. / **Details:** www.mr-underhills.co.uk; 8.15 pm; D only, closed Mon & Tue; no Amex; children: 8+. **Accommodation:** 6 rooms, from £140.

The Dartmoor Inn £46 Ⓐ
Moorside EX20 4AY (01822) 820221
This pub is more a "restaurant with a bar" nowadays, and its New England/Swedish-style cuisine can be simply "outstanding" – "variability" is an issue, though, and even a single meal can sometimes seem "a game of two halves". / **Details:** www.dartmoorinn.com; on the A386 Tavistock to Okehampton road; 9.30 pm; closed Mon L & Sun D.
Accommodation: 3 rooms, from £110.

Harbour Inn £38 Ⓐ
Marine Pde DT7 3JF (01297) 442299
A "really convivial" spot, tipped for its "great location" right on the beach and its "friendly" service; the cooking is "consistent" too.
/ **Details:** 9 pm.

Hix Oyster and Fish House £52 Ⓐ ⭐
Cobb Hs, Cobb Rd DT7 3JP (01297) 446910
"Inventive and nostalgic" dishes (in particular "fabulous fish cooked to perfection") and "views to die for" make Mark Hix's cliff-top restaurant an "idyllic" destination; if there's a gripe, it's the occasionally "patchy" service. / **Details:** www.restaurantsetcltd.co.uk; 10 pm.

East End Arms   £35   
Lymington Rd SO41 5SY (01590) 626223
*"A posh pub owned by someone from Dire Straits" (John Illsley,
the bass guitarist); its small fan club say it's "perfect in every detail" –
more reports please! / **Details:** www.eastendarms.co.uk; 9 pm; closed Sun D;
no Amex. **Accommodation:** 5 rooms, from £100.*

Egan's   £44
24 Gosport St SO41 9BE (01590) 676165
*The Egans' "welcoming" bistro near the waterfront is "loved by its
regulars", thanks to its "friendly" style and often "excellent" food –
the lunch menu, in particular, offers "superb value". / **Details:** 10 pm;
closed Mon & Sun; no Amex; booking: max 6, Sat.*

The Church Green   £65
Higher Ln WA13 0AP (01925) 752068
*No one doubts that Aiden Byrne – once chef of the Dorchester Grill –
delivers an interesting "gastronomic experience" at his "see-and-be-
seen" pub-conversion; even fans, however, note how very "overpriced"
it can appear. / **Details:** www.thechurchgreen.co.uk; 11 pm, Fri & Sat
midnight, Sun 10 pm.*

Lime Wood   £78
Beaulieu Rd SO43 7FZ (02380) 287168

*"An exciting new addition to the boutique hotel scene, in a wonderful
New Forest setting" – this "great-looking" dining room feels like
"somewhere special", and shows "great promise"; note also the "fun",
and cheaper, offshoot – The Scullery. / **Details:** www.limewoodhotel.co.uk;
9.30 pm; no shorts. **Accommodation:** 30 rooms, from £295.*

Hastings   £41
26 Hastings Pl FY8 5LZ (01253) 732400
*"A new venture from a talented chef"; there's not much dispute that
the food is "top-notch", but the atmosphere in this section of a former
Conservative club, adjacent to a busy bar, leaves much to be desired;
note limited opening hours. / **Details:** www.hastingslytham.com; sun 10.30.*

MADINGLEY, CAMBRIDGESHIRE 3–1B

Three Horseshoes £48 Ⓐ
CB23 8AB (01954) 210221
"The conservatory is great", says fans of this thatched gastropub,
long known as one of the few decent destinations near the Varsity;
it rarely excites, but standards are "reliably good".
/ **Details:** www.threehorseshoesmadingley.co.uk; 2m W of Cambridge, off A14
or M11; 9 pm, Fri & Sat 9.30 pm, Sun 8.30 pm; no Amex.

MAIDENHEAD, BERKSHIRE 3–3A

Boulters Riverside Brasserie £52 Ⓐ
Boulters Island SL6 8PE (01628) 621291
"Great place, shame about the food" – too often the feedback on this
"expensive" Thames-side venue, with views "to die for", but where the
cooking only intermittently lives up; arguably you get better value eating
in the bar (upstairs), with its "large outside terrace", than in the main
restaurant. / **Details:** www.boultersrestaurant.co.uk; 9.30 pm; closed Mon &
Sun D; no Amex.

MAIDENSGROVE, OXFORDSHIRE 2–2D

Five Horseshoes £44 Ⓐ
RG9 6EX (01491) 641282
With its superb Chilterns location, this is, for fans, "a country pub that's
well worth the drive from London"; the food's "good" too, but you may
have to wait for it – the place "can get a little busy".
/ **Details:** www.thefivehorseshoes.co.uk; off B481 between Nettlebed &
Watlington; 9.30 pm, Sun 8.30 pm; no Amex; booking essential.

MALVERN WELLS, WORCESTERSHIRE 2–1B

Outlook Ⓣ
The Cottage in the Wood £45
Holywell Rd WR14 4LG (01684) 588860
Named after its views of the Malvern Hills, a "comfortable and
pleasant" family-run small hotel, tipped for "beautifully-prepared food
using local ingredients"; more feedback please!
/ **Details:** www.cottageinthewood.co.uk; 9.30 pm, Sun 9 pm.
Accommodation: 30 rooms, from £99.

MANCHESTER, GREATER MANCHESTER 5–2B

Akbar's £27 ✪
73-83 Liverpool Rd M3 4NQ (0161) 834 8444
"Top-quality, traditional Pakistani food" is "served slickly",
and "at modest prices", at this Castlefield spot; no wonder it's always
"fantastically buzzy". / **Details:** www.akbars.co.uk; 11 pm, Fri & Sat
11.30 pm; D only; need 10+ to book.

Albert's Shed £44 Ⓐ
20 Castle St M3 4LZ (0161) 839 9818
In Castlefield, "a great place by the canal", which nowadays certainly
looks nothing like the eponymous workman's hut it once was; it serves
a "reliable" selection of dishes, mainly of Italian inspiration.
/ **Details:** www.albertsshed.com; 10 pm, Fri 10.30 pm, Sat 11 pm, Sun 9.30 pm;
no Amex.

The Angel £29 Ⓣ
6 Angel St M4 4BQ (0161) 833 4786
"Don't be put off by the exterior", say fans of this "grotty"-looking
boozer, tipped for "surprisingly good" food, and "great beer" too.
/ **Details:** www.theangelmanchester.co.uk; 9.30 pm; closed Sun; no Amex.

Armenian Taverna £33 ⭐

3-5 Princess St M2 4DF (0161) 834 9025

"The decor hasn't changed since 1971 and the music can be unspeakably bad", but this family-run, city-centre cellar can still offer a *"thoroughly enjoyable"* experience, thanks to its *"authentic"* and *"unusual"* dishes and its *"very polite and attentive service"*.
/ **Details:** www.armeniantaverna.co.uk; 11 pm; closed Mon, Sat L & Sun L; children: 3+.

Aumbry £45 ⭐

2 Church Ln M25 1AJ (0161) 7985841

This *"tiny family-run restaurant"* makes a somewhat *"unlikely"* newcomer in the suburb of Prestwich, but all reports confirm the *"marvellous"* quality of the cuisine (*"from a Blumenthal-trained chef, but much less poncy"*). / **Details:** www.aumbryrestaurant.co.uk; 10.30 pm; closed Mon, Tue & Sun D; no Mastercard.

Chaophraya Thai Restaurant & Bar £43 Ⓐ

Chapel Walks M2 1HN (0161) 832 8342

"A very busy city-centre restaurant, with notably pleasant and attentive staff"; its Thai cuisine is arguably *"not the best in Manchester"* any more, but the *"great overall experience it offers"* make it a notably *"reliable"* choice. / **Details:** www.chaophraya.co.uk; 10.30 pm.

Choice £45 ⭐

Castle Quay M15 4NT (0161) 833 3400

"A hidden gem that's somehow out of fashion"; this Castlefield quay-sider is a *"friendly"* place with *"fantastic"* service, and where the food is almost invariably *"of good quality, and accurately cooked"*.
/ **Details:** www.choicebarandrestaurant.co.uk; 9.30 pm, Fri & Sat 10 pm.

City Cafe £40 Ⓣ

One Piccadilly Pl, 1 Auburn St M1 3DG (0161) 228 0008

In a hotel right by Piccadilly Station, *"a good all-rounder for those seeking a good but unsophisticated meal"*, and tipped especially for its *"excellent-value lunch menu"*. / **Details:** www.cityinn.com; 10.30 pm.
Accommodation: 285 rooms, from £79.

Croma £29 Ⓐ

1-3 Clarence St M2 4DE (0161) 237 9799

Nestling in the shadow of the Town Hall, *"the classic Manchester pizzeria"* is *"still the best"*, for its army of fans; it's been a *"lively"* hub of city-centre life for many years now, and remains notably *"popular with groups of all ages"*. / **Details:** www.croma.biz; off Albert Square; 10.45 pm.

Dimitri's £36 Ⓐ

Campfield Arc M3 4FN (0161) 839 3319

"A good stand-by", in a pretty Victorian arcade, off Deansgate; it's *"a lively little place"*, where the Greek/Mediterranean mezze are, say fans, just *"great"*. / **Details:** www.dimitris.co.uk; near Museum of Science & Industry; 11.30 pm.

East Z East £32 ⭐

Princess St M1 7DL (0161) 244 5353

"Mouthwatering" dishes *"packed full of fresh spice, herbs and flavour"* make this *"striking-looking"* and *"buzzing"* modern Indian an *"unlikely"* find beneath a decidedly budget city-centre hotel; there's also a *"functional"* riverside branch. / **Details:** www.eastzeast.com; midnight; D only.

Eighth Day Café £21
111 Oxford Rd M1 7DU (0161) 273 1850
"Speaking as a veggie, this is one of the few places I feel spoilt for choice!"; this city-centre spot remains a "very popular" cheap 'n' cheerful favourite (although the odd reporter does believe it is "over-rated"). / Details: www.eighth-day.co.uk; 7.30 pm; closed Sun; no booking.

French Restaurant
Midland Hotel £66
Peter St M60 2DS (0161) 236 3333
This famous dining room of the hotel where Mr Rolls first met Mr Royce has the potential again to be "the most impressive restaurant in the North West"; it inspires limited feedback nowadays, but much of it suggests its "improved" cooking may finally be putting it back on the map. / Details: www.themidland.co.uk; 10.30 pm, Fri & Sat 11 pm; D only, closed Mon & Sun; no jeans or trainers. Accommodation: 311 rooms, from £145.

Gaucho £58
2a St Mary's St M3 2LB (0161) 833 4333
"An automatic choice for anyone wanting top-quality steak", and in a "top-notch" ambience too; it's just a shame this outpost of the funky Argentinean chain, by House of Fraser, charges such "ridiculous" prices. / Details: www.gauchorestaurants.com; 10.30 pm, Fri & Sat 11 pm.

Grado £46
Piccadilly M1 4BD (0161) 238 9790

Paul Heathcote's "beautiful and understated" city-centre Spanish operation continues to under-achieve; some of its tapas dishes are of "top quality", but even fans can find them "massively overpriced". / Details: www.heathcotes.co.uk; 10 pm, Sat 11 pm; closed Sun.

Great Kathmandu £26
140 Burton Rd M20 1JQ (0161) 434 6413
A recent expansion has "taken away some of the charm" of this stalwart West Didsbury subcontinental; likewise the food rating has been hit by reports that it's "nothing special" nowadays, but one regular is optimistic: "yes they had big problems when they refitted, but it's back on top form". / Details: www.greatkathmandu.com; near Withington hospital; midnight.

Green's £36
43 Lapwing Ln M20 2NT (0161) 434 4259
"As veggie places go, this is one of the best!"; this Didsbury stalwart continues to serve some "very interesting and imaginative dishes". / Details: www.greensdidsbury.co.uk; 4m S of city centre; 10.30 pm; closed Mon L; no Amex.

Grill on the Alley £40

5 Ridgefield M2 6EG   (0161) 833 3465

This "vibrant" hang-out is on quite a scale, and – thanks to its atmospheric style and "very good steak and fish" – makes one of the best city-centre options; there are echos of its London stable-mate, Smithfield Bar & Grill, however, with the occasional reporter finding it "overpriced and noisy". / **Details:** www.blackhouse.uk.com; 11 pm.

Grinch £32

5-7 Chapel Walks, off Cross St M2 1HN   (0161) 907 3210

Just off St Anne's Square, a large and "atmospheric" café/bar that's tipped for its "consistently good" food (with pizza the speciality); "for a pre-Royal Exchange Theatre" dinner, the location is certainly hard to beat. / **Details:** www.grinch.co.uk; 11 pm.

Gurkha Grill £29

194-198 Burton Rd M20 1LH   (0161) 445 3461

"Excellent value" and "interesting" Nepalese food have won a deserved following for this straightforward West Didsbury institution. / **Details:** www.gurkhagrill.com; midnight, Fri & Sat 1 pm; D only.

Jem and I £38

1c, School Ln M20 6RD   (0161) 445 3996

"Nearly taking the Lime Tree's crown" – with his "fantastic", "no-fuss" cuisine, Jem O' Sullivan continues to give the longer-established Didsbury restaurant (where he formerly worked) a run for its money; his restaurant is a "very welcoming" place too, offering "good all-round value". / **Details:** www.jemandirestaurant.co.uk; 10 pm, Fri & Sat 10.30 pm.

Katsouris Deli £10

113 Deansgate M3 2BQ   (0161) 819 1260

A "bustling modern café" – where the dishes come "with a Greek flavour profile!" – that's often "packed out", thanks to its "great weekend breakfasts", "exciting salad bar", and "really good sandwiches"; there's also a branch (the original) in Bury. / **Details:** L only; no Amex.

Koh Samui £35

16 Princess St M1 4NB   (0161) 237 9511

"The service is nothing to write home about, so it must be the food that keeps drawing me back!" – on the culinary front at least, this well-established Thai restaurant, on the fringe of Chinatown, continues to please all who comment on it; top-value lunch.
/ **Details:** www.kohsamuirestaurant.co.uk; opp City Art Gallery; 11.30 pm; closed Sat L & Sun L.

The Lime Tree   £42   Ⓐ★

8 Lapwing Ln M20 2WS   (0161) 445 1217
"No. 1 in Manchester"; this "long-standing local favourite",
in West Didsbury, has been "consistently brilliant for years", offering
a straightforward formula of "fantastic" brasserie fare and "relaxed but
respectful" service in a "lovely", "sociable" setting.
/ **Details:** www.thelimetreerestaurant.co.uk; 10 pm; closed Mon L & Sat L.

Little Yang Sing   £35   Ⓐ

17 George St M1 4HE   (0161) 228 7722
"Head 'n' shoulders above the rest, including its big brother", say fans
of this "always-busy" Chinatown basement; not everyone would agree,
though, and some "distinctly average" meals have also been recorded
of late. / **Details:** www.littleyangsing.co.uk; 11.30 pm, Sat midnight,
Sun 10.45 pm.

Livebait   £45   Ⓐ

22 Lloyd St M2 5WA   (0161) 817 4110
It looks "clinical", prices are "slightly high" and the food is somewhat
"predictable"... yet this city-centre outlet of the London-based chain
wins very respectable ratings thanks to its "consistent" performance
(and, we suspect, for being the city's only fish specialist of any
prominence at all). / **Details:** www.livebaitrestaurant.co.uk; 10.15 pm,
Sat 11 pm , Sun 9 pm.

The Living Room   £36   Ⓣ

80 Deansgate M3 2ER   (0161) 832 0083
"Busy, and cheerfully noisy", this city-centre chain-establishment
is tipped as a "great lunch location" (and also as a handy destination
for a cocktail). / **Details:** www.thelivingroom.co.uk; Mon & Tue 11 pm, Wed &
Thur 11.30 pm, Fri & Sun mi.

Lounge 10   £45   Ⓐ

10 Tib Ln M2 4JB   (0161) 834 1331
With its "dark and brooding" looks, this "romantic" city-centre venue
"can't be beaten for atmosphere" – pity the same can't be said about
the "average" food! / **Details:** www.loungetenmanchester.com; 10.30 pm,
Fri & Sat 11 pm, Sun 9 pm; closed Sat L & Sun.

Luso   £46   Ⓐ

63 Bridge St M3 3BQ   (0161) 839 5550
The "Portuguese-with-a-twist" cooking at this small, central spot
(near House of Fraser), continues to divide opinion; to fans its
"innovative" dishes are "top-notch", but even they can sometimes find
them "a bit variable" – others say they "simply don't work".
/ **Details:** www.lusorestaurant.co.uk; 10.30 pm; closed Sun; children: 12+.

The Mark Addy   £41   ★

Stanley St M5 5EJ   (0161) 832 4080
"It could do with a lick of paint", but the arrival of local-hero chef
Robert Owen-Brown has led to "quite a turn-around" at Manchester's
(read Salford's) 'first riverside pub' (or that's what they say).
/ **Details:** www.markaddy.co.uk; 9.30 pm, hot food 7 pm; closed Sun D; no Amex.

The Market   £46   Ⓣ

104 High St M4 1HQ   (0161) 834 3743
Under new owners, this long-established English restaurant in the
Northern Quarter attracts less feedback than once it did;
fans (the majority) say its "regional/seasonal cuisine" is "still powering
away", but there's also the odd complaint that "it's gone right downhill".
/ **Details:** www.market-restaurant.com; 9.30 pm; closed Mon & Sun D.

Metropolitan £37

2 Lapwing Ln M20 2WS (0161) 438 2332

With its "good food and great beer", this "noisy" and "crowded" West Didsbury gastropub stands out (not least in a city where the phenomenon curiously refuses to 'take off').
/ **Details:** www.the-metropolitan.co.uk; near Withington hospital; 9.30 pm, Fri & Sat 10 pm, Sun 9 pm.

Michael Caines
ABode Hotel £64

107 Piccadilly M1 2DB (0161) 200 5678

Handily located near Piccadilly Station, this "gloomy" hotel basement is "probably Manchester city-centre's best restaurant, certainly of a non-ethnic variety"; top billing goes to the "sensational" £12 lunch menu.
/ **Details:** www.michaelcaines.com; 10 pm; closed Sun; no shorts.
Accommodation: 61 rooms, from £79.

The Modern £39

Urbis, Cathedral Gdns M4 3BG (0161) 605 8282

"Great views over Manchester" from its 8th-floor location, plus "well-executed" locally-sourced dishes – some "traditional", others "with a twist" – combine to make this city-centre all-rounder a handy destination for business, and one that can be "very romantic" by night too. / **Details:** www.themodernmcr.co.uk; 10 pm; closed Sun D.

Moss Nook £65

Ringway Rd M22 5NA (0161) 437 4778

"Very expensive, but just about worth it", this veteran French restaurant, near the Airport, "has maintained a high standard of cooking for many years"; service often impresses too.
/ **Details:** www.mossnookrestaurant.co.uk; on B5166, 1m from Manchester airport; 9.30 pm; closed Mon, Sat L & Sun; no jeans or trainers; children: 12+.
Accommodation: 0 rooms, from £.

Mr Thomas's Chop House £38

52 Cross St M2 7AR (0161) 832 2245

"Vast", "solid", "yummy" traditional British dishes (corned beef hash, steak 'n' kidney pud', etc) have long made this popular, pub-like Victorian institution "a good, reliable standby in the city-centre".
/ **Details:** www.tomschophouse.com; 9.30 pm, Sun 8 pm.

The Ox £35

71 Liverpool Rd M3 4NQ (0161) 839 7740

A "busy" boozer, near the Museum of Industry, "which advertises itself as a gastropub"; even a reporter who notes that the place "has more people enjoying (very good) pints than eating" concedes the food is "very acceptable". / **Details:** www.theox.co.uk; 9.30 pm, Sun 7 pm; closed Sun D; no Amex; children: 14+ after 7 pm, 18+ after 9 pm.
Accommodation: 10 rooms, from £49.95 MW.

Pacific £35 🅣
58-60 George St M1 4HF (0161) 228 6668
*Declining feedback on this once-so-popular warehouse-style operation,
not far from Piccadilly Station, which offers Thai food on the upper
floor, Chinese below; even the least positive report, though, praises
"generous portions at reasonable prices".*
/ **Details:** www.pacificrestaurant.co.uk; midnight, Sun 11 pm.

Piccolino £45 🅐
8 Clarence St M2 4DW (0161) 835 9860
*This Italian restaurant is one of the more popular outposts of the
national chain, and its "real buzz" helps make it "a pleasant and
reliable place", and in the heart of the city too; the food, though, tends
to "run-of-the-mill".* / **Details:** www.piccolinore.co.uk; 11 pm, Sun 10 pm.

Punjab Tandoori £32 ⭐⭐
177 Wilmslow Rd M14 5AP (0161) 225 2960
*"Top dosas" and "interesting curries" continue to make this "authentic"
stalwart probably the best Indian on the Curry Mile.* / **Details:** midnight;
closed Mon L.

Red Chilli £29 ⭐
70-72 Portland St M1 4GU (0161) 236 2888
*"Exotic", "hot" and "spicy" Sichuanese dishes make the cooking at this
Chinatown spot "very different from run-of-the-mill Chinese
restaurants" (though there's also a large selection of more familiar
Cantonese fare); a second branch is located near the university (403-
419 Oxford Rd, tel 0161 273 1288).*
/ **Details:** www.redchillirestaurant.co.uk; 11 pm; need 6+ to book.

El Rincon £29 🅐
Longworth St, off St John's St M3 4BQ (0161) 839 8819
*"Off the beaten track, yet in the centre of Manchester", this stalwart
Deansgate tapas bar doesn't always wow reporters foodwise, but it
does arguably offer "the closest thing in the UK to genuine Spanish
buzz".* / **Details:** off Deansgate; 11 pm.

Room £38 🅐
81 King St M2 4AH (0161) 8392005
*It's not just the "sumptuous" location – on the 'piano nobile' of a
wonderfully High Victorian edifice (the former Reform Club) –
that makes this city-centre restaurant of note; its "club-style" cuisine
also pleases most reporters (and, when prix-fixe menus are available,
it can be "excellent value" too).* / **Details:** www.roomrestaurants.com;
10 pm, Sat 11 pm; closed Sun.

Rosso £36 🅐
43 Spring Gdns M2 2BG (0161) 8321400
*The "impressive surroundings" of a grand Victorian building set the
scene at this "buzzing" city-centre venue; fans say it offers a "superb"
all-round experience, but occasional "careless" dishes are reported too.*
/ **Details:** www.rossorestaurants.com; midnight.

Sam's Chop House £43 🅣
Back Pool Fold, Chapel Walks M2 1HN (0161) 834 3210
*An English restaurant in a rather pub-like city-centre basement, tipped
as a destination for fabulous British food (of a decidedly old-fashioned
variety) and its "cosy" atmosphere.* / **Details:** www.samschophouse.com;
9.30 pm, Sun 7 pm.

San Carlo £47

40 King Street West M3 2WY (0161) 834 6226

*Invariably "buzzy" and "atmospheric", the city-centre's "best Italian"
(and certainly "the liveliest") is "a great place to hob-nob",
not least with the local footie-boys; the food – with pasta and fish the
highlights – is "pretty strong" too. / **Details:** www.sancarlo.co.uk; 11 pm.*

**Second Floor Restaurant
Harvey Nichols** £55

21 New Cathedral St M1 1AD (0161) 828 8898

*"Still one of the best daytime dining experiences in the city-centre",
this "buzzing" department store dining room – currently top dog
among the HN operations – offers more than just "an ideal spot for
a break from shopping" (or "great views" for that matter), the food is
"excellent" and it's "good value" too. / **Details:** www.harveynichols.com;
9.30 pm; closed Mon D & Sun D.*

Stock £46

4 Norfolk St M2 1DW (0161) 839 6644

*Critics can find the style a bit "pretend posh", but this Italian housed
in the "grand" old (Victorian) Stock Exchange building impresses
most reporters – fish and seafood is a highlight, with lunch, early-
evening and opera night menus especially worth seeking out.
/ **Details:** www.stockrestaurant.co.uk; 10 pm; closed Sun.*

Tai Pan £30

81-97 Upper Brook St M13 9TX (0161) 273 2798

*"You come here for the food not the atmosphere" –
this "characterless", if "lively", "hangar"-sized Longsight operation
is "popular with the local Chinese community", thanks to its "excellent
dim sum" and its "marvellous banquets". / **Details:** 11 pm, Sun 9.30 pm.*

Tai Wu £27

44 Oxford Rd M1 5EJ (0161) 236 6557

*"Fast-moving dim sum carts" help set an "authentic" tone at this "vast"
city-centre Chinese, which "feels like a cavernous works canteen"; in the
basement, there's a good-value all-you-can-eat buffet.
/ **Details:** www.tai-wu.co.uk; 2.45 am.*

Tampopo £28

16 Albert Sq M2 5PF (0161) 819 1966

*For "fast food with a difference", this "reliable" city-centre canteen
(also at the Triangle) is still "the best noodle bar around", with food
that's "often really quite good". / **Details:** www.tampopo.co.uk; 11 pm,
Sun 10 pm; need 7+ to book.*

This & That £10

3 Soap St M4 1EW (0161) 832 4971

*"Beautifully-cooked curries" at "astonishingly good-value prices" ensure
a "heaving" throng – "of 'suits', hipsters and local residents too" –
at this unlikely "backstreet café"; "now open later at weekends and
with a website detailing each day's menu and opening hours".
/ **Details:** www.thisandthatcafe.com; 4 pm, Fri & Sat 8 pm; no credit cards.*

Umami £24

147 Oxford Rd M1 1EE (0161) 273 2300

*Just north of the university, a "noodle bar and sushi house" tipped for
the "very reasonably priced food" – "easily up to the Wagamamas
of the world" – dished up to "vast numbers of students".
/ **Details:** www.umami.cc; 11 pm.*

Vermilion £43

Hulme Hall Lord North St M40 8AD   (0161) 202 0055

*"In an unlikely area of the city" (a couple of miles west of the centre), this "super-posh" bar/restaurant – remarkably – survives without any support from the super-casino which was supposed to be built nearby; it's owned by a seafood importer, and fish dishes, in particular, can be "great". / **Details:** www.vermilioncinnabar.com; 10 pm, Sat 11 pm; no trainers.*

Wagamama £30

1 The Printworks, Corporation St M4 2BS   (0161) 839 5916

*"Despite the large size and rapid turnover of customers", this Mancunian outpost of the famous chain makes a useful tip for those in search of "cheap and cheerful" nosh that's "wholesome" too. / **Details:** www.wagamama.com; 11 pm; no booking.*

Wing's £46

1 Lincoln Sq M2 5LN   (0161) 834 9000

*"Probably better than the Yang Sing nowadays" – this elegant city-centre Cantonese is an all-round crowd-pleaser, consistently acclaimed for its "superb" cuisine. / **Details:** www.wingsrestaurant.co.uk; midnight, Sun 11 pm; closed Sat L; no trainers; children: 11+ after 8 pm Mon-Fri, 21+ D.*

Yakisoba £33

360 Barlow Moor Rd M21 8AZ   (0161) 862 0888

*Not enough reports for a full review, but fans of this "basic" Chorlton spot say it "takes inspiration from across Asia and knocks Wagamama into a cocked hat". / **Details:** www.yakisoba.co.uk; 11 pm, Fri & Sat midnight; closed weekday L.*

Yang Sing £38

34 Princess St M1 4JY   (0161) 236 2200

*"Still the benchmark by which others are judged" – this Chinatown landmark has for decades been Manchester's greatest culinary claim to fame (with dim sum and banquets the top tips); there's the odd gripe of "production line" experiences, here, but "at its best, there's nowhere better". / **Details:** www.yang-sing.com; 11.30 pm.*

MANNINGTREE, ESSEX 3–2C

Lucca Enoteca £33

39-43 High St CO11 1AH   (01206) 390044

*An 'Italy-comes-to-East-Anglia' operation, where "the pizzas can be excellent"; it's located in a "lovely building", and they're good with kids too. / **Details:** www.luccafoods.co.uk; 9.30 pm, Fri & Sat 10 pm; no Amex.*

The Harrow at Little Bedwyn   £66

Little Bedwyn SN8 3JP   (01672) 870871

"A brilliant wine list to suit all tastes and budgets" is the stand-out attraction at this *"intimate"* and *"well-run"* inn; the *"seasonally-led"* menus is generally *"excellent"* too (although since the receipt of the dreaded Michelin star, there seems to be a greater tendency to *"formality"* and *"over-elaboration"*).
/ **Details:** www.theharrowatlittlebedwyn.co.uk; 9 pm; closed Mon, Tue & Sun D; no Amex.

Adam Simmons
Danesfield House Hotel   £85

Henley Rd SL7 2EY   (01628) 891010

The *"wonderful setting"* – a 65-acre estate in the Chilterns, within sight of the Thames – is a particular attraction of this Victorian country house hotel; for most reporters, Adam Simmonds's food *"nearly matches the surroundings"*, though critics can find it *"unmemorable"*.
/ **Details:** www.danesfieldhouse.co.uk; 3m outside Marlow on the A4155; 9.30 pm; closed Mon, Tue L & Sun; no jeans or trainers. **Accommodation:** 84 rooms, from £195.

Hand & Flowers   £55

West St SL7 2BP   (01628) 482277

Tom Kerridge's *"amazing, yet unpretentious"* food (and in particular a set lunch offering *"unmatched value"*) inspires many rapturous reports on this *"wonderful"* gastropub – an *"unfussy"* establishment, but one that's *"full of character"*. / **Details:** www.thehandandflowers.co.uk; 9.30 pm; closed Sun D. **Accommodation:** 4 rooms, from £140.

Marlow Bar & Grill   £46

92-94 High St SL7 1AQ   (01628) 488544

"Always buzzy" (and very *"noisy"*), this town-centre hang-out remains a big local hit (especially on the days when the charming courtyard comes in to its own); the menu, though, can seem rather *"samey"*.
/ **Details:** www.therestaurantbarandgrill.co.uk; Towards the river end of the High Street; 11 pm, Sun 10.30 pm; booking essential.

The Royal Oak   £41

Frieth Rd, Bovingdon Grn SL7 2JF   (01628) 488611

Just outside the town, a whitewashed inn that's *"always buzzing"*, and tipped for *"home cooking"* which makes *"good use of local produce"*; regulars, though, can find the menu a little *"unimaginative"*.
/ **Details:** www.royaloakmarlow.co.uk; half mile up from Marlow High Street; 9.30 pm, Fri & Sat 10 pm.

The Vanilla Pod £60 ★★
31 West St SL7 2LS (01628) 898101
"Back on top form after the recent refurb"; Michael Macdonald is undoubtedly a "talented" chef, and fans say his "tiny" town-centre restaurant (occupying a house once home to TS Elliot) offers truly "memorable" food. / **Details:** *www.thevanillapod.co.uk; 10 pm; closed Mon & Sun; no trainers.*

MASHAM, NORTH YORKSHIRE 8–4B

Black Sheep Brewery Bistro £32 Ⓐ
Wellgarth HG4 4EN (01765) 680101
"A friendly microbrewery" with a large, popular café manned by "helpful staff"; "it's not only the beer which is good, though, but the food too, and there's a wide selection". / **Details:** *www.blacksheep.co.uk; 9 pm; Sun-Wed L only, Thu-Sat L & D; no Amex.*

Samuel's
Swinton Park Hotel & Spa £60 Ⓐ★
HG4 4JH (01765) 680900
"Fabulous walks around the lake" form part of the "tranquil and perfectly relaxing" experience of visiting this castellated country house hotel, and all accounts say its "beautiful" dining room offers a "superb" all-round experience. / **Details:** *www.swintonpark.com; 9.30 pm, Fri & Sat 10 pm; no jeans or trainers; booking: max 8; children: 8+ at D.* **Accommodation:** *30 rooms, from £175.*

Vennells £38 ★
7 Silver St HG4 4DX (01765) 689000
"An unexpected find" in this rural town – Jon and Laura Vennell's "calm and efficient" five-year-old offers "superb cooking at very fair prices". / **Details:** *www.vennellsrestaurant.co.uk; 9.30 pm; closed Mon, Tue–Sat D only, closed Sun D.*

MATLOCK, DERBYSHIRE 5–2C

Stones £45 Ⓐ★
1C Dale Rd DE4 3LT (01629) 56061
Only positive reports on Kevin and Jade Stone's "intimate" family-owned river-sider (with terrace), where local produce is used to "fantastic" effect; junior customers get especially well treated.
/ **Details:** *www.thestones-restaurant.co.uk; 9 pm; closed Mon, Tue–Sat D only, closed Sun D; no Amex; no shorts.*

MELBOURNE, DERBYSHIRE 5–3C

Bay Tree £49 Ⓐ
4 Potter St DE73 8HW (01332) 863358
Rex Howell's "romantic" (although arguably slightly "dated") destination of over two decades' standing still inspires many reports of "very good" cooking; even fans, though, can sometimes find the food "ordinary" or "overpriced". / **Details:** *www.baytreerestaurant.co.uk; 9.30 pm; closed Mon & Sun D.*

MELLOR, LANCASHIRE 5–1B

Cassis
Stanley House Hotel £50 Ⓐ
Off Preston New Rd BB2 7NP (01254) 769200
"Up with the best in the North West", this "luxurious" country house hotel pleases almost all reporters with its "enjoyable" cuisine, and its "lovely grounds and views"; even fans can find it "overpriced" however. / **Details:** *www.stanleyhouse.co.uk; 9.30 pm, Fri & Sat 9.45 pm; closed Mon, Tue, Sat L & Sun D; no trainers.* **Accommodation:** *12 rooms, from £185.*

T

Nant Ddu Lodge   £35
Brecon Rd CF48 2HY   (01685) 379111
"A busy bar in a small country hotel in the Brecon Beacons National Park", tipped for *"pub food with flair"*, and at *"reasonable prices"* too. / **Details:** www.nant-ddu-lodge.co.uk; 6m N of Merthyr on A470; 9.30 pm. **Accommodation:** 30 rooms, from £99.

T

The Running Horses   £47
Old London Rd RH5 6DU   (01372) 372279
"Just what a pub should be" – *"a busy and attractive old building"* tipped for its *"friendly"* service, and for food that's usually a cut above the norm. / **Details:** www.therunninghorses.co.uk; 9.30 pm, Sun 9 pm; children: 14+ in bar. **Accommodation:** 5 rooms, from ££110.

A **★**

Brasserie Blanc   £42
Chelsea Hs, 301 Avebury Boulevard MK9 2GA   (01908) 546590
"A real find for MK" – this branch of Raymond Blanc's brasserie chain *"pleasantly surprises"* some reporters, with its *"simple rustic food"*, and its *"it-could-be-Paris"* ambience (well, nearly); the set lunch offers particular value. / **Details:** www.miltonkeynesbrasserieblanc.com; 9 pm.

T

Jaipur   £35
599 Grafton Gate East MK9 1AT   (01908) 669796
"In the Milton Keynes gastronomic desert", a vast Indian restaurant with *"stunning"* OTT decor, tipped for its sometimes *"excellent"* food, and *"unobtrusive"* service too. / **Details:** www.jaipur.co.uk; near the train station roundabout; they are the big white building; 11.30, Sun 10.30; no shorts.

T

The Black Boy Inn   £42
OX15 4HH   (01295) 722111
A *"gentrified"* country inn, consistently tipped for its *"imaginatively-presented"* cuisine. / **Details:** www.blackboyinn.com; 9 pm; closed Sun D.

T

56 High St.   £38
56 High St CH7 1BD   (01352) 759225
"Excellent fresh local seafood and fish" again wins a tip for this well-reputed venture, in the county town. / **Details:** www.56highst.com; 9.30 pm, Fri & Sat 10.30 pm; closed Mon & Sun; no Amex.

A

Glasfryn   £33
Raikes Ln CH7 6LR   (01352) 750500
"Something of an oasis in this part of the world" – a *"large"* and *"convivial"* pub *"handy for the Theatr Clwyd"*; true to the Brunning & Price formula, the food is *"robust"*, rather than anything more, but there are *"decent"* wines and *"numerous"* real ales to wash it down. / **Details:** www.glasfryn-mold.co.uk; 9.30 pm, Sun 9 pm.

MONKS ELEIGH, SUFFOLK

3–1C

The Swan Inn £34

The St IP7 7AU (01449) 741391

"Nothing leaves the kitchen which is not first-rate", says one of the many fans of *"one of Suffolk's best gastropubs"*; if you're staying, be sure not to miss out on the *"outstanding"* breakfasts.

/ **Details:** www.monkseleigh.com; 9 pm; closed Mon & Sun D; no Amex.

MORECAMBE, LANCASHIRE

5–1A

Midland Hotel £39

Marine Road central LA4 4BU (08458) 501240

This *"tastefully restored"* hotel is worth a visit for its *"beautiful"* and *"nostalgic"* Art Deco interior, and *"great views across Morecombe Bay"*; most reporters are *"pleasantly surprised"* by the food too.

/ **Details:** www.elh.co.uk; 10.30 pm; booking essential. **Accommodation:** 44 rooms, from £120.

MORETON-IN-MARSH, GLOUCESTERSHIRE

2–1C

Horse & Groom £38

GL56 0XH (01451) 830584

A *"not-too-pubby"* Cotswold inn, tipped for its *"simple and fresh"* dishes with *"big flavours"*, and an *"invariably friendly welcome"*.

/ **Details:** www.horseandgroom.uk.com; 11 pm; no Amex.

MORSTON, NORFOLK

6–3C

Morston Hall £72

Main Coast Rd NR25 7AA (01263) 741041

Galton Blackiston's country house hotel continues to divide opinion; for most reporters, it's a *"beautiful"* and *"comfortable"* location, offering *"gorgeous"* cooking; a vocal minority, though, find it a *"huge disappointment"*, with *"bland"* food and excessive prices.

/ **Details:** www.morstonhall.com; between Blakeney & Wells on A149; 8 pm; D only, ex Sun open L & D. **Accommodation:** 13 rooms, from £145 pp.

MOULSFORD, OXFORDSHIRE

2–2D

The Beetle & Wedge Boathouse £48

Ferry Ln OX10 9JF (01491) 651381

"Get a window seat, and you'll never want to leave" this former boathouse, which has a *"delightful"* setting on a picture-book stretch of the Thames; the food may be *"simple"*, but it is consistently well done. / **Details:** www.beetleandwedge.co.uk; on A329 between Streatley & Wallingford, take Ferry Lane at crossroads; 9.45 pm. **Accommodation:** 3 rooms, from £90.

Carrington Arms £39
Cranfield Rd MK16 0HB (01908) 218050
"Good ingredients, perfectly cooked" inspire consistently positive feedback on this country inn, just off the M1; steaks get special mention. / **Details:** www.thecarringtonarms.co.uk; 10 pm. **Accommodation:** 8 rooms, from £29.50.

Black Bull £51
DL10 6QJ (01325) 377289
"A very handy escape from the A1 near Scotch Corner"; this "warm and friendly" pub is known for its "really good fish", and also for its indubitably "special" dining room – an old Pullman railway carriage. / **Details:** www.blackbullmoulton.com; 1m S of Scotch Corner; 9.30 pm, Fri & Sat 10 pm; closed Sun D; no Amex; children: +7.

Cornish Range £42
6 Chapel St TR19 6SB (01736) 731488
It may have a "backstreet" location, but all reporters approve the "high quality" food at this attractive little restaurant-with-rooms, with cute courtyard garden; it's a "child-friendly" place too (and offers "special prices for early diners"). / **Details:** www.cornishrange.co.uk; on coast road between Penzance & Lands End; 9.30 pm, 9 pm in Winter; no Amex. **Accommodation:** 3 rooms, from £80.

2 Fore Street Restaurant £39
2 Fore St TR19 6PF (01736) 731164
A "tasteful but relaxed" small bistro, near the harbour, again applauded for its "great" cooking; "the charming back garden makes a perfect lunch venue". / **Details:** www.2forestreet.co.uk; 9.30 pm.

The Nut Tree Inn £46
Main St OX5 2RE (01865) 331253
"Hard-to-find, down dark and narrow roads", this "remote thatched pub" ("with duck pond out front, and a farmyard with their own pigs out back") is nonetheless firmly on the map nowadays; for most reporters, it remains "a great find", but the occasional let-down is not unknown. / **Details:** www.nuttreeinn.co.uk; 9 pm.

The Foxhunter £46
Abergavenny NP7 9DN (01873) 881101
"The best of local produce, lovingly prepared" has made a big name for Matt Tebbutt's "stylish pub/restaurant" in a former stationmaster's house; standard, however, remain a little inconsistent. / **Details:** www.thefoxhunter.com; 9.30 pm; closed Mon & Sun D; no Amex. **Accommodation:** 2 cottages rooms, from £145.

Y Polyn Bar & Restaurant £43
SA32 7LH (01267) 290000
"A popular gastropub, with something for everyone" – this "genuinely friendly" rural establishment wins praise for its "high standard of local produce and cooking", and pleases all of the many reporters who've truffled it out; (the room can get "chilly" in winter, though). / **Details:** www.ypolyn.co.uk; 9 pm; closed Mon & Sun D; no Amex.

Ultracomida £31
7 High St SA67 7AR   (01834) 861491
*"A surprising find, in the middle of this tiny town" – a notably "jolly"
tapas bar, "in the back of very good deli", which – lunch only – serves
some "great, gutsy and authentic" Spanish dishes; there's also
an Aberystwyth branch.* / **Details:** *www.ultracomida.co.uk.*

The Highwayman £36 ⭐
LA6 2RJ   (01524) 273338
*Part of the sons-of-Northcote group, Ribble Valley Inns, this large
gastropub boasts "many log fires"; it has nonetheless made a big name
as a "a place to chill", and the quality of its cuisine is "consistent".*
/ **Details:** *www.highwaymaninn.co.uk; 9 pm, Sun 8.30 pm.*

Chewton Glen £84
Christchurch Rd BH25 6QS   (01425) 275341

*This "impressive" country house hotel "oozes class", and a meal here
is, for the vast majority of reporters, "a truly memorable experience";
in the past, however, culinary standards were more impressive – at the
astronomical prices, sceptics find them a touch "pedestrian" nowadays.*
/ **Details:** *www.chewtonglen.com; on A337 between New Milton & Highcliffe;
9.30 pm; no jeans; children: 5+ at D.* **Accommodation:** *58 rooms, from £329.*

Café Bleu £44
14 Castle Gate NG24 1BG   (01636) 610141
*This "charming" restaurant has quite a name locally for its "wonderful"
ambience and "imaginative" and "flavourful" cuisine; service
is "erratic", though, and takes the gloss off a number of basically
upbeat reports.* / **Details:** *www.cafebleu.co.uk; 9.30 pm; closed Sun D;
no Amex.*

Thanal £24 🅣
19 St Marks Ln NG24 1XS   (01636) 706230
*"For guaranteed fast and tasty food", fans tip this "tiny" venue where
"excellent Japanese dishes are served quickly and cheaply".*
/ **Details:** *www.thanalrestaurant.com; 11 pm.*

The Crab at Chieveley   £58   Ⓐ ★

Wantage Rd RG20 8UE (01635) 247550
An "extensive", "interesting" and "imaginative" fish menu maintains
an impressive and by and large enthusiastic following for this famous
inn; service can occasionally be "patronising" though, and the odd total
let-down is not unknown. / **Details:** www.crabatchieveley.com; M4 J13
to B4494 – 0.5 mile on right; 9 pm, Sat & Sun 9.30 pm. **Accommodation:** 13
rooms, from £125.

Yew Tree Inn   £57   ★

Hollington Cross, Andover Rd RG20 9SE (01635) 253360
It's rare for celebrity spin-offs to be worth seeking out, but this
"relaxed" MPW-branded inn has proved a "welcome addition" to the
area; the "classic" English fare can seem "over-seasoned", or "on the
pricey side", but on most accounts its "gorgeous".
/ **Details:** www.yewtree.net; Off the A343, near Highclere Castle; 9 pm.
Accommodation: 6 rooms, from £110.

Barn Asia   £42   ★

Waterloo Sq, St James Boulevard NE1 4DN (0191) 221 1000
The latest in a succession of 'Barn' ventures over the years is a boldly-
themed venue where an "interesting and very different" Asian-mix
menu reliable serves up some "great flavours".
/ **Details:** www.barnasia.com; 9.45 pm; closed Mon L, Tue L, Wed L, Thu L,
Sat L & Sun.

Blackfriars Restaurant   £41   Ⓐ

Friars St NE1 4XN (0191) 261 5945
A "very atmospheric" setting in an old monastic cloister sets the scene
at this "lovely" venue in the heart of Newcastle; its "honest, and not
unduly complicated" food wins a general (if not universal) thumbs-up.
/ **Details:** www.blackfriarsrestaurant.co.uk; 10 pm; closed Sun D.

Brasserie Black Door   £44   Ⓐ

Biscuit Factory, Stoddard St NE2 1AN (0191) 260 5411
"Supreme" dishes are still sometimes reported at this brasserie in a
former biscuit factory; there's some feeling, though, that "it would have
been better if it had stayed in its former location – what once was
a perfect place is now merely adequate".
/ **Details:** www.blackdoorgroup.co.uk; 9.30 pm, Sat 10 pm; closed Sun D.

Café 21   Ⓐ
Fenwick   £50

39 Northumberland St, First Floor NE1 7DE (0191) 384 9969
This "bright" café spin-off from the famous Café 21 did not shine this
year; fans still say that it's a "lovely" place, where "everything is done
well", but others discern a "careless attitude" amongst staff,
and complain of food that's "not what it was".
/ **Details:** www.cafetwentyone.co.uk; 0; L only.

Café 21   £49   Ⓐ ★

Trinity Gdns NE1 2HH (0191) 222 0755
Terry Laybourne's "sophisticated" local favourite – still by far the
most reported-on place in town – moved a few years ago to these large
Quayside premises; it's a "lively" place, offering an "excellent all-round
experience", including "top-quality" food.
/ **Details:** www.cafetwentyone.co.uk; 10.30 pm, Sun 8 pm.

Café Royal £35

8 Nelson St NE1 5AW   (0191) 231 3000
*"When shopping in Newcastle", or for "breakfast with the papers",
this "local-favourite" grand café is an institution worth knowing about –
it's a sometimes "overwhelmingly busy" place, where highlights include
"excellent cakes and scones" and "the best coffee in town".*
/ **Details:** www.sjf.co.uk; 6 pm; L only, ex Thu open L & D; no booking, Sat.

The Cherry Tree £39

9 Osborne Rd NE2 2AE   (0191) 239 9924
*This "buzzy" two-tier Jesmond Dene local attracts quite a few reports –
"good grub" features in most of 'em, but it can also sometimes appear
rather "average".* / **Details:** www.thecherrytreejesmond.co.uk; 9.30 pm,
Sat 10 pm, Sun 9 pm; no Amex.

Fisherman's Lodge £48

Jesmond Dene NE7 7BQ   (0191) 281 3281
*Still slightly mixed messages on the new régime at this rather grand
restaurant, which benefits from a setting "which feels countrified,
but which is actually very close to the city-centre" – overall, however,
the message is that this is a "professional" operation that generally
satisfies.* / **Details:** www.fishermanslodge.co.uk; 2m from city centre on A1058,
follow signposts to Jesmond Dene; 9.30 pm.

Francesca's £29

Manor House Rd NE2 2NE   (0191) 281 6586
*A big reputation for "great food on a budget" precedes this
"very friendly" pizza house; it's easy to spot – look out for "nightly
queues of Jesmond trendies".* / **Details:** 9.30 pm; closed Sun; no Amex;
no booking.

Hotel Du Vin £50

Allan Hs, city road NE1 2BE   (0191) 229 2200

*This "classy new branch" suggests there is some hope for the wine-led
boutique-hotel/brasserie chain (which has generally been drifting
in recent times); all reports confirm that it's a "busy, bustling" sort
of place, looking down on the Quayside, where the food is "well-
presented" and "cooked to a high standard".*
/ **Details:** www.hotelduvin.com; 9.45. **Accommodation:** 42 rooms, from £160.

Jesmond Dene House £69

Jesmond Dene Rd NE2 2EY   (0191) 212 3000
*"It's a triumph for Newcastle", say fans of Terry Laybourne's county
house hotel, who praise its "beautiful setting" and cuisine that's
"absolutely spot-on"; the year also saw some niggles recorded, though,
about "inattentive" service and poorly-judged (and, in particular, "over-
salted") dishes.* / **Details:** www.jesmonddenehouse.co.uk; out of the city centre,
towards Jesmond, which is clearly signposted; 10 pm. **Accommodation:** 40
rooms, from £210.

Oldfields £38 ⭐

Milburn House (G Floor), Dean St NE1 1LF (0191) 212 1210

A spin-off from the Durham original — this large, slightly "functional"-looking, "sub-ground" city-centre newcomer offers "casual dining to an excellent standard, using locally-sourced ingredients"; it certainly makes a handy location for business. / Details: www.oldfieldsrestaurants.com.

Pan Haggerty £44 🅐⭐

21 Queen St NE1 3UG (0191) 221 0904

"Modern Geordie food at relatively cheap prices", and "prompt and helpful service" too, earns all-round satisfaction for this modern bistro (on the original site of Café 21). / Details: www.panhaggerty.com; 9.30 pm; closed Sun D.

Pani's £27 🅐

61-65 High Bridge NE1 6BX (0191) 232 4366

"Consistently reliable as the best cheap 'n' cheerful option in town" — this "boisterous" Sardinian remains impressively popular, thanks to its "invigorating" style and "very fresh", "ultra-rapid" pasta and other light dishes. / Details: www.paniscafe.co.uk; off Gray Street; 10 pm; closed Sun; no Amex; no booking at L.

Paradiso £33 🅐

1 Market Ln NE1 6QQ (0191) 221 1240

"A typical jolly and welcoming Italian", whose "humorous" staff and "good-value" dishes have won it a big following among reporters. / Details: www.paradiso.co.uk; opp fire station; 10.30 pm, Fri & Sat 10.45 pm; closed Sun D.

Rasa £33 ⭐⭐

27 Queen St NE1 3UG (0191) 232 7799

"Out-of-this-world" south Indian cuisine makes this outpost of a London-based Keralan chain "very different from your typical cuzza", and it comes at "reasonable prices" too. / Details: www.rasarestaurants.com; 11 pm; closed Sun L.

Red Mezze £55 🅐

34-36 Leaze park Rd NE1 4PG (0191) 261 9646

"A cheap and cheerful new Turkish restaurant", already being tipped as a place where "willing staff" serve up "a great selection of mezze" at "excellent-value" prices. / Details: www.restaurantturkish.co.uk; 10.30 pm.

Sachins £31 🅐

Forth Banks NE1 3SG (0191) 261 9035

"A long-standing favourite", five minutes' walk from the Central railway station; "the flavours of its Punjabi cuisine are so different", say fans, and it "offers better value-for-money that the other top Indians in town". / Details: www.sachins.co.uk; behind Central Station; 11.15 pm; closed Sun.

Secco Ristorante Salentino £39 🅐⭐

86 Pilgrim St NE1 6SG (0191) 230 0444

This "high class" city-centre Italian occupies a large townhouse with an "eclectic" interior; the food can vary "from gob-smackingly fantastic to mediocre", but on most accounts is "surprisingly good" (set lunch and early-evening meals offer "incredible" value). / Details: www.seccouk.com; 10.30 pm; closed Sun.

Six
Baltic Centre £50
Gateshead Quays, South Shore Rd NE8 3BA   (0191) 440 4948

*"Much improved" under its new régime, the restaurant atop
Gateshead's Baltic Centre is no longer of note only for its "fantastic
views" (especially "from the ladies' loos", apparently) – it's a "friendly"
place, where the food is generally rated somewhere between "quite
reasonable" and "superb".* / **Details:** www.sixbaltic.com; 9.30 pm, Fri & Sat
10 pm; closed Sun D; no Amex.

A Taste of Persia £28
14 Marlborough Cr NE1 4EE   (0191) 221 0088
*A "quiet family-run" restaurant in the city-centre, which attracts
universal praise from reporters for its "delicious Middle Eastern fare";
the "cramped" setting, though, is no more than "pleasant enough".*
/ **Details:** www.atasteofpersia.com; 10 pm; closed Sun.

Tyneside Coffee Rooms
Tyneside Cinema £24
10 Pilgrim St NE1 6QG   (0191) 227 5520
*"Super Art Deco surroundings" are the highlight at this popular café –
a "comfortable and comforting spot" for "good-value", if very "basic",
standard fare.* / **Details:** www.tynecine.org; 9 pm; no Amex.

Valley Junction 397 £29
Old Jesmond Stn, Archbold Ter NE2 1DB   (0191) 281 6397
*A novelty tip – this consistently well-rated Indian is located in a railway
carriage, and a former signal box too.*
/ **Details:** www.valleyrestaurants.co.uk; near Civic Centre, off Sandyford Rd;
11.30 pm; closed Mon, Fri L & Sun L.

Vujon £34
29 Queen St NE1 3UG   (0191) 221 0601
*A "very good Quayside Indian", again acclaimed for its "most superior"
food – some of the highest-rated in town – "attentive" service and
"pleasant" atmosphere.* / **Details:** www.vujon.com; 11.30 pm; closed Sun L.

NEWENT, GLOUCESTERSHIRE 2–1B

Three Choirs Vineyards £45
GL18 1LS   (01531) 890223
*"The views across the vineyard are worth the visit alone", say fans
of this rural dining room; that's not to overlook the food, though
("much improved" of late), or the "excellent-value" wine list.*
/ **Details:** www.threechoirs.com; 8.45 pm; no Amex. **Accommodation:** 8, &
3 lodges rooms, from £115.

301

The Ostrich Inn   £39

T

GL16 8NP   (01594) 833260
"A lovely country pub" (with large garden), on the edge of the
Forest of Dean, tipped for its "wide choice of food to suit all budgets".
/ **Details:** www.theostrichinn.com; 2m SW of Coleford; 9.30 pm.

The Chandlery   £50

T

77-78 Lower Dock St NP20 1EH   (01633) 256622
"Anywhere else, this might be unremarkable", but in the environs
of Newport, this design-hotel dining room is tipped as a culinary
"oasis". / **Details:** www.thechandleryrestaurant.com; at the foot of George
St bridge on the A48 (hospital side); 10 pm; closed Mon & Sun D.

A ★ ★

Llys Meddyg   £48

East St SA42 0SY   (01239) 820008

An "imaginative" menu with "wonderful use of local ingredients" again
wins high praise for this "stylish" restaurant-with-rooms, in a Georgian
townhouse. / **Details:** www.llysmeddyg.com; 9 pm; closed Mon L; no Amex.
Accommodation: 8 rooms, from £150.

A

Fistral Blu   £39

Fistral Beach, Headland Rd TR7 1HY   (01637) 879444
"Fabulous views over the beach" ("amazing at sunset") set the scene
at this smart contemporary spot; there's the occasional let-down on the
food front, but most reports say it's "better than you might expect from
the location". / **Details:** www.fistral-blu.co.uk; 10 pm.

A ★

Crooked Billet   £43

2 Westbrook End MK17 0DF   (01908) 373936
"You can dress up or down, have a simple sarnie or a gourmet meal",
at this picturesque inn, which impresses almost all who comment on it;
the "top cheeseboard and wine list" rate special mention.
/ **Details:** www.thebillet.co.uk; 11 pm, Sat 9.30 pm; D only, ex Sun open L only.

A

Cook & Barker   £41

NE65 9JY   (01665) 575234
"Worth knowing about", just off the A1, a "pleasant" boozer where the
food is "pretty consistent", and "reasonably priced"; they're "great with
children" too. / **Details:** www.cookandbarkerinn.co.uk; 12m N of Morpeth,
just off A1; 9 pm. **Accommodation:** 19 rooms, from £80.

NOMANSLAND, WILTSHIRE   2–3C

Les Mirabelles   £42   A ⭐ ⭐

Forest Edge Rd SP5 2BN (01794) 390205

"Excellent and authentic" ("rather rich") French cooking is dished up by "largely French staff" at this "beautifully-located" restaurant – "though not the most expensive place in the New Forest, it's arguably the best". / **Details:** *www.lesmirabelles.co.uk; off A36 between Southampton & Salisbury; 9.30 pm; closed Mon & Sun.*

NORDEN, LANCASHIRE   5–1B

Nutter's   £45   A ⭐

Edenfield Rd OL12 7TT (01706) 650167

"They know how to look after people", at the Nutter family's old manor house, which enjoys impressive views across the moors, and it won consistent praise this year for its "always-excellent" cuisine; top tips include the "amazing-value" business lunch, and the "really special" afternoon tea. / **Details:** *www.nuttersrestaurant.com; between Edenfield & Norden on A680; 9 pm; closed Mon.*

NORTH BOVEY, DEVON   1–3C

                                                          T

Bovey Castle   £55

TQ13 8RE (01647) 445016

A decidedly "grand" hotel with impressive facilities, on the fringe of Dartmoor, tipped for food that's "absolutely delicious" (but "expensive" too). / **Details:** *www.boveycastle.com; 9.15 pm.* **Accommodation:** *65 rooms, from £154.*

NORTH SHIELDS, TYNE AND WEAR   8–2B

                                                          ⭐

Kristian Fish   £12

3-9 Union Quay NE30 1HJ (0191) 258 5155

"A traditional fish and chip shop with restaurant attached" – "always good", and "always crowded" too. / **Details:** *9 pm; closed Sun D; no credit cards.*

NORTHALLERTON, NORTH YORKSHIRE   8–4B

                                                          A

McCoys at the Tontine   £53

DL6 3JB (01609) 882 671

This "quirky" county house venture has been going for yonks and still wins praise for its "fun" style and "great food every time" (not least, for those who stay, "the best breakfast"). / **Details:** *www.mccoystontine.co.uk; junction of A19 & A172; 9.30 pm; bistro L & D every day, restaurant Sat D only.* **Accommodation:** *7 rooms, from £140.*

NORTHAMPTON, NORTHAMPTONSHIRE   2–1D

                                                          A ⭐

Buddies New York Cafe   £29

Dychurch Ln NN1 2AB (01604) 620300

A real, genuine offshoot of a New York diner of the same name, this "amazing" place lives up to all the stereotypes you might possibly hope for, not least "great burgers", which come with "an amazing range of toppings". / **Details:** *www.buddiesrestaurants.com.*

NORTHAW, HERTFORDSHIRE   3–2B

                                                          T

The Sun at Northaw   £41

1 Judges Hill EN6 4NL (01707) 655507

"A small village pub that's been nicely decorated", and is tipped for its "above-average pub fayre". / **Details:** *www.thesunatnorthaw.co.uk; 6 pm, Sun 4 pm; closed Mon & Sun D.*

The Vine Tree   £35

T

Foxley Rd SN16 0JP   (01666) 837654
*A classic country inn, tipped for its "friendly and relaxed" style,
"interesting" cooking and "good range of real ales and wine".
/ Details: www.thevinetree.co.uk; 9.30 pm, Fri & Sat 9.45 pm; closed Sun.*

Last Wine Bar   £39

A

70-76 St Georges street NR3 1AB   (01603) 626626
*"A good wine bar in an old shoe factory"; it's usually "very busy and
noisy", thanks not least to food that's "well-cooked and well-served",
and there is an "extensive wine list" too.
/ Details: www.thelastwinebar.co.uk; 10.30 pm; closed Sun.*

Waffle House   £25

T

39 St Giles St NR2 1JN   (01603) 612790
*"A Norwich institution", which "has not changed in the last 20 years";
"don't go if you don't like waffles", but – assuming you do – a meal
here can offer "a great combination of taste and value";
breakfast is especially commended. / Details: www.wafflehouse.co.uk;
10 pm; no Amex; need 6+ to book.*

Anoki   £45

A

Barker Gate NG1 1JU   (01159) 483888
*Opposite the National Ice Centre, this sibling to the excellent Derby
subcontinental wins similarly stellar ratings for its "great",
"very reasonably priced" food and "interested" service.
/ Details: www.anoki.co.uk.*

Atlas   £12

A **★**

9 Pelham St NG1 2EH   (0115) 950 1295
*"There should be one in every town!" – this "lovely, and great-value"
café near the Council House is just "what all sandwich shops should
aim to be". / Details: www.atlastdelhi.co.uk; L only.*

Bistrot Pierre   £34

★

13-17 Milton St NG1 3EN   (0115) 9412850
*For the "best French food at a great price!", this "cheap and cheerful"
bistro makes a "lively" choice – "on Saturdays, there's a queue out the
door!" / Details: www.lebistrotpierre.co.uk; 10.30 pm, fri & sat 11 pm.*

Broadway Café Bar   £27

T

14-18 Broadway, Broad St NG1 3AL   (0115) 952 1551
*"A nice café in a busy arts cinema"; a "cheerful" place for pre-film
(don't miss the special deal), it's also tipped as a good place for a "lively
beer". / Details: 9 pm; no Amex.*

Chino Latino
Park Plaza Hotel   £56

A

41 Maid Marian Way NG1 6GD   (0115) 947 7444
*Off the lobby of a city-centre hotel, a "trendy Asian-fusion dining room",
where the food can be "stunning"; it can also seem "overpriced",
however, not helped by "unsatisfactory" service, or decor that somtimes
seems plain "seedy". / Details: www.chinolatino.co.uk; 10.30 pm; closed Sun.
Accommodation: 178 rooms, from £-.*

Crème £38

12 Toton Ln NG9 7HA (0115) 939 7422

"An unexpected dining experience in a Nottingham suburb"; this Stapleford "gem" offers "incredible value for money", say fans – "no surprise that it's usually very busy".
/ *Details:* www.cremerestaurant.co.uk; 9.30 pm; closed Mon, Sat L & Sun D; children: 10+.

Edins £27

15 Broad St NG1 3JA (0115) 9241112

"A tapas bar, café and restaurant", whose "value-for-money" formula has won quite a local following; indeed, the proprietor already has plans to create something of a local empire… / *Details:* midnight; no Amex.

4550 Miles From Delhi £30

Maid Marian Way NG1 6HE (0115) 947 5111

"Strange name, but gorgeous food"; all reporters are impressed by the "exceptional" cuisine on offer at this "very buzzy and vibrant modern Indian" in the city-centre. / *Details:* www.milesfromdelhi.com; Mon-Thu 10 pm, Fri & Sat 11 pm, Sun 10.30 pm.

French Living £36

27 King St NG1 2AY (0115) 958 5885

A "cosy", bare-walled cellar (plus pavement café) where the Corsican chef "maintains a high standard of regional cuisine, and a good wine list too", all at "realistic prices"; it's "the closest thing you can get to a trip to France"… well, in Nottingham anyhow.
/ *Details:* www.frenchliving.co.uk; near Market Square; 10 pm; closed Mon & Sun; no Amex; booking: max 10.

Hart's £47

Standard Ct, Park Row NG1 6GN (0115) 911 0666

Still Nottingham most commented-on place – Tim Hart's "efficient" operation near the Castle has long been one of the slickest modern brasseries outside London; with its "consistently high-quality" cuisine, and its "upmarket, but not OTT" style, it's particularly popular as a business destination. / *Details:* www.hartsnottingham.co.uk; near Castle; 10.30 pm, Sun 9 pm. **Accommodation:** 33 rooms, from £120.

Iberico £34

The Shire Hall, High Pavement NG1 1HN (01159) 410410

"Entirely at home in its gloomy location" (the "cellar of an historic building in the Lace Market"), this "excellent all-round" Hispanic bar offers a cuisine which puts a "creative 'world' spin" on the "basic tapas formula". / *Details:* www.ibericotapas.com; 10 pm; closed Mon & Sun; no Amex; children: 16+ D.

Kayal £29

8 Broad St NG1 3AL (0115) 941 4733

"Wonderful", "light" and "interesting" – the south Indian cuisine at this city-centre spot is well worth seeking out.
/ *Details:* www.kayalrestaurant.com; 11 pm, Sun 10 pm.

Laguna Tandoori   £31   ⭐

43 Mount St NG1 6HE   (0115) 941 1632

"A very long-standing Nottingham venue for North Indian delights" –
a good number of reports confirms it "maintains its standards very
well". / Details: www.lagunatandoori.co.uk; nr Nottingham Castle; 11 pm; closed
Sat L & Sun L.

The Library Bar Kitchen   £28   Ⓐ ⭐

Beeston NG9 2NG   (0115) 922 2268

"An exciting place to eat", this "buzzy" Beeston 'tapas' joint pleases all
reporters with its "outstanding" small (non-Spanish) dishes.
/ Details: www.thelibrarybarkitchen.co.uk; 10 pm; closed Sun; no shorts.

Loch Fyne   £40   Ⓐ

15-17 King St NG1 2AY   (0115) 988 6840

With its "buzzy" style and "reliably fresh fish", this "handily-located"
city-centre branch of the national chain makes "a useful choice for
a swift, unfussy meal". / Details: www.lochfyne.com; 10 pm, Fri & Sat
10.30 pm.

MemSaab   £38   Ⓐ ⭐

12-14 Maid Marian Way NG1 6HS   (0115) 957 0009

"Creative Indian food with subtle flavours" (albeit in rather "small
portions") has won a huge following for this "smart", if slightly
"cavernous", city-centre spot. / Details: www.mem-saab.co.uk; near Castle,
opposite Park Plaza Hotel; 10.30 pm, Fri & Sat 11 pm, Sun 10 pm; D only;
no shorts.

Merchants   Ⓣ
Lace Market Hotel   £46

29-31 High Pavement NG1 1HE   (0115) 958 9898

Despite its "impressive" design, this dining room in a boutique hotel
in the heart of the Lace Market inspires relatively little feedback; all of
it is positive, though, and one reporter who feels the place "lost its way"
some time ago now feels it's "back on form".
/ Details: www.lacemarkethotel.co.uk; 10 pm; closed Sat L.
Accommodation: *42 rooms, from £160.*

Petit Paris   £32   Ⓐ

2 Kings Walk NG1 2AE   (0115) 947 3767

A "city-centre fixture of some years' standing", where "Franco/Italian
dishes come in hearty portions"; it remains especially popular for lunch
and pre-theatre. / Details: www.petitparisrestaurant.co.uk; near Theatre Royal;
10.15 pm; closed Sun.

Restaurant Sat Bains   £99   ⭐ ⭐

Old Lenton Ln NG7 2SA   (0115) 986 6566

"Textures, tastes and eye-appeal in spades" can make a meal chez
Bains a "fantastic experience"; as a fan notes, though, his restaurant
"polarises opinion" – critics diss the style ("self-important"),
the environs ("dreadful" with "fly-over, pylons, etc") and the prices,
especially of wine (a "rip-off"). / Details: www.restaurantsatbains.com;
8.30 pm; D only, closed Mon & Sun; children: 8+. **Accommodation:** *8 rooms,*
from £129.

Victoria Hotel   £36   Ⓐ

Dovecote Ln NG9 1JG   (0115) 925 4049

Only positive reports on this "real gem" of a "real ale pub", by Beeston
station, which has been offering "reliably good food for years"; "sitting
outside in the marquee in the back yard can be cold in winter",
however. / Details: www.victoriabeeston.co.uk; by Beeston railway station;
9.30 pm, Sun-Tue 8.45 pm; no Amex; no booking, Sun; children: 18+ after 8 pm.

The Wollaton £37

Lambourne Drive NG8 1GR (0115) 9288610

"Decent traditional British food" (including "the best chips anywhere")
wins a tip for this pleasant gastropub, which is named after its
suburban location. / Details: www.thewollaton.co.uk.

World Service £54

Newdigate Hs, Castle Gate NG1 6AF (0115) 847 5587

"A great place for almost all occasions"; this "swanky" stalwart near
the Castle – "a lovely building, with a summer garden for drinks" –
is the town's best all-rounder; service is "impeccable", and "some lovely
ideas come out of the kitchen – some unsuccessful, but with more
plusses than minuses". / Details: www.worldservicerestaurant.com; 10 pm,
Sun 9 pm; children: 12+ at D.

OARE, KENT 3–3C

The Three Mariners £36

2 Church Rd ME13 0QA (01795) 533633

An "unpretentious foodie pub", near the water, where the food
(with "lots of locally-caught fish") is sometimes "fantastic", and rarely
less than "very enjoyable"; "generous portions" too.
/ Details: www.thethreemarinersoare.co.uk; 11 pm, Fri & Sat midnight,
Sun 9 pm; closed Mon; no Amex.

OBAN, ARGYLL AND BUTE 9–3B

Ee-Usk (Seafood Restaurant) £37

North Pier PA35 5QD (01631) 565666

With its "seafront location" (brilliant views), and its "wonderful fish,
fresh-from-the-sea", this waterside café can do no wrong for some
reporters; sceptics, however, caution that it is "not outstanding"
nowadays. / Details: www.eeusk.com; 9 pm; no Amex; children: children 10+
at L, not welcome at dinner .

OCKLEY, SURREY 3–4A

Bryce's at the Old School House £47

Stane St RH5 5TH (01306) 627430

"Still the best fish in the South East despite the land-locked location" –
this "very reliable" Surrey Hills inn continues to inspire
almost unanimously positive reports; "good veggie fare too, plus the
odd meat dish". / Details: www.bryces.co.uk; 8m S of Dorking on A29; 9 pm;
no Amex.

The Neptune   £60

AO

85 Old Hunstanton Rd PE36 6HZ   (01485) 532122

"Relaxed", "friendly" and "tasteful", this old coaching inn is a "great place to enjoy a small selection of mostly local produce, cooked with skill and care". / Details: www.theneptune.co.uk; 9 pm; closed Mon, Tue–Sat D only, Sun open L & D; no Amex; booking essential; children: 10.
Accommodation: 6 rooms, from ££110.

Smiths Brasserie   £56

AO

Fyfield Rd CM5 0AL   (01277) 365578

On most accounts, this popular suburban destination is a "fantastic seafood restaurant" that's "improved in recent years", and is now "well worth travelling for"; for a minority of refuzniks, though, it remains "pricey" and "average". / Details: www.smithsbrasserie.com; left off A414 towards Fyfield; 10 pm, Fri & Sat 10.30 pm; closed Mon L; no Amex; children: 12+.

Loch Leven Seafood Cafe   £41

OO

PH33 6SR   (01855) 821048

"You couldn't possibly get fresher produce" – "really stunningly fresh seafood, cooked simply to perfection" – at this waterside café; "the view over Loch Leven raises it to a five-star dining experience", and one that's "well worth a major detour". / Details: www.lochlevenseafoodcafe.Co.uk; no Amex.

Butley Orford Oysterage   £37

O

Market Hill IP12 2LH   (01394) 450277

"I've been dining here since 1973, and in some ways this good and honest fish restaurant hasn't changed at all" – one reporter tells almost the whole story on the Pinney family's "time warp", which "feels like a cross between a greasy spoon and a doctor's waiting room"; "wonderful" own-smoked fish is a highlight. / Details: www.butleyorfordoysterage.co.uk; on the B1078, off the A12 from Ipswich; 9 pm; no Amex.

The Crown & Castle   £45

A

IP12 2LJ   (01394) 450205

Ruth Watson's "really good food at very sensible prices" and a "quirky and unpretentious wine list" win majority support from reporters for this popular coastal hotel; the "crowded" setting, however, is no particular attraction. / Details: www.crownandcastle.co.uk; on main road to Orford; 9.15 pm; closed Sun D in winter; no Amex; booking: max 8; children: 9+ at D. ***Accommodation: 19 rooms, from £125.***

Xian   £30

O

324 High St BR6 0NG   (01689) 871881

This veteran Chinese is one where reporters find little to fault, thanks to the "reliably good" food, wide selection of dishes, "super presentation" and "lively atmosphere"; prices are "realistic" too. / Details: Near the war memorial; 11 pm; closed Mon & Sun L.

Ⓐ

The Bush Inn   £36
SO24 0RE   (01962) 732764
*A pretty pub that's particularly tipped for its "welcoming" service,
and having "plenty of atmosphere" too; the food plays rather
a supporting role. / **Details:** www.wadworth.co.uk; just off A31 between
Winchester & Alresford; 9 pm.*

Ⓐ

Al Shami   £26
25 Walton Cr OX1 2JG   (01865) 310066
*Is it "the best Lebanese outside of London"? – not everyone is quite
convinced, but many reporters do praise the "absolute reliability" of this
Jericho veteran, and its "amazing prices" too; an "outstanding"
selection of Château Musar is also a feature.
/ **Details:** www.al-shami.co.uk; midnight. **Accommodation:** 12 rooms,
from £50.*

Ⓐ

Ashmolean Dining Room   £43
Beaumont St OX1 2PH   (01865) 553 823
*This "airy new rooftop restaurant" has a "spectacular" location,
and offers "good value, for the café of a museum", so it's no surprise
that it's already "very popular" (book ahead); service, though,
can sometimes be "very slow". / **Details:** www.ashmoleandiningroom.com.*

Ⓐ

Aziz   £33
228-230 Cowley Rd OX4 1UH   (01865) 794945
*"Consistency is everything", at this "unpretentious" East Oxford
"institution", whose "tasty" curries are "still tops" for many local
reporters. / **Details:** www.aziz.uk.com; 11.15 pm; closed Fri L.*

Ⓣ

Big Bang   £32
124 Walton St OX2 6HA   (01865) 511441
*"Quirky" it certainly is, but this "casual" and "friendly" spot is tipped
for its "brilliant choice of sausages"; they can be enjoyed at "a good
and hearty breakfast", or for breakfast or lunch.
/ **Details:** www.thebigbangrestaurant.co.uk; Opposite Cocktail Bar Raoul's;
10.30 pm; no credit cards.*

Ⓐ

The Black Boy   £37
91 Old High St OX3 9HT   (01865) 741137
*"Simple cuisine is very well-cooked" at this well-renovated roadside
boozer, on the fringes of the town – "a great little gastropub that's
always busy". / **Details:** www.theblackboy.uk.com; 9 pm.*

Ⓐ

Bombay   £24
82 Walton St OX2 6EA   (01865) 511188
*"One of Oxford's better Indians", this "friendly" and "no-nonsense"
Jericho institution is always "busy and noisy", and even critics may
admit that "the BYO policy makes it good value". / **Details:** 11 pm; closed
Fri L; no Amex.*

Ⓐ

Branca   £39
111 Walton St OX2 6AJ   (01865) 556111
*"Tasty Italian food in a fun and vibrant atmosphere" generally proves
a winning formula for this Jericho Italian; some reporters, though,
are beginning to see it as "a victim of its own success".
/ **Details:** www.branca-restaurants.com; 11 pm.*

Brasserie Blanc £42 Ⓐ

71-72 Walton St OX2 6AG (01865) 510999

"Really not so bad, for a chain"; the original Jericho outlet bearing the name of the chef from nearby Great Milton is a "reliable" sort of place, with "a real sense of brasserie about it" – it helps, no doubt, that "Raymond is often there"! / **Details:** www.brasserieblanc.com; 10 pm, Sat 10.30 pm, Sun 9.30 pm.

Browns £38 ⓧ

5-11 Woodstock Rd OX2 6HA (01865) 511995

"Disappointing because it used to be so good" – this once-legendary English brasserie is "totally average and seriously overpriced" nowadays; there's "not much to recommend it".
/ **Details:** www.browns-restaurants.com; 11 pm, Fri & Sat 11.30 pm, Sun 10.30 pm; need 5+ to book.

Cherwell Boathouse £42 Ⓐ

Bardwell Rd OX2 6ST (01865) 552746

"The wine list is sensational" ("hardly surprising as the owner is a famous merchant"), and this popular spot has "a delightful setting overlooking punts on the river"; must be catch? – yes, the food can be "woeful". / **Details:** www.cherwellboathouse.co.uk; 9.30 pm.

Chiang Mai £35 Ⓐ ⭐ ⭐

Kemp Hall Pas, 130a High St OX1 4DH (01865) 202233

Fans are not shy in their praise for the "fresh" and "flavoursome" Thai fare at what is still often hailed as "the best restaurant in Oxford"; it occupies an "interesting" (if sometimes "noisy") Tudor building, just off the High – "sounds like a tourist trap, but nothing could be further from the truth". / **Details:** www.chiangmaikitchen.co.uk; 10.30 pm.

Chutney's Indian Brasserie £32 Ⓐ

36 St Michael's St OX1 2EB (01865) 724241

"Poppadoms to die for" and a "fantastic range of dosas" win a strong following for this city-centre curry house, which attracts a "large student clientele". / **Details:** www.chutneysoxford.co.uk; Between high street and town centre; 11 pm, Fri & Sat 11.30 pm.

La Cucina £34 Ⓐ

39-40 St Clements OX4 1AB (01865) 793811

A "popular" St Clement's destination, that serves up "solid rustic Italian cuisine", and in "huge" portions too; parents NB – "they adore children". / **Details:** www.lacucinaoxford.co.uk; 10.30 pm.

Edamame £20 ⭐

15 Holywell St OX1 3SA (01865) 246916

"Small and simple, but homely and welcoming" – this tiny café is praised by most reporters for its "fresh" Japanese fare (albeit from an "unchanging" menu); Thursday night is sushi night.
/ **Details:** www.edamame.co.uk; opp New College; 8.30 pm; L only, ex Fri & Sat open L & D, closed Mon; no Amex; no booking.

Fishers Seafood £40 Ⓐ

36-37 St Clements OX4 1AB (01865) 243003

"Excellent fresh fish that's not overpriced" plus "friendly" service win solid ratings for this seafood bistro, near Magdalen Bridge.
/ **Details:** www.fishers-restaurant.com; by Magdalen Bridge; 10.30 pm, Sun 10 pm.

The Fishes £39 Ⓐ

North Hinksey OX2 0NA (01865) 249796

"A very busy" and "lively" pub (with service that can be "VERY slow" as a result), praised for its "reliable" cuisine.
/ **Details:** www.fishesoxford.co.uk; just off the A34; 10 pm; no Amex.

Gee's £48
61 Banbury Rd OX2 6PE   (01865) 553540

"The wonderful setting of a Victorian conservatory" is the star of the show at this atmospheric destination – "with someone special, it's the most romantic place in Oxford"; the food – "good, rather than great" – is a bit incidental. / *Details:* www.gees-restaurant.co.uk; 10 pm, Fri & Sat 10.30 pm.

Grand Café £25
84 High St OX1 4BG   (01865) 204463
Handily-located on the High, an elegant establishment tipped by a number of reporters for "great coffee, eggs and pastries" and "the best afternoon tea in Britain"! / Details: www.thegrandcafe.co.uk; L only.

Jamie's Italian £38
24-26 George St OX1 2AE   (01865) 838383
"Be prepared" to queue, to gain entry to this "noisy and packed" outlet of the Naked Chef's national chain; it says a lot about Oxford, though, that this "pleasant but uninspired" Italian – below-average for the group – is the most reported-on place in town!
/ *Details:* www.jamiesitalian.com; 11 pm, Sun 10.30 pm.

The Magdalen Arms £36
243 Iffley Rd OX4 1SJ   (01865) 243 159
"An astonishing newcomer"; this "handsome" Iffley Road boozer has "metamorphosed" at the hands of alumni of London's Anchor & Hope, and its "imaginative and robust" gastropub cuisine is the highest-rated in town; it's a "buzzy" place too… or, to put it another way, "the only problem is the noise". / *Details:* 10 pm; closed Mon, Tue L & Sun D; no Amex.

Malmaison £50
3 Oxford Circle OX1 1AY   (01865) 268400
The rather "fabulous" setting of a former prison houses this "very busy" hotel brasserie, in the city-centre, praised by fans as a "fun place to eat"; however, "like most Oxford restaurants, the quality of the food does not live up to the prices". / *Details:* www.malmaison.com; 10 pm. **Accommodation:** 94 rooms, from £160.

The Nosebag £19
6-8 St Michael's St OX1 2DU   (01865) 721033
A "good stand-by" whose "large portions of mainly vegetarian food" (including "a wide selection of salads") are tipped by some reporters as offering "the best value in Oxford"; the word is out, so – for comfort – "avoid peak times". / *Details:* www.nosebagoxford.co.uk; 9.30 pm, Fri & Sat 10 pm, Sun 8.30 pm.

The Old Parsonage £51

T

1 Banbury Rd OX2 6NN (01865) 292305

All reporters agree on the "potential" of this medieval building, just north of the city-centre; feedback remains mixed, however, but the place is certainly tipped as a good choice for a "tasty and traditional Sunday lunch". / Details: www.oldparsonage-hotel.co.uk; 0.5m N of city centre; 10.30 pm. Accommodation: 30 rooms, from £190.

The Perch £45

A

Binsey Ln OX2 0NG (01865) 728891

"An old pub with a large garden by the river"; it makes "a great stop-off for a walk", and is praised by most (if not quite all) reporters for its "delicious and most interesting food". / Details: www.the-perch.co.uk; 9.30 pm, Sun 8.30 pm; no Amex.

Pierre Victoire £43

A

Little Clarendon St OX1 2HP (01865) 316616

A "no-frills" Gallic brasserie (one of the last survivors in the once-national chain), particularly tipped for its "excellent-value, prix-fixe lunch menu"; in general "the food is not outstanding, but does the job". / Details: www.pierrevictoire.co.uk; 11 pm, 10 pm Sun; no Amex.

Quod

X

Old Bank Hotel £45

91-94 High St OX1 4BN (01865) 799599

"It's usually rammed with undergrads, plus their maters and paters" – and has a "very buzzy" ambience – but this "vast" and "clattery" central Italian achieved an even lower food rating this year than last, along with an impressive volume reports that it is simply "dire". / Details: www.oldbank-hotel.co.uk; opp All Souls College; 11 pm, Sun 10.30 pm; no booking at D. Accommodation: 42 rooms, from £175.

Shanghai 30s £33

A

82 St Aldates OX1 1RA (01865) 242230

This "beautiful old dining room" had such a promising re-launch as a Chinese restaurant; even fans can find it a "contrived" and "expensive" place, however, and to critics the food is no more than "bog-standard". / Details: www.shanghai30s.com; 11 pm; closed Mon L.

Sojo £35

★

8-9 Hythe Bridge St OX1 2EW (01865) 202888

Can this be Oxford? – this "wonderful and authentic" venture wins resounding praise from reporters for its "stunning and piquant" Sichuan fare; "my Chinese friend feels this is one of the best restaurants she's been to!"

OXTED, SURREY	3–3B

The Gurkha Kitchen £31

★

111 Station Road East RH8 0AX (01883) 722621

An "evolving" Nepalese menu served "with flair and enthusiasm" (if occasionally "rather slowly") makes for a "very enjoyable" experience at this self-explanatory spot. / Details: www.moolirestaurant.co.uk; 11 pm, Sun 10 pm; no Amex.

OXTON, CHESHIRE	5–2A

Fraiche £52

★★

11 Rose Mount CH43 5SG (0151) 652 2914

"A really special place", which offers "an extraordinary eating experience" – Mark Wilkinson's "exceptional" cuisine wins consistent raves for this "minimalist but comfortable" foodie haven. / Details: www.restaurantfraiche.com; 8.30 pm, Sun 7 pm; closed Mon, Tue, Wed L, Thu L & Sun L; no Amex.

Custard   £47   Ⓐ
1A, The Strand PL28 8AJ   (01841) 532565

"A little oasis, hidden-away from the summer chaos of the town";
fans say this attractive diner "puts many grander places to shame" with
its "good-value" bistro fare. / **Details:** www.custarddiner.com; 9.30 pm, Fri &
Sat 10 pm; no Amex.

Margot's   £37   Ⓐ⭐
11 Duke St PL28 8AB   (01841) 533441
"The freshest of food, mainly fish, simply served, and at affordable
prices too" – that's the formula which allows Adrian Oliver's "tiny" (22-
seat) but "excellent" bistro "to compete well with the Stein operations".
/ **Details:** www.margots.co.uk; On the back street behind the Inner Harbour,
on the same road as the Post Office; 9.30 pm; closed Mon & Sun; booking:
max 10.

Paul Ainsworth at No 6   £42   ⭐⭐
6 Middle St PL28 8AP   (01841) 532093
"The best dining in Padstow" is, say Paul Ainsworth's fans, not to
be found at the Stein empire, but at this "intimate" townhouse-
restaurant, where the cooking is "fabulous", and the service
is "so welcoming" too. / **Details:** www.number6inpadstow.co.uk; Off the main
square in Padstow, next door to Rick Stein's; 10 pm; closed Mon & Sun; no Amex.

Rick Stein's Café   £42   Ⓐ⭐
10 Middle St PL28 8AP   (01841) 532700
"I know it's not the 'Seafood', but I prefer it here" – Rick Stein's
"buzzy" all-day bistro may lack its famous parent's polish, but it has
a "casual" appeal which, for many reporters, makes it "the best all-
rounder in Padstow". / **Details:** www.rickstein.com; 9.30 pm; no Amex.
Accommodation: 3 rooms, from £90.

St Petroc's Hotel & Bistro   £47   ⭐
4 New St PL28 8EA   (01841) 532700
Rick Stein's lesser-known (and cheaper) Padstow outfit is a "relaxed"
bistro that wins very consistent praise for its "zingy" fare, and for
"great value" too. / **Details:** www.rickstein.com; 9.30 pm; no Amex.
Accommodation: 10 rooms, from £135.

Seafood Restaurant £72

Riverside PL28 8BY (01841) 532700

"Better than ever after the refurb" (of a couple of years ago) –
Rick Stein's renowned quayside restaurant is often applauded
by reporters for "the best seafood anywhere"; even so, prices can seem
"inflated", so keep an eye out for "winter lunch deals".
/ Details: www.rickstein.com; opp harbourmaster's car park; 10 pm; no Amex;
booking: max 14; children: 3+. **Accommodation:** 16 rooms, from £135.

Stein's Fish & Chips £32

South Quay PL28 8BL (01841) 532700
"Fabulous fish in perfect batter" make this Padstein chippy "a really
buzzing and happy place" – "arrive before opening to avoid a long
queue". / **Details:** www.rickstein.com; 10 pm; no Amex.

PANTYGELLI, ABERGAVENNY 2–1A

The Crown £36

Old Hereford Rd NP7 7HR (01873) 853314
Notably consistent reports on this "beautifully-located" rural inn on the
edge of town, tipped for its "above-average" pub grub.
/ **Details:** www.thecrownatpantygelli.com; 9pm; closed Mon & Sun D; no Amex.

PAR, CORNWALL 1–3B

Sams On The Beach £39

14 Polkerris Nr Fowey PL24 2TL (01726) 812255
You get "amazing views of St Austell Bay" and "outstanding food too",
at this former lifeboat station – now a fish-and-seafood offshoot of the
similarly named Fowey restaurant; "book – you can go there and find
it full at the oddest time of day!" / **Details:** www.samsfowey.co.uk;
closed Mon.

PARKGATE, CHESHIRE 5–2A

Marsh Cat £38

1 Mostyn Sq CH64 6SL (0151) 336 1963
Especially if you can get a table with "great views of the Dee Estuary"
("partially silted", though it is), this cheerful bistro can make
a "wonderful" rendezvous, especially for lunch; "the food varies",
though, and "service can struggle at busy times".
/ **Details:** www.marshcat.com; 10 pm, Tue-Sun 9 pm.

PEEBLES, SCOTTISH BORDERS 9–4C

Cringletie House £38

Edinburgh Rd EH45 8PL (01721) 725750
Still not the volume of feedback we'd like on dining at this impressive
Borders hotel... which fans tip as being "truly outstanding".
/ **Details:** www.cringletie.com; between Peebles and Eddleston on A703, 20m S
of Edinburgh; 9 pm; D only, ex Sun open L & D; booking essential.
Accommodation: 13 rooms, from £180.

Osso   **£39**   ⭐

Innerleithen Rd EH45 8BA   (01721) 724477

*"An absolute gem", this "cafe/tapas bar by day/fine-dining restaurant
by night" pleases all reporters; not much feedback as yet, but some
"stunning" dishes have been recorded. / **Details:** www.ossorestaurant.com;
9 pm; closed Mon D & Sun D.*

PENSHURST, KENT   3–3B

Spotted Dog   **£40**   Ⓐ

Smarts Hill TN11 8EE   (01892) 870253

*"A lovely traditional pub" (dating from the 15th century),
with "beautiful views"; reports are all good but, as it changed hands
in 2010, we've left it unrated for the moment.
/ **Details:** www.spotteddogpub.co.uk; near Penshurst Place; 9 pm, Fri & Sat
9.30 pm, Sun 7 pm.*

PENZANCE, CORNWALL   1–4A

The Honey Pot   **£15**   Ⓐ⭐

5 Parade St TR18 4BU   (01736) 368686

*"For a complete meal or just cake and coffee", this "fun" café with
invariably "tasty" food – is well worth seeking out; "at lunchtime,
booking is recommended". / **Details:** L only, closed Sun; no credit cards.*

PERTH, PERTH AND KINROSS   9–3C

Cafe Tabou   **£38**   Ⓐ⭐

4 St John's Pl PH1 5SZ   (01738) 446698

*"Right in the middle of the town", this "bustling" and "popular" bistro
attracts unanimous praise for its can't-go-wrong formula – "all the
classics, at very reasonable prices". / **Details:** www.cafetabou.com; 9 pm,
Wed & Thu 9.30 pm, Fri & Sat 10 pm; closed Mon D & Sun; no Amex.*

PETERSFIELD, HAMPSHIRE   2–3D

JSW   **£62**   Ⓐ

20 Dragon St GU31 4JJ   (01730) 262030

*Jake Saul Watkins's former coaching inn is a "peaceful" and "refined"
foodie "oasis" nowadays, and most reporters feel it lives up to its
reputation for "superb" and "original" cuisine; even fans, though,
may sometimes feel it's "not as good as it used to be".
/ **Details:** www.jswrestaurant.com; On the old A3; 8 min walk from the railway
station; 9.30 pm; closed Mon & Sun; no Amex; children: D 8+.*
Accommodation: *3 rooms, from £110.*

PETWORTH, WEST SUSSEX   3–4A

The Noahs Ark Inn   **£40**   Ⓐ

Lurgashall GU28 9ET   (01428) 707346

*"Possibly the perfect pub on a summer evening, overlooking the village
green"; the food is "very good, for the price" too.
/ **Details:** www.noahsarkinn.co.uk; 9.30 pm; closed Sun D.*

Well Diggers Arms   **£39**   new   ⭐

Lowheath GU28 0HG   (01798) 342287

*The name does not lie – a "hearty appetite" is needed best to enjoy
this "brilliant" canal-side local, which inspires only positive reports.
/ **Details:** 1m out of town on Pulborough Road; 9 pm; closed Mon, Tue D,
Wed D & Sun D.*

The White Swan £45 Ⓐ ⭐

Market Pl YO18 7AA (01751) 472288

"A great hotel with a fabulous restaurant" – this tastefully updated inn is "informal" in style, but all reports extol its "wonderful" food (from "excellent ingredients"). / Details: www.white-swan.co.uk; 9 pm. Accommodation: 21 rooms, from £150.

Clog And Billycock £36 Ⓐ

Billinge End Rd BB2 6QB (01254) 201163

With its "vibrant" atmosphere and "honest" local food ethos, the Northcote team has scored another hit with this latest – "huge" – addition to the Ribble Valley Inns group; moderate overall food ratings, however, do suggest the law of diminishing returns is beginning to set in. / Details: www.theclogandbillycock.com; 9pm mon - sat 830 sunday.

Plockton Inn £33 ⭐

Innes St IV52 8TW (01599) 544222

A loch-side inn (plus smokery) tipped for the quality of its seafood ("straight out of the ocean and on to the plate"); it has a "great location" too. / Details: www.plocktoninn.co.uk; 9 pm, Winter 8.30 pm; no Amex. Accommodation: 14 rooms, from ££94.

The Barbican Kitchen Brasserie £33 Ⓐ

60 Southside St, The Barbican PL1 2LQ (01752) 604448

This "light and airy warehouse location" – the former Plymouth Gin Distillery, nowadays a brasserie run by the Tanner brothers – wins praise from all who report on it; it offers an "interesting choice of food", and often "great value" too. / Details: www.barbicankitchen.com; 10 pm.

Platters £39 Ⓐ

12 The Barbican PL1 2LS (01752) 227262

"Fresh traditional seafood at its best" wins high praise for this "small and cosy" café of long standing; critics, though, just dismiss it as "a chippy with pretensions". / Details: www.platters-restaurant.co.uk; 10.30 pm.

Tanners Restaurant £53 Ⓐ ⭐

Prysten Hs, Finewell St PL1 2AE (01752) 252001

"Plymouth's smallest, and just about only, really good restaurant" – the eponymous brothers' "small but beautiful" establishment, "in one of the city's oldest houses", pleases almost all reporters with its "very high standard of cuisine at reasonable prices". / Details: www.tannersrestaurant.com; 9.30 pm; closed Mon & Sun.

Guildhall Tavern £44 Ⓐ ⭐

15 Market St BH15 1NB (01202) 671717

"Spectacular seafood" and "very friendly and knowledgeable service" make this Gallic-run former boozer a "real little gem", all the more worth knowing about as an "oasis" in a thin area. / Details: www.guildhalltavern.co.uk; 9.30 pm; closed Mon; no Amex.

Storm   **£44** ⭐

16 High St BH15 1BP   (01202) 674970
*It may only have "a small, unprepossessing shop front in the old High Street", but this "basic" outfit is well-liked for its "cosy", "rustic" and "impressively unpretentious" style; its fish dishes are undoubtedly "very competent" too. / **Details:** www.stormfish.co.uk; 9.30 pm, Fri & Sat 10 pm; closed Mon L, Tue L & Sun L.*

POPHAM NR WINCHESTER, HAMPSHIRE   2–3D

Little Chef   **£30** Ⓐ

Micheldever SO21 3SP   (01256) 398490
*"Heston's worked wonders", say fans of the Fat Duck chef's revitalised roadside diner, who praise its "outstanding" staples, kid-friendly attitude and "big breakfasts"; even some supporters feel "it's slipped a bit" since the TV cameras left, though, and others just find it a "massive disappointment". / **Details:** www.littlechef.co.uk; A303 West; 11 pm; no booking.*

PORLOCK, SOMERSET   1–2D

Andrews On The Weir   **£47** Ⓐ

Porlock Weir TA24 8PB   (01643) 863300
*The "beautiful location" is a high point, at this dramatically-sited restaurant-with-rooms; for most reporters, its "delicious" food is "always consistent" too, but not everyone is impressed.
/ **Details:** www.andrewsontheweir.co.uk; 9.30 pm; closed Mon & Tue; no Amex; children: 12+. **Accommodation:** 5 rooms, from £75.*

PORT APPIN, ARGYLL AND BUTE   9–3B

Airds Hotel   **£70** Ⓐ ⭐⭐

PA38 4DF   (01631) 730236
*This "remote but brilliant" foodie hotel – picturesquely situated on the side of Loch Linnhe – again wins impressively positive reports for its "locally-sourced fresh ingredients, beautifully presented".
/ **Details:** www.airds-hotel.com; 20m N of Oban; 9.30 pm; no jeans or trainers; children: 8+ at D. **Accommodation:** 11 rooms, from £245.*

Pierhouse Hotel   **£47** Ⓐ ⭐

PA38 4DE   (01631) 730302

*"A fantastic location overlooking the pier" ("what a view!") helps "justify the detour" to visit this popular spot; a further incentive is the "spanking fresh seafood" – "just as you hope it would taste, but so rarely does!" / **Details:** www.pierhousehotel.co.uk; just off A828, follow signs for Port Appin & Lismore Ferry; 9.30 pm. **Accommodation:** 12 rooms, from £120.*

317

The Shed   £52
SA62 5BN   (01348) 831518
"Well-cooked and imaginative seafood at a cosy, but very rustic, restaurant" (and "superb fish 'n' chips" too) – the formula that makes this seaside spot very popular; even a fan who says that "on a good day it makes Rick Stein look like an amateur", however, concedes that it's "not always on form". / **Details:** *www.theshedporthgain.co.uk; 9 pm; no Amex.*

Kota   £41
Harbour Head TR13 9JA   (01326) 562407
Seafood with a light Asian twist is the highlight of the "very good" cuisine at this harbour-side venture, into which a half-Maori proprietor injects an Antipodean twist. / **Details:** *www.kotarestaurant.co.uk; 9.30 pm; closed Mon L, Tue L, Wed L, Thu L & Sun; no Amex.* **Accommodation:** *2 rooms, from £55.*

Yr Hen Fecws   £18
16 Lombard St LL49 9AP   (01766) 514625
A Snowdonia restaurant-with-rooms tipped for its "very good" food. / **Details:** *www.henfecws.com; L only, closed Sun.* **Accommodation:** *7 rooms, from £67.*

The Oystercatcher   £44
Main St IV20 1YB   (01862) 871560
Situated "right by the beach", this "small" restaurant-with-rooms is an "atmospheric" spot, tipped for its consistently high quality cooking; it majors in fish, but even the breakfast selection involves "a whole range of possibilities"! / **Details:** *www.the-oystercatcher.co.uk; 11 pm; closed Mon & Tue; no Amex.* **Accommodation:** *3 rooms, from ££70.*

Portmeirion Hotel   £53
LL48 6ET   (01766) 770000

On top form of late, the "wonderfully located" dining room of the hotel, in Clough Williams-Ellis's fantasy-Italianate village, offers "fantastic" cooking (if with too many "smears and foams" for some tastes). / **Details:** *www.portmeirion-village.com; off A487 at Minffordd; 9 pm.* **Accommodation:** *14 rooms, from £215.*

Knockinaam Lodge   **£72**   Ⓣ

DG9 9AD   (01776) 810471

*Tipped not least for its "beautiful location", this remote hunting lodge
(with view) attracts few reports, but all of them report food of a notably
"high standard"; Churchill and Eisenhower plotted D Day here!
/ Details: www.knockinaamlodge.com; off A77 at Colfin Smokehouse, follow signs
to lodge; 8.30 pm; no jeans or trainers; children: 12+ after 7 pm.*
Accommodation: *10 rooms, from £280.*

PORTSMOUTH, HAMPSHIRE   2–4D

abarbistro   **£35**   ★

58 White Hart Rd PO1 2JA   (02392) 811585

*It's "always reliable for fresh fish" (in particular), but this "lively" and
"comfortable" harbour-side bistro in fact offers a "very tasty" menu
which "caters for all requirements". / Details: www.abarbistro.co.uk; 2 min
walk from Portsmouth Cathedral; midnight, Sun 10.30 pm.*

Le Café Parisien   **£27**   new   Ⓣ

1 Lord Montgomery Way PO1 2AH   (023) 9283 1234

*"Cosmopolitan", "lively" and "always packed" – this University Quarter
snackery is highly tipped as a "fantastic" breakfast or lunch destination
(including for business); it offers a "massive range of ciabattas, wraps
and panninis and salads, plus more substantial mains".
/ Details: www.lecafeparisien.com; 8 pm; closed Sun; no Amex.*

Loch Fyne   **£28**   Ⓐ

Unit 2 Vulcan Buildings PO1 3TY

*"One of the better branches" in the national seafood chain,
this "handsome" outpost wins consistently good reports for its well-
prepared seafood.*

PRESTON BAGOT, WARWICKSHIRE   5–4C

The Crabmill   **£44**   Ⓐ

B95 5EE   (01926) 843342

*"Sophisticated pub food" and an "excellent summer garden" are the
twin features which win consistent – and widespread – popularity
among reporters for this "trendy" boozer. / Details: www.thecrabmill.co.uk;
on main road between Warwick & Henley-in-Arden; 9.30 pm; closed Sun D;
no Amex; booking essential.*

PRESTON, LANCASHIRE   5–1A

Bukhara   **£19**   ★

154 Preston New Rd PR5 0UP   (01772) 877710

*"Still the best Indian in central Lancashire"; if you're looking for "tasty
food in a fun family environment", this "consistently good" Samlesbury
spot rarely disappoints (assuming you can put up with the absence
of booze, obviously). / Details: www.bukharasamlesbury.co.uk; 11pm; D only;
no Maestro.*

PRIORS HARDWICK, WARWICKSHIRE   2–1D

The Butchers Arms   **£50**   Ⓐ

Church End CV47 7SN   (01327) 260504

*Go with a Portuguese friend for the full – "somewhat bizarre" –
experience of encountering an Iberian pub in the middle of nowhere;
it's "a tad expensive nowadays", but its "warm" service and good
atmosphere win consistent praise. / Details: www.thebutchersarms.com;
off J11/12 of the M40; 9.30 pm; closed Sat L & Sun D.*

Plas Bodegroes £60 ⒶⒶⒶ
Nefyn Rd LL53 5TH (01758) 612363
A veritable "oasis" of "great food at sensible prices"; this "very cosy" and attractive restaurant-with-rooms, just outside the town, is an "excellent all-rounder". / Details: www.bodegroes.co.uk; on A497 1m W of Pwllheli; 9.30 pm; closed Mon, Tue-Sat D only, closed Sun D; no Amex; children: . Accommodation: 11 rooms, from £150.

Dakota Forth Bridge £40 ⒶⒶ
FERRIMUIR RETAIL PARK EH30 9QZ (0870) 423 4293
This "ultra-modern and chic" hotel is something of a surprise just off the M90, near the Forth Road Bridge – even more surprising, it has a "great ambience" and the food's "really very good" too. / Details: www.dakotaforthbridge.co.uk; 10 pm; booking essential. Accommodation: 132 rooms, from £99.00.

Three Horseshoes £40 Ⓐ
Horsehoe Rd, Bennett End HP14 4EB (01494) 483273
"A small restaurant-with-rooms in a former village pub, with nice views and a well-executed, varied menu" – one reporter says it all about this "good-value" Chilterns destination. / Details: www.thethreehorshoes.net; 9.30 pm; closed Mon L & Sun D; no Amex.

Ramsons £68 ⭐
18 Market Pl BL0 9HT (01706) 825070
A "passionate" owner risks doing this potentially "superlative" restaurant no favours at all; nearly all reports extol "unquestionably fine" food and wine ("with an Italian accent"), but this is only a "cramped" little place, and the "exuberant" service can sometimes seem "too full of itself" for comfort. / Details: www.ramsons-restaurant.com; 9.30 pm; closed Mon & Tue L; no Amex; booking: max 10.

Age & Sons £39 Ⓐ
Charlotte Ct CT11 8HE (01843) 851515
"A fantastic find in a bleak town!"; this "improving" restaurant has an "unusual menu", based on "imaginative" use of "fresh local ingredients", and a "good wine list" too; service can be "erratic", though – "sometimes justifying its local nickname: 'Ages to Eat'". / Details: www.ageandsons.com; 10 pm.

Eddie Gilbert's £32 ⭐
32 King St CT11 8NT (01843) 852 123
"Most definitely a find"; this "winning" fish shop/chippy/restaurant attracts almost universally glowing reports; all the dishes are "full of flavour", with "extremely fresh fish", inevitably, the highlight. / Details: www.eddiegilberts.com; 11 pm; closed Sun D.

Yorke Arms £79
HG3 5RL (01423) 755243
"A picture-perfect village in the Yorkshire Dales" provides the setting for Frances & Gerald Atkins's "faultless" country inn; the former is the survey's highest-rated female chef, receiving amazingly consistent acclaim for her "fabulous" food ("brilliant" game, in particular). / *Details:* www.yorke-arms.co.uk; 4m W of Pateley Bridge; 8.45 pm; no Amex. **Accommodation:** 12 rooms, from £150.

READING, BERKSHIRE 2–2D

Forbury's Restaurant & Wine Bar £45
1 Forbury Sq RG1 3BB (0118) 957 4044
"Competent" Gallic cuisine – somewhat "less pretentious" than in the early days – and "excellent" wine has won quite a following for this "formal" city-centre destination; there's a small minority, though, for whom it's a "ghastly" place, with staff who "have an unduly high impression of themselves". / *Details:* www.forburys.com; 10 pm; closed Sun.

London Street Brasserie £47

2-4 London St RG1 4SE (0118) 950 5036

A "friendly" old-favourite near the city-centre, which benefits from a "lovely riverside terrace"; it continues to attract praise for its "fantastic British food", and "prompt" service too. / *Details:* www.londonstbrasserie.co.uk; On the corner of the Oracle shoping centre; 10.30 pm.

Mya Lacarte £39
5 Prospect St, Caversham RG4 8JB (0118) 946 3400
"Simple" dishes from "seasonal, local ingredients" have carved out a big local reputation for this "friendly" Caversham bistro; critics do fear, however, that it's becoming rather "over-rated". / *Details:* www.myalacarte.co.uk; Mon-Thu 10 pm, Fri & Sat 10.30 pm; closed Sun D.

REIGATE, SURREY 3–3B

La Barbe £47
71 Bell St RH2 7AN (01737) 241966
"Always reliable, friendly and busy", this suburban Gallic bistro – in business for over a quarter of a century – continues to please almost all reporters with its "competent" cuisine. / *Details:* www.labarbe.co.uk; 9.30 pm; closed Sat L & Sun D.

Tony Tobin @ The Dining Room £63
59a High St RH2 9AE (01737) 226650
"Still going strong", this TV chef's town-centre veteran continues to offer "well-judged" cuisine (and some "excellent prix-fixe menus"); "standards can occasionally slip", says one regular, "but the service generally saves the day". / *Details:* www.tonytobinrestaurants.co.uk; 10 pm; closed Sat L & Sun D.

The Westerly £42
2-4 London Rd RH2 9AN (01737) 222733
John Coombe's cooking is "outstanding" and his wife Cynthia
is "a perfect front of house", say fans of this town-centre venture;
the room can seem rather "dull", though, and it's "noisy" too.
/ Details: www.thewesterly.co.uk; 10 pm; closed Mon, Tue L, Sat L & Sun.

REYNOLDSTON, SWANSEA   1–1C

Fairyhill £64
SA3 1BS (01792) 390139

"A fine, if not exceptional, meal in absolutely exceptional surroundings"
– that's still the verdict of fans on this remote country house hotel,
known in part for its "large and varied" wine list; not everyone's
convinced though – "problem is, it's not really as good as initial
appearances suggest". / Details: www.fairyhill.net; 20 mins from M4, J47 off
B4295; 9 pm; no Amex; children: 8+ at D. Accommodation: 8 rooms,
from £180.

RICHMOND, SURREY   3–3A

Pizzeria Rustica £34
32 The Quadrant TW9 1DN (020) 8332 6262
"The best pizza in Richmond, and reasonably priced too" –
this restaurant by the railway station attracts a good number of reviews,
and almost invariably positive. / Details: www.pizzeriarustica.co.uk;
11.15 pm.

RIPLEY, SURREY   3–3A

Drakes £65
The Clock Hs, High St GU23 6AQ (01483) 224777
Steve Drake's "striking" flavour combinations gave one reporter his
"best meal ever" this year, and almost all feedback acclaims his cuisine
as "by far the best in the area"; the catch – does the dining room really
need to be so "boring"? / Details: www.drakesrestaurant.co.uk; just beyond
the intersection of A3 and M25 (J10) heading towards Guildford; 9.30 pm; closed
Mon, Sat L & Sun; no Amex; booking: max 12; children: 12+.

RIPON, NORTH YORKSHIRE   8–4B

Bruce Arms £38
Main St HG4 5JJ (01677) 470325
This "traditional Yorkshire pub", on the edge of the Dales, was recently
taken over by a new team; with a chef formerly of the Yorke Arms,
it's already tipped as "one to watch". / Details: www.brucearms.co.uk;
9.30 pm; closed Mon; no Amex. Accommodation: 3 rooms, from £80.

The Old Deanery £37 Ⓐ ✪

Minster Rd HG4 1QS (01765) 600003
*Right by the cathedral, this rambling restaurant-with-rooms occupies
an old building, with panelling and open fires, that's undergone
a "smart", modern make-over; its "imaginative" and "tasty" dishes
impress all who comment on them.* / **Details:** www.theolddeanery.co.uk;
9 pm, Fri & Sat 9.30 pm; closed Sun D; no Amex. **Accommodation:** 11 rooms,
from £130.

RIPPONDEN, WEST YORKSHIRE   5–1C

El Gato Negro Tapas £38 Ⓐ ✪ ✪

1 Oldham Rd HX6 4DN (01422) 823070
*"Better than Barcelona!"... "a revelation" – fans are not shy in their
praise for this "superb" tapas bar in a cheery former boozer, which
"can compete with the big names in London"; NB: "very difficult to get
a table now, after its success on the f-word".*
/ **Details:** www.elgatonegrotapas.com; 9.30 pm, 10 pm Fri & Sat; closed Mon,
Tue, Wed L, Thu L, Fri L & Sun D; no Amex.

ROADE, NORTHAMPTONSHIRE   3–1A

Roade House £46 Ⓣ

16 High St NN7 2NW (01604) 863372
*"A good choice for avoidance of M1 service areas"; it may
be somewhat "austere", but – for those in search of "wholesome" fare
– this restaurant (and hotel) is a "reliable" stand-by.*
/ **Details:** www.roadehousehotel.co.uk; 9 pm; closed Sat L & Sun D; no shorts;
booking essential. **Accommodation:** 10 rooms, from £75.

ROCK, CORNWALL   1–3B

L'Estuaire £45 ✪

Rock Rd PL27 6JS (01208) 862622
*"The food shows great attention to detail" and the service is "genuinely
friendly", at this very highly-rated venture, run by a husband (French)
and wife (Cornish) team; if there's a quibble, it is that the dining room
is rather "poorly proportioned".* / **Details:** www.lestuairerestaurant.com;
9 pm; closed Mon & Tue; no Amex.

Restaurant Nathan Outlaw ✪
The St Enodoc Hotel £95

Pl27 6LA (01208) 863394
*Nathan Outlaw may change restaurants like most people do socks,
but he has still won a reputation as "one of the UK's top dozen chefs";
his latest restaurant (plus brasserie) – with "stunning views across the
Camel estuary" – is hailed by fans as "even better than in Fowey",
but early-days reports (few) also include the odd "unremarkable"
experience.* / **Details:** www.nathan-outlaw.co.uk; midnight; D only, closed
Mon & Sun.

ROCKBEARE, DEVON   1–3D

Jack in the Green Inn £45 Ⓐ

London Rd EX5 2EE (01404) 822240
*"Beloved of those en route to Cornwall", this "always-buzzing" inn
is sought out by many reporters in search of "tasty" fare on the great
journey west.* / **Details:** www.jackinthegreen.uk.com; 2 miles from Exeter airport
on the old A30; 9.30 pm; no Amex.

ROMALDKIRK, COUNTY DURHAM 8–3B

The Rose & Crown £42
DL12 9EB (01833) 650213
"A lovely old hotel and restaurant in a great location" – amidst three
village greens, and with a "lovely country atmosphere";
the worst complaint this year? – "service is sometimes a little too jolly!"
/ **Details:** www.rose-and-crown.co.uk; 6m NW of Barnard Castle on B6277;
9 pm; no Amex; children: 6+ in restaurant. **Accommodation:** 12 rooms,
from £140.

ROSEVINE, CORNWALL 1–4B

Driftwood
Driftwood Hotel £62
TR2 5EW (01872) 580644

A "beautiful coastal location", "well-executed seafood dishes",
and "exemplary service" – the formula that inspires consistently
positive reports on the dining room of this stylish, modern hotel.
/ **Details:** www.driftwoodhotel.co.uk; Off the A30 to Truro, towards St Maees;
9.30 pm; D only; booking: max 6; children: 8+. **Accommodation:** 15 rooms,
from £195.

ROWDE, WILTSHIRE 2–2C

George & Dragon £44
High St SN10 2PN (01380) 723053
A "well-run" and "attractive" old pub, where the "serious" menu –
featuring "lots of fish" – is generally notably well realised.
/ **Details:** www.thegeorgeanddragonrowde.co.uk; on A342 between Devizes &
Chippenham; 10, Sat 6.30; closed Sun D; booking: max 8. **Accommodation:** 3
rooms, from £55 week 105 wkend.

ROWHOOK, WEST SUSSEX 3–4A

Chequers Inn £41
RH12 3PY (01403) 790480
"Attractive", "reliable" and "good for lunch or dinner" – this recently-
refurbished inn is a destination rated "reliable" or better by all who
comment on it. / **Details:** www.chequersrowhook.com; 9 pm; closed Sun D;
no Amex.

RYE, EAST SUSSEX 3–4C

Landgate Bistro £36
5-6 Landgate TN31 7LH (01797) 222829
"A joy to find such accomplished food and helpful service on a day-trip
to the coast!" – so say all reports on this "tiny" venture, where the
menu is "simple", "honest" and locally-sourced.
/ **Details:** www.landgatebistro.co.uk; below Landgate Arch; 9.30 pm; closed Mon,
Tue, Wed L, Thu L, Fri L & Sun D.

Tuscan Kitchen £50   Ⓐ✪✪

8 Lion St TN31 7LB (01797 223269) 223269
A "cosy, small, beamed" newcomer from Tuscan chef Franco and his
wife Jen, with a formula that lives up to the name – a "warm welcome"
and "no frills, but excellent food with a varied menu that changes
regularly". / **Details:** www.tuscankitchenrye.co.uk; 10 pm; closed Mon,
Tue, Wed, Thu L & Sat L.

Webbes at the Fish Café £40   Ⓐ

17 Tower St TN31 7AT (01797) 222210
Tipped for "fresh and well-cooked fish dishes" – a café sibling to the
Wild Mushroom and Webbe's Rock-a-Nore.
/ **Details:** www.thefishcafe.com; 9 pm; children: 10+ at D.

SALISBURY, WILTSHIRE 2–3C

Anokaa £36   Ⓐ✪✪

60 Fisherton St SP2 7RB (01722) 414142
"A voyage of discovery for the tongue!" – this "classy and creative"
Indian serves up some "beautiful" and "exotic" dishes, and "with a
flourish" too. / **Details:** www.anokaa.com; 10.30 pm; no shorts.

SALTAIRE, WEST YORKSHIRE 5–1C

Salts Diner £30   Ⓐ

Salts Mill, Victoria Rd BD18 3LB (01274) 530533
"A great destination for seeing industrial heritage mixed with good
contemporary food and shopping" – this mill-turned-arts-centre serves
"really good" food, which it dishes up with surprising consistency.
/ **Details:** www.saltsmill.org.uk; 2m from Bradford on A650; L & afternoon tea
only; no Amex.

SALTHOUSE, NORFOLK 6–3C

Cookies Crab Shop £16   ✪✪

The Grn, Coast Rd NR25 7AJ (01263) 740352
"No-frills dining in an outdoor shed" – the deal that makes this coastal
operation a "real little gem" for those in search of "plates packed full
of fresh tasty fish", plus "very good salads", and all at "reasonable
prices"; "wrap up warm", though. / **Details:** www.salthouse.org.uk; on A149;
7.30 pm; no credit cards.

SANDSEND, NORTH YORKSHIRE 8–3D

Estbek House £57   Ⓐ✪

East Row YO21 3SU (01947) 893424
"Fish dishes prepared with a light touch using the local catch" are the
highlight culinary attraction at this "especially friendly" restaurant-with-
rooms, "right by the beach"; notable New World wine list too.
/ **Details:** www.estbekhouse.co.uk; 9 pm; D only; no Amex. **Accommodation:** 4
rooms, from £125.

SAPPERTON, GLOUCESTERSHIRE 2–2C

The Bell at Sapperton £44   Ⓐ✪

GL7 6LE (01285) 760298
It's quite a smart destination – "first pub I've encountered with copies
of Tatler!" – and this "beautiful old inn" is consistently well-rated
by reporters for its sometimes "excellent" fare, and its "lovely"
atmosphere too. / **Details:** www.foodatthebell.co.uk; from Cirencester take the
A419 towards Stroud, turn right to Sapperton; 9.30 pm; no Amex; no booking
at L; children: 10+ at D.

The Straw Hat Oriental   £42   **T**
Harrow Rd CM21 0AJ (01279) 722434
This Asian-fusion restaurant in a thatched cottage attracts frustratingly little feedback… all reports there are suggest that it's of the highest quality! / **Details:** www.strawhat-oriental.co.uk; On the A1184, 1m south of Sawbridgeworth; 11 pm, Sun 9.30 pm; no shorts; children: no children after 9 pm.

The Spread Eagle   £36   **A**
BB7 4NH (01200) 441202
"Completely restyled by the new owners", this "lovely" pub overlooking the River Ribble has yet to attract a huge volume of reports, but all say the food is "really good". / **Details:** www.spreadeaglesawley.co.uk; 9.30 pm, Sun 7.30 pm.

Bell Hotel   £37   ⭐
31 High St IP17 1AF (01728) 602331
"Good food, but lacking in atmosphere"; there's not much doubt that Andrew Blackburn is an "extremely talented" chef, but neither setting nor service at this "sombre" 17th-century coaching inn really live up. / **Details:** www.bellhotel-saxmundham.co.uk; 9 pm. **Accommodation:** 10 rooms, from £90.

Lanterna   £52   ⭐
33 Queen St YO11 1HQ (01723) 363616
There's a good number of reports on this "authentic" and "friendly" family-run Italian fish-specialist – "an old favourite" that's something of "an unexpected gem" hereabouts. / **Details:** www.giorgioalessio.co.uk; near the Old Town; 9.30 pm; D only, closed Sun; no Amex.

The White Room   **A**
Seaham Hall   £80
Lord Byron's Walk SR7 7AG (0191) 516 1400
Just as he was making a real name for the place, the former chef at this grand (von Essen) country house hotel (and spa) left during our survey year; early reports on the new régime are somewhat conflicting, to the extent that we've 'ducked' a rating till next year. / **Details:** www.seaham-hall.co.uk; 9.45 pm; D only, ex Sun open L & D; no trainers; booking: max 8. **Accommodation:** 19 rooms, from £300.

The Vine   £53   **A**
11 Pound Ln TN13 3TB (01732) 469510
"This lovely place overlooks England's oldest cricket ground, and a couple of the original 'seven oaks' too!" – a bright restaurant with "consistently good" food (with puddings rating special mention); service was quite a "let-down", though, for a couple of reporters this year. / **Details:** www.vinerestaurant.co.uk; 11 pm; closed Sun D; no Amex.

Ode £52

Fore St TQ14 0DE (01626) 873977
"A Devon gem!"; Tim Bouget's establishment in an "attractive" village
is tipped as "lovely small bistro" (if possibly on the expensive side for
what it is). / **Details:** www.odetruefood.co.uk; 9.30 pm; closed Mon, Tue L,
Wed L, Sat L & Sun; no Amex; booking essential.

Aagrah £30

Unit 1 Leopold Sq, Leopold St S1 2JG (0114) 279 5577
With its "great range of well-made dishes", this superior modern curry
house is a worthy outpost of the famous NE chain, and one of the
best places to eat in the city-centre. / **Details:** www.aagrah.com; Mon-Thu
11.30 pm, Fri & Sat midnight; D only.

Artisan £44

32-34 Sandygate Rd S10 5RY (0114) 266 6096
Richard Smith's "classy-modern-suburban" bistro is tipped for its
"very well prepared" dishes, from "excellent local produce".
/ **Details:** www.relaxeatanddrink.com; 10 pm; no Amex.

Café Ceres £18

390 Sharrowvale Rd S11 8ZP (0114) 267 9090
Looking for a "real French bistro"? - with its "Gallic-provincial cooking"
and "cramped French-style setting", this village eatery is tipped
as just the place. / **Details:** Fri & Sat 9.30 pm; Mon-Thu L only, closed Sun.

The Milestone £39

84 Green Lane At Ball St S3 8SE (0114) 272 8327
There's a "more formal" restaurant upstairs, but it's the "buzzing" bar
which inspires most reports on this "excellent" gastropub, which serves
"comfort food" in "hearty portions". / **Details:** www.the-milestone.co.uk.

Nirmals £30

189-193 Glossop Rd S10 2GW (0114) 272 4054
This "welcoming" family-run Indian veteran is still sometimes tipped for
its "delicious" cuisine; of late, however, reports have been more
inconsistent. / **Details:** www.nirmals.com; near West St; Mon-Thu Midnight,
Fri & Sat 1 am; closed Sun L.

Nonna's £37

539-541 Eccleshall Rd S11 8PR (0114) 268 6166

If you're looking for "a genuine Mediterranean flavour", this Eccleshall
spot is "the best Italian" hereabouts — "slightly crazy" and "frenetic",
"but with great food"; it now also has an offshoot in Chesterfield.
/ **Details:** www.nonnas.co.uk; M1, J33 towards Bakewell; 9.45 pm; no Amex.

The Old Vicarage £72

Ridgeway Moor, Ridgeway S12 3XW (0114) 247 5814

Recent reports on this celebrated restaurant – which is "somehow Michelin-starred" – have once again turned overwhelmingly negative; even those who speak of "superb" cooking may find the wine list "vastly overpriced" and service "very poor", and some visits are described as simply "nightmarish". / **Details:** www.theoldvicarage.co.uk; 10 mins SE of city centre; 9.30 pm; closed Mon, Sat L & Sun; no Amex.

Rafters £47

220 Oakbrook Rd, Nether Grn S11 7ED (0114) 230 4819

"Probably Sheffield's best" – this "intimate" restaurant in Ranmoor ("which looks nothing from the outside") is acclaimed by most reporters for its "very good" food and (especially) service; not everyone is quite convinced, though, and the ambience of its first-floor premises is "variable". / **Details:** www.raftersrestaurant.co.uk; 10 pm; D only, closed Tue & Sun.

Silversmiths £29

111 Arundel St S1 2NT (0114) 270 6160

A two-year-old venture in the city's 'Cultural Quarter', tipped for its sometimes "brilliant" dishes. / **Details:** www.silversmiths-restaurant.com; 11.30 pm, Fri & Sat midnight; D only, closed Sun; no Amex.

SHELLEY, WEST YORKSHIRE 5–2C

Three Acres £50

Roydhouse HD8 8LR (01484) 602606

Despite a "bleak" and "isolated" location on Emlyn Moor, this rural inn ("which feels a lot like a restaurant") still pulls in the crowds; fans say it's a "cracking" place "ticking all the boxes for quality", but a minority (mainly former fans) fear it has "expanded so much" of late that its approach smacks of "mass catering". / **Details:** www.3acres.com; near Emley Moor TV tower; 9.30 pm; no Amex. **Accommodation:** 20 rooms, from £120.

SHEPTON MALLET, SOMERSET 2–3B

Charlton House £44

Charlton Rd BA4 4PR (01749) 342008

A sizable country house hotel, whose dining room is tipped as a "good if expensive" destination for "fresh, local food cooked to perfection" (and "a great kids' menu" too). / **Details:** www.charltonhouse.com; on A361 towards Frome; 9 pm, Fri & Sat 10 pm. **Accommodation:** 27 rooms, from £95.

Fortune Palace £28 **T**
Yeovil Rd DT9 4RB (01935) 414380
*Too few reports for a grading, but this Chinese restaurant in a
converted car showroom is tipped for its "authentic" cuisine,
and "helpful" service. / Details: www.fortunepalace.info; A30 Dual
carriageway ; closed Tue.*

The Green £41 ★
The Green DT9 3HY (01935) 813821
*An "elegant" restaurant where the service is "very attentive" and the
wines "well-priced"; the cooking is "very enjoyable" too, "albeit from
a rather limited menu". / Details: 9 pm; closed Mon & Sun; no Amex.*

King's Arms £39 **A**
Charlton Horethorne DT9 4NL (01963) 220281
*"The best newcomer hereabouts" – this "sumptuously refurbished
gastropub and hotel" offers "well-presented" food, and "attentive"
service too. / Details: www.thekingsarms.co.uk; mon - thur 930 pm fri -sat
10pm sun 9pm; no Amex. Accommodation: 10 rooms, from £105.*

Three Wishes £30 **T**
78 Cheap St DT9 3BJ (01935) 817777
*Tipped for its "good bistro-type fare", a simple outfit, with "excellent
staff"; parents NB – they are "very understanding of their junior
customers". / Details: www.thethreewishes.co.uk; 9 pm; closed Sun-Thu D;
no Amex.*

Kinghams £52 **A**
Gomshall Ln GU5 9HE (01483) 202168
*This "picture-postcard" cottage-restaurant impresses most reporters
with its "interesting" cuisine and its "cosy" (some people think
"too cosy") ambience; critics, however, may find the style a little
"dated". / Details: www.kinghams-restaurant.co.uk; off A25 between Dorking &
Guildford; 9 pm; closed Mon & Sun D.*

L'Ortolan £91 **A**
Church Ln RG2 9BY (0118) 988 8500
*Alan Murchison's '10 [stars] in 8 [years]' group bizarrely measures its
prospective success in Michelin terms – no surprise, then, that the
atmosphere at his original venture, in a former refectory, is often rather
"hushed", or that the food comes at prices which can seem "sky-high"
for what it is. / Details: www.alanmurchisonrestaurants.co.uk; J11, take first exit
left on all three roundabouts, then follow sign posts; 9 pm, 9.30 pm; closed
Mon & Sun.*

The Chaser Inn £35 ★
Stumble Hill TN11 9PE (01732) 810360
*"Consistently good food" is the drift of almost all commentary on this
"good-value" gastroboozer (which is "fun for a grown-up night out,
and good with children at the weekend too"); now, if they just put a bit
more effort in on the service front… / Details: www.thechaser.co.uk;
9.30 pm, Sun 9 pm; no Amex.*

Aagrah £32

4 Saltaire Rd BD18 3HN (01274) 530880

"Top-quality food with an extra twist" makes this *"consistently excellent"* curry house – amongst the highest rated in this impressive Yorkshire chain – *"one of the stand-outs in the Bradford area"*.
/ **Details:** www.aagrah.com; 11.30 pm; closed Sat L.

Chesters £32

LA22 9NN (01539) 432553

"Only a café, but a really really nice one" (with a *"lovely"* river-edge setting); it's tipped for *"gorgeous cakes"*, but the savouries can satisfy too. / **Details:** www.chesters-cafebytheriver.co.uk; 5 pm, Sat & Sun 5.30 pm; no Amex.

The Bell at Skenfrith £46

NP7 8UH (01600) 750235

"In the middle of nowhere", it may be, but this *"sophisticated"* gastropub has made quite a name for its *"very good, inexpensive and well chosen wine list"*; the food is usually good, too, although portions can be *"small"* (*"like you might find in the metropolis!"*).
/ **Details:** www.skenfrith.co.uk; on B4521, 10m E of Abergavenny; 9.30 pm, Sun 9 pm; no Amex; children: 8+ at D. **Accommodation:** 11 rooms, from £110.

Kinloch Lodge £ 45

IV43 8QY (01471) 833333

"Going from strength to strength", the *"welcoming"*, loch-side ancestral home of the Macdonald of Macdonald continues to extend a *"peerless"* welcome to visitors; the food almost invariably satisfies too – the multi-course lunch menu, in particular, offers *"exceptional value for money"*.
/ **Details:** www.kinloch-lodge.co.uk; 9 pm; no Amex. **Accommodation:** 14 rooms, from £150.

Richard Phillips at Chapel Down £46

Tenterden Vineyard TN30 7NG (01580) 761616

Most accounts praise *"beautiful"* dishes, made from *"excellent ingredients"*, at this *"delightful"*, *"relaxed"* and *"airy"* vineyard restaurant (and *"great English wines too, of course"*); critics say the food is *"fine, rather than inspiring"*, though, and don't really rate the service. / **Details:** www.richardphillipsatchapeldown.co.uk; 9.45 pm; closed Mon D, Tue D, Wed D & Sun D.

The Crown Inn £36

Bridge Rd IP17 1SL (01728) 688324

Owned by Adnams, this village inn, near the Snape Maltings concert hall, is strongly tipped by its small local fan club for the consistency of its cuisine. / **Details:** www.snape-crown.co.uk; off A12 towards Aldeburgh; 9.30 pm, Sat 10 pm; no Amex.

SOLIHULL, WEST MIDLANDS   5–4C

Town House   £39   ★
727 Warwick Rd B91 3DA (0121) 704 1567
"A gem in a sea of tourist tat"; "fabulous locally-sourced food"
("some of it from only 20 yards away") is utilised to create some "great
pub food" at this recently-revamped boozer.
/ **Details:** www.thetown-house.com.

SONNING-ON-THAMES, BERKSHIRE   2–2D

Bull Inn   £41   Ⓐ
High St RG4 6UP (0118) 969 3901
A "fantastic olde-worlde pub", which "hasn't any pretensions to being
a gastropub" – with its "robust and tasty food", however,
some reporters feel that it should have!
/ **Details:** www.bullinn@fullers.co.uk; off A4, J10 between Oxford & Windsor;
9.30 pm; no booking. **Accommodation:** 7 rooms, from £85.

The French Horn   £81   Ⓐ
RG4 6TN (0118) 969 2204
"Stuck in a time warp" it may be, but this "old-school" fixture still quite
a name for its "perfect setting by the Thames", and for the
quality of its spit-roast duck; critics may decry the atmosphere
as "stuffy" and "unimaginative", but for most reporters this remains
a "wonderful" treasure. **Details:** www.thefrenchhorn.co.uk; M4, J8 or J9,
then A4; 9.30 pm; booking: max 10. **Accommodation:** 21 rooms, from £170.

SOUTH SHIELDS, TYNE AND WEAR   8–2B

Colman's   £28   ★★
182-186 Ocean Rd NE33 2JQ (0191) 456 1202
"They can't be faulted for freshly cooked fish and chips", and, if you eat
in, the ambience in the "sparkling clean" restaurant is judged
"wonderful" too ("by chippy standards", obviously).
/ **Details:** www.colmansfishandchips.com; L only; no Amex.

SOUTHAMPTON, HAMPSHIRE   2–3D

Kuti's   £32   Ⓣ
37-39 Oxford St SO14 3DP (023) 8022 1585
Again tipped as "still the best restaurant in Southampton", an Indian
'brasserie' commended by all reporters for its "continuing high
standards". / **Details:** www.kutis.co.uk; near Stanley Casino; 11 pm.

Vatika   £55   Ⓐ★
Botley Rd SO32 2HL (01329) 830 405
Quite "a find" overlooking a "glorious" Hampshire vineyard,
this "beautiful" contemporary restaurant serves up "top-notch" dishes
created by Atul Kochar, of Benares (a top London Indian) fame;
the prices, though, would seem equally at home in Mayfair.
/ **Details:** www.vatikarestaurant.com; 9.30 pm; closed Mon, Tue, Wed L, Thu L &
Sun D.

SOUTHEND-ON-SEA, ESSEX   3–3C

The Pipe of Port   £35   Ⓣ
84 High St SS1 1JN (01702) 614606
"A Southend institution", this sawdust-floored cellar wine bar is tipped
for its "great wine list", and "the best steak and mushroom pie in the
world" too. / **Details:** www.pipeofport.co.uk; basement just off High Street;
10.30 pm; closed Sun; no Amex; children: 16+.

Michael's   £36   **A** ✪ ✪
47 Liverpool Rd PR8 4AG   (01704) 550886
*It may look "just like a café", but Michael Wichmann's modestly-scaled
venture is "wonderful from start to finish" — the setting is "convivial",
service "friendly without being intrusive", and the "expert" cooking
simply "a delight". / **Details**: www.michaelsbirkdale.co.uk; 2 minutes walk from
Birkdale train station; 10 pm; D only, closed Mon & Sun.*

The Swan at Southrop   £41   **A** ✪
GL7 3NU   (01367) 850205
*"Worth a trip down the winding country lanes", this "rustic" operation
"brings top-end food to the backwoods of Gloucestershire";
"it's supposed to be a gastropub", says one reporter, "but it's more like
a proper restaurant with a great menu".
/ **Details**: www.theswanatsouthrop.co.uk; 10 pm; closed Sun D; no Amex.*

Coasters   £42   **T**
Queen street IP18 6EQ   (01502) 724734
*"A great find"; this "unpretentious and welcoming" small restaurant
(with courtyard) is tipped for its "lovely British food", and service that's
"friendly without being over-familiar".
/ **Details**: www.coastersofsouthwold.co.uk; 2 min walk from seafront and Market
square; 9pm; closed Mon & Sun D; no Amex; booking essential.*

The Crown   **A**
Adnams Hotel   £41
High St IP18 6DP   (01502) 722275
*With its "welcoming" and "bustling" style, Adnams' famous inn "still
pulls in the crowds"; most of the credit for that must go to the "great
atmosphere", however, and the "very good wines" (with a large
selection by the glass) — the "reliable" food is something of a supporting
attraction. / **Details**: www.adnamshotels.co.uk; 9 pm, Fri & Sat 9.30 pm.
Accommodation: 14 rooms, from £145.*

Sole Bay Fish Company   £29   **T**
22e Blackshore IP18 6ND   (01502) 724241
*"The fish is so fresh but then, it is right by the side of the harbour so it
should be!" — this basic shop/café is tipped for its "great seafood
platter"; BYO — both bread and wine. / **Details**: www.solebayfish.co.uk;
closed Mon.*

Sutherland House   £43   **A** ✪
56 High St IP18 6DN   (01502) 724544
*"Fantastic cooking" (so locally-sourced the menu shows food miles!)
is complemented by a "rounded and interesting wine list", at this
"friendly" restaurant in a 15th-century building; the only reservation? —
"it's best when the owners are about".
/ **Details**: www.sutherlandhouse.co.uk; 9.30 pm; closed Mon.
Accommodation: 3 rooms, from £140.*

Gimbals   £38   **T**
76 Wharf St HX6 2AF   (01422) 839329
*"In a valley crowded with strong competition", a family-run bistro tipped
for its "imaginative" cuisine; "thanks to the new mid-week offers,
it's never empty". / **Details**: www.gimbals.co.uk; 9.15 pm; D only, closed Sun;
no Amex.*

The Millbank £40 ⭐

Millbank Rd HX6 3DY (01422) 825588

*"Idyllic" location, "cracking" views and "great" food – the gist of all commentary on this "hidden-away" inn. / **Details:** www.themillbank.com; The M62, between junctions 22 and 23; 9.30 pm, Fri & Sat 10 pm, Sun 8 pm; closed Mon; no Amex.*

SPARSHOLT, HAMPSHIRE 2–3D

The Plough Inn £42 🅣

SO21 2NW (01962) 776353

*This "always-welcoming" hostelry is tipped for its "consistently reliable" and "fresh-tasting" food, and its "charming" staff; "to call it a gastropub would be unfair – it's a proper pub with great food!" / **Details:** www.theploughsparsholt.co.uk; 9 pm, Sun & Mon 8.30 pm, Fri & Sat 9.30 pm; no Amex.*

SPEEN, BUCKINGHAMSHIRE 3–2A

The Old Plow £44 🅐

Flowers Bottom Ln HP27 0PZ (01494) 488300

*"A great place... once you find it" – this "comfortable" Chilterns pub-conversion offers high-quality food in both a bistro and a grander restaurant; it "verges on expensive", however, and service can seem a touch "stern". / **Details:** www.yeoldplow.co.uk; 20 mins from M40, J4 towards Princes Risborough; 9 pm; closed Mon & Sun.*

ST ALBANS, HERTFORDSHIRE 3–2A

The Albany £39 🅐

7 George St AL3 4ER (01727) 730888

*This "good local" has quite a name hereabouts, and most (if not quite all) reporters praise its "excellent" food, "attentive" service and "lovely ambience". / **Details:** www.albanyrestaurant.co.uk; 10.30 pm; closed Mon, Tue L, Wed L, Thu L & Sun D.*

La Cosa Nostra £32 🅐

62 Lattimore Rd AL1 3XR (01727) 832658

*This "frenetic" Italian is renowned locally as "a lovely friendly place", offering "above-average pasta" and the "best pizza around"; even the odd fan, though, can find its formula "a little stale". / **Details:** near railway station; 10.30 pm; closed Sat L & Sun; no Amex.*

Darcy's £48 🅐

2 Hatfield Rd AL1 3RP (01727) 730777

*An "enjoyable" city-centre option; some reporters feel it "tries to be too trendy", but on most accounts it's "a good local" serving "reliable" fare "without fuss". / **Details:** www.darcysrestaurant.co.uk; 9 pm, Fri & Sat 10 pm.*

Kashu £38

9 Hatfield Rd AL1 3RR (01727) 854436

"A well-designed brasserie-style operation in the town centre" – this "light and airy" operation, in a former club, is already being tipped as "a very welcome addition to the local scene".
/ **Details:** www.kashu.co.uk; 10.30 pm; closed Sun D.

Lussmanns £40

Waxhouse Gate, High Street AL3 4EW (01727) 851941

For "an OK meal in a city over-run with run-of-the-mill Italians", this "modern" venture generally wins a thumbs-up from reporters – it offers "well-presented food", a "relaxed" style and a "good location" too (opposite the Abbey).
/ **Details:** www.lussmans.com; Off the High Street, close to the cathedral; 10 pm, Fri & Sat 10.30 pm, Sun 9 pm.

Mumtaj £26

115 London Rd AL1 1LR (01727) 843691

*"It looks ordinary on the outside", but this "old-school curry house" is worth seeking out for its "good range of dishes" (which include "some interesting options"). / **Details:** midnight.*

St Michael's Manor £58

Fishpool St AL3 4RY (01727) 864444

A "lovely" riverside setting provides the "beautiful" backdrop to a meal at this country house hotel; even fans, though, say the "food doesn't justify the prices", and service can sometimes be a let-down too.
/ **Details:** www.stmichaelsmanor.com; near the Cathedral; 9 pm.
Accommodation: 30 rooms, from £180.

Sazio £32

5a, High St AL3 4ED (01727) 812683

*"A crowded and very popular Italian"; "it can be a bit hit-and-miss", but mostly it's tipped as the former. / **Details:** www.sazio.co.uk; 10.30 pm.*

The Waffle House
Kingsbury Water Mill £24

St Michael's St AL3 4SJ (01727) 853502

*"In a beautiful old water mill" with an "olde-worlde interior", this long-standing snackery is tipped as absolutely "great" ("so long as you like waffles!"). / **Details:** www.wafflehouse.co.uk; near Roman Museum; 6 pm; L only; no Amex; no booking.*

ST ANDREWS, FIFE 9–3D

Seafood Restaurant £70

The Scores KY16 9AB (01334) 479475

It's not just the "stunning location" – with "spectacular views over the bay" – that wins praise for this striking glass box, which literally (or perhaps 'littorally'?) hangs over the water; its "simple" seafood ("so fresh it's only just dead") is "full of flavour".
/ **Details:** www.theseafoodrestaurant.com; 9.30 pm; no shorts; children: 12+ at D.

Vine Leaf £46

131 South St KY16 9UN (01334) 477497

*"In a time warp, but undoubtedly well run", the Hamilton family's veteran bistro offers "a huge menu for such a small restaurant", but "everything is good". / **Details:** www.vineleafstandrews.co.uk; 9.30 pm; D only, closed Mon & Sun. **Accommodation:** 3 guest apartments rooms, from £80.*

(A)

Warpool Court
Warpool Court Hotel £56
SA62 6BN (01437) 720300
*"A slightly old-fashioned hotel" on the coast, tipped for its "fabulous"
views and "excellent" restaurant; "can't work out why it's not featured
in the guide before", says one reporter... "we must have been keeping
it to ourselves". / **Details:** www.warpoolcourthotel.com; 9 pm.*
Accommodation: 22 rooms, from £105.

(T)

The Kinmel Arms £47
The Village LL22 9BP (01745) 832207
*"There's always a good welcome", say fans of this former inn; it "tries
hard", and – even if "standards vary a little" – is tipped for its
"interesting" menu. / **Details:** www.thekinmelarms.co.uk; From Chester,
J24a on A55, turn left into village; 9.30 pm; closed Mon & Sun; no Amex.*
Accommodation: 4 rooms, from £135.

(★)

Alba Restaurant £39
The Old Life Boat Hs, Wharf Rd TR26 1LF (01736) 797222
*"Book early, and ask for an upstairs window seat for the best views",
at this waterside spot, overlooking St Ives bay; fans say it "never
disappoints" for "very fresh and delicious fish", and the early-evening
menu offers "good value" too. / **Details:** www.thealbarestaurant.com;
9.30 pm.*

(A)

Porthgwidden Beach Café £38
Porthgwidden Beach TR26 1SL (01736) 796791
*"Perfect at any time of day, but especially for breakfast and dinner" –
this lesser-known sibling to the Porthminster Café is a "relaxed" and
"well-priced" spot, with "phenomenal" views.
/ **Details:** www.porthgwiddencafe.co.uk; 10 pm; no Amex; booking: max 10.*

(A)(★)(★)

Porthminster Café £45
Porthminster Beach TR26 2EB (01736) 795352
*"Fabulous" Asian/modern European fish dishes and "a perfect location
with the most exquisite views" combine to make this beachside fish
restaurant one of the UK's most consistently popular destinations;
the worst criticism? – the friendly service "can sometimes be a bit
casual". / **Details:** www.porthminstercafe.co.uk; near railway station; 10 pm;
no Amex.*

(★)

The Seafood Café £32
45 Fore St TR26 1HE (01736) 794004
*"Outstanding" fish draws many admirers to this "cheerful" and
"brightly-lit" café, where "you choose your dish from the chill cabinet,
then pick 'n' mix with veg' and sauces". / **Details:** www.seafoodcafe.co.uk;
map on website; 10.30 pm; no Amex.*

(T)

Tate Cafe
Tate Gallery £25
Porthmeor Beach TR26 1TG (01736) 791122
*"Perched on the top floor", with "amazing" sea views, this "simply-
furnished café" is often tipped as a super spot for "tasty snacks and
cakes"; at peak times, though, you may feel as if you're being processed
on a "a very busy conveyor belt". / **Details:** www.tate.org.uk; L only;
no Amex.*

A

St Kew Inn   £36
PL30 3HB   (01208) 841259
*Local hero chef Paul Ripley is in charge at this "cosy" north Cornwall gastropub "gem", in a tiny hamlet; the occasional doubter "expected better of an ex-Seafood Restaurant chef", but on most accounts the place is going "from strength to strength". / **Details:** www.stkewinn.co.uk; just off the A39, between Wadebridge and Camelford; 11 pm; no Amex; children: no children in bar.*

T

St Clement's   £43
3 Mercatoria   TN38 0EB   (01424) 200355
*A short walk from the front – a simple, modern fish bistro consistently tipped for the high standard of its cuisine. / **Details:** www.stclementsrestaurant.co.uk; 10 pm; closed Mon & Sun D; no Amex.*

A

Walletts Court   £55
Westcliffe   CT15 6EW   (01304) 852424
*A short hop from the White Cliffs, this county house hotel (and spa), has long been one of the area's culinary 'heavy-hitters'; recent reports, however, suggest the food risks becoming "pedestrian" and "expensive". / **Details:** www.wallettscourt.com; on A258 towards Deal, 3m NE of Dover; 9 pm; children: 8+ at D. **Accommodation:** 17 rooms, from £120.*

A ⭐

Hotel Tresanton   £57
27 Lower Castle Rd   TR2 5DR   (01326) 270055
*If only the UK had more spots like Olga Polizzi's seaside "stunner", with its "idyllic setting" (especially on the "relaxed outside terrace", from which you can best enjoy the view), its "delightful" food and its "wonderfully laid-back" style; "surprisingly child-friendly" too. / **Details:** www.tresanton.com; near Castle; 9.30 pm; booking: max 10; children: 6+ at dinner. **Accommodation:** 29 rooms, from £240.*

A ⭐⭐

The Seafood Restaurant   £52
16 West End   KY10 2BX   (01333) 730327
*"A small and cosy dining room" (sibling to the striking St Andrews restaurant of the same name) "with lovely views over the harbour to the Firth of Forth"; as the name hints, there's "plenty of fresh fish on the menu", and fans say "nowhere does it better". / **Details:** www.theseafoodrestaurant.com; 9.30 pm; closed Mon & Tue; children: 5+.*

A

The Crazy Bear   £53
Bear Ln   OX44 7UR   (01865) 890714
*"Quirky" and decadent decor creates an interior "with a charm all of its own", at this "fun" and "bustling" gastropub; opinions differ on whether the "rustic English" menu is to be preferred to the Thai one, but either way the bill can end up seeming "exorbitant". / **Details:** www.crazybeargroup.co.uk; 10 pm; children: Not D FRi, Sat. **Accommodation:** 17 rooms, from £235.*

Fratellis   £38   Ⓐ
13 St Mary's Hill PE9 2DP   (01780) 754333
*"Sound" cooking (including "rustic and hearty pizza and pasta") makes this town-centre Italian a very useful destination; its interior – part of a 12th century building – is "very good" too, and includes an atmospheric cellar. / **Details:** www.fratellis.co.uk; 9.30 pm.*

The George Hotel   £65   Ⓐ
71 St Martins PE9 2LB   (01780) 750750
*"One of the country's great coaching inns – from its panelled dining room to the cobbled courtyard"; this "old-fashioned" bastion "in a gem of a Georgian town" is most notable for its "beautiful" interior and its "wide and varied" wine list – the food, though, can rather "pricey" for what it is. / **Details:** www.georgehotelofstamford.com; off A1, 14m N of Peterborough, onto B1081; 10 pm; jacket and/or tie; children: 8+ at D. **Accommodation:** 47 rooms, from £140.*

Jim's Yard   £41   Ⓐ⭐
3 Ironmonger St PE9 1PL   (01780) 756080
*"Quietly located" in the centre of this charming town, a "very pleasant feeling", "semi-bistro-style" operation in a conservatory praised for its "attentive, but not overpowering" service and "quality" dishes at "affordable" prices. / **Details:** www.jimsyard.biz; 9.30 pm; closed Mon & Sun; no Amex.*

Leaping Hare Vineyard   £42   Ⓐ⭐
Wyken Vineyards IP31 2DW   (01359) 250287

*An "all-round great experience" is to be had at this café within a beautiful old high-ceilinged barn "in the middle of nowhere"; the "superb" food is "a steal", and "with the added bonus of a very good wine list". / **Details:** www.wykenvineyards.co.uk; 9m NE of Bury St Edmunds; follow tourist signs off A143; 9 pm; L only, ex Fri & Sat open L & D; no Amex.*

Red Lion Inn   £39   Ⓐ⭐
2 Red Lion St LE14 4HS   (01949) 860868
*"More pubby than its more famous sibling, the Olive Branch, Clipsham", this extremely popular rural gastropub, near Belvoir Castle, is "a really genuine" kind of place, offering "good, country-style cooking", "excellent local beers" and "interesting wines". / **Details:** www.theredlioninn.co.uk; 9.30 pm; closed Sun D; no Amex.*

Clos du Marquis   £48   ⭐
London Rd   SO20 6DE   (01264) 810738
"What good restaurants in France used to be like!" – this "small and excellent" rural place offers "appetising Gallic country cooking" (in "hearty" portions), and "very good" service too. / **Details:** *www.closdumarquis.co.uk; 2m E on A30 from Stockbridge; 9 pm; closed Mon & Sun D.*

Greyhound   £41   Ⓐ⭐
31 High St   SO20 6EY   (01264) 810833
"A fabulous pub/restaurant in a part of the world where such things are a rarity" – on all accounts a "delightful place with delicious food". / **Details:** *www.thegreyhound.info; 9 pm; closed Sun D; no Amex; booking: max 12.* **Accommodation:** *7 rooms, from £95.*

Mayfly   £38   Ⓐ
Testcombe   SO20 6AZ   (01264) 860283
"A great riverside spot for a summer pub lunch"; this "friendly and efficient" pub, very scenically located on the River Test, makes a great sunny-day destination, offering "good standard pub fare" at "reasonable prices". / **Details:** *9 pm; no Amex; no booking, except weekday L.*

The Vineyard at Stockcross   £96   Ⓐ
RG20 8JU   (01635) 528770
Daniel Galmiche's take-over of the stoves at this modern ("rather 'Hollywood'") country house hotel has yet to enable it really to square up against its top-price peers; "one of the UK's best New World wine lists" – much of it from owner Sir Peter Michael's own estate – is, however, an undisputed attraction. / **Details:** *from M4, J13 take A34 towards Hungerford; 9.30 pm; no jeans or trainers.* **Accommodation:** *49 rooms, from £125.*

The Wildebeest Arms   £35   Ⓐ
82-86 Norwich Rd   NR14 8QJ   (01508) 492497
"An oasis in a culinary desert" – this "accomplished" gastropub a short drive from Norwich (part of a local group, Animal Inns) was consistently praised this year for "hearty servings" of "competent" scoff, and notably "warm" service too. / **Details:** *www.animalinns.co.uk; from A140, turn left at Dunston Hall, left at T-junction; 9 pm.*

The Crooked Billet   £48   Ⓐ⭐
Newlands Ln   RG9 5PU   (01491) 681048
An "ancient" and "lovely" country hide-away, with "great food, really friendly service and a sublime setting", and offering an "extensive" menu of "eclectic" food of "high quality". / **Details:** *www.thecrookedbillet.co.uk; off the A4130; 10 pm; no Amex.*

The Angel Inn   £33   Ⓣ
Polstead St   CO6 4SA   (01206) 263245
Early days for the new régime at this pretty 16th-century coaching inn in Constable country; initial reports, though, tip the food as "great". / **Details:** *www.theangelinn.net; 5m W of A12, on B1068; 9.45 pm.* **Accommodation:** *6 rooms, from £50.*

The Crown £43 (A) (★)
Palk St CO6 4SE (01206) 262346
*"A well-established and nicely furnished gastropub", where the food
is "always well-cooked", and sometimes "exceptional"; beware, though
– "the best dishes tend to run out early!" / Details: www.eoinns.co.uk;
on B1068; 9.30 pm, Fri & Sat 10 pm, Sun 9 pm; no Amex.*

STOKESLEY, NORTH YORKSHIRE 8–3C

Howards £37 (★)
30 College Sq TS9 5DN (01642) 713391
*"A perfect little bistro nestled in a market town at the foot of the
Cleveland Hills", praised for overall "good value", and decent wines too.
/ Details: www.howards-eatery.co.uk; Mon-Weds 8 pm, Thu-Sun 9 pm; closed
Sun D.*

STONEHAVEN, ABERDEENSHIRE 9–3D

Marine Hotel £39 (T)
9-10 Shore Head AB39 2JY (01569) 762155
*A harbourside pub, tipped for its "great choice of fish" at "reasonable
prices"... plus the "best range of beers for miles".
/ Details: www.britnett-carver.co.uk/marine; 9 pm. **Accommodation:** 6 rooms,
from £110.*

STOW ON THE WOLD, GLOUCESTERSHIRE 2–1C

The Old Butchers £39 (A)
7 Park St GL54 1AQ (01451) 831700
*This "informal" brasserie on the main drag of a pretty town
is "a Cotswold favourite" for some reporters; doubters, however,
can find its standards rather "variable". / Details: www.theoldbutchers.com;
9.30 pm; closed Mon; booking essential.*

STRACHUR, ARGYLL AND BUTE 9–4B

Inver Cottage Restaurant £37 (A) (★)
Stracthlachlan PA27 8BU (01369) 860537
*"Superb food, great service and the most entrancing views over Loch
Fyne and ruined Castle Lachlan" justify a trip to "the middle
of nowhere", to this "small but perfectly formed" waterside croft which,
say fans, is simply "brilliant" all-round. / Details: www.invercottage.com;
8.30; closed Mon & Tue; no Amex.*

STRATFORD UPON AVON, WARWICKSHIRE 2–1C

Lambs £40 (A)
12 Sheep St CV37 6EF (01789) 292554
*"Watch your head on the low beams", when you visit this "olde-worlde"
house; with its "willing" staff and "well-prepared and -presented
dishes", it's the safest choice in town – "you must book pre-theatre".
/ Details: www.lambsrestaurant.co.uk; 9.30 pm, Sun 10 pm; closed Mon L;
no Amex.*

The Oppo £42 (T)
13 Sheep St CV37 6EF (01789) 269980
*"Charming historic surroundings", "engaging" staff and "good, tasty
food"... no wonder this "bustling" central restaurant, near the
Courtyard Theatre, is tipped as a "good choice for a pre-show meal".
/ Details: www.theoppo.co.uk; 10 pm, Sun 9.30 pm; closed Sun L; no Amex;
booking: max 12.*

The Vintner £34

4-5 Sheep St CV37 6EF (01789) 297259

For "unpretentious but good food with variety", this "delightful" spot – from the same stable as The Oppo and Lambs – is again tipped as the best of the trio. / **Details:** www.the-vintner.co.uk; 10 pm, Sun 9 pm; no Amex.

STRATHCARRON, HIGHLAND 9–2B

Kishorn Seafood Bar £29

Kishorn IV54 8XA (01520) 733240

"A wooden hut on the coast", with sea-views to the Isle of Skye; it is tipped for its "limited but good" selection of local fish and seafood. / **Details:** www.kishornseafoodbar.co.uk.

STUCKTON, HAMPSHIRE 2–3C

Three Lions £51

Stuckton Rd SP6 2HF (01425) 652489

"High-quality local ingredients are cooked beautifully", and served by "totally lovely" staff, at Michael Womersley's New Forest inn – even those complaining of "London prices" say it's "well worth a visit". / **Details:** www.thethreelionsrestaurant.co.uk; 1m E of Fordingbridge off B3078; 9 pm, Fri & Sat 9.30 pm; closed Mon & Sun D; no Amex. **Accommodation:** 7 rooms, from £80.

STUDLAND, DORSET 2–4C

Shell Bay Seafood £38

Ferry Rd BH19 3BA (01929) 450363

You get "views over Poole Harbour to di(n)e for" at this "modest-looking" restaurant, near the ferry, which has sometimes seemingly traded on the "location-is-everything" principle; new owners took over during the survey year, however, and initial feedback is encouraging (but too scant, as yet, for a rating). / **Details:** www.shellbay.net; just near the Sandbanks to Swanage ferry; 9 pm.

SUNBURY ON THAMES, SURREY 3–3A

Indian Zest £38

21 Thames St TW16 5QF (01932) 765 000

"Many notches above a neighbourhood restaurant" – Manoj Vasaikar's "sprawling Victorian mansion" is a worthy sibling to his acclaimed Hammersmith venture (Indian Zing), and offers food that's often outstanding; it's a "busy" place, though, and "over-stretched" service can grate. / **Details:** www.indianzest.co.uk; 12.00.

SUNNINGDALE, BERKSHIRE   3–3A

Bluebells   £69   🅐 ⭐
Shrubs Hill SL5 0LE   (01344) 622990
"Reliably brilliant food" is twinned with a "great wine list" ("from top-end classics to interesting New Worlds"), at this "slick" but "intimate" restaurant, which attracts only positive reviews; the set lunch is of particular note for its "incredible value".
/ **Details:** www.bluebells-restaurant.com.

SURBITON, SURREY   3–3A

The French Table   £48   ⭐ ⭐
85 Maple Rd KT6 4AW   (020) 8399 2365
Eric Guignard's "exciting" cuisine has won an enormous following for this "casual" – but "brilliant" and "great value" – Surbiton spot; it had something of a make-over this year, from which it emerged with its "tinny acoustics" much improved. / **Details:** www.thefrenchtable.co.uk; 10.30 pm; closed Mon & Sun D.

Joy   £29   ⭐
37 Brighton Rd KT6 5LR   (020) 8390 3988
"Not your typical Indian by a long way" – this particular example offers "a more modern dining experience", with "subtly different" cooking and "very helpful" staff. / **Details:** www.joy-restaurant.co.uk; 11.30 pm.

Red Rose   £26   🅐
38 Brighton Rd KT6 5PQ   (020) 8399 9647
It's not just the décor ("in the style of a Greek taverna") that makes this "lively" spot a change from the norm – its solid cooking means "it's usually very busy, even though there are many competitors nearby". / **Details:** www.redroseofsurbiton.co.uk; midnight.

SUTTON GAULT, CAMBRIDGESHIRE   3–1B

The Anchor   £41   🅐 ⭐
Bury Ln CB6 2BD   (01353) 778537
"Back on song" of late – this "reliable", "traditional" and "atmospheric" inn, "beside the Ouse washes", is hailed in all reports as a "top-quality" destination. / **Details:** www.anchorsuttongault.co.uk; 7m W of Ely, signposted off B1381 in Sutton; 9 pm, Sat 9.30 pm, Sun 8.30 pm. **Accommodation:** 4 rooms, from £79.5.

SUTTON GREEN, SURREY   3–3A

Olive Tree   £42   🅐
Sutton Green Rd GU4 7QD   (01483) 729999
"Scrumptious" cooking and "consistent good value-for-money" is the gist of most commentary on this "always-packed" gastropub; the odd cynic, though, does suspect that its popularity is a function of its location in "a particularly parched foodie desert". / **Details:** 9.30 pm; closed Mon D & Sun D; no Amex.

SWANSEA, SWANSEA   1–1C

Morgans
Morgans Hotel   £38   🅐
Somerset Pl SA1 1RR   (01792) 484848
The high-ceilinged dining room of this city-centre boutique hotel is tipped as a "beautiful" location, and all reports acknowledge the venue's potential; whereas fans praise the "high-quality" food and "experienced" staff, though, critics say it's "lost its way" and "can't cope at busy times". / **Details:** www.morganshotel.co.uk; 9.45 pm; children: 12+. **Accommodation:** 42 rooms, from £100.

T

Masons Arms   £38
Banbury Rd OX7 4AP   (01608) 683212
*An old inn that's been modernised "without being over-gentrified",
and is tipped for cooking that "can be very good".*
/ **Details:** www.masons-arms.com; 9 pm; closed Sun D; no Amex; no shorts.

A

The Terrace
Cliveden House   £80
Cliveden Rd SL6 0JF   (01628) 668561
*Fans of this "fantastic room" – "idyllically-located" within the famous
palazzo, and with "wonderful views" – extol it as an "excellent all-
round experience"; it has almost as many critics, though, who find the
food "very disappointing", and prices "ludicrous".*
/ **Details:** www.clivedenhouse.co.uk; 9.30 pm; no trainers. **Accommodation:** 38
+ cottage rooms, from £240.

A

Waldo's
Cliveden House   £82
Clivedon Rd SL6 0JF   (01628) 668561
*Still astonishingly little, and mixed, feedback on the fine-dining room
at this "stunning" ex-Astor palazzo-hotel; to fans its "first-class all
round" – critics ask "why shove it in the basement?… and the food
isn't much better than the location!"* / **Details:** www.clivedenhouse.co.uk;
M4, J7 then follow National Trust signs; 9.30 pm; D only, closed Mon & Sun;
no trainers; booking: max 6; children: 12+. **Accommodation:** 38 + Spring
Cottage rooms, from £195.

A ★

The Castle Hotel   £65
Castle Grn TA1 1NF   (01823) 272671
*"A classic hotel dining room in a classic hotel"; this picture-book,
wisteria-clad castle has been in the Chapman family since 1950 and its
main dining room offers cooking that's "always competent,
and sometimes very fine"; there's also a brasserie.*
/ **Details:** www.the-castle-hotel.com; follow tourist information signs; 9.30 pm;
closed Sun D. **Accommodation:** 44 rooms, from £230.

A ★

The Willow Tree   £42
3 Tower Ln TA1 4AR   (01823) 352835
*"Still going strong", a "small" and "always reliable" local favourite,
where "seasonal ingredients form the basis of beautifully-executed
modern cuisine".* / **Details:** www.willowtreerestaurant.co.uk; 10 pm; D only,
closed Sun & Mon; no Amex.

★

Imperial China   £35
196-198 Stanley Rd TW11 8UE   (0208) 9778679
*"A real find in a pretty dismal parade of shops", which attracts
"many Chinese customers" with its "first-rate dim sum" (and many
other "excellent" dishes too).* / **Details:** www.imperialchinalondon.co.uk;
11 sun 10.

TEFFONT EVIAS, WILTSHIRE 2–3C

Howards House Hotel £62
SP3 5RJ (01722) 716392
In the "beautiful" surroundings of a quiet village, "a good, honest hotel restaurant, which, as a local, you'd be pleased to have on your doorstep, and, as a traveller, you're very pleased to find".
/ **Details:** *www.howardshousehotel.co.uk; 9m W of Stonehenge off A303; 9 pm.*
Accommodation: *9 rooms, from £165.*

TENTERDEN, KENT 3–4C

The Raja Of Kent £34
Bibbenden Rd TN30 6SX (01233) 851191
Heading up a trio of Kentish Indians, an establishment tipped for its "interesting" dishes ("such as game curries"), and its consistent standards overall. / **Details:** *www.therajaofkent.com; midnight.*

TETBURY, GLOUCESTERSHIRE 2–2B

Calcot Manor £60
GL8 8YJ (01666) 890391

The main dining room of this "refined" yet "relaxed" Cotswold hotel, famous for its child-friendliness, is still sometimes tipped for its "high-quality" cuisine; even fans, though, can find it "on the pricey side" for what it is. / **Details:** *www.calcotmanor.co.uk; junction of A46 & A4135; 9.30 pm, Sun 9 pm.* **Accommodation:** *35 rooms, from £260.*

Calcot Manor (Gumstool Inn) £56
GL8 8YJ (01666) 890391
"Same kitchen, but more basic and busy" than the main dining room, this Ye-Olde-Boozer-style operation wins unanimously positive feedback on its "tremendous family dining", from a menu of "old pub favourites" which are realised to "a really high standard".
/ **Details:** *www.calcotmanor.co.uk; cross roads of a46 & A41345; 9.30 pm, Sun 9 pm; no jeans or trainers; children: 12+ at dinner in Conservatory.*
Accommodation: *35 rooms, from £240.*

THAMES DITTON, SURREY 3–3A

The Albany £35
Queens Rd KT7 0QY (020) 8972 9163
Tipped for its "wonderful view" over the Thames, a "busy" pub, near Hampton Court, which serves a wide-ranging menu that's generally "well executed". / **Details:** *www.the-albany.co.uk; 10 pm.*

Ronnie's £44 Ⓐ

11 St Mary St BS35 2AR (01454) 411137

Quite a lot of feedback on this recently-opened and well-acclaimed establishment (in a former 17th century barn), most of it praising the "well-executed" menu and the "carefully balanced" wine list; it can seem "a bit over-rated", though, and "small portions" seem to be something of a bugbear. / **Details:** *www.restaurant-ronnies.co.uk; 930 tue thur 1030 thur -sat; closed Mon & Sun D; no Amex.*

Thornbury Castle £67 Ⓣ

Castle St BS35 1HH (01454) 281182

Fewer reports than we'd like on this castle in its own vineyard; they do tend to confirm, however, that – with its "outstanding" setting, "imaginative" food and "impeccable" service – it makes "a great place for a special celebration". / **Details:** *www.thornburycastle.co.uk; near intersection of M4 & M5; 9.30 pm; no jeans or trainers.* **Accommodation:** *27 rooms, from £165.*

Bakers Arms £38 Ⓐ

Main St LE16 7TS (01858) 545201

This thatched cottage in an attractive village is "extremely popular" thanks to its "reliable" nature and "all-round" appeal; even fans, though, can find it "pricey" or "predictable". / **Details:** *www.thebakersarms.co.uk; near Market Harborough off A6; 9.30 pm; D only, ex Sat open L & D & Sun open L only, closed Mon; no Amex; children: 12+.*

An Lochan Ⓐ⭐
An Lochan Hotel £54

PA21 2BE (01700) 811239

"The best seafood ever" and "wonderful views" too continue to impress all who comment on this beautiful loch-side hotel, which enjoys views across the Kyles of Bute. / **Details:** *www.anlochan.co.uk; 8.30 pm; no Amex.* **Accommodation:** *11 rooms, from ££110.*

Stagg Inn £43 Ⓐ⭐⭐

HR5 3RL (01544) 230221

"All that fine dining should be about" – this "versatile" gastroboozer is widely praised for its "superb" food and its "very decent value"; it maintained its rating this year, despite the odd gripe that it's "beginning to get a bit so-so". / **Details:** *www.thestagg.co.uk; on B4355, NE of Kington; 9 pm; closed Mon & Sun D; no Amex.* **Accommodation:** *6 rooms, from £85.*

The King John Inn £50 Ⓣ

SP5 5PS (01725) 516 207

"A busy local pub", tipped by a number of reporters for its "good gastro-menu"; "book ahead". / **Details:** *www.kingjohninn.co.uk.*

TONBRIDGE, KENT   3–3B

The Little Brown Jug   £41
Chiddingstone Causeway TN11 8JJ   (01892) 870318
*A "great choice" of "interesting" dishes in "generous" portions make
this "family-favourite" gastropub popular with all who report on it;
"well-kept ales" too. / **Details:** www.thelittlebrownjug.co.uk; 11 pm,
Sat midnight; no Amex.*

TOPSHAM, DEVON   1–3D

The Galley   £54   **T**
41 Fore St EX3 0HU   (01392) 876078
*A nautically-themed restaurant, well-located on the quayside, tipped for
"the freshest fish, carefully cooked with flair".
/ **Details:** www.galleyrestaurant.co.uk; 9.30 pm; closed Mon & Sun; booking
essential; children: 12+.*

La Petite Maison   £49   **T**
35 Fore St EX3 0HR   (01392) 873660

*Fans of this family-run restaurant hail it for its "top quality, value,
presentation and informality"; it's temporarily closed as we go to press,
set to re-open in November 2010. / **Details:** www.lapetitemaison.co.uk;
Next to The Globe Hotel; 10 pm; closed Mon & Sun; no Amex; booking essential
at L.*

TORBERMORY, ARGYLL AND BUTE   9–3A

Cafe Fish   £38
The Pier PA75 6NU   (01688) 301253
*"A lovely little shack on the waterfront of this picturesque town", tipped
for a blackboard menu of "fish that's so beautifully fresh, you couldn't
possibly pick anything else". / **Details:** www.thecafefish.com; 30-40 min drive
north from the ferry pier at Criagnure; 9 pm; no Amex.*

TORCROSS, DEVON   1–4D

Start Bay Inn   £29
TQ7 2TQ   (01548) 580553
*"What could be better than sitting on the esplanade with a plate
of Start's Bay fish 'n' chips and a pint of bitter?"; this waterfront boozer
is "great for all fish dishes" – be prepared to queue.
/ **Details:** www.startbayinn.co.uk; on beach front (take A379 coastal road
to Dartmouth); 10 pm; no Amex; no booking.*

Elephant Restaurant & Brasserie   £60

3-4 Beacon Ter, Harbourside TQ1 2BH   (01803) 200044
"Accomplished cooking" has carved out a good reputation for the
upstairs dining room (with views) of this town-centre *"gem"* (which also
has a downstairs brasserie); the occasional disappointment, however,
is not unknown. / **Details:** www.elephantrestaurant.co.uk; 9.30 pm; closed
Mon & Sun; children: 14+ at bar.

No 7 Fish Bistro   £47

Beacon Ter TQ1 2BH   (01803) 295055
*"Tucked-away on the hill overlooking the harbour, definitely the venue
for really fresh, really good fish"* – an *"uncomplicated"*, *"genial"* and
"consistent" bistro-style operation that impresses all who comment
on it. / **Details:** www.no7-fish.com; 9.30 pm; D only Sun-Tue.

Gurnards Head   £35

TR26 3DE   (01736) 796928

Some *"stunning"* meals are reported at this *"cosy"*, if isolated, coastal
inn, which has *"lovely views"*; *"dismissive"* service can let the place
down, though, and – while it's still *"good in terms of value"* –
enthusiasm for the food declined this year.
/ **Details:** www.gurnardshead.co.uk; on coastal road between Land's End &
St Ives, near Zennor B3306; 9.30 pm; no Amex. **Accommodation:** 7 rooms,
from £90.

The Akeman   £40

9 Akeman St HP23 6AA   (01442) 826027
In the heart of the town, an *"atmospheric"* gastropub that's *"always
bustling"*; there's the odd complaint about *"erratic"* results, but more
common are compliments for the *"authentic Italian cuisine"*.
/ **Details:** www.theakeman.co.uk; 10.30 pm.

Olive Limes   £35

60 High St HP23 5AG   (01442) 828283
"A real find"; housed on a positively imperial scale (with a ballroom
overlooking Tring Park sometimes used for overflow!), this Indian
restaurant offers a *"careful"* cuisine that's *"a little different from the
norm"*. / **Details:** www.olivelimes.co.uk; 11 pm, fri & sat 11.30 pm.

A

Queen's Head £45
Townhead LA23 1PW (01539) 432174
*A "cosy and cavernous" old pub, praised for its "varied menu with
plenty to choose from"; it doesn't please everyone though, and even
one or two fans concede its cooking can be "hit-and-miss".
/ Details: www.queensheadhotel.com; A592 on Kirkstone Pass; 9 pm; no Amex.*
Accommodation: *15 rooms, from £110.*

T

One Eyed Cat £33
116 Kenwyn St TR1 3DJ (01872) 222122
*Impressively-housed in a former church – right next to a rather good
local museum – 'Truro's Only Bar and Brasserie' is tipped for its
"fantastic range of local food and drink", and "wonderful atmosphere".
/ Details: www.oneeyedcat.co.uk; 9 pm; closed Sun D; no Amex.*

★

Saffron £41
5 Quay St TR1 2HB (01872) 263771
*A "great, small restaurant", offering an "inventive" and "ever-changing"
menu, in which fish and seafood are the stars, and praised for its
overall "good value". / Details: www.saffronrestauranttruro.co.uk; 10 pm;
closed Sun.*

A

The Black Pig £39
18 Grove Hill Rd TN1 1RZ (01892) 523030
*A "minimalist" gastropub in the heart of the town, generally praised for
its "enthusiastic" staff and "interesting" cuisine.
/ Details: www.theblackpig.net; 9.30 pm, Sat 10.30pm, Sun 9 pm; no Amex.*

A

Hotel du Vin et Bistro £50
Crescent Rd TN1 2LY (01892) 526455
*"Still a nice place to dine, but waiters can be stand-offish and food
is sometimes mediocre" – a typically ambivalent report on this
attractive branch of the boutique hotel/bistro chain, where an "excellent
wine list" is now the only certain attraction. / Details: www.hotelduvin.com;
opp Assembly Hall; 10 pm, Fri & Sat 10.30 pm; booking: max 10.*
Accommodation: *34 rooms, from £120.*

★

Thackeray's £60
85 London Rd TN1 1EA (01892) 511921
*"One of the best-value set lunches in the country" – "superb food with
perfect wine pairings" – is the special reason to seek out Richard
Phillips's restaurant, in a "wonderful" Regency villa; dinners inspire
relatively little commentary. / Details: www.thackerays-restaurant.co.uk;
near Kent and Sussex hospital; 10.30 pm; closed Mon & Sun D.*

T

Lunesdale Arms £34
LA6 2QN (01524) 274203
*In the Lune valley, a "reliable" pub tipped for its "well-prepared food"
and its "genuine country atmosphere". / Details: www.thelunesdale.co.uk;
15 min from J34 on M6 onto A683; 9pm; closed Mon.*

Alexander House Hotel £64

East St RH10 4QD   (01342) 714914

We wish we had more reports on this trendified country house hotel (and spa); feedback – both on the "romantic" restaurant and the "seriously nice" brasserie – is invariably positive.

*/ **Details:** www.alexanderhouse.co.uk; off M23 J10, follow signs to E. Grinstead and Turners Hill, on B2110; 9.30 pm; no jeans or trainers. **Accommodation:** 38 rooms, from £185.*

Pallavi £26

Unit 3, Cross Deep Ct, Heath Rd, TW1 4QJ   (020) 8892 2345

Not just "a good place to hang out on match days", this "authentic" spot is tipped for its "very good South Indian cuisine".

Groes Inn £38

Nr Conway LL32 8TN   (01492) 650545

"A beautiful historic pub", with a "fantastic cosy ambience", and a lovely rural setting; "good food and beer", too.

*/ **Details:** www.groesinn.co.uk; on B5106 between Conwy & Betws-y-coed, 2m from Conwy; 9 pm; children: 10+ in restaurant. **Accommodation:** 14 rooms, from £105.*

Sharrow Bay £91

CA10 2LZ   (01768) 486301

For a "cosseting" experience, it's still hard to beat the Lake District's original country house hotel, which is still flourishing after several years of group ownership (Von Essen); the setting is as "dramatic" as ever, and the rich, traditional cooking remains "first-class".

*/ **Details:** www.sharrowbay.co.uk; on Pooley Bridge Rd towards Howtown; 8 pm; children: 10+. **Accommodation:** 24 rooms, from £175.*

Lords of the Manor £82

GL54 2JD   (01451) 820243

*This "charming" Cotswold country house has a very "beautiful location", and even its critics say it can serve "great food"; even so, "haughty" or "totally inept" service made some visits this year simply a "disaster". / **Details:** www.lordsofthemanor.com; 4m W of Stow on the Wold; 9.30 pm; D only, ex Sun open L & D; no jeans or trainers; children: 7+ at D in restaurant. **Accommodation:** 26 rooms, from £195.*

The Lake Isle £46

16 High Street East LE15 9PZ   (01572) 822951

*"A small and attractive restaurant-with-rooms" with "an appealing setting on the high street" – a "comfortable" sort of place, whose "quite traditional" fare generally pleases. / **Details:** www.lakeisle.co.uk; past the Market place, down the High Street; 9 pm, Fri & Sat 9.30 pm; closed Mon L & Sun D. **Accommodation:** 12 rooms, from £75.*

UTTOXETER, STAFFORDSHIRE 5–3C

Restaurant Gilmore £58 ⭐
Strine's Farm ST14 5DZ (01889) 507100
*"Really punching above its weight" – this "quiet farmhouse-restaurant"
is one of Staffordshire's few culinary attractions, offering
"very accomplished" food and service that's "always friendly and
efficient" too. / Details: www.restaurantgilmore.com; 9 pm; closed Mon,
Tue, Wed L, Sat L & Sun D; no Amex; booking essential.*

VENTNOR, ISLE OF WIGHT 2–4D

The Hambrough £79 ⭐⭐
Hamnorough Rd PO38 1SQ (01983) 856333

*"The view over the Channel is sensational", and so is Robert
Thompson's "elaborate but delicate" cooking, at this "fabulous hotel
restaurant"; its contemporary decor, however, elicits a somewhat muted
response. / Details: www.thehambrough.com; 9.30 pm; closed Mon & Sun;
no Amex; children: 5+ at D. Accommodation: 7 rooms, from £170 b&b.*

WADEBRIDGE, CORNWALL 1–3B

Relish £28 🅣
Foundry Ct PL27 7QN (01208) 814214
*"The best coffee in the South West" is – say fans – to be found at this
café/deli (plus courtyard); it's tipped as "a great place for a light lunch"
too. / Details: www.relishwadebridge.co.uk; closed Mon & Sun; no Amex.*

WAKEFIELD, WEST YORKSHIRE 5–1C

Aagrah £34 🅐
Barnsley Rd WF1 5NX (01924) 242222
*Even fans concede this branch is "not the best-looking Aagrah", and it's
not one of the higher-scoring ones either, but this outpost of the
eminent chain is still consistently praised for its "inventive and authentic
tastes of the subcontinent". / Details: www.aagrah.com; from M1, J39 follow
Barnsely Rd to A61; 11.30 pm, Sun 11 pm; D only. Accommodation: 10 rooms,
from £35.*

WALBERSWICK, SUFFOLK 3–1D

The Anchor £39 ⭐
Main St IP18 6UA (01502) 722112
*A "friendly coastal gastropub", where there's "always a bit of a buzz",
and where the garden comes with sea views; its "reliable and sensibly-
priced" fare almost invariably satisfies.
/ Details: www.anchoratwalberswick.com; 9 pm. Accommodation: 10 rooms,
from £100.*

Mill Race   £36   **T**
Ross on Wye HR9 5QS   (01989) 562891
*This village pub in the Wye valley doesn't please all reporters, but is
tipped by most for its good locally-sourced food and beers.*
/ **Details:** www.millrace.info; 930pm; no Amex.

The Art Kitchen   £36   **A** **★** **★**
7 Swan St CV34 4BJ   (01926) 494303
*"Beautifully-cooked Thai food using top-class ingredients" and "helpful
staff" help win the highest praise for this "always-popular" ("you need
to book") "gem" in the middle of town – a friendly, informal place
decked out not unlike a tapas bar.* / **Details:** www.theartkitchen.com;
10 pm.

Saffron   £28   **★**
Unit 1 Westgate Hs, Market St CV34 4DE   (01926) 402061
*"Just ignore the location" of this Indian on the edge of a shopping
precinct – it's worth braving it for food that "never fails to impress".*
/ **Details:** www.saffronwarwick.co.uk; 11.30 pm; D only.

Saxon Mill   £35   **T**
Coventry Rd, Guys Cliffe CV34 5YN   (01926) 492255
*"A lovely waterside pub, with a vibrant atmosphere", tipped for bar
food that's "among the best in the area".* / **Details:** www.saxonmill.co.uk;
9.30 pm, Sun 9 pm.

Tailors   £47   **T**
22 Market Place CV34 4SL   (01926) 410590
*"A small but up-and-coming restaurant in the market square"; fans tip
it as a "marvellous find" in this under-served town.*
/ **Details:** www.tailorsrestaurant.co.uk; 9.30 pm; closed Mon & Sun.

A

The Beach Hut
Watergate Bay Hotel   £41
On The Beach TR8 4AA   (01637) 860543
*"A great setting on the beach" is the star feature of this "noisy and
brash, but fun" venue (which is not remotely hut-like); the "fresh" and
"simple" fare includes a "stunning breakfast".*
/ **Details:** www.watergatebay.co.uk; 9 pm; no Amex.

Fifteen Cornwall
Watergate Bay Hotel   **£60**
TR8 4AA   (01637) 861000

"Astounding views", a "funky" interior and "laid-back" service help create a "delightful" experience at J Oliver's beachside chef-training operation; as ever, though, even those who praise a "good concept" may find the food "too ordinary for the gourmet prices".
/ **Details:** www.fifteencornwall.co.uk; on the Atlantic coast between Padstow and Newquay; 9.15 pm; children: 7+ before 7 pm only.

WATH-IN-NIDDERDALE, NORTH YORKSHIRE   8–4B

Sportsman's Arms   **£47**
HG3 5PP   (01423) 711306
"One of the best of the Dales pub/restaurants"; this cosy and slightly old-fashioned riverside inn (reached by a narrow bridge) has long been in the ownership of the same family, and is still acclaimed for its "very good pub grub". / **Details:** take Wath Road from Pateley Bridge; 9 pm, Sun 8 pm; no Amex; booking essential. **Accommodation:** 11 rooms, from £120.

WELLS, SOMERSET   2–3B

Goodfellows   **£50**
5 Sadler St BA5 2RR   (01749) 673866
Adam Fellows's restaurant makes an "astonishing" find, thanks to the quality of his "creative" ("but not necessarily complicated") dishes, often involving fish; it's situated on a "lovely old street" in the town-centre too. / **Details:** www.goodfellowswells.co.uk; Near the Cathedral and the Market Square; 9.30 pm; closed Mon, Tue D & Sun. **Accommodation:** 0 rooms, from £0.

WELWYN, HERTFORDSHIRE   3–2B

Auberge du Lac
Brocket Hall   **£78**
AL8 7XG   (01707) 368888
A "beautiful lakeside setting" and a "wonderful terrace" contribute to the "really special" and "romantic" atmosphere of this former hunting lodge; most reporters also praise the "consistent high quality" of Phil Thompson's cuisine – to the occasional sceptic, however, it's merely "acceptable". / **Details:** www.brocket-hall.co.uk; on B653 towards Harpenden; 9.30 pm; closed Mon & Sun; no jeans or trainers. **Accommodation:** 16 rooms, from £175.

Brocket Arms   **£32**
Ayot St Lawrence AL6 9BT   (01438) 820250
"Worth the drive down single-track roads" – this "characterful country inn, in a lovely village" is a "helpful" sort of place, where Andrew Knight (who's trained with some really big names) prepares dishes that are usually "superbly cooked and presented". / **Details:** www.brocketarms.com; 9 pm; closed Sun D; no Amex. **Accommodation:** 6 rooms, from £85 b&b.

⭐

Larwood And Voce
Fatcat   **£45**
Fox Rd NG2 6AJ   (0115) 981 9960
*"Backing onto the famous Trent Bridge ground", a "very worthy
gastropub" that's "strong on local ingredients"; "deals and special
nights" (including "impressive wine tastings") are especially worth
seeking out. / **Details:** www.larwoodandvoce.co.uk; 9pm.*

Ⓐ

Chu Chin Chow   **£34**
63 Old Woking Rd KT14 6LF   (01932) 349581
*"A very good basic Chinese, that does sushi too" – "it's spacious, long-
established, well-managed and very consistent".
/ **Details:** www.chuchinchow.com; 11 pm.*

Ⓐ

The Cat Inn   **£37**
Queen's Sq RH19 4PP   (01342) 810369
*With Gravetye Manor's former chef at the stove, it's perhaps no great
surprise that this "beautifully restored ancient building" is increasingly
recommended for its "excellent gastropub fare"; it can end
up "extraordinarily busy". / **Details:** www.catinn.co.uk; 9 pm, Fri-Sun
9.30 pm; closed Sun D.*

Ⓣ

Loch Fyne   **£39**
Ring O Bells, Village Rd CH48 7HE   (01592) 96750
*Some of "the best seafood on the Wirral" – something of a double-
edged compliment, admittedly! – is to be found at this outlet in an old
seaside town; locals tip it as "surprisingly OK, for a chain".
/ **Details:** www.lochfyne.com.*

Ⓐ

The Swan   **£46**
35 Swan St ME19 6JU   (01732) 521910
*This "pleasant" and "popular" brasserie, in a former coaching inn, risks
'coasting' a bit; dishes – served in either the "pleasant" courtyard
or the "comfortable" dining room – can still be "beautifully cooked and
presented", but there are a few gripes about "small portions" and
"high prices". / **Details:** www.theswanwestmalling.co.uk; 11 pm, Sun 8 pm.*

⭐⭐

The Company Shed   **£19**
129 Coast Rd CO5 8PA   (01206) 382700
*"Be warned, it really is a shed!", but it's the "seafood straight off the
boat" which makes this "idiosyncratic", "zero-frills" gem popular with
all of the many reporters who comment on it; "arrive early in summer"
to miss the "daunting queues", and don't forget to BYO (including
bread). / **Details:** L only, closed Mon; no credit cards; no booking.*

⭐

West Mersea Oyster Bar   **£30**
Coast Rd CO5 8LT   (01206) 381600
*"More used by many locals than the famous Company Shed" –
this nearby operation has its plus points; for one thing, it's licensed,
for another the queue's shorter, and, finally, it offers hot food (notably
"great fish and chips"), as well as "fresh and cheap oysters".
/ **Details:** www.westmerseaoysterbar.co.uk; 5pm, Fri & Sat 10pm; Sun-Thu closed
D; no shorts.*

WEST WITTON, NORTH YORKSHIRE 8–4B

The Wensleydale Heifer £53

Main St DL8 4LS (01969) 622322

"The mainly fish menu is a dream" at this *"marvellous restaurant-with-rooms"* which has two rooms – *"one formal, one more relaxed, same menu"*; practically all reports attest to its *"attractive maritime atmosphere"*, *"down-to-earth"* service and *"very fine"* cooking. / **Details:** www.wensleydaleheifer.co.uk; 9.30 pm. **Accommodation:** 13 rooms, from £110.

WESTCLIFF-ON-SEA, ESSEX 3–3C

Oldhams £28
13 West Rd SS0 9AU (01702) 346736
"A great chippy", in the town-centre – a *"basic"* place, tipped for *"top value"*. / **Details:** On the A13; no Amex.

WESTFIELD, EAST SUSSEX 3–4C

The Wild Mushroom £42
Westfield Ln TN35 4SB (01424) 751137
Paul and Rebecca Webbe's *"peaceful"*, *"no-pretensions"* roadside ex-farmhouse serves up *"good local and seasonal produce"*, and at *"excellent-value"* prices too. / **Details:** www.webbesrestaurants.co.uk; 9.30 pm; closed Mon & Sun D; children: 8+ at D.

WEYMOUTH, DORSET 2–4B

Perry's £43
4 Trinity Rd, The Old Harbour DT4 8TJ (01305) 785799
"Excellent fish" often stars in meals at this *"pleasant"*, but sometimes *"quiet"*, harbour-view restaurant. / **Details:** www.perrysrestaurant.co.uk; 9.30 pm; no Amex; children: 7+.

WHALLEY, LANCASHIRE 5–1B

Food by Breda Murphy £36
41 Station Rd BB7 9RH (01254) 823446
The setting may be *"a bit café-like"* (with portions sometimes in keeping), but this bistro/deli from a former Inn at Whitewell chef is otherwise a real crowd-pleaser, thanks to its *"very courteous"* service and *"excellent"* food (including particularly *"brilliant"* cakes). / **Details:** www.foodbybredamurphy.com; 5 pm; closed Mon & Sun, Tue-Sat D; no Amex.

Three Fishes £37
Mitton Rd BB7 9PQ (01254) 826888
"Real, regional classically British food done very well" is part of the formula that's made this Northcote-offshoot (the first of the Ribble Valley Inns) the *"definitive gastropub"* for many reporters, and it remains *"incredibly popular"*. / **Details:** www.thethreefishes.com; 9 pm, Sun 8.30 pm.

WHITBY, NORTH YORKSHIRE   8–3D

Greens   £55   ⭐

13 Bridge St YO22 4BG (01947) 600284

A restaurant and bistro which "just gets better and better", utilising "the best of local produce" to produce dishes (with fish the highlight) which are often "superb"; the occasional reporter does wonder, though, whether it isn't "getting a little pricey". / Details: www.greensofwhitby.com; 9.30 pm, Fri & Sat 10 pm.

Magpie Café   £35   ⭐⭐

14 Pier Rd YO21 3PU (01947) 602058

"Still the best fish and chips in the UK, and worth the queue!" – that's about all there is to say about this "tremendous" harbourside institution, "Whitby's No. 1 tourist attraction", and one of the country's best-loved eateries. / Details: www.magpiecafe.co.uk; opp Fish Market; 9 pm; no Amex; no booking at L.

Trenchers   £39   Ⓐ

New Quay Rd YO21 1DH (01947) 603212

"A modern-style chippy", that's a favourite for some reporters, who praise its "consistently high standards"; "no queueing on the pavement" either! / Details: www.trenchersrestaurant.co.uk; opp railway station, near marina; 8.30 pm; need 7+ to book.

WHITE WALTHAM, BERKSHIRE   3–3A

Royal Oak   £45   ⭐⭐

Paley St SL6 3JN (01628) 620541

"Michael Parkinson's lovely country gastropub" ("or is it a restaurant...?") charges "reasonable prices" ("given the celeb status"), and is an all-round hit, with locals as much as the "DFL (down from London) crowd", serving food that's "a real step up from usual pub fare", and "particularly friendly and efficient service". / Details: www.theroyaloakpaleystreet.com; 9.30 pm, Fri & Sat 10 pm; closed Sun D.

WHITEBROOK, MONMOUTHSHIRE   2–2B

The Crown at Whitebrook   £63   ⭐

NP25 4TX (01600) 860254

"Hidden-away in a valley", this "simple" restaurant-with-rooms has won a very big reputation with its "accomplished" cuisine; "slow" or "overly fussy" service, though, can sometimes take the edge off the experience. / Details: www.crownatwhitebrook.co.uk; 2m W of A466, 5m S of Monmouth; 9 pm; closed Sun D; no Amex; children: 12+. Accommodation: 8 rooms, from £125.

A ⭐

The Pear Tree Inn   £42
Top Ln SN12 8QX   (01225) 709131
"The quality of the food matches the surroundings", say fans of this
"impressive" gastropub, which all reports proclaim to be a *"top-quality"*
operation. / **Details:** www.maypolehotels.com; 9.30 pm, Sun 9 pm; no Amex.
Accommodation: 16 rooms, from £125.

T

Crab & Winkle   £40
South Quay, Whitstable Harbour CT5 1AB   (01227) 779377
A café above the fish market, tipped for its *"great fresh fish, especially
the catch of the day"*; the setting, though, is *"rather barn-like"* –
"grab a window table if you can". / **Details:** www.crab-winkle.co.uk;
9.30 pm; no Amex.

A

JoJo   £25
2 Herne Bay Rd CT5 2LQ   (01227) 274591
"A fantastic ever-changing tapas menu" commended this *"cheap and
cheerful"* favourite in its former location; sadly, however, the
new venture opened post-survey, so no ratings are appropriate.
/ **Details:** www.jojosrestaurant.co.uk; 9.30 pm; closed Mon, Tue L & Sun D;
no credit cards.

A ⭐

The Pearson's Arms   £36
The Horsebridge, Sea Wall CT5 1BT   (01227) 272005
"Don't judge a book by its cover!"; this pub, next to the Oyster
Company, *"may look like an old man's boozer"*, but all reporters like its
first-floor dining room, which has *"a wonderful location overlooking the
sea"*, and makes impressive use of *"good local produce, especially fish"*.
/ **Details:** www.pearsonsarms.com; 9 pm, Fri & Sat 9.30 pm; closed Sun D;
no Amex.

T

Samphire   £37
4 High St CT5 1BQ   (01227) 770075
A *"small, café-like place"*, tipped for its *"good"* fish dishes; brace
yourself, though, for *"uncomfortable chairs"*.
/ **Details:** www.samphirerestaurant.co.uk; 9.30 pm, Sat & Sun 10 pm; no Amex.

A ⭐ ⭐

Sportsman   £45
Faversham Rd, Seasalter CT5 4BP   (01227) 273370
"What an amazing find"; Stephen Harris's old inn on the salt marshes
outside Whitstable may look (very much) *"like a normal pub"* – and a
"totally unpretentious" and *"convivial"* one at that – but his food
is *"world-class"*; *"everyone who runs a gastropub should come here,
and see how it's done"*. / **Details:** www.thesportsmanseasalter.co.uk; 8.45 pm;
closed Mon & Sun D; no Amex; children: 18+ in main bar.

A ⭐ ⭐

Wheeler's Oyster Bar   £42
8 High St CT5 1BQ   (01227) 273311
"A joyous find for fish lovers"; the following for this *"truly remarkable"*
16-seater *"gem"* (est. 1856) is out of all proportion to its *"tiny"*,
"quaint" and *"jam-packed"* premises; it's all down to *"exquisite"* fish
and seafood that's among the best in the UK; the BYO policy
is *"the icing on the cake"*. / **Details:** www.seewhitstable.com; 7.30 pm,
Sun 7 pm; closed Wed; no credit cards.

Whitstable Oyster Fishery Co. £50 Ⓐ⭐

Horsebridge CT5 1BU (01227) 276856

This "pure Dickens" destination, with its "perfect" waterside setting, continues to please many reporters with its "simple fresh fish", as well as the "unbeatable oysters" for which the town is famous; it's "expensive", though, and service can be "slow" (or off-hand) at busy times. / **Details:** www.oysterfishery.co.uk; on the seafront; 8.45 pm, Fri 9.30 pm, Sat 9.15 pm, Sun 8.15 pm; closed Mon .

WILLIAN, HERTFORDSHIRE 3–2B

The Fox £42 Ⓐ

SG6 2AE (01462) 480233

"Never a bad meal", say fans of this "smart" rural "gem", where the cuisine – which includes some "well thought-out dishes" – is "a step above normal pub grub". / **Details:** www.foxatwillian.co.uk; 1 mile from junction 9 off A1M; 9 pm; closed Sun D; no Amex.

WILMSLOW, CHESHIRE 5–2B

Chilli Banana
Kings Arms Hotel £42 Ⓐ⭐

Alderley Rd SK9 1PZ (01625) 539100

"Highly recommended"; some reporters may think it "odd" to have a "top-of-the-range" Thai restaurant as part of a pub – not really, nowadays! – but all attest to the "authenticity" and "quality" of the cuisine. / **Details:** www.chillibanana.co.uk; 11 pm; closed Mon, Tue-Thu D only. **Accommodation:** 7 rooms, from £60.

WINCHCOMBE, GLOUCESTERSHIRE 2–1C

5 North Street £61 ⭐⭐

5 North St GL54 5LH (01242) 604566

Marcus Ashenford's "awesome", "truly accomplished" cuisine, twinned with "unobtrusive" and "efficient" service, wins many fans for this "great little restaurant"... even if prices are "on the high side", and critics find the setting rather "cramped". / **Details:** just off the high street; 9 pm; closed Mon, Tue L & Sun D.

Wesley House £49 Ⓐ⭐

High St GL54 5LJ (01242) 602366

"A real find"; many reports attests to the "good-quality ingredients" and "imaginative cooking" at this "friendly" restaurant, in a beautiful Tudor building; the conservatory is sometimes found "more inviting than the main restaurant". / **Details:** www.wesleyhouse.co.uk; next to Sudeley Castle; 9 pm; closed Sun D. **Accommodation:** 5 rooms, from £90.

The Black Rat £47 ⭐

88 Chesil St SO23 0HX (01962) 844465

A former pub – nowadays a 'fine dining restaurant' – which inspires praise from reporters for its "light and fresh-tasting" cuisine and "interesting" wines; don't miss the tropical beach huts (we kid you not) in the back yard. / Details: www.theblackrat.co.uk; 9.30 pm; closed weekday L; children: Weekend L only.

The Chesil Rectory £48 Ⓐ

1 Chesil St S023 0HU (01962) 851555

In a Tudor building in the centre of the city, this is – say fans – "a stylish restaurant that offers good food and great value for money"; compared to its former incarnation, the style can seem rather "downmarket", though, and critics dismiss the cuisine as "not very special". / Details: www.chesilrectory.co.uk; 9.30 pm, Fri & Sat 10 pm; closed Sun D; children: 12+ at D Sat & Sun.

The Chestnut Horse £42 Ⓐ

Easton Village SO21 1EG (01962) 779257

This "olde-worlde village pub" remains a big hit with reporters; it's a "lovely" place offering fare of "consistent quality" – no wonder if can be "hard to get a table". / Details: www.thechestnuthorse.com; Junction M3 Newbury exit right hand lane; 9.30 pm, Sun 8 pm; closed Sun D; no Amex.

Hotel du Vin et Bistro £50 Ⓐ

14 Southgate St SO23 9EF (01962) 841414

The founder member of the wine-led hotel/bistro chain occupies a "lovely" building, and fans still like its "relaxed brasserie style"; there's a large school of thought, however, that, if you leave out of account the "vast and superb wine list", this is an establishment "on the slide". / Details: www.hotelduvin.com; Central Winchester, top of high street, near the Cathedral; 9.45 pm; booking: max 12. Accommodation: 24 rooms, from £140.

Avenue Ⓐ
Lainston House Hotel £75

SO21 2LT (01962) 776088

The surroundings are "exquisite", and the cooking is "of a high standard" too – shame, then, that this classy country house is just so "very expensive" that most reporters conclude it's just "not worth the price". / Details: www.lainstonhouse.com; 9.30 pm, 10 pm Fri & Sat; children: 18 + after 7pm. Accommodation: 50 rooms, from £245.

Loch Fyne £40 Ⓐ

18 Jewry St SO23 8RZ (01962) 872930

It's hardly news that it is "not particularly exciting or innovative", but this chain outlet is still "the best fish restaurant in Winchester", and it has a surprisingly broad following among reporters (thanks not least to its "real-food" menu for kids). / Details: www.loch-fyne.com; 10 pm.

The Old Vine £37 Ⓣ

8 Great Minster St SO23 9HA (01962) 854616

"Just as the Wykeham Arms has gone downhill, this place has come to the rescue…"; this 'other' pub near the cathedral is tipped for an experience that "good all-round". / Details: www.oldvinewinchester.com; 9.30 pm, Sun 9 pm; children: 6+. Accommodation: 5 rooms, from £100.

Wykeham Arms   £42
75 Kingsgate St SO23 9PE   (01962) 853834
*This famous and "cosy" old pub, near the Cathedral,
is just an 'atmosphere' recommendation nowadays — "the food isn't
up to the very high standards of a few years ago".*
*/ Details: www.fullershotels.com; between Cathedral and College; 8.45 pm;
booking: max 8; children: 14+.* **Accommodation:** *14 rooms, from £125.*

A

WINDERMERE, CUMBRIA   7–3D

**First Floor Café
Lakeland Limited**   £30
Alexandra Buildings LA23 1BQ   (015394) 47116

*Surprising as it may seem, the first-floor dining room of this famous
kitchen shop — presided over by its ex-Gavroche chef! — continues to be
a notable all-round crowd-pleaser, offering "excellent fresh food",
and "quick service" too. / Details: www.lakeland.co.uk; 6 pm, Sat 5 pm,
Sun 4 pm; no Amex.*

⭐

Francines   £34
22 Main Rd LA23 1DX   (015394) 44088
*Unless you know that the chef used to work at the late-lamented
'Porthole', the "wonderful" food at this "lovely" little café can come as a
"a great surprise". / Details: www.francinesrestaurantwindermere.co.uk/;
11 pm; closed Mon, Tue D & Sun D.*

⭐

Gilpin Lodge   £72
Crook Rd LA23 3NE   (01539) 488818
*For a "luxury Lakes break", this "beautiful" and "pampering" country
house hotel makes a "reliable" destination, and its "bold and
adventurous" dishes almost invariably "hit their mark".
/ Details: www.gilpinlodge.co.uk; 9.15 pm; no jeans; children: 7+.
Accommodation: 20 rooms, from £290.*

A ⭐

Holbeck Ghyll   £78
Holbeck Ln LA23 1LU   (01539) 432375
*A Lakeland "epic", where "stunning views over Windermere" have long
been part of the "ultimate country house dining experience"; given the
change of ownership during the survey year, no rating is appropriate.
/ Details: www.holbeckghyll.com; 3m N of Windermere, towards Troutbeck;
9 pm; booking essential; children: 18+ at D.* **Accommodation:** *23 rooms,
from £220.*

A

Jerichos   £52
College Rd LA23 1BX   (01539) 442522
*Jo and Chris Blaydes' "relaxed" restaurant-with-rooms has a very
dedicated fan club for its "wonderfully flavoured" cooking; there's the
odd quibble though — it can seem a tad "expensive" and the "well-
judged" service "isn't as good when Jo's not about".
/ Details: www.jerichos.co.uk; 9.00; closed L; children: 12+.
Accommodation: 10 rooms, from £85.*

⭐

The Samling **£68** A ★

Ambleside Rd LA23 1LR (01539) 431922
"Marvellous views over Windermere" help create a lovely and relaxed
atmosphere at this small luxury hotel (Von Essen); fans say the food's
"top-class" too, and even a reporter who found prices unduly *"stiff"*
rated the experience well overall. / **Details:** www.thesamlinghotel.co.uk;
take A591 from town; 9.15 pm. **Accommodation:** 11 rooms, from £190.

WINDSOR, BERKSHIRE 3–3A

Al Fassia **£34** ★

27 St Leonards Rd SL4 3BP (01753) 855370
This *"simple but comfortable"* Jericho *"neighbourhood"* Moroccan
remains popular, thanks to its *"consistently good food and friendly
service"*; *"try the interestingly decorated dining room upstairs for
a different perspective!"* / **Details:** 10.30 pm, Fri & Sat 11 pm.

WINKFIELD, BERKSHIRE 3–3A

Cottage Inn
Greens restaurant **£50** A

Winkfield St SL4 4SW (01344) 882242
It's been a year of transition to new ownership at this *"old, traditional
pub"*, whose restaurant has *"grown in stature and reputation"* in recent
years; in consequence, although initial impressions are favourable, we've
left it un-rated. / **Details:** www.cottage-inn.co.uk; 11 pm; closed Sun D; booking
essential. **Accommodation:** 10 rooms, from £100.

WINTERINGHAM, LINCOLNSHIRE 5–1D

Winteringham Fields **£96** A

1 Silver St DN15 9ND (01724) 733096
Reports on this charming restaurant-with-rooms – once among the
best in the UK – continue to dive; reporters' main complaint is that it's
nowadays *"grossly overpriced"*, with realisation simply not up to the
demands of the *"highly complex"* menu.
/ **Details:** www.winteringhamfields.com; 4m SW of Humber Bridge; 9.30 pm;
closed Mon & Sun; no Amex. **Accommodation:** 11 rooms, from £180.

WITHAM, ESSEX 3–2C

Lian **£40** A ★

5 Newland St CM8 2AF (01376) 510684
Chinese food that's *"well above-average for this part of the world"* has
won a big reputation for this long-established venture; more sceptical
reporters, however, would suggest that it's *"not bad for Essex"*.
/ **Details:** 11.30 pm; closed Sun.

WOBURN, BEDFORDSHIRE 3–2A

Paris House **£85** ★

Woburn Pk MK17 9QP (01525) 290692
This formerly *"very staid"* restaurant, beautifully located within the
Bedford Estate, has been transformed – and *"for the better"* – by Alan
Murchison (of L'Ortolan, Shinfield); the *"rather corporate"* new design
may not be to all tastes, but the *"skillful"* food and *"professional"*
service certainly are. / **Details:** www.parishouse.co.uk; on A4012; 9 pm; closed
Mon, Tue L & Sun D.

Ⓐ

Inn @ West End   **£46**
42 Guildford Rd GU24 9PW   (01276) 858652
*"Easy access from the M3" helps boost the popularity of this relaxed
gastropub, which serves "better-than-average" fare to complement its
"outstanding" wine list (which offers "many choices by the glass").*
*/ **Details:** www.the-inn.co.uk; 9.30 pm, Sun 9 pm; children: 5+.*

Ⓐ

The Trout Inn   **£36**
195 Godstow Rd OX2 8PN   (01865) 510930
*"One of the best locations in Oxford, on the river just by a weir"
ensures this "lovely" pub (of Inspector Morse fame) is "ludicrously busy
on a sunny day"; the food is "not memorable", but it is "good value".*
*/ **Details:** www.thetroutoxford.co.uk; 2m from junction of A40 & A44; 10 pm,
Fri & Sat 10.30 pm, Sun 9.30 pm.*

★

Bilash   **£46**
2 Cheapside WV1 1TU   (01902) 427762
*"Not the cheapest Indian dishes you will ever eat, but probably among
the best!" – the "consistent" reputation of "Wolverhampton's best-kept
secret" remains intact. / **Details:** www.thebilash.co.uk; opp Civic Centre;
10.30 pm; closed Sun.*

Ⓐ

Chequers Inn   **£45**
Kiln Ln HP10 0JQ   (01628) 529575
*"Very good fresh fish" (and "wonderful chips") are a menu highlight
at this "great gastropub", which inspires notably consistent reports.*
*/ **Details:** www.chequers-inn.com; 9.30 pm; closed Sun D. **Accommodation:** 17
rooms, from £87.50.*

Ⓐ

Crown   **£41**
Throughfare IP12 1AD
*Some "excellent meals" are recorded at this recently refurbished –
but still "squashed" – dining room of an ancient inn; feedback, however,
is too mixed to make it an entirely safe recommendation.*
*/ **Details:** www.thecrownatwoodbridge.co.uk; 930PM. **Accommodation:** 10
rooms, from £145.*

★

Terravina
Hotel Terravina   **£50**
174 Woodlands Rd SO40 7GL   (023) 8029 3784
*This "boutique hotel nestling in the New Forest" hit a more impressive
stride this year with acclaim growing for its "subtle" cuisine, as well
as its "personal" approach; and the wine? – let's just say patron Gerard
Basset won this year's World's Best Sommelier contest…*
*/ **Details:** www.hotelterravina.co.uk; 9.30 pm. **Accommodation:** 11 rooms,
from £145.*

WOOKEY HOLE, SOMERSET   2–3B

The Wookey Hole Inn   £44
BA5 1BP   (01749) 676677
*Near the famous caves, this quirky pub is again tipped for its
"interesting" food and "friendly" staff; impressions of the atmosphere
differ sharply, though – from "dull" to "beyond excellent"!*
*/ **Details:** www.wookeyholeinn.com; 9.30 pm; closed Sun D.*
Accommodation: *5 rooms, from £90.*

WORTHING, WEST SUSSEX   3–4A

Bryce's Seafood Brasserie   £39
The Steyne BN11 3DU   (01903) 214317

*Feedback is much more limited than we would like, but this agreeable
fish restaurant is tipped for its "very good food", and "good value-for-
money" too. / **Details:** www.seafoodbrasserie.co.uk; 9.30 pm; no Amex.*

The Fish Factory   £34
51-53 Brighton Rd BN11 3EE   (01903) 207123
*Thanks to its "wide range of extremely fresh seafood from a regularly-
changing menu", this is the sort of place that always "very busy" –
"even mid-week in the quiet season"!*
*/ **Details:** www.protorestaurantgroup.com; 10 pm.*

WREXHAM, WREXHAM   5–3A

Pant-yr-Ochain   £38
Old Wrexham Rd LL12 8TY   (01978) 853525
*The cuisine at this large and prettily-located, but "hard-to-find",
gastropub may be that of a "standard gastropub", but its all-round
charms – which include a "cracking" garden (with lake!), "comfortable"
interior and "well-trained" staff – make it a veritable "oasis" in these
parts. / **Details:** www.pantyrochain-gresford.co.uk; 1m N of Wrexham; 9.30 pm,
Sun 9 pm.*

WRIGHTINGTON BAR, LANCASHIRE   5–1A

High Moor   £39
High Moor Ln WN6 9QA   (01257) 252364
*An attractive former coaching inn, with impressive views; it's especially
tipped for lunch, when it offers "excellent value".*
*/ **Details:** www.highmoorrestaurantwigan.co.uk; J27 of the M6; 9.30 pm,
Sun 8 pm; closed Mon & Sat L.*

Mulberry Tree   £47
9 Wood Ln WN6 9SE   (01257) 451400
*"Consistently good food" from "an enormous and varied menu" makes
this former boozer popular with all who comment on it; the bar
is sometimes tipped over the restaurant.*
*/ **Details:** www.themulberrytree.info; 2m along Mossy Lea Rd, off M6,
J27; 10 pm; no Amex; booking essential.*

Hand And Trumpet £34

Main Rd CW3 9BJ (01270) 820048

"Good food in a classic country pub" – that's the deal at this "very large" operation (part of the Brunning & Price chain), which comes complete with a large garden and pond.
/ **Details:** www.handandtrumpet-wrinehill.co.uk; 10.00 sun 9.30; no Amex.

The Wife of Bath £45

4 Upper Bridge St TN25 5AF (01233) 812232

"A (very) old favourite" locally, with "attentive but not smothering" service, and food that's "always well-cooked and presented".
/ **Details:** www.thewifeofbath.com; off A28 between Ashford & Canterbury; 10 pm; closed Mon, Tue L & Sun D. **Accommodation:** 5 rooms, from £85.

Crab House Café £42

Ferrymans Way, Portland Rd DT4 9YU (01305) 788867

There are "some reservations about the look of the place", but most reporters are smitten by this "relaxing" seaside shack with its "great fresh seafood", and its "absolutely delicious" fish (with "rather tasty" chips too); "go early or all the food will be gone!"
/ **Details:** www.crabhousecafe.co.uk; 9 pm, Sat 9.30 pm; closed Tue; no Amex.

The Bell Inn £39

Green Ln HR6 0BD (01568) 780359

"Claude Bosi's brother is doing a good job", at this "small" and "quiet" establishment; it is "more than a gastropub", but certainly not seeking to compete with the family's 'other' establishment, in Mayfair.
/ **Details:** www.thebellinnyarpole.co.uk; 9.30 pm; closed Mon; no Amex.

Ate O'Clock £38

13A, High Ousegate YO1 8RZ (01904) 644080

"Difficult to find down an alleyway, off one of York's main shopping streets", this small modern bistro is tipped as "good value if you eat before 8pm"; the occasional reporter, however, left disappointed.
/ **Details:** www.ateoclock.co.uk; 9.30 pm; closed Sun.

Bettys £35

6-8 St Helen's Sq YO1 8QP (01904) 659142

A famous tearoom "institution" ("with décor by the designers of the Queen Mary"); most reporters say "its worth waiting in the long queue", but critics complain of prices reflecting the place's "tourist trap" status. / **Details:** www.bettysandtaylors.com; down Blake St from York Minster; 9 pm; no Amex; no booking, except Sun.

The Blue Bicycle   £52

⊗

34 Fossgate YO1 9TA   (01904) 673990
*It's notable how often comments on this "busy" restaurant come with
a note of reservation (usually about "hit-and-miss" service or high
prices)… to the extent that it's difficult to disagree with the reporter
who finds it "difficult to see why it's so popular"!*
/ **Details:** www.thebluebicycle.com; 9.30 pm, Sun 9 pm; closed Mon - Wed L;
no Amex; booking: max 8 Sat D. **Accommodation:** 6 rooms, from £145.

Café Concerto   £38

Ⓐ

21 High Petergate YO1 7EN   (01904) 610478
*Lots of feedback on this "buzzy and characterful bistro-style
restaurant", near the Minster, confirm its "unchanging" charm and the
quality of its cuisine; "a coat of paint might not go amiss, though".*
/ **Details:** www.cafeconcerto.biz; by the W entrance of York Minster; 9.30 pm;
booking: max 6. **Accommodation:** 1 room, at about £-.

Cafe No. 8 Bistro   £42

Ⓐ

8 Gillygate YO31 7EQ   (01904) 653074
*"A small space, big on flavoursome food", near the Minster; it's rather
"cramped", so "grab a courtyard table", if you can.*
/ **Details:** www.cafeno8.co.uk; 9.30 pm; no Amex.

City Screen Café Bar
City Screen Picturehouse   £26

Ⓣ

Coney St YO1 9QL   (01904) 612940
*Tipped as an "atmospheric venue, overlooking the river", this cinema
café is "an inexpensive place with an emphasis on vegetarian options".*
/ **Details:** www.picturehouses.co.uk; 9 pm; no Amex; no booking.

Hotel du Vin & Bistro   £50

Ⓐ

89 The Mount YO24 1AX   (01904) 557350
*"An excellent wine list, as you'd expect", "a lovely building" and
a "buzzy" ambience – this hotel bistro ticks all the usual boxes for the
brand; no surprise, then, that the menu proposes "average food
at London prices".* / **Details:** www.hotelduvin.com; 9.30 pm.
Accommodation: 44 rooms, from £110.

J Baker's Bistro Moderne   £43

⊛⊛

7 Fossgate YO1 9TA   (01904) 622688
*"Very imaginative and technically-assured cooking" – and at
"tremendous value-for-money" prices – is winning ever more praise for
Jeff Baker's "modest"-seeming three-year-old; the service is also often
"excellent" (but, as even a fan notes, "it can sometimes be a let-down"
too).* / **Details:** www.jbakers.co.uk; 10 pm; closed Mon & Sun.

La Langhe   £38

Ⓣ

36 Peasholme Grn YO1 7PW   (01904) 622584
*Run by a local firm of Italian food importers – a "combined café/deli",
tipped for its "simple menu from first-rate ingredients".*
/ **Details:** www.lelanghe.co.uk; 9.30 pm; closed Sun; no Amex.

Little Betty's   £25

Ⓣ

46 Stonegate YO1 8AS   (01904) 622865
*"Don't be a poseur, go to Little Betty's instead!"; fans tip the
"more intimate" sibling to the main gaff – in a "very attractive old
building near the Minster" – as having "shorter queues", and the tea
and cakes are "just as good".* / **Details:** www.bettys.co.uk; L only; no Amex.

Melton's   £42 ⭐

7 Scarcroft Rd YO23 1ND   (01904) 634 341
*In a terrace house on the way to the racecourse, Michael Hjort's
popular venture is still often recommended as "the city's
best restaurant"; despite a feeling that it's "slipped a bit over the
years", the "sheer dependability" of its "robust local fare"
(not least "top puddings") underpins its enduring success.
/ Details: www.meltonsrestaurant.co.uk; 10 mins walk from Castle Museum;
10 pm; closed Mon & Sun; no Amex.*

Melton's Too   £33 Ⓐ

25 Walmgate YO1 9TX   (01904) 629 222
*This large café/bar/bistro won steady praise this year for its
"interesting" dishes — the array of tapas and mezze it offers alongside
the more conventional menu attracts particular praise.
/ Details: www.meltonstoo.co.uk; 2 minutes from the City centre; 10.30 pm,
Sun 9.30 pm; no Amex.*

Middlethorpe Hall   £72 Ⓣ

Bishopthorpe Rd YO23 2GB   (01904) 641241
*This grand country house hotel, on the fringe of the city, attracts only
positive feedback; it's tipped as a "special place for breakfast", lunch
is said to offer "exceptional value" and tea is good too — on dinner,
however, reports are curiously silent... / Details: www.middlethorpe.com;
next to racecourse; 9.30 pm; no shorts; children: 4+. Accommodation: 29
rooms, from £199.*

UK Maps

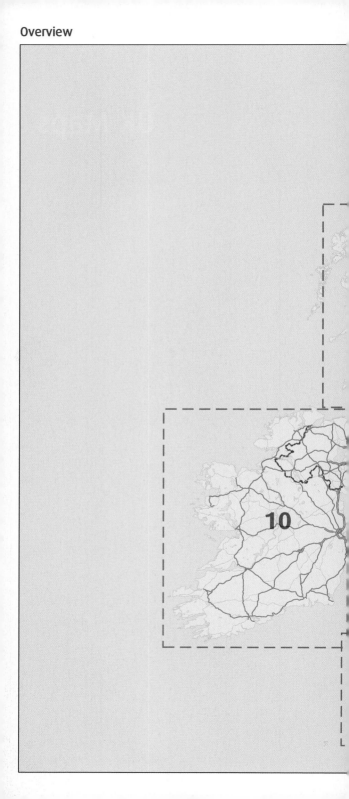

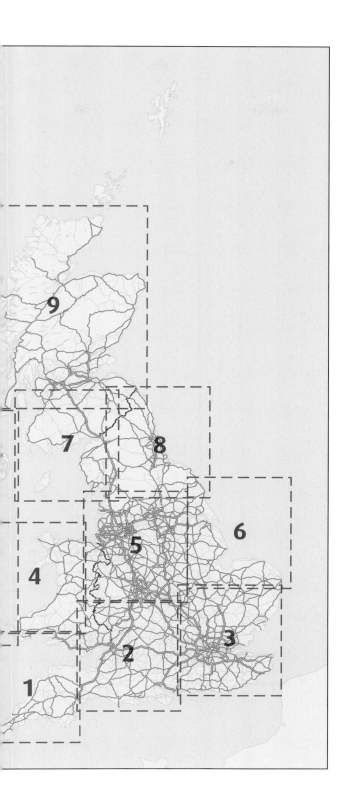

MAP 1

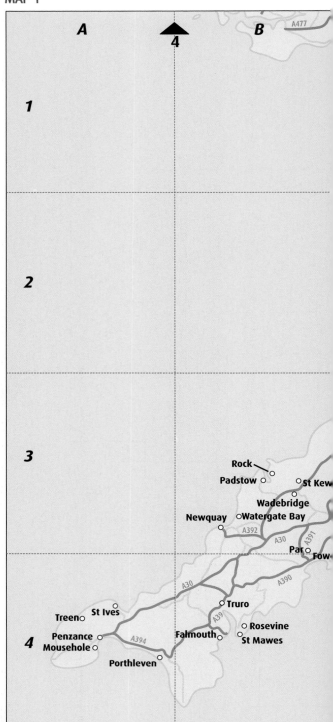

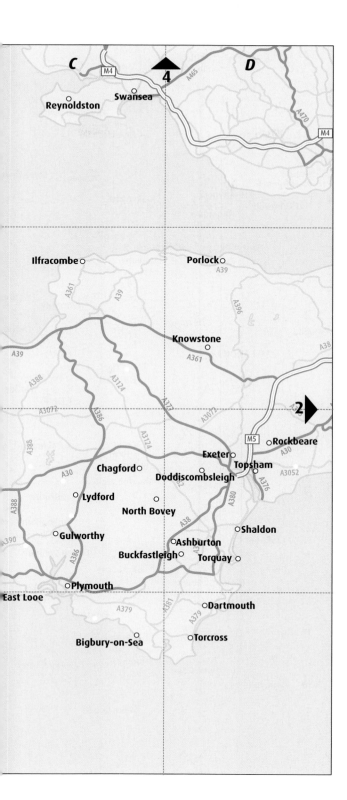

MAP 2

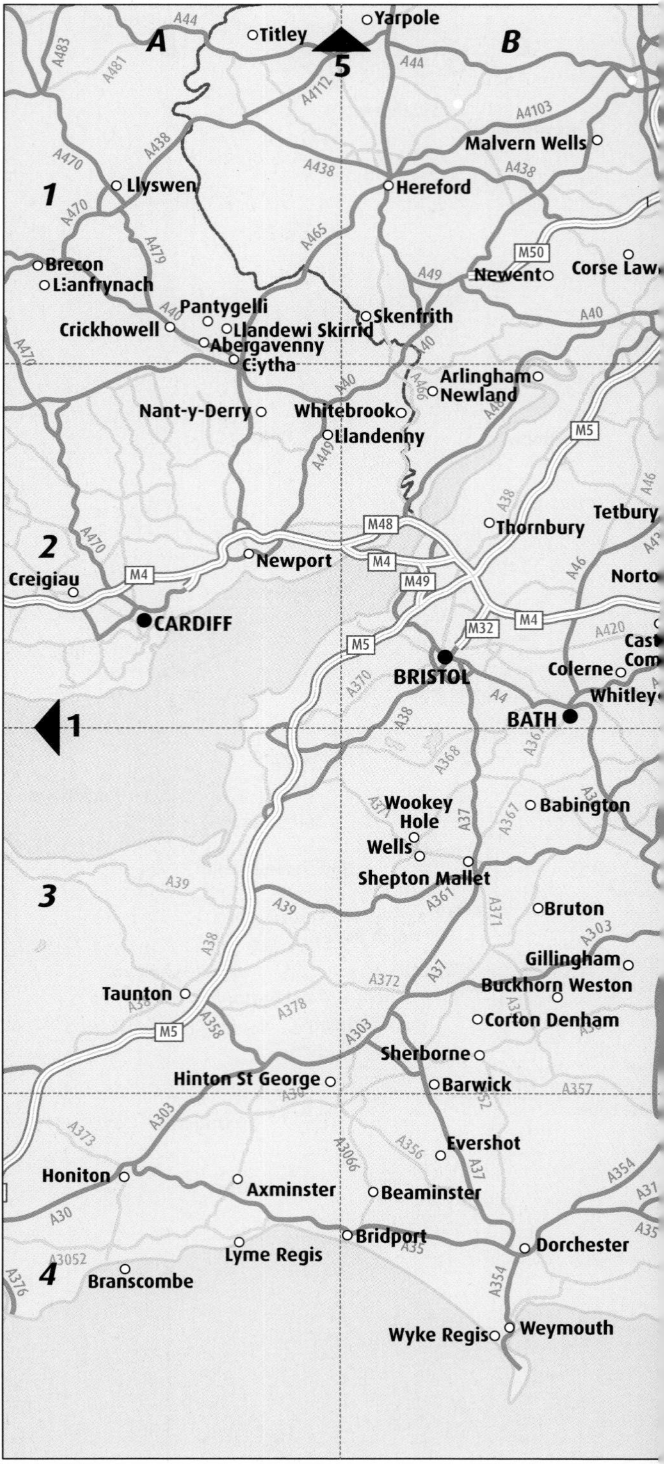

A   B

5

Titley Yarpole

Malvern Wells

1   Llyswen Hereford Newent Corse Law

Brecon
Llanfrynach
Pantygelli
Crickhowell Llandewi Skirrid Skenfrith
Abergavenny
Clytha Arlingham
Newland

Nant-y-Derry Whitebrook
Llandenny

Tetbury

2 Thornbury

Newport Norto

Creigiau Cas
CARDIFF Colerne Com
BRISTOL Whitley

1 BATH

Wookey
Hole Babington

Wells
Shepton Mallet

3 Bruton

Gillingham
Buckhorn Weston

Taunton Corton Denham

Sherborne
Hinton St George Barwick

Evershot

Honiton Axminster Beaminster

Bridport Dorchester

4 Lyme Regis
Branscombe

Wyke Regis Weymouth

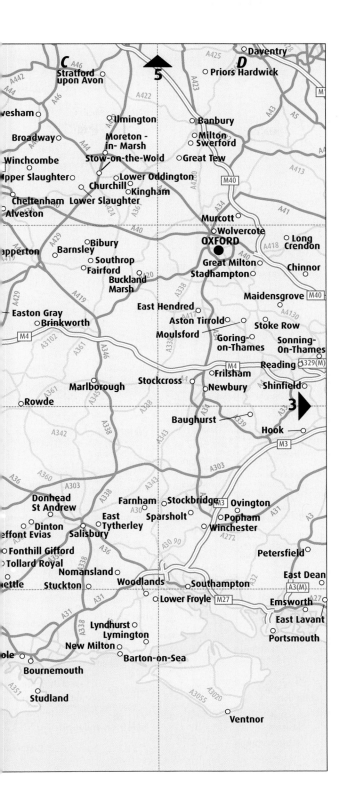

MAP 3

A 6

B

Sutton Gault   Ely

Keyston   Huntingdon
Hemingford Grey

Histon
Little Wilbral

Bolnhurst   Madingley   CAMBRIDGE

Roade

Fowlmere

Moulsoe

Milton Keynes
Woburn   Willian   Clavering

Newton Longville

2   Welwyn Sawbridgeworth   Bishop's Stortford

Aylesbury   Harpenden   Hemel   Hunsdon
Tring   Frithsden   Hempstead
Berkhamsted   St Albans
Radnage   Ongar
Amersham Flaunden   Northaw
Speen   Chandler's Cross   Chigwell
Henley-on-Thames   High Wycombe   Bushey
    Barnet

Great Missenden   Bushey Heath

Marlow   Beaconsfield
    Denham
Taplow   Cookham Flackwell Heath   LONDON
Hurley   Henley on Thames   M25
Winkfield   Bray   Maidenhead Teddington   Brentford
    Windsor   Eton   Hounslow   Richmond   Bromley
White Waltham   Wooburn Common   Kingston   Beckenham
3   Egham   Sunningdale   Twickenham   upon Thames
Ascot   Church Crookham   Surbiton   Croydon   Locksbotto
Bagshot   Sunbury on Thames   Esher   Thames
    West Byfleet   Hersham   Ditton   Epsom   Orpington   Addington
Woking   Cobham
Sutton Green   Ripley
Guildford   Reigate   M25
    Hammer Mickleham   Oxted   Shipbo
Shere   Dorking   Sevenoaks
Godalming   Tonbridge
    Penshurst
Forest Green   Ockley   East Grinstead   Tunbridge Wells
Rowhook   Turner's Hill   Forest Row
    West Hoathly   Crowboroug
Horsham   Cuckfield   Danehill
Petworth   Haywards   Fletching
    Heath
4   East Chiltington
Lavant   Amberley   Albourne   Lewes
Chilgrove
Chichester   Arundel   BRIGHTON and Hove
Bosham
Littlehampton   Worthing   Eastbourn

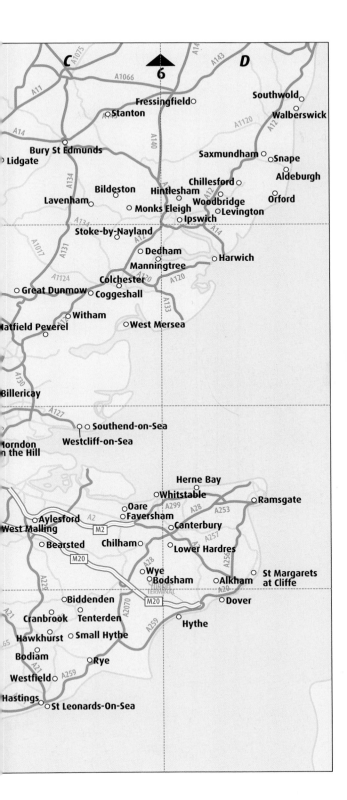

MAP 4

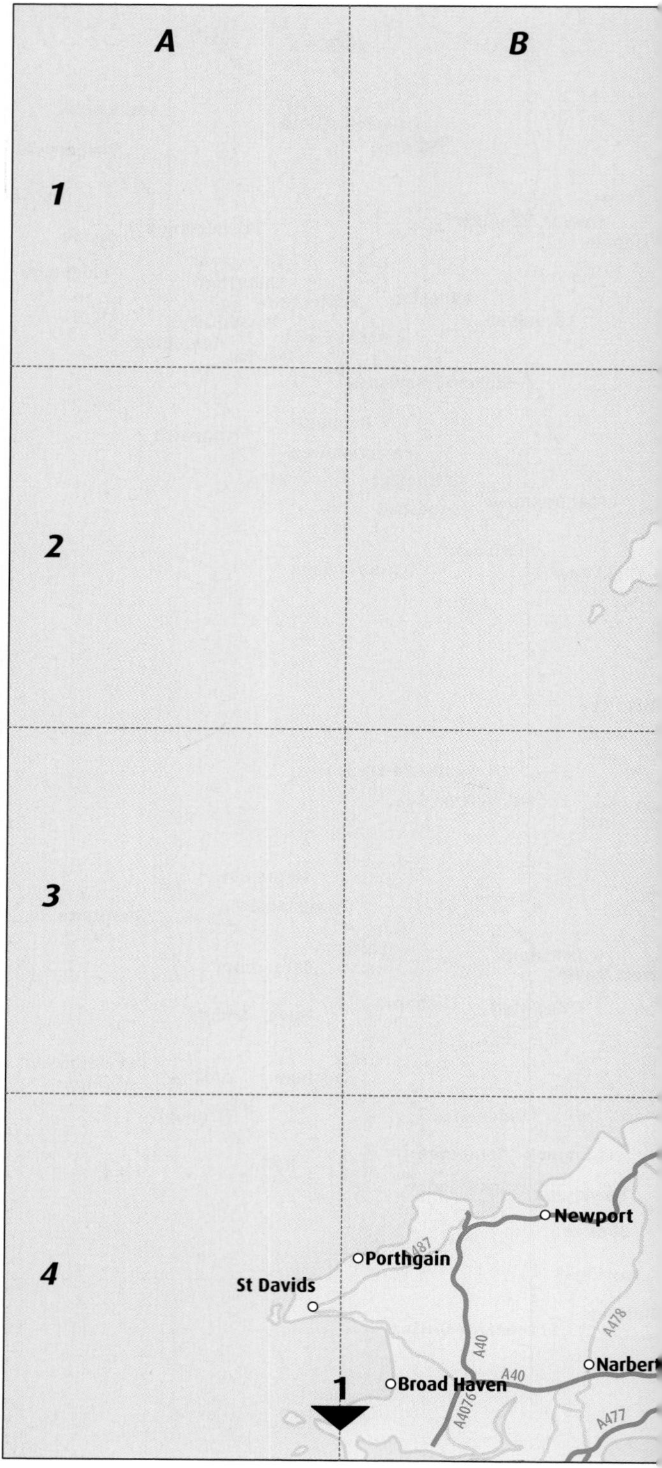
A
B
1
2
3
4
Newport
Porthgain
A487
St Davids
A478
A40
Narberth
A40
Broad Haven
A4076
A477
1

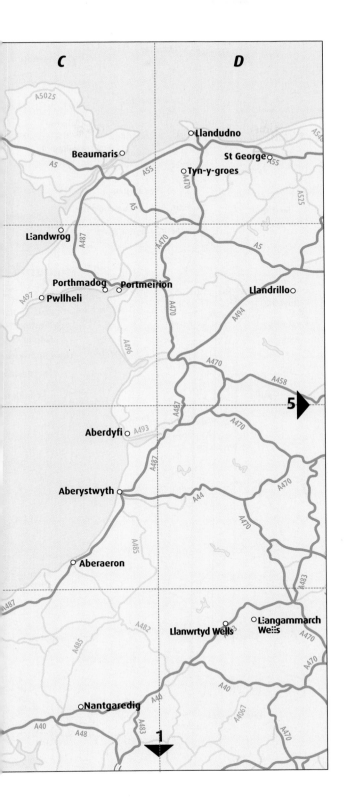

MAP 5

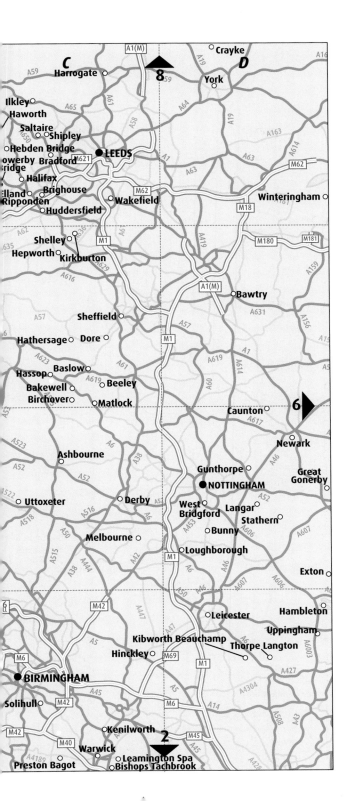

MAP 6

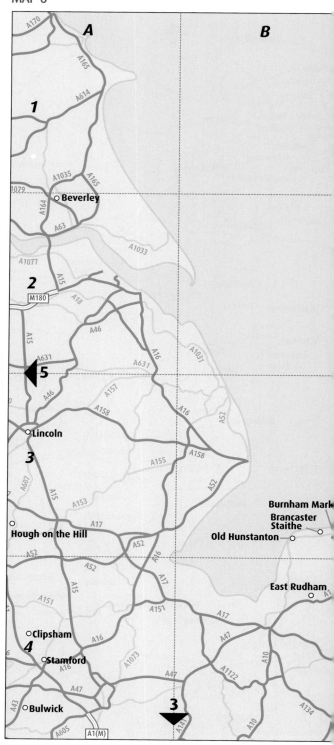

C

D

lkham
A149 Morston oSalthouse
Holt *A148*

oItteringham

A149

A140

A1067

A47 Norwich o **Brundall**
o *A47*

Stoke Holy Cross o *A146*

3 ▼ *A143*

A11

A140

A1075 *A143*

MAP 7

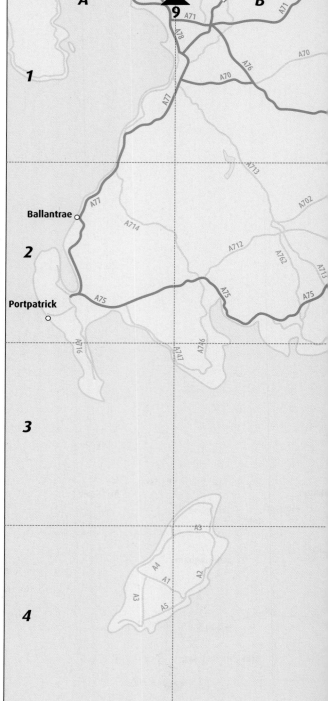

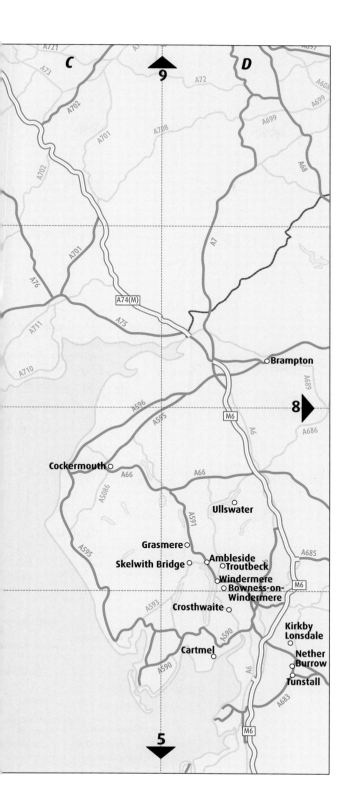

MAP 8

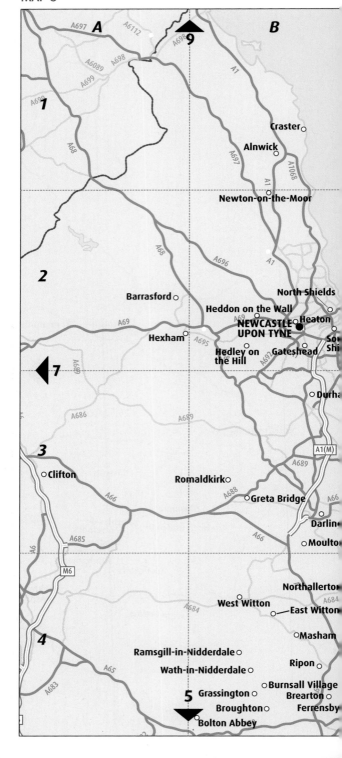

A697 **A** A6112 **B**

A6089 A698

A6089

A699 A698

1

A68

A697

Craster

Alnwick

Newton-on-the-Moor

A1

A696 A1

2 A68

Barrasford

North Shields

Heddon on the Wall

A69 NEWCASTLE Heaton
UPON TYNE

Hexham A695 South
Shi

Hedley on Gateshead
the Hill

7 A68

Durha

A686

A689

3

A1(M)

Clifton A689

Romaldkirk

A66 A688

Greta Bridge A66

A685

Darlin

M6 A66 Moulto

Northallerton

West Witton A684

East Witton

4 A684

Masham

Ramsgill-in-Nidderdale

A65 Ripon

Wath-in-Nidderdale

A683 **5** Grassington Burnsall Village

Broughton Brearton

Bolton Abbey Ferrensby

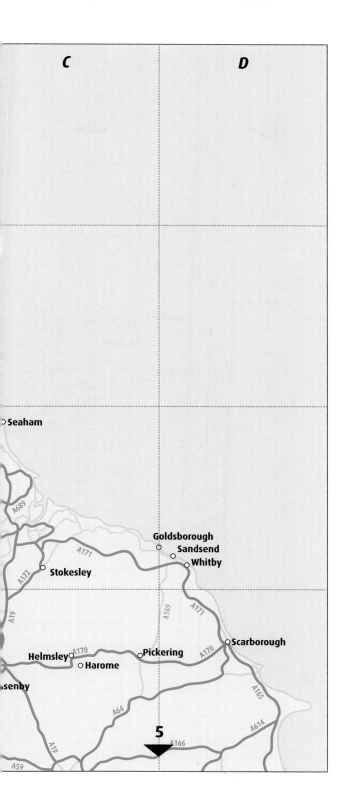

MAP 9

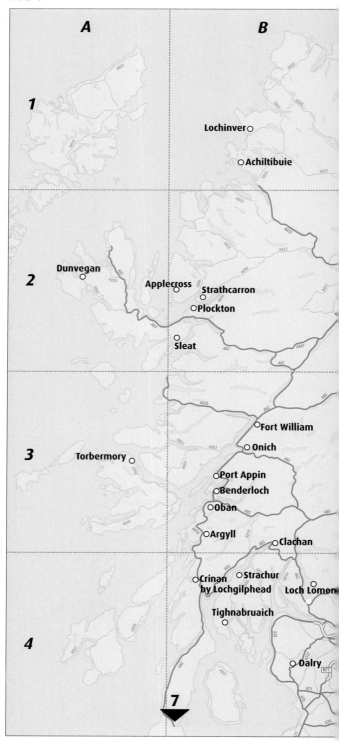

A

B

1

Lochinver ○

○ Achiltibuie

2

Dunvegan ○

Applecross ○   ○ Strathcarron
○ Plockton

○ Sleat

3

Torbermory ○

○ Fort William

○ Onich

○ Port Appin
○ Benderloch
○ Oban

○ Argyll

○ Clachan

Crinan ○   ○ Strachur
by Lochgilphead   Loch Lomon ○

Tighnabruaich ○

4

○ Dalry

▼ 7

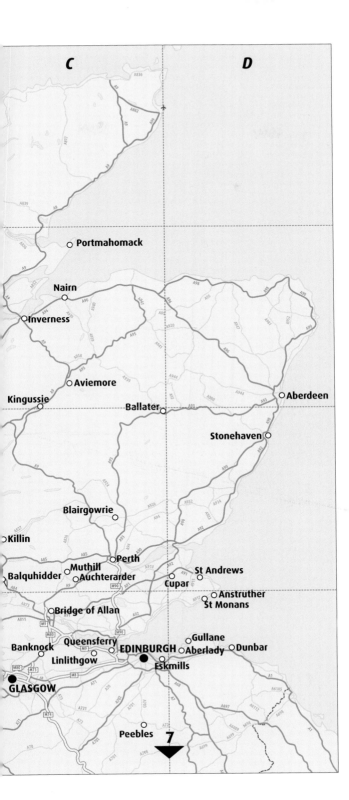

C

D

○ Portmahomack

Nairn ○

○ Inverness

○ Aviemore

Kingussie ○

Ballater ○

Stonehaven ○

○ Aberdeen

Blairgowrie ○

○ Killin

Muthill ○   ○ Perth

Balquhidder ○   ○ Auchterarder

Cupar ○   ○ St Andrews

○ Bridge of Allan

○ Anstruther
St Monans

Banknock ○   Queensferry ○   ● EDINBURGH

○ Gullane
Aberlady   ○ Dunbar

Linlithgow ○

Eskmills

● GLASGOW

Peebles ○

7 ▼

MAP 10

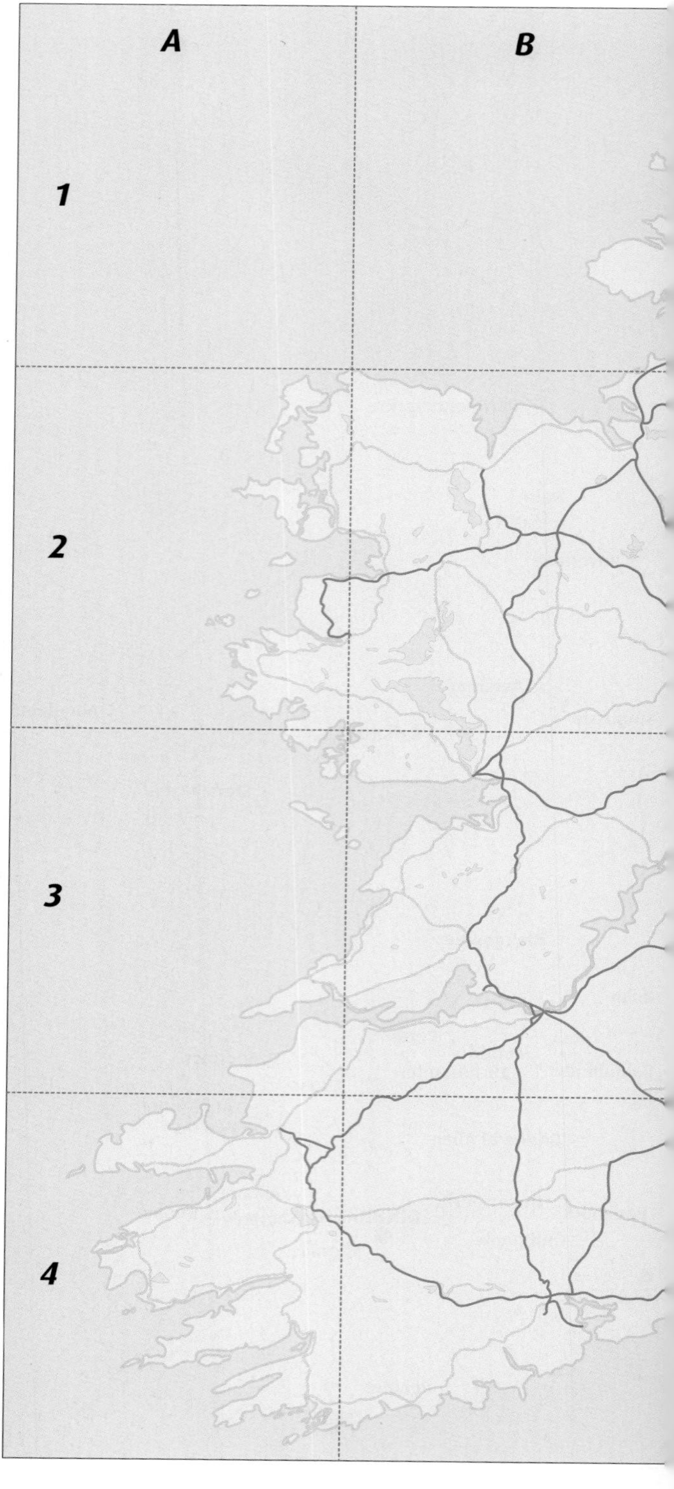

A   B

1

2

3

4

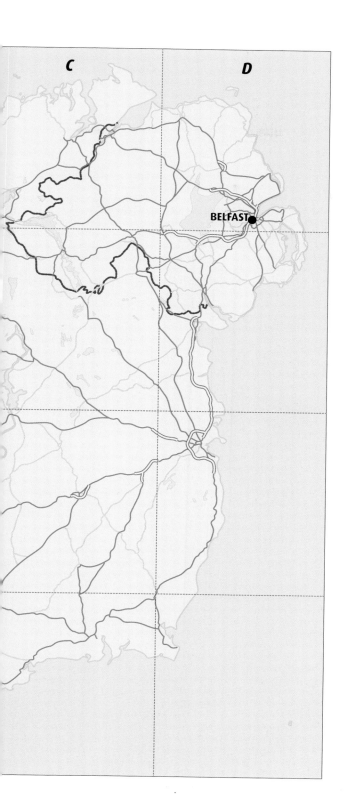

C

D

BELFAST

Alphabetical Index

ALPHABETICAL INDEXES

Goodman 71
Goods Shed
Canterbury 213
Gordon Ramsay
London 71
**Gordon Ramsay at
Claridge's** *London* 71
Gordon's Wine Bar
London 72
The Goring Hotel
London 72
Gourmet San *London* 72
Gourmet Spot
Durham 230
The Gowlett *London* 72
Grado *Manchester* 285
Graffiti *Cambridge* 212
Grain Store *Edinburgh* 235
Grand Café *Oxford* 311
The Grapes *London* 72
**Graveley's Fish & Chip
Restaurant** *Harrogate* 253
Gravetye Manor *East
Grinstead* 231
Graze *Brighton* 201
**Great Eastern Dining
Room** *London* 72
The Oak Room
Egham 239
The Great House
Hawkhurst 254
Great House
Lavenham 268
Great Kathmandu
Manchester 285
Great Queen Street
London 72
The Green *Sherborne* 329
Green Inn *Ballater* 181
Green Papaya *London* 72
Green Room
Colchester 222
Green's *Manchester* 285
Green's Dining Room
Bristol 205
The Greenhouse
London 73
Greens *Whitby* 354
Greyhound
Stockbridge 338
The Griffin Inn
Fletching 243
Grill on the Alley
Manchester 286
La Grillade *Leeds* 271
Grinch *Manchester* 286
Groes Inn *Tyn-y-Groes* 348

The Grosvenor Arms
Aldford 175
Guildhall Tavern
Poole 316
The Guinea Grill
London 73
Gung-Ho *London* 73
Gurkha Grill
Manchester 286
The Gurkha Kitchen
Oxted 312
Gurnards Head *Treen* 346
Gwesty Cymru
Aberystwyth 173
Haché 73
Hakkasan 73
The Half Moon *Haywards
Heath* 255
Hambleton Hall
Hambleton 251
The Hambrough
Ventnor 349
**The Hammer And
Pincers** *Loughborough* 280
Hand & Flowers
Marlow 292
Hand And Trumpet
Wrinehill 362
**The Hand At
Llanarmonn** *Llanarmon
Dc* 277
Hansa's *Leeds* 271
Haozhan *London* 74
Happy Gathering
Cardiff 214
Harbour Inn *Lyme
Regis* 281
Harbourmaster
Aberaeron 172
The Hardwick
Abergavenny 173
**The Harrow at Little
Bedwyn** *Marlborough* 292
Harry's Place *Great
Gonerby* 248
Hart's *Nottingham* 305
Hartwell House
Aylesbury 180
Harwood Arms
London 74
Hassop Hall *Hassop* 254
Hastings *Lytham* 282
Havana *Brighton* 201
The Havelock Tavern
London 74
Hawksmoor 74
Hélène Darroze

ALPHABETICAL INDEXES

ALPHABETICAL INDEXES

ALPHABETICAL INDEXES